Human Attention in Digital Environments

Digital systems, such as phones, computers and PDAs, place continuous demands on our cognitive and perceptual systems. They offer information and interaction opportunities well above our processing abilities, and often interrupt our activity. Appropriate allocation of attention is one of the key factors determining the success of creative activities, learning, collaboration and many other human pursuits. This book presents research related to human attention in digital environments. Original contributions by leading researchers cover the conceptual framework of research aimed at modelling and supporting human attentional processes, the theoretical and software tools currently available, and various application areas. The authors explore the idea that attention has a key role to play in the design of future technology and discuss how such technology may continue supporting human activity in environments where multiple devices compete for people's limited cognitive resources.

CLAUDIA RODA is Professor of Computer Science and Global Communication and Director of the Division of Arts and Sciences at the American University of Paris.

Human Attention in Digital Environments

Edited by

Claudia Roda

American University of Paris

CAMBRIDGE
UNIVERSITY PRESS

CAMBRIDGE UNIVERSITY PRESS
Cambridge, New York, Melbourne, Madrid, Cape Town, Singapore,
São Paulo, Delhi, Tokyo, Mexico City

Cambridge University Press
The Edinburgh Building, Cambridge CB2 8RU, UK

Published in the United States of America by Cambridge University Press,
New York

www.cambridge.org
Information on this title: www.cambridge.org/9780521765657

First published 2011
Reprinted 2012

Printed at MPG Books Group, UK

A catalogue record for this publication is available from the British Library

ISBN 978-0-521-76565-7 Hardback

To my favourite distractors:
Andrew, Matteo, Marco and Pietro

Contents

The colour plates appear between pages 204 and 205

Acknowledgements

This book was originally conceived with the objective of disseminating the results of the AtGentive project, an international research project sponsored by the European Commission. As the book evolved, the desire to provide a wider view of the research and applicative work in the area of *attention aware systems* resulted in the inclusion of many chapters coming from other applied research projects. I am grateful to the authors who have contributed not only with their excellent chapters but, very often, also by providing comments and suggestions to authors of other chapters. This has resulted in creating those bridges that are often missing between different disciplines and between specific aspects of inquiry within this area of research. It has been a pleasure and a rewarding learning experience to be able to coordinate this work.

I also would like to thank the many reviewers who have commented on individual chapters. The quality of this book has certainly gained from their insights. I extend my appreciation to the publisher's anonymous reviewers who have provided comments and suggestions about the overall structure and content of the book.

My gratitude goes to Jan Steyn and Antal Neville whose patient and thorough work in proofreading and organizing references has been invaluable.

Special thanks to Hetty Reid, Commissioning Editor, and Tom O'Reilly, Production Editor for Cambridge University Press, who have supported and guided me during the whole process of creating this book, together with Joanna Garbutt, Carrie Cheek and Oliver Lown. Finally, I am sincerely grateful for the professional, careful and timely copy-editing work of Diane Ilott, who has spent many hot summer days patiently fixing the small details that make all the difference.

Notes on contributors

LAURENT ACH is the CTO of the French company Cantoche that engages in research and development for the Living Actor™ software suite. He leads the implementation of software solutions, tools and services. After graduating as a software engineer from the École Centrale de Lyon in 1990, he worked for ten years in Thales Group where he was first in charge of neural networks projects for the French Navy and later joined a team of 3D engineers arriving at Thales from Thomson Digital Image. He led several 3D and virtual reality projects in design and ergonomics studies for car manufacturers and contributed to industrial prototypes in virtual reality for the European Commission. He was later in charge of visualization technologies at Visiospace, a start-up that created innovative 3D streaming software. Before joining Cantoche in 2005, Laurent Ach was responsible at Sagem for the compliance of mobile phone product lines with operators' requirements. More information about Laurent is available at www.ach3d.com.

PHIL J. BARNARD is a programme leader at the Medical Research Council's Cognition and Brain Sciences Unit in Cambridge. Over the course of his career, he has carried out research on how memory, attention, language, body states and emotion work together in the normal healthy, human mind. He is committed to seeing the types of basic cognitive theory developed in scientific laboratories put to good use in the real world. His theoretical model of the architecture of the human mind (Interacting Cognitive Subsystems) has been used to research problems of designing 'easy-to-use' everyday technologies and computer interfaces. He has also applied the same theory to help understand and treat emotional disorders like depression, as well as using it to account for the way in which human mental and emotional skills have developed over the long-term course of evolution.

CARLA VAN BOXTEL is Senior Researcher at the Graduate School of Teaching and Learning at the University of Amsterdam and Endowed Professor of Historical Culture and Education at the Center for

Historical Culture of the Erasmus University Rotterdam (EUR). She manages the Dutch Center for Social Studies Education. She has published on collaborative learning, visual representations and the learning of history.

HOWARD BOWMAN is Professor of Cognition and Logic at the University of Kent at Canterbury and he is joint Director of the Centre for Cognitive Neuroscience and Cognitive Systems at Kent. He has worked for over twenty years in the field of formal methods, contributing to both their theoretical development and their application. In particular, he has championed the application of formal methods (such as LOTOS) analysing human–computer interaction. More recently, he has undertaken research in cognitive neuroscience, focused on understanding human attention, emotions and decision making. This research has involved both behavioural and electrophysiological experimentation, as well as computational modelling. In particular, he has developed both formal methods and neural network models of human cognition. He also recently led the Salience Project at the University of Kent, which is the subject of his contribution.

AULIKKI HYRSKYKARI is a lecturer in computer science at the University of Tampere. She obtained her Lic.Phil. degree in computer science in 1995 and her Ph.D. in interactive technology in 2006 at the University of Tampere. She worked as a coordinator in the EU FP5 IST Project iEye, a three-year project which focused on studying gaze-assisted access to information. She has also acted as a programme and organizing committee member in several international HCI conferences, most recently as the co-chair of the programme committee of the ACM Symposium on Eye-Tracking Research and Applications, ETRA 2010.

PUTAI JIN serves at the University of New South Wales. His research interest is in applied psychology. His current research areas include technology-aided learning, memory, cognitive styles and stress reactivity.

UWE KIRSCHENMANN has been working as a researcher at the Fraunhofer Institute for Applied Information Technology since 2008. He received a diploma in psychology in 2007 and a diploma in philosophy in 2008 at the University of Hamburg. His main interest is the application of psychological knowledge on usage data.

FRANK KOOI is coordinator of the 'applied perception' group at TNO which combines fundamental knowledge of the human visual and auditory systems with applied technological developments. His personal work consists of the design, development and evaluation of innovative display systems. His scientific work includes ten refereed articles (240+ citations). His applied work includes patents on display systems (head-mounted, peripheral and dual-layer), visual conspicuity and NVG simulation.

ANDREA KULAKOV enrolled at university at the age of sixteen and graduated as the best student at the Faculty of Electrical Engineering, Computer Science Department, of the University of Sts Cyril and Methodius, Skopje, Macedonia, in 1995. He received his M.Sc. degree in cognitive science from the New Bulgarian University in Sofia, Bulgaria in 1998. He defended his Ph.D. thesis in 2006 at the University of Sts Cyril and Methodius, Skopje, Macedonia, where he works at the moment as an assistant professor. He received the Walter Karplus Summer Research Grant of the IEEE Computational Intelligence Society for 2005, for part of his Ph.D. research.

RENAE LOW serves at the University of New South Wales. Her research interest is in educational psychology. Her current research involves the intersection of cognition, motivation and multimedia learning.

NICOLAS MAISONNEUVE is an associate researcher at the Sony Computer Science Laboratory in Paris. He received master's degrees in computer science and artificial intelligence. Previously he was involved in research projects on information retrieval and robotics in France. He also worked on visualization and data mining for supporting e-collaboration at the University of Sydney. Recently he participated, as a research associate at the INSEAD school, in an EU project about the management of social attention in online communities (AtGentive). His current interest mixes organization sciences, sustainability and computer science. He is working on a new participatory approach empowering citizens to monitor noise pollution using their mobile phones (NoiseTube). He also worked at the Guiana Space Centre in Kourou and co-founded two internet start-ups.

PÄIVI MAJARANTA was the scientific coordinator of the five-year European Network of Excellence on Communication by Gaze Interaction (COGAIN, 2004–2009). Her research interests are computer-aided communication, multimodal interaction, and especially eye-aware and eye-operated computer interfaces. She obtained her M.Sc. in computer science in 1998 from the University of Tampere and completed her Ph.D. research on text entry by eye gaze. Päivi is currently a researcher in the TAUCHI unit at the University of Tampere, Finland.

INGE MOLENAAR is the initiator and CEO of the e-learning application Ontdeknet, which has been developed since 2001. She received different national and international awards for the development of Ontdeknet and was the project manager of Ontdeknet in the EC-sponsored project AtGentive. She is a Ph.D. student at the University of Amsterdam, in the department of educational sciences. Her research is dealing with scaffolding of self-regulated learning in innovative learning arrangements.

BENOÎT MOREL is the co-founder and CEO of the French company Cantoche, which is a world leader in embodied agent technology and has created the patented technology Living Actor^{TM}. Following his career as sound engineer and producer at Radio France, Benoît worked in the video games industry for ten years, producing CGI animation in a variety of formats – notably video games, interactive shows, Internet websites and, particularly, character animation. He is the creator of the most-downloaded agent, 'James the Butler'. Benoît has published several articles and has been consulted by multinational organizations, companies, research institutes and universities on embodied agent design and deployment. More information about Benoît and his company Cantoche is available in both English and French at www.cantoche.com.

THIERRY NABETH is a senior research fellow at INSEAD. His research is centred on the study of social platforms and social systems for supporting the social process in the context of Web 2.0. He investigates concepts such as social attention, online social identity, motivation to participate in an interaction, and the profiling of activities in social platforms. Thierry has worked on projects in the domain of knowledge management, learning systems and agent-based systems. He was, for instance, the coordinator of AtGentive, a project aimed at investigating how to support attention using ICT, and a participant in the network of excellence FIDIS (Future of Identity in the Information Society) in which his role was more particularly focused on the management of online identity and collaborative conceptualization.

KATJA NIEMANN received her diploma in computational linguistics and computer science from the University of Heidelberg (Germany) in 2007. Since then she has been working in the 'Information in Context' research group at Fraunhofer FIT. Her research interests include human–computer interaction and information retrieval.

KARI-JOUKO RÄIHÄ obtained his Ph.D. in computer science at the University of Helsinki in 1982. Since 1985 he has been a full professor of computer science at the University of Tampere. He was the department head in 1991–8 and vice-rector of the university in 1999–2004. He founded Tampere Unit for Computer–Human Interaction (TAUCHI), a unit of about forty-five people, in the mid-1990s and has led it since. He has chaired several conferences in the field and led more than forty research projects funded through competitive funding sources.

RONALD A. RENSINK is an associate professor in the departments of computer science and psychology at the University of British Columbia (UBC). His interests include human vision (particularly visual attention), computer vision, visual design and human–computer interaction. He has done work on visual attention, scene perception, computer graphics and consciousness. He obtained his Ph.D. in computer science from UBC in 1992, followed by a two-year postdoctoral fellowship in the psychology department at Harvard University. For several years he was a research scientist at Cambridge Basic Research, a lab sponsored by Nissan Motor Co. Ltd. He returned to UBC in 2000, and is currently part of the UBC Cognitive Systems Program, an interdisciplinary programme that combines computer science, linguistics, philosophy and psychology.

CLAUDIA RODA is Professor of Computer Science and Global Communication at the American University of Paris, and founder of the Technology and Cognition Lab. She obtained her bachelor degree in computer science from the University of Pisa, Italy, and her master's degree and Ph.D. from the University of London. Claudia's current research focuses on theoretical and computational models for attention computing. She has edited collections and published her work on attention-aware systems in many journals, books and conferences. She has extensive experience in the design, implementation and validation of multi-agent systems supporting cognitive and social processes related to learning and collaboration. This earlier work has also been widely published. She has been a member of the organizing and programme committees of numerous international conferences and organized the workshops on 'Designing for attention' at HCI-2004 and on 'Attention management in ubiquitous computing environments' at Ubicomp 2007. Claudia has collaborated with many universities, research institutions and industries worldwide; several institutions, including the Mellon Foundation and the European Commission, have funded her research on attention computing.

HANS-CHRISTIAN SCHMITZ is a member of the Fraunhofer Institute for Applied Information Technology in St Augustin, Germany.

Previously he worked as a member of the Institute of Cognitive Linguistics (University of Frankfurt am Main) and of the Institute for Communication Research and Phonetics (University of Bonn). In Bonn, he earned his Ph.D. with work on 'accentuation and interpretation'. His current research focus is on contextualized attention metadata and the criteria of relevance and informativity for recommender systems.

PETER SLEEGERS is Professor of Educational Sciences at the University of Twente. He has published extensively on leadership, innovation and educational policy in more than forty refereed journal articles and several edited books. His current research projects are studies into the effects of educational leadership on student motivation for school, longitudinal research into sustainability of reforms and design studies into professional learning communities.

GEORGI STOJANOV received his master's degree in 1993 and his Ph.D. in computer science from the Faculty of Electrical Engineering, Sts Cyril and Methodius University in Skopje, Macedonia in 1997. During his graduate studies, he held posts of research and teaching assistant at the University in Skopje. He spent one year as a research postdoctoral fellow in the Laboratory for Human–Computer Interaction at the University of Trieste, Italy. In 2000 he founded the Cognitive Robotics Group at the Faculty of Electrical Engineering in Skopje. In 2001 he was appointed Associate Professor at the same faculty. He was a visiting scholar at Les Archives Jean Piaget in Geneva, at the Université de Versailles Saint-Quentin-en-Yvelines, Paris, and at the Institute for Non-linear Science, University of California at San Diego. He has been Associate Professor at the American University of Paris since autumn 2005. Georgi is co-founder of the Institute for Interactivist Studies, www.interactivism.org, and member of the organizing committee of the bi-annual Interactivist Summer Institute (ISI). He is a member of AAAI (American Association for Artificial Intelligence), ACM (Association for Computing Machinery), ISAB (International Society for Adaptive Behavior), ACM (Association for Computing Machinery) and JPS (Jean Piaget Society). His main interests lie in: learning in artificial and natural agents; modelling cognitive phenomena in robotic systems; constructivism; metaphors; languages and translation. He has published more than forty scholarly articles in journals and books, as well as in the proceedings of various scientific meetings in the above-mentioned fields.

LI SU is a postdoctoral researcher at the Institute of Psychiatry (IOP) and the Cognition and Brain Sciences Unit at King's College London.

He is a computational neuroscientist working on implementing and piloting real-time functional magnetic resonance imaging (rt-fMRI) at the IOP. He has a degree in computer science, and his Ph.D. focused on computational modelling of human cognition, e.g., temporal attention, learning, electrophysiology and emotion. His model has been applied to human–computer interaction during the course of the Salience Project. His current research interests also involve clinical applications of neural feedback, in particular developing rt-fMRI techniques to target persistent attenuated affect in both clinical and non-clinical groups.

JOHN SWELLER is Emeritus Professor of Education at the University of New South Wales. His research is associated with cognitive load theory. The theory is a contributor to both research and debate on issues associated with human cognition, its links to evolution by natural selection, and the instructional design consequences that follow.

MARTIN WOLPERS holds a Ph.D. in electrical engineering and information technology from the University of Hanover. He is leading the Context and Attention for Personalized Learning Environments Group at FIT ICON, dealing with trend and user-goal identification from contextualized attention metadata streams. His main engagements in research projects include the project management of the FP6 EU/ICT TEL NoE PROLEARN, the coordination of the EC eContent+ MACE project and the FP7 EU/ICT TEL Integrated Project ROLE. His research focuses on how to use metadata in order to improve technology-enhanced learning scenarios. Specifically, he focuses on contextualized attention metadata and knowledge representation in education. His further research interests include conceptual modelling, databases and information extraction.

BRAD WYBLE is a postdoctoral fellow in the department of brain and cognitive sciences at the Massachusetts Institute of Technology in Cambridge, Massachusetts. His research focuses on computational, behavioural and electrophysiological study of the interaction of temporal factors in visual attention, working memory and emotions. After his undergraduate education in computer science at Brandeis University, he obtained his Ph.D. in the psychology department of Harvard University, where he recorded and analysed theta oscillations in the hippocampus of the rat. Before moving to the MIT in Boston, Brad worked in the UK to study visual attention at the University of Kent at Canterbury and University College London.

Illustrations

Tables

1   Introduction

Claudia Roda

In recent years it has been increasingly recognized that the advent of information and communication technologies has dramatically shifted the balance between the availability of information and the ability of humans to process information. During the last century information was a scarce resource. Now, *human attention* has become the scarce resource whereas information (of all types and qualities) abounds. The appropriate allocation of attention is a key factor determining the success of creative activities, learning, collaboration and many other human pursuits. A suitable choice of focus is essential for efficient time organization, sustained deliberation and, ultimately, goal achievement and personal satisfaction. Therefore, we must address the problem of how digital systems can be designed so that, in addition to allowing fast access to information and people, they also support human attentional processes. With the aim of responding to this need, this book proposes an interdisciplinary analysis of the issues related to the design of systems capable of supporting the limited cognitive abilities of humans by assisting the processes guiding attention allocation. Systems of this type have been referred to in the literature as Attention-Aware Systems (Roda and Thomas 2006), Attentive User Interfaces (Vertegaal 2003) or Notification User Interfaces (McCrickard, Czerwinski and Bartram 2003) and they engender many challenging questions (see, for example, Wood, Cox and Cheng 2006).

The design of such systems must obviously rest on a deep understanding of the mechanisms guiding human attention. Psychologists have studied attention from many different perspectives. In the nineteenth century, when attention was mainly studied through introspection, William James (considered by many the founder of American psychology) devoted a chapter in his *Principles of Psychology* to human attention and observed:

Everyone knows what attention is. It is the taking possession by the mind, in clear and vivid form, of one out of what seem several simultaneously possible objects or trains of thought... It implies withdrawal from some things in order to deal effectively with others (James 1890: 403–4).

1

However, as for many other *things* that 'everyone knows', such as rationality, intelligence, memory and love, attention escapes a precise definition, and more than a century after James' writing, its mechanisms still generate debates and controversy in the scientific community.

Since the mid-twentieth century, attention allocation has been viewed as the process of *selecting* stimuli for processing, and research has focused on the question of *when and how* this selection takes place. Proponents of *early selection theory* (Broadbent 1958) argue that stimuli are filtered early, at the perceptual level, on the basis of their physical properties so that irrelevant (unattended) stimuli are not further processed. Proponents of the *modified early selection theory* (Treisman 1960) maintain that the early filter is not just *on* or *off* but that some stimuli are just attenuated rather than completely filtered out, so that some irrelevant stimuli may reach consciousness. Proponents of *late selection theory* (Deutsch and Deutsch 1963) argue that all stimuli are analysed (i.e., there is no filter at perceptual level) but only pertinent stimuli are selected for awareness and memorization. More recently some of the fundamental assumptions of the early/late selection dichotomy have been questioned (Awh, Vogel and Oh 2006; Vogel, Luck and Shapiro 1988) and the debate over early and late selection has directly or indirectly raised many other related questions: e.g., does attention modify the manner in which we perceive the environment, or does it impact on our response to what we perceive? This is an important question for the design of attention-aware systems. For example, Posner (1980) suggests that cueing facilitates perception and that different cues activate brain areas devoted to alerting and to orienting attention (Posner and Fan 2007). This implies that it is possible to help the user redirect attention, maintain attention on a certain item, or simply alert him to possibly relevant stimuli. However, psychological literature also tells us that certain stimuli may be perceived if uncued and even if they are actively blocked. For example, in a noisy environment such as a cocktail party we are able to block out noise and listen to just one conversation amongst many (Cherry 1953), but why will some of us very easily and almost necessarily notice our name if mentioned in a nearby but unattended conversation? In trying to address this question, Conway and his colleagues showed that 'subjects who detect their name in the irrelevant message have relatively low working-memory capacities, suggesting that they have difficulty blocking out, or inhibiting, distracting information' (Conway, Cowan and Bunting 2001: 331). Similar results, relating working-memory capacity and the ability to block distractors, have been reported in the visual modality with experiments employing neurophysiological measures (Fukuda and Vogel 2009). A better understanding of these mechanisms could help us design systems that help

users who have more difficulties in maintaining focus with obvious applications in, for example, in-car support systems, technology enhanced
learning applications, control room systems, etc. The study of this very
close relationship between attention and working memory has been a
very active area of research (Awh, Vogel and Oh 2006; Baddeley 2003;
Buehner *et al*. 2006; Engle 2002; Shelton, Elliott and Cowan 2008).
However, both attention and working memory realize multiple functions
implemented by a variety of processes that physically correspond to multiple areas in the brain and therefore the interaction between attention
and working memory is difficult to grasp. Some of the chapters in this
book take different stands on this interaction. In chapter 4, Low, Jin
and Sweller base their analysis of the relationship between attention and
learning on an assumption of 'equivalence between working memory
and attentional processes'; in chapter 5, Bowman and his colleagues see
attention as a mechanism that mediates the encoding and consolidation
of information in working memory; in chapter 9, Stojanov and Kulakov
indicate that activated items in working memory guide the perception
processes.

Another area of research in cognitive psychology that has had a significant impact on the field of human–computer interaction addresses the
question of whether all types of stimuli are treated by a central system or,
instead, several different systems manage different types of input. The
organization of attention over several channels associated with different
modalities was first proposed by Allport, Antonis and Reynolds (1972),
who suggested that a number of independent, parallel channels process
task demands. Users' responses to messages in different modalities have
consequently been studied in relation to the optimization of interaction in
various applications (see, for example, chapters 4 and 7 of this volume).
The interaction between, and the integration of, these different channels
has not yet been extensively studied. The large majority of the studies of
attention have concentrated on either the sound modality or the visual
modality. Recent research, expecially when related to human–computer
interaction, is for the most part focused on visual attention. This greater
focus on visual attention is reflected in this book, with many chapters (3,
5, 7, 10) reporting results in this modality.

A final important issue, recurrent in this volume, addresses how to
facilitate the user in his perception and understanding of messages coming from digital devices. It is commonly accepted that two types of
processes, bottom-up and top-down, guide attention and visual attention in particular. Bottom-up processes, also called exogenous processes, guide attention to *salient* elements of the environment; and top-
down, or endogenous, processes guide attention to elements of the

environment that are relevant to the current task. The definition of what determines the saliency of elements of the environment, and the creation of models that integrate both bottom-up and top-down processes, has been a very active area of research (Cave 1999; Itti 2005; Peters and Itti 2007). These issues are central to chapters 3 and 5 of this book.

A challenge that this book aims to address is the creation of a bridge (or a set of bridges) between the research work carried out in cognitive psychology and neuroscience, which reports fundamental results on specific aspects of attentional processes, and the work carried out in human–computer interaction that endeavours to apply these results. The difficulty of this effort is mainly due to the fact that, in the former work, experiments are carried out in controlled environments where the conditions under which subjects are working are known, and effects are observed over periods of time that are often very short (down to the millisecond). Instead, in real-world situations, such as the ones addressed by research in human–computer interaction, there is very little or no control over the conditions under which users are working, and the time lengths are much longer with effects that may span hours, days or even months. To make things worse, addressing the problems faced by human–computer interaction would require a holistic theory of attention, which is still far from being achieved. As a result, the tools and systems proposed in the chapters of this book necessarily focus only on some aspects of attention. For example, chapter 8 focuses on the effects of contextual information, chapter 10 on the conspicuity of visual information, and chapter 12 on social aspects of attention. Nevertheless, attention-aware applications have been shown to be greatly beneficial in several areas, including the control of appliances and desktop interfaces (chapter 7), robotics (chapter 9), visualization for decision making (chapter 10), learning and training (chapters 8 and 11), and online collaborative environments (chapter 12).

The book is organized in three parts, with chapters that focus mainly on concepts in part I, chapters that focus mainly on theoretical and software tools in part II, and chapters describing applications in part III.

Part I (Concepts) introduces the conceptual framework of research aimed at modelling and supporting human attentional processes. The chapters in this part analyse human attention in digital environments, integrating results from several different disciplines, including cognitive psychology, neuroscience, pedagogy and human–computer interaction.

Chapter 2 sets the scene by providing a broad overview of the main issues addressed by attention research in cognitive psychology and neuroscience, and their relevance for the design of digital devices.

In chapter 3, Ronald Rensink reviews one of the prevalent areas of attention research, vision science. Drawing on his vast experience in this subject, Rensink guides the reader through an exploration of visual attention and the many processes involved in scene perception. Based on this knowledge of scene perception, Rensink proposes that displays may be designed so that they elicit particularly efficient users' responses.

John Sweller, who co-authors chapter 4 with Renae Low and Putai Jin, has developed *cognitive load* theory, one of the most influential theories relating attention and learning. Cognitive load theory was originally designed 'to provide guidelines intended to assist in the presentation of information in a manner that encourages learner activities that optimize intellectual performance' (Sweller, Merrienboer and Paas 1998: 251). In chapter 4 the authors discuss the impact of cognitive load theory on the design of digital tools supporting learning.

Part I closes with a chapter by Howard Bowman, Li Su, Brad Wyble and Phil J. Barnard. The authors report on the results obtained in the Salience Project,[1] and elegantly analyse some aspects of attention that have been the focus of recent research, including its temporal organization, its redirection, and the role of long-term goals and emotional significance in determining saliency.

Part II (Theoretical and software tools) analyses the theoretical and computational mechanisms currently available for supporting human attentional processes. These tools span very different areas of attention-related services to users.

Chapter 6, contributed by Benoît Morel and Laurent Ach, focuses on the design of artificial characters that adapt to the attentional state of the user. On the strength of over a decade of practice in creating 3D embodied agents, the authors explain the role that attention plays in creating engaging agents 'that are capable of natural, intuitive, autonomous and adaptive behaviours that account for variations in emotion, gesture, mood, voice, culture and personality'.

In chapter 7, Kari-Jouko Räihä, Aulikki Hyrskykari and Päivi Majaranta discuss eye-tracking technology based on their long experience of leading some of the most successful research endeavours in this field, including the European Network of Excellence COGAIN and the EYE-to-IT project. Eye-tracking technology has historically been central to the development of attention-aware applications because of the very close relationship between gaze direction and attention. After reviewing the psychological foundation of visual attention, the authors

[1] www.cs.kent.ac.uk/~hb5/attention.html.

address the question of the relation between attention and the point of gaze as well as the use of the latter for the implementation of adaptive applications.

Chapter 8, authored by Hans-Christian Schmitz, Martin Wolpers, Uwe Kirschenmann and Katja Niemann, proposes that metadata about attention allocation can be captured and exploited to personalize information and tasks environments. Significantly, on the basis of their extensive application studies, the authors argue for the important role of attention metadata for the support of cooperative work.

In chapter 9, Georgi Stojanov and Andrea Kulakov analyse how attention may be modelled within a complete cognitive architecture. After reviewing how attentional processes are represented in several known cognitive architectures, the authors present their own cognitive architecture, founded on robotics research, and they highlight the role played by attentional processes.

Part III (Applications) presents several computing applications designed to support attention in specific environments. The applications presented in this part cover a wide variety of fields, showing the relevance of attention-aware systems to fields as different as command-and-control displays, technology-enhanced learning, and the support of online communication and collaboration.

The application described by Frank Kooi in chapter 10 is the result of the author's very long experience in researching and implementating visual displays. The objective of the two-depth layer display presented by the author is to increase the amount of information available to the user without increasing clutter. Based on knowledge of visual attentional processes, Kooi proposes that, by using dual layer displays, search may be made much more efficient in command-and-control displays.

Chapter 11, authored by Inge Molenaar, Carla van Boxtel, Peter Sleegers and Claudia Roda, reports on a system designed to supply adaptive and dynamic scaffolding through the analysis and support of learners' attentional processes. The experimental results clearly show the potential of the application of attention management in technology-enhanced learning environments.

Finally, in chapter 12, Thierry Nabeth and Nicolas Maisonneuve propose an implementation of the general attention support model originally proposed by Roda and Nabeth (2009). This model is based on four levels of support: perception, deliberation, operation and metacognition. Chapter 12 explains how this model may be implemented to support social attention and describes the attention-aware social platform AtGentNet.

1.1 References

Allport, D. A., Antonis, B., and Reynolds, P. 1972. On the division of attention: A disproof of the single channel hypothesis, *Quarterly Journal of Experimental Psychology* 24(2): 225–35

Awh, E., Vogel, E. K., and Oh, S. H. 2006. Interactions between attention and working memory, *Neuroscience* 139(1): 201–8

Baddeley, A. 2003. Working memory: Looking back and looking forward, *Nature Reviews Neuroscience* 4: 829–39

Broadbent, D. E. 1958. *Perception and Communication*. London: Pergamon Press

Buehner, M., Krumm, S., Ziegler, M., and Pluecken, T. 2006. Cognitive abilities and their interplay: Reasoning, crystallized intelligence, working memory components, and sustained attention, *Journal of Individual Differences* 27(2): 57–72

Cave, K. R. 1999. The FeatureGate model of visual selection, *Psychological Research* 62(2–3): 182–94

Cherry, E. C. 1953. Some experiments on the recognition of speech, with one and with two ears, *Journal of the Acoustical Society of America* 25(5): 975–9

Conway, A. R. A., Cowan, N., and Bunting, M. F. 2001. The cocktail party phenomenon revisited: The importance of working memory capacity, *Psychonomic Bulletin and Review* 8(2): 331–5

Deutsch, J., and Deutsch, D. 1963. Attention: Some theoretical considerations, *Psychological Review* 70: 80–90

Engle, R. W. 2002. Working memory capacity as executive attention, *Current Directions in Psychological Science* 11(1): 19–23

Fukuda, K., and Vogel, E. K. 2009. Human variation in overriding attentional capture, *Journal of Neuroscience* 29(27): 8726–33

Itti, L. 2005. Models of bottom-up attention and saliency, in L. Itti, G. Rees and J. K. Tsotsos (eds.), *Neurobiology of Attention*. San Diego, CA: Elsevier: 576–82

James, W. 1890. *Principles of Psychology*. New York: Holt

McCrickard, D. S., Czerwinski, M., and Bartram, L. (eds.) 2003. Notification user interfaces, special issue of *International Journal of Human–Computer Studies* 58(5): Elsevier

Peters, R. J., and Itti, L. 2007. Beyond bottom-up: Incorporating task-dependent influences into a computational model of spatial attention. Paper presented at the IEEE Conference on Computer Vision and Pattern Recognition (CVPR). Minneapolis, MN: 1–8

Posner, M. 1980. Orienting of attention, *Quarterly Journal of Experimental Psychology* 32(1): 3–25

Posner, M. I., and Fan, J. 2007. Attention as an organ system, in J. Pomerantz (ed.), *Neurobiology of Perception and Communication: From Synapse to Society. The IVth De Lange Conference*. Cambridge, UK: Cambridge University Press

Roda, C., and Nabeth, T. 2009. Attention management in organizations: Four levels of support in information systems, in A. Bounfour (ed.), *Organisational Capital: Modelling, Measuring and Contextualising*. Abingdon: Routledge: 214–33

Roda, C., and Thomas, J. (eds.) 2006. Attention aware systems, special issue of *Computers in Human Behavior* 22(4): Elsevier

Shelton, J. T., Elliott, E. M., and Cowan, N. 2008. Attention and working memory: tools for understanding consciousness, *Psyche* 14. Retrieved July 2010 from: www.theassc.org/journal_psyche/archive/vol_14_2008

Sweller, J., van Merrienboer, J. J. G., and Paas, F. G. W. C. 1998. Cognitive architecture and instructional design, *Educational Psychology Review* 10(3): 251–96

Treisman, A. 1960. Contextual cues in selective listening, *Quarterly Journal of Experimental Psychology* 12: 242–8

Vertegaal, R. (ed.) 2003. Attentive user interfaces, special issue of *Communications of the ACM* 46(3): ACM

Vogel, E. K., Luck, S. J., and Shapiro, K. L. 1988. Electrophysiological evidence for a postperceptual locus of suppression during the attentional blink, *Journal of Experimental Psychology: Human Perception and Performance* 24(6): 1656–74

Wood, S., Cox, R., and Cheng, P. 2006. Attention design: Eight issues to consider, *Computers in Human Behavior* 22(4): 588–602

Part I

Concepts

2 Human attention and its implications for human–computer interaction

Claudia Roda

Remembering planned activities, resuming tasks previously interrupted, recalling the names of colleagues, sustaining focused performance under the pressure of interruptions, ensuring that we don't miss important information . . . these are only a few examples of critical activities whose performance is guided by attentional processes. This chapter proposes that knowledge about attentional processes can help us design systems that support users in situations such as those described above. The first part of the chapter gives an overview of some of the essential theoretical findings about human attention. The second part analyses attentional breakdowns and how those theoretical findings may be applied in order to design systems that either help avoid attentional breakdowns or assist in recovering from them.

2.1 Introduction

Current information and communication technologies concentrate on providing services to users performing focused activities. However, focused activity is no longer the norm. Users are often interrupted, they switch between the contexts of different devices and tasks, maintain awareness about the activity of distant collaborators and manage very large quantities of information. All this results in high cognitive load that may hinder users' overall achievements.

In order to address interaction in a more realistic manner, we have been working on the development of systems that are capable of supporting the processes that govern human cognitive resources allocation: attentional processes.

Attention plays an essential role in task performance and interaction. It enables us to act, reason and communicate, in physical or virtual environments that offer us stimuli exceeding, probably by several orders of magnitude, what we are actually capable of processing. Attention makes it possible for us to pursue goals without being distracted by the immense variety of available alternative stimuli and actions and undeniably mediates our interaction with the world.

Many years of research, within several fields of study, have demonstrated that attention is a surprisingly complex and multifaceted phenomenon. However, as we discover more about the processes involved in attention, we are also increasingly provided with the knowledge necessary to design systems that take into account the limitations and characteristics of such processes. This is particularly important because people interact with a growing number of devices while involved in many parallel activities. Hence the strategies and means employed for allocating and shifting attention play a major role in performance and satisfaction.

In our approach, the essential cues enabling the understanding of user activity are the user interactions with the environment. Such interactions are managed by attentional processes, which guide the allocation of cognitive and physical resources, allowing one to both perceive the environment and act upon it. Attention allocation can be used as the proxy that both reveals and guides interactions enabling us to build *attention-aware systems* (Roda and Thomas 2006). These systems recognize that attentional processes play an important role in many of the problematic situations faced by users of digital environments and aim at reducing information overload, limiting the negative effects of interruptions, increasing situation awareness (especially in the case of virtual environments) and supporting users in situations of multi-tasking (Roda and Nabeth 2007). In our work, for example, we have been able to show that attention management may effectively guide interaction in digital learning environments. The results obtained show that attention-based scaffolding improves students' results, while fostering a more proactive attitude towards the learning activity and increased motivation (Molenaar and Roda 2008 and Molenaar *et al.* in chapter 11 of this book). Similar results highlighting the positive effects of attention support have been obtained by others in situations of cooperative problem solving (Velichkovsky 1995) and in contexts where the user needs proactive assistance (Eisenhauer *et al.* 2005).

One problem that has often been encountered in designing attention-aware systems is that current knowledge about the cognitive and perceptual processes underlying attention allocation is, if seen from an HCI (human–computer interaction) point of view, very scattered. At the macro-level, many different theories, based on diverse hypotheses, describe individual aspects of attention, but no unified view of attentional phenomena exists. At the micro-level, research results about individual attentional phenomena are often analysed for very simple tasks and environments which, while allowing for sound and well-controlled experimental settings, do not reflect at all the conditions of users in real-world applications. Unfortunately this situation is not likely to change in the short term. The integration of the different aspects of attention in a single theory capable not only of describing individual phenomena but also of predicting their effects and interactions seems currently out of our reach. Perhaps easier to achieve is the scaling-up of some of the findings reported on individual phenomena so that they are a closer approximation of real-world settings in which users select their own goals, read documents composed of many words, see screens whose content depends on previous operations, etc.

The aim of this chapter is to collect the findings of psychological research that appear most relevant to the design of attention-aware systems (section 2.2) and then to show how these findings have been, or could be, used in design (section 2.3). Given the breadth of this review, it is necessarily very partial, but it will hopefully give the reader a feeling for the issues involved in designing systems that take into consideration human cognitive and perceptual limitations.

We set the scene with the classic endogenous versus exogenous perspective on attention and then explore two important areas of study: divided attention and automaticity. Understanding divided attention is essential to the design of attention-aware systems because, under this heading, we find research highlighting the constraints under which we perform multiple tasks and attend to multiple sensory input. Automaticity, on the other hand, explores what we appear to be able to do more easily, although the subsection on 'what we may miss' mitigates the view of our efficiency. Section 2.2 concludes with an overview of the important relationship between attention and memory and a discussion of long-term attention which is almost completely excluded from current studies in cognitive psychology and neuroscience. In section 2.3 we turn to the application of psychological theories to system design. In order to do this, we consider common situations of failure, which we name *attentional breakdowns*, and describe how attention-aware systems may help avoid, or recover from, such breakdowns. In particular we consider: prospective memory failures; retrospective memory failures; task resumption failures; disruption of primary tasks; missing important information; and habituation errors. In discussing recovery and avoidance of these breakdowns, we consider several types of systems; however, we don't discuss here three large application domains: machine vision, robotics and virtual reality. We believe that most of the discussion in this chapter would also apply to these domains, but a treatment of their specific requirements is outside the scope of the chapter.

2.2   The many faces of attention

Attention has been extensively studied for many years. However, the answer to the question *what is attention?* is not a straightforward one. *Attention as selection* has been the most common paradigm guiding research in this field (Baddeley and Weiskrantz 1993; Driver 2001; Lavie and Tsal 1994; Parasuraman and Davis 1984; Posner 1982), although some authors stress that attention selectivity covers a variety of very different purposes and functionalities (see, for example, Allport 1993). Within the *attention as selection* paradigm attention is seen as the set of mechanisms that allows the allocation of cognitive resources, which are assumed to be limited. In the literature, attentional selection has been associated with a variety of – possibly overlapping – functions, including influence over (1) which stimuli will be processed, (2) which information will enter working memory (Awh, Vogel and Oh 2006; McNab and Klingberg 2008), (3) which stimuli will reach a level of conscious availability (Koch and Tsuchiya 2007; O'Regan and Noë 2001; Posner 1994) and (4) which internal and external actions will be performed (Hommel 2010; Hommel, Ridderinkhof and Theeuwes 2002; Norman and Shallice 1986).

With respect to visual attention, for example, Desimone and Duncan (1995: 194) summarize attentional selection as follows: 'At some point (or several points) between input and response, objects in the visual input compete for representation, analysis, or control. The competition is biased, however, towards information that is currently relevant to behaviour. Attended stimuli make demands on processing capacity, while unattended ones often do not.' With respect to action, Norman and Shallice (1986: 3) propose that 'two complementary processes operate in the selection and control of action. One is sufficient for relatively simple or well-learned acts. The other allows for conscious, attentional control to modulate the performance.'

This section discusses three aspects of attention that are particularly relevant to HCI. First, in section 2.2.1, we are concerned with the issue of how attention may be affected by the environment and by the internal state of the user (e.g., his goals, intentions, motivation) and how these effects may interact. This knowledge will provide us with a better understanding of how, by acting on the user environment, devices may direct or *protect* users' attention. Second, in section 2.2.2, we explore how attention may be divided among several targets. This aspect of attention is obviously related to multi-tasking, which is a normal condition of operation in most computing environments. The objective is to gain an understanding of how the organization and presentation of several tasks and information may affect user performance. Third, in section 2.2.3, we consider the issue of automaticity. Automatic processes are those that can take place without disturbing ongoing activity. If a device can communicate with users by activating automatic processes then the communication is very efficient and does not disturb the user. Fourth, section 2.2.4 explores the relationship between attention and memory through two constructs: working memory and prospective memory. The former has often been correlated with intelligence; it significantly impacts on the efficiency with which we can treat information and defines the limits to the amount of information we can elaborate at one time (Buehner *et al.* 2006; Conway *et al.* 2002; Engle 2002; Engle, Kane and Tuholski 1999; Engle, Tuholski *et al.* 1999). The latter controls our ability to perform planned actions; because of its high failure rate, supporting prospective memory is particularly important. Finally, section 2.2.5 briefly discusses the time span of attention over which digital support takes place.

2.2.1   *Endogenous/exogenous – top-down/bottom-up processes*

Attention selectivity can be considered as guided by two main mechanisms. Either attention is captured, in a 'bottom-up' manner, by external events – as when one notices a sudden loud noise in the silence – or it is controlled voluntarily, in a 'top-down' manner, by the subject – as when one follows the sequence of words in a text one is reading. The two types of control are often called respectively exogenous and endogenous to stress the fact that either external or internal (to the subject) events regulate attention allocation. This dichotomy, bottom-up versus top-down, is in many ways related to the classic dichotomy, recurrent in twentieth-century psychology, focusing on either conscious control of human behaviour, as proposed by humanist theories, or behaviour which is determined by environmental factors, as in early behaviourist theories, and unconscious choices, as proposed by Freud. Many current theories of attention assume that both aspects intervene, so that some human experiences and behaviours are automatic responses to environmental stimuli, whilst other experiences and behaviours are under the control of the subject. The top-down, bottom-up dichotomy has also been the source of a debate related to the fact that some authors see attention as a *cause*, others see it as an *effect*, and others yet as a combination of both (Fernandez-Duque and Johnson 2002; Stinson 2009). Under the causal interpretation, attention is seen as an engine capable of orienting perception and guiding cognitive processes. Such a motor is generally modelled through some 'executive system' which, some authors dispute, is none other than a homunculus because no clear account is given of its functioning. Effect theories of attention, instead, see attention allocation as the result of various sensory and cognitive processes. These theories, rooted in neuroscience, maintain that no executive system exists and perceptual stimuli compete in order to activate cortical areas, and attention is merely a side effect of these competitive processes. So, while cause theories associate attention with top-down processes and dispute whether attention plays a role in bottom-up processes as well (i.e., whether there can be any processing of sensorial input without attention), effect theories merely see attention as a by-product of bottom-up processes (i.e., attention plays no role in the processing of sensorial input). Whilst the main objection to cause theories is the homunculus issue, the main objection to effect theories is their alleged inability to account for situations in which very salient stimuli are not attended, or vice versa, low-saliency stimuli are.

As we return to the discussion of top-down (or endogenous) and bottom-up (or exogenous) processes, we will see that, although this chapter mainly reports on causal theories, the themes mentioned above will recur often.

An important difference between the two attentional mechanisms is that exogenous processes are assumed to be capable of processing several stimuli in parallel, while endogenous processes are considered to be sequential; consequently the former are much faster than the latter. Chun and Wolfe (2001: 279) stress the fact that 'endogenous attention is voluntary, effortful, and has a slow (sustained) time course; . . . exogenous attention draws attention automatically and has a rapid, transient time course'.

The interaction between exogenous and endogenous processes has been the subject of much research and it is often studied through models based on the observations of subjects' physical and/or neurological activity. Following most theories, overall attentive behaviour cannot be determined by one or the other type of processes individually. However, from the point of view of HCI, it is important to note that exogenous processes are triggered by changes in the environment, i.e., something a device may be able to provoke, whereas endogenous processes are under the subject's internal control which a device may only be able to influence indirectly.

Following this classic differentiation between endogenous (top-down) and exogenous (bottom-up) processes, many authors have proposed more detailed models describing how these processes may work.

Bottom-up processes select stimuli on the basis of their *saliency*, where saliency is determined by how much an item stands out from its background based on *basic features* (e.g., colour, shape, etc.), luminance, level of detail or extended configurations (Rensink, chapter 3 in this volume). Other factors that appear to influence bottom-up selection may be learned – e.g., hearing one's own name in a conversation is very salient, and a famous face generates more interference than an unknown one (Lavie 2005) – or are instinctively important – such as translating and looming stimuli (Franconeri and Simons 2003) or novel signals (Fahy, Riches and Brown 1993). Note, in passing, that this strictly bottom-up definition of saliency is not shared by all authors. Bowman *et al.* in chapter 5 of this book, for example, define saliency in terms both of bottom-up and top-down processes, including factors such as relevance to long-term goals and emotional significance.

Top-down processes, instead, select stimuli on the basis of their relevance to the current task or goal. This selection may be done by enhancing the quality of the signal of stimuli that have certain task-relevant features at a given time. Top-down processes are based on information describing which characteristics of the input are relevant to the current task. Duncan and his colleagues call this information *the attentional template* (Desimone and Duncan 1995; Duncan and Humphreys 1989). It also appears that the strength of the bias associated with certain input characteristics 'depends on the difficulty of the task performed at the attended location' (Boudreau, Williford and Maunsell 2006: 2377) so that, for example, if a stimulus is more difficult to recognize, the top-down signal supporting its selection will be stronger.

An important aspect of selective attention is related to the control of action. In order to explain how action may be controlled, including the cases in which action performance may be considered automatic, Norman and Shallice propose that two different and complementary sets of processes are involved. The first set of processes controls actions that are 'relatively simple or well learned' (Norman and Shallice 1986: 3); in this case, action sequences are represented by sets of *schemas* that may be activated or inhibited by perceptual input without the need for attention. Different levels of activation enable the selection of schemas through a mechanism called *contention scheduling*. The second set of processes depends on a *supervisory attentional system* (SAS) and provides for the management of novel or complex actions for which no schema is available. The SAS intervenes by supplying extra activation or inhibition of schemas so that the appropriate sequence of actions may be selected that responds to the situation.

This model fits well with the bottom-up, top-down paradigm described earlier. Sensory-based (bottom-up) and volition-based (top-down, involving the SAS) activation processes interact to guide action.

Along with Norman and Shallice's, several other models have been proposed which aim to articulate this interaction between attention, perception, consciousness and action (e.g., Hommel, Ridderinkhof and Theeuwes 2002; LaBerge 2002).

Based on results of functional neuroimaging, Posner and his colleagues propose that three distinct functions of the attentional system should be recognized: alerting, orienting and executive control. 'Alerting is defined as achieving and maintaining a state of high sensitivity to incoming stimuli; orienting is the selection of information from sensory input; and executive attention involves mechanisms for monitoring and resolving conflict among thoughts, feelings, and responses' (Posner and Rothbart 2007: 7; see also Posner and Fan 2007; Hussain and Wood 2009).

Within this framework we can imagine that signals such as alarms and warning road signs would vary the state of alertness; the provision of spatial cues for where a target will appear would orient attention; and executive control may be activated when planning is needed, to detect errors (e.g., attention is needed for one to realize that one has chosen the wrong road), to respond appropriately to novel situations or to overcome habitual actions (e.g., typing on an English qwerty keyboard when used to a French azerty one).

The analysis proposed by Posner and his colleagues provides important insights for human–device interaction. The first of these is the existence of a general alertness state that would make a user more sensitive to incoming stimuli. Second, there is the possibility of using cue-based orienting of attention to support users in making selections without reducing available choices (see section 2.3.4 of this chapter). Third, there is the need to take into consideration the increased effort the user will have to invest in *novel situations* and in *overcoming habitual actions* (see section 2.3.6).

As a result of the activation of bottom-up and top-down processes, a selection takes place that enables only the strongest signals to influence subsequent processing. Note that this type of selection in fact happens at many levels between sensory input and higher level processing.

In certain situations bottom-up priority may be so high that a signal takes over attention even if it is irrelevant to the current task. The involuntary shift of attention to a target that is not relevant to the current task is called *attention capture* (Franconeri and Simons 2003; Yantis 2000). The issue of whether attention may be captured in a purely bottom-up manner, and what exactly are the characteristics of the stimuli that may trigger such a capture, is still a subject of research: see Gibson *et al.* 2008 for an account of the many aspects and interpretations of *attention capture*. It is clear, however, that under certain conditions, certain stimuli – e.g., sudden luminance changes or noise – cause a shift of attention in a manner that appears to be independent of the current task. Lavie and her colleagues propose a theory that aims at clarifying the different roles played by perception and cognitive control in attention capture. On the basis of a set of experiments, they argue that high perceptual load reduces distractor interference, whilst high cognitive load increases distractor interference (Lavie *et al.* 2004).

Attention capture is very important for the design of human–device interfaces because, on the one hand, devices may be able to 'protect' users from undesired attentional shifts (e.g., someone's phone ringing in a lecture theatre may distract a whole audience), but, on the other hand, devices may be able to provoke attention capture when a user's attention needs to be drawn to a particular event (e.g., calling an operator's attention to a fault in the system he is controlling): see section 2.3.4 of this chapter.

2.2.2   Divided attention

Attention may be concentrated on a single item (focused attention) or it may be divided between multiple targets (divided attention, split attention). The majority of the work on divided attention addresses one or both of two related issues: (1) multi-tasking, in particular dual-task performance; and (2) the identification of multiple sensory inputs. In both cases divided attention has been shown frequently to induce errors and delays in response. The questions addressed are: Which cognitive processes are involved in the performance of two or more tasks simultaneously or in attending multiple sensory inputs? And what are the factors intervening in the performance of multiple tasks? The answers to these questions have important consequences for device design and for how information should be presented in order to facilitate learning (this latter aspect is discussed by Low, Jin and Sweller in chapter 4 of this volume).

Two main theories have tried to explain the problems we may encounter in divided attention situations: capacity theories and cross-talk theories. Another hypothesis which is relevant to divided attention is that multi-tasking involves switching from one task to another and that the switch itself may generate interference.

2.2.2.1 Capacity theories

Capacity theories argue that a limited pool of cognitive resources is available. Some authors postulate that we have a single set of mental resources (Kahneman 1973) and, consequently, as we increase the number of targets, we necessarily reduce the resources available to attend each one of them. Other theorists argue for a *multiple resources theory* by which different cognitive and perceptual processes are supported by different sets of resources and therefore performance under divided attention varies depending on whether the targets require the same resources or not. Wickens (2002) identifies four types of resources (dimensions) influencing task interference: processing stages, perceptual modalities, visual channels and processing codes.

The processing stage dimension predicts that perceptual and cognitive activities share the same resources while selection and execution of responses pulls from a separate set.

The perceptual modalities dimension predicts that different perceptual modalities (visual, auditory, etc.) pull from separate resources. For example, Duncan and his colleagues (Duncan, Martens and Ward 1997) found that targets in different modalities do not generate the same level of interference as multiple sensory input presented in the same modality. Note that, although multiple task performance is obviously affected by the limit of perceptual analysis of multiple stimuli, there are situations, such as split visual attention over easily discriminated targets, in which it appears possible simultaneously to attend stimuli at non-adjacent locations (Bichot, Cave and Pashler 1999; Cave and Bichot 1999; McMains and Somers 2004).

The visual channels dimension predicts that focal vision requires a different set of resources than ambient vision.

Finally, the processing codes dimension predicts that analogue/spatial processes use a different set of resources than categorical/symbolic (e.g., linguistic) processes.

2.2.2.2 Cross-talk theories   Cross-talk theories attribute the errors and delays that one may experience in divided attention situations not to the fact that there is, so to speak, not enough fuel to support multiple cognitive activities, but rather to the interference between the contents of the information being processed. These theories relate performance to the information involved in the specific tasks, so that similar tasks are more likely to interfere with each other. Several experiments show that dual-task performance improves when the two tasks are dissimilar. Navon and Miller (1987: 435) report experimental results supporting the hypothesis that reduced performance in dual-task situations may be due to interference when 'the outcome of the processing required for one task conflicts with the processing required for the other task (e.g., cross-talk)'.

2.2.2.3 Task switching   Multi-tasking is also closely related to task switching (Pashler 2000). Many experiments demonstrate that if two tasks must be attended in sequence, the response to the second task is slowed down as the interval between the two tasks is reduced. This effect is termed the *psychological refractory period* (PRP) (Welford 1952). One possible explanation of the delay observed when people try to divide attention between two or more tasks is that only one active task-set (i.e., the configuration of mental resources necessary to perform the task (Anderson 1996; Monsell 2003)) can be maintained at a time. Under this hypothesis, multi-tasking amounts to frequent switches of attention between the attended tasks. The task-set is changed at each switch. The multi-tasking activity is therefore affected by the delayed response times due to the PRP. The PRP, and task-switching delays in general, have been extensively studied and several alternative explanations of this effect have been proposed (Meiran, Chorev and Sapir 2000; Pashler 1994; Pashler and Johnston 1998). Rogers and Monsell (1995) present a set of experiments indicating that both task-set updating costs and cross-talk effect intervene in task switching.

Altmann and Trafton (2002) have performed experiments on a task requiring frequent switches between goals (the Tower of Hanoi puzzle) and formulate a *goal-activation* model. The main hypotheses guiding this model are that goals have different levels of activation in memory, that decay of memory traces is not instantaneous but gradual, and that the most active goal is the one that will guide behaviour. The authors argue that three elements can be used to predict performance: first, the interference between goals due to decay time for old goals in memory; second, the time needed to encode the new goals; and third, the cues available for retrieving pending goals. We will see that these three predictive constraints play an important role in the design of attention-aware systems, in particular with respect to prospective memory failures and disruption of primary task.

2.2.2.4 Diffusion of attention   Recent research has reported an opposite effect of divided attention that, although frequently experienced, has rarely been studied. Exploring the *attentional blink*, an effect by which subjects fail to identify the second of two visual targets presented in close succession, Olivers and Nieuwenhuis (2005: 265) found that this effect 'is significantly ameliorated when observers are concurrently engaged in distracting mental activity, such as free-associating on a task-irrelevant theme or listening to music'. In order to explain these results they formulate the hypothesis that the task-irrelevant mental activity generates a *diffusion of attention* which could be attributed to a higher state of arousal, a positive affective state or the multi-tasking situation itself.

Another study reports that complex choices (e.g., deciding which car or apartment to buy) may actually benefit from the lack of attention, and subjects may achieve more satisfactory results if, during the decision-making time, their attention is engaged in an unrelated demanding task. These results were explained by the fact that conscious thought, which can be very precise, is also limited by the boundary of what we can attend to at any given time. Unconscious thought, instead, can process and summarize very large amounts of information (Dijksterhuis *et al.* 2006).

2.2.3   *Automaticity*

The discussion in the previous section has highlighted the existence of two types of processes: those that can, in a sense, be considered *automatic* and those that require a closer control on the side of the subject. Automaticity is pervasive in human behaviour and extends to the automatic effect of perception on action, automatic goal pursuit and a continual automatic evaluation of one's experience (Bargh and Chartrand 1999). In this chapter, however, we will only concentrate on two aspects of automaticity that are particularly relevant to HCI: the lower effort required to perform automatic processes as compared to non-automatic ones, and the high effort required to override automatic reactions. Although the discussion so far has given an indication that bottom-up processes are automatic whilst top-down ones are not, a clearer definition of what automaticity is and which processes actually correspond to this definition would be helpful.

In the literature automaticity has been defined in many different ways and factors of very diverse nature have sometimes been considered. In fact automaticity can be defined along at least three different sets of parameters: (1) the behaviour induced; (2) the neuronal mechanisms involved; and (3) the cognitive mechanisms underlying the processes. So, for example, on a behavioural basis we can say that an automatic process will induce a fast response to a stimulus, on a neuronal basis we can say that amplified activity takes place in a certain area of the brain, and on a cognitive mechanism basis we can say that the process does not require the intervention of an executive attentional system. With respect to our objectives, the distinction between the three sets of parameters is important because behavioural and neuronal parameters enable us to give a measurable definition of the occurrence of automatic processes. This means that on the basis of behavioural or neurophysiologic observations of the user we will be able to predict the likelihood that certain environmental conditions will trigger automatic processes. In particular we will concentrate on behavioural parameters, which can give us a sense of how users may respond to certain types of interaction.

Historically, several different behavioural parameters have been used to define automatic processes. First, automaticity is normally associated with fast *response times*. Response time measures the time interval between the presentation of a stimulus and the response of the subject (e.g., pressing a button in response to seeing a certain object on the screen). Second, automaticity is normally associated with obligatory execution, i.e., the subject may not be able to avoid executing the process. Third, automatic processes are assumed to have no interaction with other concurrent processes, i.e., in situations of divided attention, the performance of other processes is not affected by the automatic process. Fourth, it has been argued that automaticity is normally associated with high transferability so that the performance level of automatic processes remains constant across different types of tasks. Fifth, automaticity is normally associated with no awareness, i.e., the subject will not be able to report that the process is taking place. Note also the relation between choice and awareness: no awareness requires that the process be obligatory. Sixth, automaticity is normally associated with no sensitivity to distractors so that the presence of multiple stimuli will not affect the level of performance of the automatic process.

Most authors consider only the first two of these parameters and automatic processes are defined as obligatory processes resulting in fast response times.

Although these parameters have frequently been defined as taking discrete values (e.g., processes are parallel and fast or serial and slow, interaction takes place or not), there is increasing evidence that they may take continuous values, so that a process may generate a continuum of response times or may interact with other processes at different levels under different conditions.

Behavioural and neuronal measures are often used to deduce underlying cognitive mechanisms. However, there is no widespread agreement on what combinations of such measures imply which cognitive mechanisms. For example, in order to assess whether certain subjects' responses to stimuli are purely due to bottom-up cognitive mechanisms (i.e., purely controlled by external stimuli irrespective of the subjects' attentional state), many experiments rely on *response time* or *stimulus exposure duration*. Following the experimental technique employed by Treisman and Gelade in defining *feature integration theory* (Treisman and Gelade 1980), many authors consider that if the response time is relatively short and constant, unrelated to the number of distractors, then the process is bottom-up (and pre-attentive in particular) because subjects are obviously not performing a serial search through the items but a parallel one. Similarly, for stimulus exposure duration, pre-attentive processing is assumed to take place when subjects to whom a stimulus is shown for a short and fixed exposure duration (about 200 ms) accurately report on the presence of the target stimulus, regardless of the number of distractors. However, these types of definitions have caused confusion between pre-attentive processes and, what we will call here, learned-response processes which, along other dimensions of automaticity, behave significantly differently from pre-attentive processes (see section 2.2.3.2).

2.2.3.1 On what we perceive fast   Early selection theories (Broadbent 1958) and modified early selection theories (Treisman 1960), which are briefly discussed in the introduction to this book, stipulate that essential information about sensory input is extracted by one type of automatic processes, pre-attentive processes, and is then processed by attentive processes. Pre-attentive processes are defined as bottom-up processes dealing with simple information about the input signals and, importantly, they are very fast because input is processed in parallel (Treisman 1985; Wolfe 2001; see also Rensink, chapter 3 of this volume).

Response time in pre-attentive processing is fast and not significantly affected by the size of the display, and it can take place when focused attention is prevented (e.g., by the simultaneous performance of an attention-demanding task, or by extremely brief exposure to the stimulus). According to Treisman and Gelade's feature integration theory (Treisman and Gelade 1980), pre-attentive processes are the bottom-up processes that detect *basic features* of the visual input, such as colour, orientation and size. It is still a matter of research which *basic features*, and under which conditions, are systematically detected by pre-attentive processes: see Wolfe 2001 for an overview.

Several authors (see, for example, Logan 1992: 317; Wright 1998: 111) define pre-attentive processes as being obligatory, stimulus-driven, parallel, independent of attention and preceding attentional selection: the output of pre-attentive processes is assumed to be the input for attentive ones. However, a classic question in the attention literature is whether, and if so which, bottom-up processes really act independently of top-down control, i.e., can take place in the absence of attention.

In the visual modality Treisman (Treisman 1985; Treisman and Gelade 1980) has proposed that individual features are processed in parallel and, at a later stage, attention intervenes to *integrate* these features into objects. Consequently, searches for targets defined by individual features are parallel and not affected by variations in the number of distractors, whilst searches along multiple features require attention and are therefore sequential. For example, the red spot and the diagonal bar in figures 2.1a–d (see plate) can be found pre-attentively, both targets *pop out* and their retrieval time is not significantly different whether they are surrounded by few distractors (figures 2.1a and c) or many (figures 2.1b and 2.1d). On the other hand, attention needs to be applied to find the blue diagonal bar in figure 2.1e and the response time will be much higher in the case of a larger number of distractors as shown in figure 2.1f. The red spot and the diagonal bar of figures 2.1a–d are said to be *visually salient* because they stand out from their background of homogenous blue spots in figures 2.1a and 2.1b, or horizontal bars in figures 2.1c and 2.1d.

Similarly to the visual modality, research in the sound modality has demonstrated that parallel processing supports the recognition of auditory features such as frequency, intensity and duration of acoustic stimuli (see, for example, Takegata *et al.* 2005; Winkler *et al.* 2005).

Other authors, however, note that visual saliency is not an absolute property of a stimulus but it describes how a certain element stands out with respect to its background (Itti 2005). For example, the saliency of the diagonal bar in figures 2.1c and 2.1d is significantly reduced amongst non-homogenous distractors in figure 2.1g, and amongst distractors that are very similar to the target as shown in figure 2.1h. On the basis of these observations, Duncan and Humphreys (1989: 433) suggest that in visual searches 'difficulty increases with increased similarity of targets to nontargets and decreased similarity between nontargets producing a continuum of search efficiency'. This is a departure from the classic dichotomy (feature/parallel versus conjunctions/serial) governing theories about visual searches that stipulate that searches for individual features proceed in parallel, whilst searches for conjunction of features take place serially. Automaticity is no longer simply associated with searches for individual features. The quality of the distractors, and not only whether the search is for single/multiple features, comes into play in deciding whether the search can be performed fast, obligatorily and without interacting with other processes. A related question is that of how different features contribute to overall perceptual saliency. Several computational models of bottom-up attention have represented different featural contributions and control mechanisms (see Itti 2005 for a review), providing a better understanding of feature interaction. These models are based on *saliency maps* representing stimulus saliency in every point of a two-dimensional space: see, for example, Itti, Koch and Niebur 1998. Recently, models integrating both bottom-up and top-down attentional control have been developed (e.g., Navalpakkam and Itti 2006; Schill, Zetzsche and Hois 2009). These models not only contribute to the field of machine vision but also enable the testing of hypotheses about the functioning of human attentional mechanisms.

Another line of research departing from feature integration theory has aimed at establishing what other types of information, beside pre-attentive features, can be extracted automatically from images. Evidence from neuroscientific observations, for example, supports the hypothesis that fairly complex facts, such as determining whether an image contains the picture of an animal, can be extracted very quickly (within 150 ms) upon presentation of a stimulus (Thorpe, Fize and Marlot 1996) and, in general, the gist of a scene can be determined very rapidly (Rensink, chapter 3 of this volume). Other work suggests that in some cases discrete objects may be recognized with the same efficiency as individual features (see, for example, review in Scholl 2001).

Although the application of these laboratory results to interface design is not always straightforward, they imply that certain information can be made available to the user by presenting it in a manner that triggers automatic processes, thereby minimizing the demands on the attentional system (as discussed in section 2.3.4, this would be particularly useful for notification systems). In fact, the discussion so far would place us in an ideal situation, allowing the design of interfaces that present information in a manner that does not disturb the user and where interaction could be mostly automatic, requiring little or no attention from the user.[1] Unfortunately, as our experience tells us, this is not always possible. In the following sections we will see that attention may be necessary to detect stimuli even if they are very salient, and that the performance of concurrent tasks may be negatively affected even by well-known interaction patterns.

2.2.3.2 On what we can learn to do rapidly   In the classic perception literature automatic processes have often been equated to pre-attentive processes and defined as processes that do not require attention. More recent accounts (Logan 1992; Treisman, Vieira and Hayes 1992) distinguish between pre-attentive processes and what we here call *learned-response* processes. Learned-response processes are associated with learning. The idea is that performing a well-rehearsed action (e.g., recognizing a well-known object, eating with fork and knife, washing your hands) will require less attentional effort than performing a new or less known one. Logan believes that this difference in cognitive demand may be explained by a theory in which 'novice (nonautomatic) performance is based on a general algorithm for solving the problems the task presents, whereas

---

[1] Note that interfaces controlled mostly on automatic feedback are not unusual and include, for example, the dashboard and control system used to drive a car.

automatic performance is based on single-step, direct-access retrieval of past solutions from memory . . . Automatic processing has the properties of well-practiced memory retrieval. It is fast and effortless' (Logan 1988; 1992: 321). This dual nature of automaticity is also evident in the analysis of automatic self-regulation proposed by Bargh and Chartrand, as they state: 'Some of the automatic guidance systems . . . are "natural" and don't require experience to develop . . . Other forms of automatic self-regulation develop out of repeated and consistent experience; they map onto the regularities of one's experience and take tasks over from conscious choice and guidance when that choice is not really being exercised' (Bargh and Chartrand 2000: 476).

For our purposes it is important to note that there appear to be two types of processes allowing fast access to information. First, there are pre-attentive processes (such as single-feature visual searches), which are either innate or acquired at a very early age. These processes maintain performance in situations of divided attention and in the context of different tasks. Second, there are learned-response processes (such as the recognition of some danger symbols in a display), which may become automatic but only after practice. These processes bring no advantages to performance in divided-attention settings (Logan 1992) and don't transfer well to novel tasks (Treisman, Vieira and Hayes 1992).

This implies that in display design certain pop-out effects can only be achieved through training whereas others, based on single features, come *for free* as they are innate.

2.2.3.3 On what we may miss   We have seen that a question motivating the research work mentioned above is that of whether automatic processes, and bottom-up processes in general, require attention, i.e., the intervention of some executive attentional system. Whilst the work presented in sections 2.2.3.1 and 2.2.3.2 implies that attention may not be involved in early processing of sensorial input, some neuroscientific experiments support the hypothesis that attention operates from the very early stages of visual processing (Awh, Vogel and Oh 2006; Hillyard, Vogel and Luck 1998), with amplified responses to attended visual stimuli beginning within 60 ms of stimulus onset. The results of some behavioural experiments may also be explained as refuting the hypothesis that certain visual processes occur *without attention* (Gibson and Peterson 2001). Several authors (Mack and Rock 1998; Simons and Chabris 1999), for example, argue that there is no conscious perception of the visual world without attention to it (but see also discussion in Driver *et al.* 2001). Mack bases her argument on the *inattentional blindness* phenomenon which 'denotes the failure to see highly visible objects we may be looking at directly when our attention is elsewhere' (Mack 2003: 180). Several experiments demonstrate that highly salient (from a sensory point of view) stimuli can be completely missed if they are not the explicit targets of a visual search; therefore it is argued that, unless attention is allocated to the target, the subject develops no conscious perception of the stimuli.

The possibility of a subject completely missing certain parts of a stimulus is accompanied by another, similar phenomenon, *change blindness*, i.e., the 'failure to see large changes that normally would be noticed easily' (Simons and Rensink 2005: 16). Changes in the visual environment are normally salient because they produce a transient motion or flicker. However, in a series of, sometimes very surprising, experiments (Simons) the authors show that even very large changes may go unnoticed if they are not attended when they occur (see also Rensink in chapter 3 of this volume).

Interestingly, the factors that may prevent change detection are not only related to the current attentional focus (a subject concentrating on a target may miss a change occurring in the environment), or sensory input (e.g., the change is hidden by an occluding object, the flicker of a display or an eye movement), but could also be cultural. Nisbett and Masuda, for example, report that East Asian subjects are more likely to detect changes in the relationships between objects in a scene, whereas Westerners are more likely to detect changes to objects' attributes (Nisbett and Masuda 2003).

Taken together, the main result of this research is that human vision does not create a *copy* or *complete representation* of the world in the mind, as has been assumed for many years. Human vision rather seems to be a more dynamic process that binds elements of the external world in models that satisfy the needs of the viewer on the basis of the current task. As O'Regan puts it, 'the outside world is . . . a kind of external memory store which can be accessed instantaneously by casting one's eyes (or one's attention) to some location' (O'Regan 1992: 461).

2.2.3.4 Automaticity in action   So far we have mainly concentrated on the role of attention in the selection of perceptual input. The question of automaticity, however, naturally highlights another important aspect of attention: the role it plays in action control. In their seminal paper studying this aspect of attention, Norman and Shallice argue that the term *automatic*

has at least four different meanings. First, it refers to the way that certain tasks can be executed without awareness of their performance (as in walking along a short stretch of flat, safe ground). Second, it refers to the way an action may be initiated without deliberate attention or awareness (as in beginning to drink from a glass when in conversation). Third, it is used in cases such as the orienting response, in which attention is drawn automatically to something, with no deliberate control over the direction of attention. And finally, [it refers] to situations in which a task is performed without interfering with other tasks' (Norman and Shallice 1986: 1–2).

As we have seen earlier, it may happen that the sensory-based activation is strong enough to override volition-based activation. In these cases actions that may be unrelated or even inappropriate for the performance of the current task may be initiated or completely carried out (as when one walks to a place out of habit when, in fact, one should have gone somewhere else). These situations correspond to the first two types of automaticity described by Norman and Shallice. As the authors note, the third type of automaticity – 'attention is drawn automatically to something' – is significantly different from the previous two types because, instead of guiding action without involving attention allocation, it automatically redirects attention.

We may therefore (in the first two cases of automaticity) have stimuli that provoke certain actions but don't involve any attentional shifts. The subject maintains his attention on the current task. In the third case, however, the automatic process triggers a change in the supervisory system that may provoke a lasting change of attentional focus. In terms of human–device interaction, if we assume that some device produces the stimulus, the latter case of automaticity corresponds to the generation of a very salient stimulus that attracts attention to the device itself (for example, to provide information about an emergency situation). The former two cases instead correspond to a stimulus capable of producing an automatic action that will not disturb (or, more likely, bring minimal disturbance to) the user's current activity such as when, for example, one stops or starts walking at the change of a traffic light. This type of automatic behaviour requires some learning on the side of the user but the resulting interaction is very efficient.

2.2.4   Attention and memory

Human thought and action are obviously influenced by past experience. Memory is the system that enables us to record past experience and use it in the present. Attention is strictly related to memory in two manners: on the one hand, our memories may influence attention allocation; on the other hand, attention allocation may determine which sensory input is stored in memory.

The study of human memory has a long history and memory has been defined along many different dimensions.

One classic differentiation is between explicit memory and implicit memory: see Eichenbaum 1997, Polster, Nadel and Schacter 2007 and Schacter 1987 for influential reviews. Implicit memory is not available for conscious retrieval but influences task performance; one example of implicit memory is procedural memory which enables us to perform actions, such as riding a bicycle, without explicitly remembering the individual components of the action. Explicit memory enables us to bring facts and experiences of the past to mind and then express them in some format. The memory of facts such as *Rome is the capital of Italy*, which are theoretical knowledge independent from a specific context, has been named *semantic memory*; the memory of personal experiences, which are related to specific contexts in time and space and carry some emotional value, has been named *episodic memory* (Tulving 1972).

Although the distinction between implicit and explicit memory is important and has influenced research in human–computer interaction (e.g., Oulasvirta 2004; Oulasvirta, Kärkkäinen and Laarni 2005), this chapter will mainly focus on two other characteristics of the memory system that are more immediately related to attention: the relationship between long-term memory and working memory, and the distinction between retrospective memory and prospective memory.

2.2.4.1 Working memory   Memory is normally seen as fulfilling two different functions: collecting information for long-term retrieval and holding information for immediate usage. These two different functions can be exemplified by the memory of the number 313 that may be created to remember the date when Constantine issued the Edict of Milan; and the memory of the number 313 created if asked to add 213 and 100. The former type of memory is called *long-term* memory (LTM), referring to the fact that the number 313 is stored for retrieval possibly hours, days or even years after it is memorized. The latter type of memory is meant for immediate use and the number 313 (which, by the way, may be retrieved from long-term memory as the date of the Edict of Milan) is only remembered for the time necessary to perform the calculation. Memory for immediate use is characterized by fast decay (it does not last long) and very limited capacity which, in a very influential paper, Miller (1956) evaluated at 7 ± 2 *chunks* of information (for a more recent discussion of working-memory capacity limits, see also Cowan *et al.* 2008).

In the seventies Baddeley and Hitch (1974) proposed a model of this memory for immediate use, which they called *working memory*. Since then the term working memory has been adopted widely. Baddeley and

Hitch emphasized the fact that working memory includes several components, that it combines processing and storage, and that it forms the basis for most cognitive activities. The authors proposed that working memory is a three-component system, including 'a control system of limited attentional capacity, termed the *central executive*, which is assisted by two subsidiary storage systems: the *phonological loop*, which is based on sound and language, and the *visuospatial sketchpad*' (Baddeley 2003: 830). Subsequently Baddeley (1986) proposed that the central executive system could be implemented with the model proposed by Norman and Shallice (1986) (also discussed in sections 2.2.1 and 2.2.3.4 of this chapter).

The Baddeley and Hitch model has been fundamental for the development of much research addressing how attention and working memory relate to other aspects of cognition, including language learning and processing, fluid intelligence, consciousness and many other cognitive processes (Engle 2002). The model has also been supported by much neuroscience research, notably by the findings of Goldman-Rakic (1987). However, some authors have argued for a dynamic, functional view of working memory, by which working memory is the 'active portion of LTM, coupled with mechanisms for cognitive control' (Conway, Moore and Kane 2009: 262). In this view, the content of working memory may lose its discrete characteristic and, as Anderson has proposed, because of 'the continuous nature of activation . . . membership in working-memory is a matter of degree. Less active working-memory elements are processed less rapidly, for instance, in a recognition task' (Anderson 1983: 263). Items are available for processing, not because they are stored in a special component, but because they have reached a threshold value of activation in long-term memory. In this view, control mechanisms of working memory are not achieved through a specialized system but rather due to 'coordinated recruitment, via attention, of brain systems that have evolved to accomplish sensory-, representation-, or action-related functions' (Postle 2006: 23).

Cowan's model (Cowan 1988) integrates some aspects of the classic Baddeley and Hitch model with the view of degrees of activation in long-term memory. Cowan argues that what really distinguishes short-term from long-term memory is the processes necessary to maintain activation, e.g., rehearsal for short-term memory, and semantic elaboration for long-term memory. Memory can be activated either automatically by external stimuli, or through attention. These two types of activations may interact so that 'automatic activation may direct attention, and attention may in turn influence the amount of memory activation' (Cowan 1988: 172). Further, Cowan argues that the *focus of attention* is a part of the active portion of memory, and that items in the focus of attention are immediately available for processing. Cowan's model has subsequently inspired similar models that include a *focus of attention* component: see, for example, Oberauer 2002.

Complementary to activation, another aspect of memory is very important for the good functioning of cognition, that is decay. Decay reduces activation and eventually results in forgetting (or losing the memory trace). Altmann and Gray (2000) argue that, in task environments, we need to forget a task (at least partially) in order to perform another one. In particular, if one task has reached a below-threshold state before a new one becomes current, then there will be no interference between the two tasks. Literature in this area has concentrated on addressing the question of what are the factors that intervene in forgetting: see Wixted 2004 for a survey.

2.2.4.2 Prospective memory Prospective memory, closely related to intentionality (Marsh, Hicks and Bryan 1999; Sellen *et al.* 1997), is the mechanism that allows us to remember planned activities in the future (e.g., go to a meeting, complete writing a paper, turn off the oven in thirty minutes, give a message to a friend when we meet him). Whilst retrospective memory is the mechanism that allows us to remember facts of the past (e.g., people's names, the lesson studied yesterday), prospective memory requires remembering to remember, i.e., remembering something at an appropriate moment in the future. Such a moment may be represented by an actual time (e.g., going to a meeting at 2 p.m.) or by the occurrence of an event or a series of events (e.g., publishing the minutes once everyone has approved them). This has brought about the distinction between 'event-based and time-based remembering tasks' (Sellen *et al.* 1997: 484). Studies in prospective memory have mostly concentrated on event-based remembering and analyse the two aspects of 'acting when encountering the correct circumstances (prospective component) and . . . remembering the correct action to perform (retrospective component)' (Kardiasmenos *et al.* 2008: 746).

Kliegel *et al.* describe prospective memory mechanisms as organized in four phases: '(1) intention formation – the point at which a future activity is planned; (2) intention retention – the period during which the intended action is retained in memory while other ongoing activities are performed (i.e., the ongoing task); (3) intention initiation – the moment at which execution of the intention is initiated; and (4) intention execution – the actual execution of the intended action(s) according to a previously formed plan' (Kliegel, Mackinlay and Jäger 2008: 612). As in the case of other cognitive processes discussed above, the question arises of the cognitive effort required in order to complete prospective memory tasks. In particular, several authors have studied how one may go from intention retention to intention initiation. This process, often named *prospective memory retrieval*, requires matching some event in the environment to target events in prospective memory (e.g., it's 2 p.m., thirty minutes have elapsed, all approvals to the minutes have arrived) and initiating the task to be executed (e.g., go to the meeting, turn off the oven, publish the minutes). Some authors (e.g., Burgess and Shallice 1997) see prospective memory retrieval as an attention-demanding process and have proposed that the executive attentional system (such as Norman and Shallice's supervisory attentional system or Baddeley's central executive) monitor the environment for events that would match prospective memory target events. Other authors have proposed that prospective memory retrieval may be an automatic process that does not require attention allocation except perhaps in specific situations such as when the task is very important. In the latter interpretation, events in the environment may act as cues that, rather than requiring focused attention, are accepted by an automatic-associative memory and, if activated enough, may bring to awareness the associated intended action (Einstein and McDaniel 1996).

'Critical for purposes of prospective memory, this information is retrieved rapidly, obligatorily, and with few cognitive resources [and,] in contrast to the cue-focused views, the target event is not necessarily recognized as a cue' (McDaniel *et al.* 2004: 606). However, a set of experiments proposed by McDaniel and his colleagues (McDaniel *et al.* 2004) support the hypothesis that both types of processes may intervene in prospective memory retrieval. In particular, they argue that retrieval is more likely to be attained through automatic – i.e., reflexive and obligatory – processes if the target event is sufficiently associated with the intended action (e.g., write the word 'house' whenever the picture of a house appears), whilst attentive processes are more likely to intervene when the target event is not as well associated with the intended action (e.g., write the word 'house' whenever the number 56 appears). There appears to be no single rule deciding the type of process applied in retrieval; rather, the degree of monitoring versus spontaneous retrieval depends on task complexity and individual differences.

Einstein (Einstein and McDaniel 1996) found that factors intervening in the selection of automatic or attentive processes include: (1) whether the target event is focal, i.e., whether the ongoing activity encourages focal processing of the prospective memory target; (2) the importance of the prospective memory task, as reflected by the level of emphasis given to the prospective memory task when instructing the subjects;

(3) the number of target events; (4) the duration of the ongoing task; and (5) individual differences. In their experiments, spontaneous retrieval processes took place with focal prospective memory target events and when the prospective memory task was moderately emphasized. On the other hand, attentive monitoring of the target event took place 'with a nonfocal target or high-emphasis instructions or both' (Einstein and McDaniel 1996: 331). A single target event was retrieved automatically, whilst a test with six target events revealed that attentive monitoring was engaged. Consistently with previous results indicating that capacity for maintaining controlled processing is limited (e.g., Bargh and Chartrand 1999), the authors found that attentive monitoring declined over trials in the nonfocal condition. Optimal performance of the prospective memory task, with minimal costs (least disturbance to the ongoing task), were obtained in the focal target moderate-emphasis condition.

2.2.5   Long-term and short-term attention

Our perception, intentionality, social situation and aesthetic sensibility all seem to concur in determining our attentional behaviour. This behaviour may be observed and analysed both in the short term and in the long term. Short-term attentional processes, strongly related to working memory and cognitive load, reflect one's immediate concentration on an object or activity. For example, short-term attention may be deployed on a specific part of an image in order to recognize an object. Long-term attentional processes refer to processes that span over a length of time of minutes, hours, days or even months. They normally involve one or more tasks, long-term memory as well as working memory. An example of long-term attention may be the cognitive effort that one makes in writing a letter, or in completing a much longer, possibly collaborative, project. Understanding short-term attention enables one to support users in the immediate selection of, and focus on, tasks or objects. Short-term attention can be evaluated by the use of behavioural and psycho-physiological measures capable, for example, of detecting the level of arousal of a user in relation to a given stimulus.

Understanding long-term attention enables one to provide individuals and groups of users with the appropriate information and guidance about their long-term allocation of cognitive resources. Long-term attention can be inferred through analysis of subjects' activities over an extended period of time. To our knowledge, long-term attention has not been investigated in psychology and neuroscience. The only research that moves in the direction of long-term attention involve those experiments requiring the performance of lengthy complex tasks under high cognitive load conditions. Examples of such tasks are complex-span tasks (Diamond 2005; Unsworth and Engle 2007) where subjects are asked to remember a list of items while performing some processing activity, e.g., calculations. Complex-span tasks are sometimes called working-memory tasks because they test the ability to maintain (or focus on) elements held in working memory. Some experiments (e.g., Colom *et al.* 2006) compare results obtained by subjects performing complex-span tasks with results obtained in simple-span tasks (or short-term memory tasks) where subjects have to remember lists of items but are not asked to perform a simultaneous processing activity. Conway and his colleagues (Conway *et al.* 2002) indicate that simple-span tasks can be performed on the basis of automatic routines such as rehearsal and chunking, whilst complex-span tasks cannot and therefore require the intervention of the supervisory attentional system.

2.3   Addressing attentional breakdowns

In the previous section we explored some of the current theories of attention which may play a significant role in the design of interactive systems. This section explores a set of situations in which breakdowns occur as a consequence of particularly demanding conditions, which in modern working environments are often due to multi-tasking and interruptions (Czerwinski, Horvitz and Wilhite 2004; Gonzalez and Mark 2004; Mark, Gonzalez and Harris 2005). Activity fragmentation stresses attentional processes, long-term memory and working memory, and has been the subject of several studies. For example, Gonzalez and Mark report that 'In a typical day . . . people spend an average of three minutes working on any single event before switching to another event [and] somewhat more than two minutes on any use of electronic tool, application, or paper document before they switch to use another tool' (Gonzalez and Mark 2004: 119).

In this section we will suggest how systems have been, or could be, designed in order to avoid, or recover from, attentional breakdowns.

In the human–computer interaction literature one finds references to attention with respect to very short time spans, as in the examples given in section 2.2.3, as well as to much longer time spans, as in the attention needed to drive a car (C. Ho, Tan and Spence 2005; Pêcher, Lemercier and Cellier 2009), perform collaborative activities (Nabeth and Maisonneuve in chapter 12 of this volume) or learn academic subjects (Molenaar *et al.* in chapter 11 of this volume). These situations are characterized by the fact that people are often involved in activities that require multiple and possibly interdependent or closely related tasks, they have to interact with many people and devices, and they have to find, create or manage very large amounts of information.

As we move from short to longer time spans, attentional processes are increasingly seen as coordinating information flow (rather than just selecting information input) so that appropriate higher-level perception and action can take place. Research in developmental cognitive neuroscience, for example, suggests that problems in initiating and monitoring task performance, in both adults and children, are due to deficits in the *central executive* (Diamond 2005; Wilson *et al.* 1998). Executive functions of attention are therefore necessary to plan activity and establish priority between multiple competing tasks. These observations are obviously based on a causal interpretation of attention. Effect theories, however, point in the same direction. For example, with respect to visual attention, Rensink states that attention is 'the establishment (and maintenance) of a coordinated information flow that can span several levels of processing' (Rensink 2007: 139).

This double aspect of *attention as selection* and *attention as coordination* is consistent with literature that sees attentional breakdowns as the cause of failure in situations that may appear very diverse. Forgetting to start or complete a task, being prone to interrupting one's primary task, difficulties in restarting an interrupted task or in establishing whether the conditions for the execution of a task are met, problems with task prioritization and inability to find and focus on relevant information, are all examples of phenomena that have been attributed to attentional breakdowns. This section analyses these failure situations and proposes how appropriate system design may reduce some of the burden on the user's cognitive system. We define the following set of typical attentional breakdowns: (1) prospective memory failures; (2) retrospective memory failures; (3) task resumption failures; (4) disruption of primary task; (5) missing important events and information; and (6) habituation-related failures. Each breakdown situation is analysed in detail.

2.3.1   Prospective memory failures

As discussed earlier, normal activity often requires remembering, at appropriate times, plans we have made in the recent or distant past. These memories enable the correct continuation of planned tasks when they have been interrupted, and the evaluation of relative priorities of concurrent tasks. In section 2.2.4.2 we saw that prospective memory is the mechanism that enables these types of recollection. Daily experience and laboratory experiments demonstrate that prospective memory is essential for professional performance, independent living and social relationships (Eldridge, Sellen and Bekerian 1992; Kardiasmenos *et al.* 2008; Lamming *et al.* 1994). However, it has been reported that prospective memory failures may account for up to 70 per cent of memory failures in everyday life (Kliegel and Martin 2003; Kvavilashvili, Messer and Ebdon 2001) and that such failures are likely to occur more frequently in older adults than in younger ones (Kliegel, Mackinlay and Jäger 2008; Kvavilashvili, Messer and Ebdon 2001; Zimmermann and Meier 2010). This situation is further aggravated in modern working and learning environments where a high level of multi-tasking increases the difficulty in keeping track of relative priorities between tasks.

Services to help users overcome these problems may include task reminder services such as those associated with many electronic calendars. The ideal reminder service, however, should provide the user with an environment where task reminders may be associated with user tasks and group tasks, as well as various types of resources. These reminders should also help users remember to resume tasks that have been interrupted, which are reported as not being resumed in 40 per cent of cases (O'Conaill and Frohlich 1995).

One approach to enhancing current reminder services is based on collecting information about people's attention allocation to task and resources (see Schmitz *et al.*, chapter 8 of this volume on such information collection) and then using this information for inferring tasks' urgency, relationships and priority. Reminder systems should be able to represent and manage information about tasks' dependencies/sequences and resource availability. This would enable the system to detect if a task represents a bottleneck for other personal or community tasks, to visualize the consequences of not completing a certain task within a certain date, and to issue reminders only if the conditions for the execution of a task are met (e.g., prerequisite tasks have been completed and resources are available). Intelligent task reminder services, implementing the above requirements, would lower the load on prospective memory, allowing users to concentrate on the task currently performed.

With respect to interrupted tasks, the *goal-activation model*, briefly introduced in section 2.2.2.3, predicts that prospective memory failures could be reduced 'if operators were taught to react to an alert by searching for a cue and associating it with the goal being suspended' (Altmann and Trafton 2002: 66). The authors also argue that the digital environment should provide those cues so that an association can be formed at interruption time and priming can take place at resumption time.

In section 2.2.4.2 other factors affecting the effort associated with prospective memory tasks were discussed. Some of these factors, such as the emphasis on importance of the prospective memory tasks, cannot be controlled through system design. Others, however, may be. These include high association between target and intended action, focal targets and single target. Under these conditions prospective memory tasks may be achieved with higher levels of automaticity, therefore reducing cognitive effort.

It seems likely that systems capable of providing semantically relevant reminder messages highly associated with the reminded tasks will prove effective in reducing users' cognitive effort in the phases of *intention initiation* and *intention execution*. Further, integration of the target (i.e., the reminder message) within the current task environment would make the target focal, and could result in the improved performance of prospective memory tasks. Finally, the aggregation of all reminder messages in a single system should promote automation since the user will be monitoring a single target area or object type. To our knowledge none of the above hypotheses has been verified through the evaluation of interfaces providing these types of services. Much work, however, has been done in the evaluation of notification methodologies (see section 2.3.4), of which reminders are a special case. It should be noted that in the design and evaluation of notification systems the emphasis is often placed on reducing the disturbance to the primary task whereas here we have been concerned with techniques that optimize the retrieval of a prospective memory task.

2.3.2   *Retrospective memory failures*

Retrospective memory failures occur when someone has difficulties remembering previously acquired information (e.g., someone's name, a lecture studied, having met someone, having visited a place). Eldridge proposes that retrospective memory problems can be classified into the following seven categories: forgetting a person's name, forgetting a word, forgetting an item in a list, forgetting a past action or event, forgetting some aspect of past actions or events, forgetting where some object (physical or electronic) was put or last seen and forgetting how to perform some action or series of actions (Eldridge, Sellen and Bekerian 1992). Several systems have been devised with the aim of reducing the negative effects of retrospective memory failures or enhancing human memory capacity (e.g., Mase, Sumi and Fels 2007). The 'Forget-Me-Not' system (Lamming *et al.* 1994; Lamming and Flynn 1994), for example, has been implemented in a PDA-like device and continuously collects data about user activity (e.g., telephone calls, documents printed, people encountered, etc.), allowing the user to search information for specific events.

For instance, one can retrieve the telephone number dialled while talking to a colleague. Because associations of this type (i.e., not remembering a telephone number but remembering that a call to that number was made in a certain context) happen frequently, services such as those offered by the 'Forget-Me-Not' system promise to be very useful to remedy retrospective memory failures. iRemember (Vemuri and Bender 2004), a 'wearable memory prosthesis', captures audio – and face-to-face conversations in particular – along with the user's location, calendar, email, commonly visited websites and weather. This data is then indexed and organized for searching and browsing so that retrieved data can act as triggers for forgotten memories.

Issues related to retrospective memory failures have concerned researchers for a long time and recur across the entire field of information management (e.g., Freeman and Gelernter 2007; Karger 2007).

2.3.3   Task resumption failure: context restore

Because multi-tasking is the condition under which we often operate, we regularly have to interrupt tasks and restart them at a later time. Mary Czerwinski and her colleagues performed a diary study analysing the effects of interruptions on task performance. They found that it is significantly more difficult to switch to tasks that require 'returning to' after an interruption, and that returned-to tasks take generally longer than more routine tasks and require 'significantly more documents, on average, than other tasks' (Czerwinski, Horvitz and Wilhite 2004: 178–9). Mechanisms for prospective memory support, such as the ones described in section 2.3.1, may be used to remind a user of the need to resume interrupted tasks. Resuming a task, however, doesn't only require remembering to restart the task but also entails being able to re-establish the context of that task (e.g., retrieving the documents necessary for the performance of the task). To this end, retrospective memory support systems such as those mentioned in the last section can be used to remind the user about the context of resumed tasks – see Czerwinski and Horvitz 2002 and Franke, Daniels and McFarlane 2002 for a review from this perspective, and Franke, Daniels and McFarlane 2002 for an example of a system implementation in the domain of military logistics tasks. However, because we are considering tasks that are performed in digital environments, the system may do more than just remind the user about the task context; it can actively save the context of interrupted tasks and restore it on demand. We expect that services of this type would significantly reduce cognitive load and minimize task resumption time.

Additionally, a complete rethinking of the metaphors used in interface design could reduce the problems related to context restore. In the current desktop interface, in order to complete a task – say, write a report – the user is forced to fragment the task into subtasks (such as using a word processor to write some text, collecting data from a spreadsheet, going back to the spreadsheet to insert the data). This fragmentation could be avoided by shifting from an *application-oriented* to a *task-oriented* approach to computer-based activities (Clauzel, Roda and Stojanov 2006; Gonzalez and Mark 2004; Kaptelinin and Czerwinski 2007; Roda, Stojanov and Clauzel 2006). The definition of real-task environments would also make it possible to evaluate their characteristics automatically and control for task interference, for example along the processing stages, perceptual modalities, visual channels and processing codes dimensions suggested by Wickens (2002) and discussed in section 2.2.2.1.

2.3.4   Disruption of primary task (distraction)

The type of breakdown situations discussed in the previous three sections all require directing the user's attention to a new primary task or to a related piece of information. This section analyses instead situations in which the objective of the system is not to help the user move from one primary task to another, but rather to help the user maintain awareness about secondary information whilst minimizing disruption of the primary task. As discussed in section 2.2.1, if task-irrelevant information is presented in a very conspicuous manner, bottom-up processes may cause enough activation to override the primary task, causing attention capture and thereby interrupting the primary task. A significant body of research reports on the negative effects of interruptions both on the effectiveness and on the agreeableness of task performance (Bailey, Konstan and Carlis 2001; Gillie and Broadbent 1989; Grundgeiger and Sanderson 2009; Zijlstra *et al.* 1999). These effects are modulated by several factors, including individual differences with respect to responses to task interruptions and restoration, the characteristics of the primary tasks, the characteristics of the interruption, and the context in which the primary task and interruption take place (Czerwinski, Horvitz and Wilhite 2004; Gievska, Lindeman and Sibert 2005; J. M. Hudson *et al.* 2002; McFarlane and Latorella 2002; Oulasvirta and Salovaara 2004; Speier, Vessey and Valacich 2003). The negative effects of interruption have also been reported to be more severe on mobile devices (Nagata 2003).

The problem of presenting information in a way that enables awareness but does not disrupt the primary task has been extensively studied within the *notification systems* literature. This literature covers several application domains, including messaging systems (Cutrell, Czerwinski and Horvitz 2001; Czerwinski, Cutrell and Horvitz 2000; Horvitz *et al.* 2003), alerting in military operations (Obermayer and Nugent 2000), shared document annotation (Brush *et al.* 2001), ambient displays (Altosaar *et al.* 2006), healthcare (Grundgeiger and Sanderson 2009), social awareness in collaborative activities (Carroll *et al.* 2003), end-user programming (Robertson *et al.* 2004), air traffic control (C.-Y. Ho *et al.* 2004; Ratwani *et al.* 2008) and many others. Frameworks for the evaluation of notification systems have been proposed in order to compare approaches and capitalize on design knowledge (Chewar, McCrickard and Sutcliffe 2004; McCrickard *et al.* 2003). McCrickard and his colleagues (McCrickard *et al.* 2003) propose to measure the effects of visual notification with respect to (1) users' *interruption* caused by the reallocation of attention from a primary task to a notification, (2) users' *reaction* to a specific secondary information cue while performing a primary task, and (3) users' *comprehension* of information presented in secondary displays over a period of time. Through a set of experiments evaluating notifications along the above parameters the authors were able to establish the fitness of specific notification mechanisms given the notification objective. For example, small-sized blast or fade-in-place animation were found to be best suited to goals of minimal attention reallocation (low interruption), immediate response (high reaction) and small knowledge gain (low comprehension) (see also McCrickard and Chewar 2003).

As this section discusses methodologies aimed at avoiding disruption of the primary task, we are particularly concerned with low interruption notifications. Ideally, in order to minimize disruption whilst ensuring that relevant content is appropriately attended to, notification systems should evaluate the relevance of the information to be delivered to the current user's context, and consequently select notification contents, timing and modality. One area of investigation that, to our knowledge, has not been explored is related to the evaluation of how different types of notification mechanisms may be affected by cross-talk effects, i.e., how the content of a notification message may interfere with the execution of the current task.

2.3.4.1 Interruption relevance   Although experimental results report that notifications that are relevant to the user's task are less disruptive than irrelevant ones (Czerwinski, Cutrell and Horvitz 2000), the automatic evaluation of relevance is obviously not a trivial task because it requires semantic knowledge about user activity and about the interruption content. In order to address this problem, Arroyo Acosta (2007) has proposed to use semantic-knowledge-based systems which allow reasoning about concepts related to the user's goal and the interruption content. Another promising approach to relevance evaluation is metadata collection and analysis, as discussed by Schmitz *et al.* in chapter 8 of this volume.

Relevance evaluation remains, however, a very open field of research.

2.3.4.2 Notification contents   An obvious design question in notification systems is how much should a notification say about the new task in order to minimize *interruption* whilst maximizing *reaction* and *comprehension*?

We distinguish three types of notification system. The first type, *pure notification*, is normally a fairly simple message providing a pointer to newly available information or tasks to be performed. Common examples include a 'jumping' icon pointing to newly available system updates, or a fading small window informing users of the arrival of email messages. The second type of notification system includes *awareness mechanisms*. Differently from pure notification, awareness mechanisms provide the information itself rather than a pointer to it. Examples include awareness displays in distributed collaborative systems and stock-monitoring systems. Finally, a notification can take the form of a *complete switch of context* (e.g., opening a new window with a new application). This last case can be considered as a notification with no task cueing or, to use McFarlane and Latorella's terminology, with no *annunciation signal* (McFarlane and Latorella 2002).

Appropriate content in pure notification mechanisms is necessary in order to supply users with enough information about the interrupting task so that they can make an informed decision on whether to redirect attention (this is one of the requirements of what Woods terms the pre-attentive reference (Woods 1995)). In other words, appropriate cueing enables *intentional dismissal* and *intentional integration* (McFarlane and Latorella 2002), which take place when the user is supplied with enough information to decide whether and when to interrupt the primary task (*intentional integration*) or to continue on it, disregarding the notification (*intentional dismissal*). A study in air traffic control environments (C.-Y. Ho *et al.* 2004) reports significant improvements in the management of interruptions with a notification system that provides users with information about the modality and timing of the prospective task. One obviously important element in the selection of notification content is ensuring that the message is informative enough whilst its comprehension can be accomplished with little disruption of the primary task. There is a continuous trade-off between providing enough information for intentional integration or dismissal and minimizing the chance of disrupting the primary task – see, for example, the discussion in Sarter 2005. This problem has been analysed, with respect to textual information, in the READY system. READY is a natural language interface that dynamically adapts to the user's time pressure and working-memory limitations by appropriately bundling messages to the user. For example, shorter messages are used if the user is under time pressure, longer ones if the user is more available (Bohnenberger *et al.* 2002; Jameson *et al.* 1999).

Awareness mechanisms are similar to pure notification signals in that they inform users about new information or pending tasks. However, awareness mechanisms may provide the user with large amounts of complex data because the core of the information is immediately made available. In order to support the extraction of relevant content from awareness displays, without disrupting performance of the primary task, Somervell and his colleagues (Somervell *et al.* 2002) propose to use peripheral visualization techniques. The authors argue that some visualization techniques, which have been shown to improve performance in situations of focused attention over large and/or complex amounts of data, could be used as peripheral mechanisms that, used under divided attention conditions, bring minimal disturbance to the primary task. In this manner, the benefits, in terms of high information comprehension, of visualization techniques can be integrated with the benefits, in terms of low interruption, of pure notification mechanisms. The use of visualization techniques to support users in situations of focused attention is briefly discussed in section 2.3.5.

2.3.4.3 Timing of interruption   Notification timing impacts significantly on whether and how the interruption is perceived and on how much disruption it will bring to the current task. McFarlane and Latorella (2002: 5) propose four design solutions to schedule notifications:

immediate, negotiated, mediated, and scheduled. Interruptions can be delivered at the soonest possible moment (immediate), or support can be given for the person to explicitly control when they will handle the interruption (negotiation). Another solution has an autonomous broker dynamically decide when best to interrupt the user (mediated), or to always hold all interruptions and deliver them at a prearranged time (scheduled)

and conclude that in most situations negotiation is the best choice: see Franke, Daniels and McFarlane 2002 and C.-Y. Ho *et al.* 2004 for examples of implementation of these strategies. The conclusions drawn by McFarlane and Latorella are in line with the prediction of the *goal-activation model* (see section 2.2.2.3) that the interval between an alert and the interruption proper is a critical period: the model in fact predicts that this time can be used to prepare to resume the interrupted task (Altmann and Trafton 2002).

More recent work has considered finer-grained analysis of interruption time, on the basis of either task knowledge or sensory input.

Task-knowledge-based timing relies on the analysis of the structure of the task being performed. Bailey and his colleagues (Bailey *et al.* 2006; Bailey and Konstan 2006; Iqbal *et al.* 2005) represent tasks as two-level hierarchies composed of coarse events which are further split into fine events, and demonstrate that interruptions are less disruptive when presented at coarse breakpoints, corresponding to the completion of coarse events. Alternative task decompositions have also been proposed to select interruption timing. Czerwinski and her colleagues, for example, identify three task phases (planning, execution and evaluation) and analyse the different effects that interruptions have on these phases (Czerwinski, Cutrell and Horvitz 2000).

Sensory-input-based timing relies on sensors' input to detect user activity and the best times for interruption. On the basis of the observation that human beings can very efficiently, and in the presence of a very small number of cues, evaluate others' interruptibility, Fogarty and Hudson propose that interruptibility evaluation is attainable from simple sensors and that speech detectors are the most promising sensors (Fogarty *et al.* 2005; S. E. Hudson *et al.* 2003). Chen and Vertegaal (2004) use more sophisticated physiological cues (heart rate variability (HRV) and electroencephalogram (EEG)) to distinguish between four attentional states of the user: at rest, moving, thinking and busy. From these, they derive the user's interruptibility.

Finally, our research group has successfully explored the integration of task knowledge and sensory input for the selection of the most appropriate interruption time by combining knowledge of a detailed task structure (Laukkanen, Roda and Molenaar 2007) with simple sensory input to evaluate the strength of breakpoints for possible interruptions (Molenaar and Roda 2008).

It should be noted that appropriate selection of interruption time is particularly critical in wireless devices because the user may be carrying/wearing such devices in a wide variety of situations. J. Ho and Intille (2005: 909) propose a context-aware mobile computing device that 'automatically detects postural and ambulatory activity transitions in real time using wireless accelerometers. This device was used to experimentally measure the receptivity to interruptions delivered at activity transitions, relative to those delivered at random times'. The authors conclude that messages are better received at times when the user is transitioning between different physical activities.

2.3.4.4 Interruption modality Interruption modality is an important factor determining how disruptive an interruption will be with respect to the primary task. In particular, multiple resource theories (see section 2.2.2) predict that cross-modal interruption presentation should generate lower disruption to the primary task. On the basis of this prediction, several cross-modality notification mechanisms have been designed and evaluated (Latorella 1998; Sarter 2006), reporting mixed results. The effects of modality, in fact, appear difficult to separate from other intervening effects.

It seems possible that the advantage obtained by certain notification mechanisms is due to automatic processing of the notification whilst, in other cases, it is due to a low interference between the primary task and the task of attending to the notification. In the latter case a task switch would intervene and therefore all costs involved in the task-switching process would contribute to the cost of processing the interruption (see section 2.2.2.3), including, in particular, the cost of returning to the primary task. As discussed in section 2.2.4.2, returning to the primary task is facilitated if an associative link is maintained with the primary task. In this situation, the advantages found in many experiments testing the effects of cross-modality notification could be ascribed to the maintenance of this link rather than to a multi-resource model (e.g., a spoken notification in a visual primary task environment would maintain the visibility of the primary task screen, thereby preserving the associative link). Support for this hypothesis has been found in several small-scale experiments (Field 1987; Ratwani *et al.* 2008).

2.3.5 Missing important events and information

Section 2.2.3.3 presents results showing that in certain situations an observer may miss very salient information. These events become increasingly common as our cognitive system is placed under greater strain due to larger or more complex perceptual input and/or increased task demands. Visualization techniques have been developed to address the needs of users working under these conditions. Results of the studies of pre-attentive and automatic processing (see section 2.2.3) supply a basis for providing information in a format that can be acquired by the user with minimal effort. Significant results have recently been achieved in addressing the question of how information can be presented so that the important elements stand out (Ware 2000), and the knowledge of specific psycho-physiological visual effects has significantly guided vision research. Healey and his colleagues (Healey, Booth and Enns 1996), for example, have shown that the use of pre-attentive features (hue and orientation) can support the discrimination of important information in the context of numerical estimation. Importantly, they highlight the fact that the use of features (especially for the representation of multi-dimensional data) should be guided by the rule of avoidance of feature interference. The authors have later extended their original work to analyse texture and colour. They show that colour discrimination is related to colour distance, linear separation and colour category, while texture is mainly discriminated by size and density (Healey and Enns 1999). Another feature used to support fast detection of visual stimuli is motion. Bartram and her colleagues (Bartram, Ware and Calvert 2003) show that icons with simple motions provide an effective notification mechanism which, especially in the periphery, is detected more easily than when the user is guided by colour and shape. Motion is reported as being effective in both the near and the far field of vision, further even small linear oscillation appears to be sufficient for discrimination and not to interfere with colour and shape coding (for a further discussion of peripheral displays supporting notification which also relates to the influence of time pressure, information density and secondary tasks, see Somervell *et al.* 2002). More recent research of perception in visualization has explored the possibilities opened up by the use of 3D displays. Kooi, in chapter 10 of this volume, demonstrates how, through the use of an extra real depth layer, it is possible to declutter the screen so that more information can be displayed whilst maintaining performance. A different approach is taken by Spence (2002), who proposes that scanning through a large amount of, possibly not organized, information can be made more efficient through Rapid Serial Visual Presentation which exploits the user's ability to recognize very quickly (in the range of 100 ms) whether some information is relevant.

Purely perceptual approaches to visualization, however, may not always be sufficient because, as discussed in section 2.2.3.3, what we see or do not see, as well as what is salient and to what degree, is dependent not only on properties of the external world, but also on our own internal state and objectives; and in particular on how we allocate attention. As a consequence, some authors move to what we call an *adaptive visualization approach* in which perceptual knowledge is integrated with knowledge related to the user's current interest, goals or focus of attention. Adaptive visualization is characterized by both the choice of perceptual techniques used for interaction and the method used to evaluate users' cognitive state. One method that has been extensively researched and applied is the use of users' gaze information as an indicator of users' attention allocation. This method is further discussed by Räihä, Hyrskykari and Majaranta in chapter 7 of this volume and a survey based on evaluation studies can be found in Toet 2006. A different method for the evaluation of the user's state is taken by Furnas (1999), who proposes to use a *degree of interest* function to evaluate which portion of the structure to be displayed is most likely to be of interest to the user. The degree of interest evaluation is applied to fisheye techniques for the display of a tree structure so that the degree of interest function aims at assigning an interest value to the tree nodes. Similar approaches include Card and Nation 2002 and Lamping and Rao 1994.

One could see search engines and ranking tools as an extreme example of adaptive visualization where the perceptual technique is extremely simple (just display relevant elements in order) and the degree of interest function is very complex and corresponds to the search algorithm. Search algorithms, however, do not take into account the past and current states of attention of the user. This could be achieved through the use of attention metadata as proposed by Schmitz and colleagues in chapter 8 of this volume.

In addition to the use of visualization techniques, the problem of users missing important events and information can be addressed due to the knowledge of cognitive effects such as change blindness. For example, particularly important changes that may be missed by the user can be made more obvious to the user through cues appearing in the focus area. To our knowledge, this technique has never been experimented with.

Pure visualization approaches are sometimes integrated with approaches relying on proactive system behaviour so that, rather than trying to attract the attention of a busy user to important events, these events are automatically treated by the system. Bosse and his colleagues (Bosse, van Maanen and Treur 2006), for example, propose a system capable of recognizing if the user is not attending to an important visual event (a track on screen representing a hostile aircraft), in which case the system takes over the task.

2.3.6   Habituation-related failures

There are two important aspects of automaticity as described in section 2.2.3 that should be considered in system design. First, automatic actions can be executed in the absence of attention and therefore without interfering with other tasks. Second, automatic actions are obligatory and therefore require an act of explicit control to be suppressed. These two observations reveal that whilst automaticity may enable the design of interfaces that, once learned, will place very little demand on cognitive processes, they will also engender situations in which actions are performed without awareness, and thus regardless of whether they are correct or not. Raskin (2000) notes, for example, that requiring a confirmation on file close is ineffective if the user always has to perform the same action to confirm. Assume that after a *file close* command a window appears in which one has to press the return key to confirm; because, in the great majority of cases, one would press the return key to confirm, the sequence *file close followed by press return* will become a habitual action and it will be executed also in the rare cases when the confirmation shouldn't have been given. The consequence is that 'any confirmation step that elicits any fixed response soon becomes useless' (Raskin 2000: 22). On the other hand, if the interface is appropriately designed its use may become automatic, with all the advantages of automatic performance discussed earlier in this chapter.

In section 2.2.3.2 we saw that learned automaticity does not transfer well; this implies that habituation is better achieved in interfaces that, given a sequence of commands, always produce the same behaviour. This constraint may interfere with designs that strive dynamically to adapt the interface to the user's need, or simply to the context of the operation. To address the latter case, Raskin proposes that operation through *modes* should be replaced by operation through *quasi-modes*. Modes are contexts in which a user action may result in different behaviours of the system. A simple example is the different behaviour the system has when typing, depending on whether the Caps Lock key is engaged. The Caps Lock key defines two modes of operation of the system. The problem of modes is that users may perform actions without being aware of the mode they are in and therefore trigger unexpected system behaviours (unawareness of the Caps Lock mode, for example, may hinder the work of even the most experienced typist). Raskin argues that quasi-modes, such as the holding of the Shift key while typing, integrate the operational context in the gesture required for the user to perform the action. In this manner the interface can operate in a context-dependent manner whilst the user can acquire action automaticity: see Raskin (2000: chapter 3) for a thorough discussion.

2.4   Other relevant research areas

Although this chapter covers a wide variety of aspects of attention, some other aspects are, at least potentially, relevant to the design of attention-aware systems. The first of these is the relation between attention and emotion. Studies in this area analyse the effects of emotional stimuli depending on their valence, including reactions to happy/sad, fearful/safe and generally positive/negative stimuli. Emotional valence appears to be evaluated both at perceptual and at semantic level; it therefore influences reaction to stimuli at all levels of processing (see Compton 2003 for a review, and Lavie 2005, Lim, Padmala and Pessoa 2008 and Pêcher, Lemercier and Cellier 2009 for examples of relevant more recent work). Interfaces that strive to manage emotional aspects include those based on animated agents. Chapter 6 of this book discusses the impact of one such interface on the support of attention allocation.

Second, findings in the area of social attention could improve our understanding of the constraints and motivations guiding attention allocation. Two aspects are particularly relevant. On the one hand there is the research covered in the field of *joint attention* (Eilan *et al.* 2005; Frischen, Bayliss and Tipper 2007; Moore and Dunham 1995), which is at the heart of communication and collaboration. On the other hand, there is the research covered in the field of *collective attention*, which addresses questions such as: How do communities of people allocate attention to a given item? What processes underlie collective attention? How can these processes be supported? Some of these aspects are treated in Huberman 2008 and in chapters 8 and 12 of this book.

Finally, several studies have addressed the question of how attention allocation may vary amongst individuals; this research goes under the name of *individual differences*. In particular, age and gender appear to be significant factors (Engle, Kane and Tuholski 1999; Frischen, Bayliss and Tipper 2007; Lavie 2005). It is conceivable that interfaces capable of adapting to these individual differences may provide for a better attention support.

2.5   Conclusions

Many years of studies in cognitive psychology and, more recently, in neuroscience have built a body of knowledge about the central role of attention in human physical and mental activity. Although theories concerning various aspects of attention are sometimes scattered and controversial, many results are very relevant to the design of attention-aware systems. In this chapter we have discussed how such results help us design systems that address the problem of *attentional breakdowns*. For example, research in the area of divided attention indicates that the time span between a notification and the actual task switch, together with the associative cues provided by the system in this period, have a significant impact on task resumption; research in perception and automatic processes has provided guidelines for the design of efficient visualization mechanisms; multiple resources theories provide a path to minimize task interference in multitasking environments; and there are many other such results.

Whilst some of these results are directly applicable to system design, many others require further research in order to evaluate their effects in real-world environments where the number of perceptual stimuli and the cognitive state of the user cannot be controlled as they are in laboratory settings.

2.6   Acknowledgements

This research was partially supported by a grant from the European Commission under the FP6 Framework project AtGentive IST 4–027529-STP.

2.7   References

Allport, A. 1993. Attention and control: Have we been asking the wrong questions? A critical review of twenty-five years, in D. E. Meyer and S. Kornblum (eds.), *Attention and Performance*. London: MIT Press: vol. XIV: 183–218.

Altmann, E. M., and Gray, W. D. 2000. Managing attention by preparing to forget. Paper presented at the IEA 2000/HFES 2000 Congress. San Diego: 152–5

Altmann, E. M., and Trafton, J. G. 2002. Memory for goals: An activation-based model, *Cognitive Science* 26(1): 39–83

Altosaar, M., Vertegaal, R., Sohn, C., and Cheng, D. 2006. AuraOrb: Social notification appliance. Paper presented at the CHI '06, *Extended Abstracts on Human Factors in Computing Systems*. New York: 381–6

Anderson, J. R. 1983. A spreading activation theory of memory, *Journal of Verbal Learning and Verbal Behavior* 22(3): 261–95

   1996. ACT: A simple theory of complex cognition, *American Psychologist* 51(4): 355–65

Arroyo Acosta, E. 2007. Mediating disruption in human–computer interaction from implicit metrics of attention. Doctoral thesis, Massachusetts Institute of Technology, Cambridge, MA

Awh, E., Vogel, E. K., and Oh, S. H. 2006. Interactions between attention and working memory, *Neuroscience* 139(1): 201–8

Baddeley, A. 1986. *Working Memory*. Oxford: Oxford University Press

   2003. Working memory: Looking back and looking forward, *Nature Reviews Neuroscience* 4: 29–39

Baddeley, A., and Hitch, G. J. 1974. Working memory, in G. A. Bower (ed.), *Recent Advances in Learning and Motivation*. New York: Academic Press: vol. VIII: 47–89

Baddeley, A., and Weiskrantz, L. (eds.) 1993. *Attention: Selection, awareness and control. A tribute to Donald Broadbent.* Oxford: Clarendon Press

Bailey, B. P., Adamczyk, P. D., Chang, T. Y., and Chilson, N. A. 2006. A framework for specifying and monitoring user tasks, *Computers in Human Behavior* 22(4): 709–32

Bailey, B. P., and Konstan, J. A. 2006. On the need for attention-aware systems: Measuring effects of interruption on task performance, error rate, and affective state, *Computers in Human Behavior* 22(4): 685–708

Bailey, B. P., Konstan, J. A., and Carlis, J. V. 2001. The effects of interruptions on task performance, annoyance, and anxiety in the user interface. Paper presented at the INTERACT '01: 593–601

Bargh, J. A., and Chartrand, T. L. 1999. The unbearable automaticity of being, *American Psychologist* 54(7): 462–79

    2000. The mind in the middle: A practical guide to priming and automaticity research, in H. T. Reis and C. M. Judd (eds.), *Handbook of Research Methods in Social and Personality Psychology.* New York: Cambridge University Press: vol. XII: 253–85

Bartram, L., Ware, C., and Calvert, T. 2003. Moticons: Detection, distraction and task, *International Journal of Human–Computer Studies* 58(5): 515–45

Bichot, N. P., Cave, K. R., and Pashler, H. 1999. Visual selection mediated by location: Feature-based selection of noncontiguous locations, *Perception and Psychophysics* 61(3): 403–23

Bohnenberger, T., Brandherm, B., Grossmann-Hutter, B., Heckmann, D., and Wittig, F. 2002. Empirically grounded decision-theoretic adaptation to situation-dependent resource limitations, *Künstliche Intelligenz* 3: 10–16

Bosse, T., van Maanen, P.-P., and Treur, J. 2006. A cognitive model for visual attention and its application. Paper presented at the International Conference on Intelligent Agent Technology. IAT '06. IEEE/WIC/ACM 255–62

Boudreau, C. E., Williford, T. H., and Maunsell, J. H. R. 2006. Effects of task difficulty and target likelihood in area V4 of macaque monkeys, *Journal of Neurophysiology* 96: 2377–87

Broadbent, D. E. 1958. *Perception and Communication.* London: Pergamon Press

Brush, B., Bargeron, D., Gupta, A., and Grudin, J. 2001. *Notification for Shared Annotation of Digital Documents* (Technical Report No. MSR-TR-2001-87): Microsoft Research

Buehner, M., Krumm, S., Ziegler, M., and Pluecken, T. 2006. Cognitive abilities and their interplay: Reasoning, crystallized intelligence, working memory components, and sustained attention, *Journal of Individual Differences* 27(2): 57–72

Burgess, P. W., and Shallice, T. 1997. The relationship between prospective and retrospective memory: Neuropsychological evidence, in M. A. Conway (ed.), *Cognitive Models of Memory.* Cambridge, MA: MIT Press: 247–72

Card, S. K., and Nation, D. 2002. Degree-of-interest trees: A component of an attention–reactive user interface. Paper presented at the Advanced Visual Interfaces Conference: 231–45

Carroll, J. M., Neale, D. C., Isenhour, P. L., Rosson, M. B., and McCrickard, D. S. 2003. Notification and awareness: Synchronizing task-oriented collaborative activity, *International Journal of Human–Computer Studies* 58(5): 605–32

Cave, K. R., and Bichot, N. P. 1999. Visuospatial attention: Beyond a spotlight model, *Psychonomic Bulletin and Review* 6(2): 204–23

Chen, D., and Vertegaal, R. 2004. Using mental load for managing interruptions in physiologically attentive user interfaces, in *Extended Abstracts of the 2004 Conference on Human Factors and Computing Systems*. Vienna, Austria: ACM Press: 1513–16

Chewar, C. M., McCrickard, D. S., and Sutcliffe, A. G. 2004. Unpacking critical parameters for interface design: Evaluating notification systems with the IRC framework. Paper presented at the Conference on Designing Interactive Systems: Processes, Practices, Methods and Techniques (DIS 2004), Slovakia: 279–88

Chun, M. M., and Wolfe, J. 2001. Visual attention, in E. B. Goldstein (ed.), *Blackwell's Handbook of Perception*. Oxford: Blackwell: 272–310

Clauzel, D., Roda, C., and Stojanov, G. 2006. Tracking task context to support resumption. Paper presented at the HCI 2006 workshop on computer assisted recording, pre-processing, and analysis of user interaction data, London: 43–54

Colom, R., Rebollo, I., Abad, F. J., and Shih, P. C. 2006. Complex span tasks, simple span tasks, and cognitive abilities: A reanalysis of key studies, *Memory and Cognition* 34(1): 158–71

Compton, R. J. 2003. The interface between emotion and attention: A review of evidence from psychology and neuroscience, *Behavioral and Cognitive Neuroscience Reviews* 2(2): 115–29

Conway, A. R. A., Cowan, N., Bunting, M. F., Therriault, D. J., and Minkoff, S. R. B. 2002. A latent variable analysis of working memory capacity, short-term memory capacity, processing speed, and general fluid intelligence, *Intelligence* 30: 163–84

Conway, A. R. A., Moore, A. B., and Kane, M. J. 2009. Recent trends in the cognitive neuroscience of working memory, *Cortex* 45(2): 262–8

Cowan, N. 1988. Evolving conceptions of memory storage, selective attention, and their mutual constraints within the human information-processing system, *Psychological Bulletin* 104(2): 163–91

Cowan, N., Morey, C. C., Chen, Z., Gilchrist, A. L., and Saults, J. S. 2008. Theory and measurement of working memory capacity limits, *The Psychology of Learning and Motivation* 49: 49–104

Cutrell, E., Czerwinski, M., and Horvitz, E. 2001. Notification, disruption, and memory: Effects of messaging interruptions on memory and performance. Paper presented at the Interact 2001 IFIP Conference on Human–Computer Interaction, Tokyo: 263–9

Czerwinski, M., Cutrell, E., and Horvitz, E. 2000. Instant messaging: Effects of relevance and time. Paper presented at the HCI 2000 – 14th British HCI Group Annual Conference: 71–6

Czerwinski, M., and Horvitz, E. 2002. An investigation of memory for daily computing events. Paper presented at the HCI 2002: 230–45

Czerwinski, M., Horvitz, E., and Wilhite, S. 2004. A diary study of task switching and interruptions. Paper presented at the SIGCHI Conference on Human Factors in Computing Systems. Vienna: 175–82

Desimone, R., and Duncan, J. 1995. Neural mechanisms of selective visual attention, *Annual Review of Neuroscience* 18: 193–222

Diamond, A. 2005. Attention-deficit disorder (attention-deficit/hyperactivity disorder without hyperactivity), A neurobiologically and behaviorally distinct disorder from attention-deficit/hyperactivity disorder (with hyperactivity), *Development and Psychopathology* 17: 807–25

Dijksterhuis, A., Bos, M. W., Nordgren, L. F., and van Baaren, R. B. 2006. On making the right choice: The deliberation-without-attention effect, *Science* 311: 1005–7

Driver, J. 2001. A selective review of selective attention research from the past century, *British Journal of Psychology* 92: 53–78

Driver, J., Davis, G., Russell, C., Turatto, M., and Freeman, E. 2001. Segmentation, attention and phenomenal visual objects, *Cognition* 80(1–2): 61–95

Duncan, J., and Humphreys, G. W. 1989. Visual search and stimulus similarity, *Psychological Review* 96(3): 433–58

Duncan, J., Martens, S., and Ward, R. 1997. Restricted attentional capacity within but not between sensory modalities, *Nature* 387(6635): 808–10

Eichenbaum, H. 1997. Declarative memory: Insights from cognitive neurobiology, *Annual Review of Psychology* 48(1): 547–72

Eilan, N., Hoerl, C., McCormack, T., and Roessler, J. (eds.) 2005. *Joint Attention: Communication and Other Minds*. Oxford: Oxford University Press

Einstein, G. O., and McDaniel, M. A. 1996. Retrieval processes in prospective memory: Theoretical approaches and some new empirical findings, in M. Brandimonte, G. O. Einstein and M. A. McDaniel (eds.), *Prospective Memory: Theory and Applications*, Mahwah, NJ: Lawrence Erlbaum Associates: 115–42

Eisenhauer, M., Lorenz, A., Zimmermann, A., Duong, T. V., and James, F. 2005. Interaction by movement – One giant leap for natural interaction in mobile guides. Paper presented at the mobileHCI 05, Salzburg: www.comp.lancs.ac. uk/~kc/mguides05/pdfs/Eisenhauer_InteractionMovement.pdf (retrieved July 2010)

Eldridge, M., Sellen, A., and Bekerian, D. 1992. *Memory Problems at Work: Their Range, Frequency, and Severity* (Technical Report EPC-1992-129) Rank Xerox Research Centre

Engle, R. W. 2002. Working memory capacity as executive attention, *Current Directions in Psychological Science* 11(1): 19–23

Engle, R. W., Kane, M. J., and Tuholski, S. W. 1999. Individual differences in working memory capacity and what they tell us about controlled attention, general fluid intelligence, and functions of the prefrontal cortex, in A. Miyake and P. Shah (eds.), *Models of Working Memory: Mechanisms of Active Maintenance and Executive Control*. New York: Cambridge University Press: 102–34

Engle, R. W., Tuholski, S. W., Laughlin, J. E., and Conway, A. R. A. 1999. Working memory, short-term memory, and general fluid intelligence: A latent-variable approach, *Journal of Experimental Psychology: General* 128(3): 309–31

Fahy, F. L., Riches, I. P., and Brown, M. W. 1993. Neuronal activity related to visual recognition memory: Long-term memory and the encoding of recency and familiarity information in the primate anterior and medial inferior temporal and rhinal cortex, *Experimental Brain Research* 96(3): 457–72

Fernandez-Duque, D., and Johnson, M. 2002. Cause and effect theories of attention: The role of conceptual metaphors, *Review of General Psychology* 6(2): 153–65

Field, G. E. 1987. Experimentus interruptus, *SIGCHI Bulletin* 19(2): 42–6

Fogarty, J., Hudson, S. E., Atkeson, C. G., Avrahami, D., Forlizzi, J., Kiesler, S., et al. 2005. Predicting human interruptibility with sensors, *ACM Transactions on Computer–Human Interaction* 12(1): 119–46

Franconeri, S. L., and Simons, D. J. 2003. Moving and looming stimuli capture attention, *Perception and Psychophysics* 65(7): 999–1010

Franke, J. L., Daniels, J. J., and McFarlane, D. C. 2002. Recovering context after interruption. Paper presented at the 24th Annual Meeting of the Cognitive Science Society (CogSci 2002): 310–15

Freeman, E., and Gelernter, D. 2007. Beyond lifestreams: The inevitable demise of the desktop metaphor, in Kaptelinin and Czerwinski: 19–48

Frischen, A., Bayliss, A. P., and Tipper, S. P. 2007. Gaze cueing of attention: Visual attention, social cognition, and individual differences, *Psychological Bulletin* 133(4): 694–724

Furnas, G. W. 1999. The FISHEYE view: A new look at structured files, in S. K. Card, J. Mackinlay and B. Shneiderman (eds.), *Readings in Information Visualization: Using Vision to Think*. San Francisco: Morgan Kaufmann: 312–30

Gibson, B. S., Folk, C., Theeuwes, J., and Kingstone, A. (eds.) 2008. Attentional capture, a special issue of *Visual Cognition* 16(2/3): Psychology Press

Gibson, B. S., and Peterson, M. A. 2001. Inattentional blindness and attentional capture: Evidence for attention-based theories of visual salience, in C. L. Folk and B. S. Gibson (eds.), *Attraction, Distraction and Action: Multiple Perspectives on Attentional Capture*. New York: Elsevier Science: 51–76

Gievska, S., Lindeman, R., and Sibert, J. 2005. Examining the qualitative gains of mediating human interruptions during HCI. Paper presented at the 11th International Conference on Human–Computer Interaction (HCI International 2005). Mahwah, NJ: 605–14

Gillie, T., and Broadbent, D. 1989. What makes interruptions disruptive? A study of length, similarity, and complexity, *Psychological Research* 50(4): 243–50

Goldman-Rakic, P. S. 1987. Circuitry of the prefrontal cortex and the regulation of behavior by representational memory, in V. B. Mountcastle, F. Plum and S. R. Geiger (eds.), *Handbook of Neurobiology*. Bethesda, MD: American Physiological Society: 373–417

Gonzalez, V. M., and Mark, G. 2004. 'Constant, constant, multi-tasking craziness': Managing multiple working spheres. Paper presented at the SIGCHI Conference on Human Factors in Computing Systems. Vienna: 113–20

Grundgeiger, T., and Sanderson, P. 2009. Interruptions in healthcare: Theoretical views, *International Journal of Medical Informatics* 78(5): 293–307

Healey, C. G., Booth, K. S., and Enns, J. T. 1996. High-speed visual estimation using preattentive processing, *ACM Transactions on Computer–Human Interaction* 3(2): 107–35

Healey, C. G., and Enns, J. T. 1999. Large datasets at a glance: Combining textures and colors in scientific visualization, *IEEE Transactions on Visualization and Computer Graphics* 5(2): 145–67

Hillyard, S. A., Vogel, E. K., and Luck, S. J. 1998. Sensory gain control (amplification) as a mechanism of selective attention: Electro-physiological and neuroimaging evidence, *Philosophical Transactions: Biological Sciences* 353(1373): 1257–70

Ho, C., Tan, H. Z., and Spence, C. 2005. Using spatial vibrotactile cues to direct visual attention in driving scenes, *Transportation Research Part F: Traffic Psychology and Behaviour* 8(6): 397–412

Ho, C.-Y., Nikolic, M. I., Waters, M. J., and Sarter, N. B. 2004. Not now! Supporting interruption management by indicating the modality and urgency of pending tasks, *Human Factors: The Journal of the Human Factors and Ergonomics Society* 46: 399–409

Ho, J., and Intille, S. S. 2005. Using context-aware computing to reduce the perceived burden of interruptions from mobile devices. Paper presented at the CHI 2005. Portland, OR: 909–18

Hommel, B. 2010. Grounding attention in action control: The intentional control of selection, in B. J. Bruya (ed.), *Effortless Attention: A New Perspective in the Cognitive Science of Attention and Action.* Cambridge, MA: MIT Press; 121–40

Hommel, B., Ridderinkhof, K. R., and Theeuwes, J. 2002. Cognitive control of attention and action: Issues and trends, *Psychological Research* 66(4): 215–19

Horvitz, E., Kadie, C., Paek, T., and Hovel, D. 2003. Models of attention in computing and communication: From principles to applications, *Communications of the ACM* 46(3): 52–9

Huberman, B. A. 2008. Crowdsourcing and attention, *Computer* 41(11): 103–5

Hudson, J. M., Christensen, J., Kellogg, W. A., and Erickson, T. 2002. 'I'd be overwhelmed, but it's just one more thing to do': Availability and interruption in research management. Paper presented at the SIGCHI Conference on Human Factors in Computing Systems. Minneapolis: 97–104

Hudson, S. E., Fogarty, J., Atkeson, C. G., Avrahami, D., Forlizzi, J., Kiesler, S., et al. 2003. Predicting human interruptibility with sensors: A Wizard of Oz feasibility study. Paper presented at the CHI 2003. Fort Lauderdale, FL: 257–64

Hussain, F., and Wood, S. 2009. Modelling the efficiencies and interactions of attentional networks, in L. Paletta and J. K. Tsotsos (eds.), *Attention in Cognitive Systems.* Berlin: Springer-Verlag: 139–52

Iqbal, S. T., Adamczyk, P. D., Zheng, X. S., and Bailey, B. P. 2005. Towards an index of opportunity: Understanding changes in mental workload during task execution. Paper presented at the SIGCHI Conference on Human Factors in Computing Systems. Portland, OR: 311–20

Itti, L. 2005. Models of bottom-up attention and saliency, in L. Itti, G. Rees and J. K. Tsotsos (eds.), *Neurobiology of Attention*. San Diego: Elsevier: 576–82

Itti, L., Koch, C., and Niebur, E. 1998. A model of saliency-based visual attention for rapid scene analysis, *IEEE Transactions on Pattern Analysis and Machine Intelligence* 29: 1254–9

Jameson, A., Schafer, R., Weis, T., Berthold, A., and Weyrath, T. 1999. Making systems sensitive to the user's time and working memory constraints, in *Proceedings of the 4th International Conference on Intelligent User Interfaces*. Los Angeles: ACM Press: 79–86

Kahneman, D. 1973. *Attention and Effort*. Englewood Cliffs, NJ: Prentice Hall

Kaptelinin, V., and Czerwinski, M. (eds.) 2007. *Beyond the Desktop Metaphor: Designing Integrated Digital Work Environments*. Cambridge, MA: MIT Press

Kardiasmenos, K. S., Clawson, D. M., Wilken, J. A., and Wallin, M. T. 2008. Prospective memory and the efficacy of a memory strategy in multiple sclerosis, *Neuropsychology* 22(6): 746–54

Karger, D. R. 2007. Haystack: Per-user information environment based on semistructured data, in Kaptelinin and Czerwinski: 49–100

Kliegel, M., Mackinlay, R., and Jäger, T. 2008. Complex prospective memory: Development across the lifespan and the role of task interruption, *Developmental Psychology* 44(2): 612–17

Kliegel, M., and Martin, M. 2003. Prospective memory research: Why is it relevant? *International Journal of Psychology* 38(4): 193–4

Koch, C., and Tsuchiya, N. 2007. Attention and consciousness: Two distinct brain processes, *Trends in Cognitive Sciences* 11(1): 16–22

Kvavilashvili, L., Messer, D. J., and Ebdon, P. 2001. Prospective memory in children: The effects of age and task interruption, *Developmental Psychology* 37(3): 418–30

LaBerge, D. 2002. Attentional control: Brief and prolonged, *Psychological Research* 66(4): 220–33

Lamming, M., Brown, P., Carter, K., Eldridge, M., Flynn, M., Louie, G., *et al.* 1994. The design of a human memory prosthesis, *Computer Journal* 37(3): 153–63

Lamming, M., and Flynn, M. 1994. 'Forget-me-not': Intimate computing in support of human memory. Paper presented at the FRIEND21 Symposium on Next Generation Human Interfaces, Tokyo. Also available as RXRC TR 94–103, 61 Regent St, Cambridge, UK

Lamping, J., and Rao, R. 1994. Laying out and visualizing large trees using a hyperbolic space. Paper presented at the 7th Annual ACM Symposium on User Interface Software and Technology. Marina del Rey, CA

Latorella, K. A. 1998. Effects of modality on interrupted flight deck performance: Implications for data link. Paper presented at the Human Factors and Ergonomics Society 42nd Annual Meeting, Santa Monica, CA: 87–91

Laukkanen, J., Roda, C., and Molenaar, I. 2007. Modelling tasks: A require-ments analysis based on attention support services. Paper presented at the workshop on contextualized attention metadata: personalized access to dig-ital resources, CAMA 2007 at the ACM IEEE Joint Conference on Digital Libraries, 17–23 June 2007, Vancouver: 1–7

Lavie, N. 2005. Distracted and confused? Selective attention under load, *Trends in Cognitive Sciences* 9: 75–82

Lavie, N., Hirst, A., de Fockert, J. W., and Viding, E. 2004. Load theory of selective attention and cognitive control, *Journal of Experimental Psychology: General* 133(3): 339–54

Lavie, N., and Tsal, Y. 1994. Perceptual load as a major determinant of the locus of selection in visual attention, *Perception and Psychophysics* 56(2): 183–97

Lim, S.-L., Padmala, S., and Pessoa, L. 2008. Affective learning modulates spa-tial competition during low-load conditions, *Neuropsychologia* 46(5): 1267–78

Logan, G. D. 1988. Toward an instance theory of automatization, *Psychological Review* 95(4): 492–527

   1992. Attention and preattention in theories of automaticity, *American Journal of Psychology* 105(2): 317–39

Mack, A. 2003. Inattentional blindness: Looking without seeing, *Current Direc-tions in Psychological Science* 12(5): 180–4

Mack, A., and Rock, I. 1998. *Inattentional Blindness*. Cambridge, MA: MIT Press

Mark, G., Gonzalez, V. M., and Harris, J. 2005. No task left behind? Examining the nature of fragmented work. Paper presented at the SIGCHI conference on Human Factors in Computing Systems. Portland, OR: 321–30

Marsh, R. L., Hicks, J. L., and Bryan, E. S. 1999. The activation of un-related and canceled intentions, *Memory and Cognition* 27(2): 320–7

Mase, K., Sumi, Y., and Fels, S. 2007. Welcome to the special issue on memory and sharing of experience for the *Journal of Personal and Ubiquitous Comput-ing*, *Journal of Personal and Ubiquitous Computing* 11(4): 213–14

McCrickard, D. S., Catrambone, R., Chewar, C. M., and Stasko, J. T. 2003. Establishing tradeoffs that leverage attention for utility: Empirically eval-uating information display in notification systems, *International Journal of Human–Computer Studies* 58(5): 547–82

McCrickard, D. S., and Chewar, C. M. 2003. Attuning notification design to user goals and attention costs, *Communications of the ACM* 46(3): 67–72

McDaniel, M. A., Guynn, M. J., Einstein, G. O., and Breneiser, J. 2004. Cue-focused and reflexive-associative processes in prospective memory retrieval, *Journal of Experimental Psychology: Learning, Memory, and Cognition* 30(3): 605–14

McFarlane, D. C., and Latorella, K. A. 2002. The scope and importance of human interruption in human–computer interaction design, *Human–Computer Interaction* 17(1): 1–62

McMains, S. A., and Somers, D. C. 2004. Multiple spotlights of attentional selection in human visual cortex, *Neuron* 42: 677–86

McNab, F., and Klingberg, T. 2008. Prefrontal cortex and basal ganglia control access to working memory, *Nature Neuroscience* 11(1): 103–7

Meiran, N., Chorev, Z., and Sapir, A. 2000. Component processes in task switching, *Cognitive Psychology* 41(3): 211–53

Miller, G. A. 1956. The magical number seven, plus or minus two: Some limits on our capacity for processing information, *Psychological Review* 63: 81–97

Molenaar, I., and Roda, C. 2008. Attention management for dynamic and adaptive scaffolding, *Pragmatics and Cognition* 16(2): 225–71

Monsell, S. 2003. Task switching, *Trends in Cognitive Sciences* 7(3): 134–40

Moore, C., and Dunham, P. J. (eds.) 1995. *Joint Attention: Its Origins and Role in Development*. Hillsdale, NJ: Lawrence Erlbaum Associates

Nagata, S. F. 2003. Multitasking and interruptions during mobile web tasks. Paper presented at the 47th Annual Meeting of the Human Factors and Ergonomics Society: 1341–5

Navalpakkam, V., and Itti, L. 2006. An integrated model of top-down and bottom-up attention for optimal object detection. Paper presented at the IEEE Conference on Computer Vision and Pattern Recognition (CVPR): 2049–56

Navon, D., and Miller, J. 1987. Role of outcome conflict in dual-task interference, *Journal of Experimental Psychology: Human Perception and Performance* 13: 435–48

Nisbett, R. E., and Masuda, T. 2003. Culture and point of view, *Proceedings of the National Academy of Sciences of the United States of America* 100(19): 11163–70

Norman, D., and Shallice, T. 1986. Attention to action: Willed and automatic control of behavior, in R. J. Davidson, G. E. Schwartz and D. Shapiro (eds.), *Consciousness and Self-Regulation*. New York: Plenum: vol. IV: 1–18

Oberauer, K. 2002. Access to information in working memory: Exploring the focus of attention, *Journal of Experimental Psychology: Learning, Memory, and Cognition* 28(3): 411–21

Obermayer, R. W., and Nugent, W. A. 2000. Human–computer interaction for alert warning and attention allocation systems of the multi-modal watchstation. Paper presented at the SPIE 2000 – The International Society for Optical Engineering: 14–22

O'Conaill, B., and Frohlich, D. 1995. Timespace in the workplace: Dealing with interruptions. Paper presented at the CHI '95 Conference, Denver, CO: 262–3

Olivers, C. N. L., and Nieuwenhuis, S. 2005. The beneficial effect of concurrent task-irrelevant mental activity on temporal attention, *Psychological Science* 16: 265–9

O'Regan, J. K. 1992. Solving the 'real' mysteries of visual perception: The world as an outside memory, *Canadian Journal of Psychology* 46(3): 461–88

O'Regan, J. K., and Noë, A. 2001. A sensorimotor account of vision and visual consciousness, *Behavioral and Brain Sciences* 24(5): 939–1031

Oulasvirta, A. 2004. Task demands and memory in web interaction: A levels-of-processing approach, *Interacting with Computers* 16(2): 217–41

Oulasvirta, A., Kärkkäinen, L., and Laarni, J. 2005. Expectations and memory in link search, *Computers in Human Behavior* 21(5): 773–89

Oulasvirta, A., and Salovaara, A. 2004. A cognitive meta-analysis of design approaches to interruptions in intelligent environments, in *Extended Abstracts of the 2004 Conference on Human Factors and Computing Systems*. Vienna: ACM Press: 1155–8

Parasuraman, R., and Davis, D. R. (eds.) 1984. *Varieties of Attention*. San Diego: Academic Press

Pashler, H. 1994. Dual-task interference in simple tasks: Data and theory, *Psychological Bulletin* 116(2): 220–44

   2000. Task switching and multitask performance, in S. Monsell and J. Driver (eds.), *Attention and Performance XVIII: Control of Mental Processes*. Cambridge, MA: MIT Press: 277–308

Pashler, H., and Johnston, J. C. 1998. Attentional limitations in dual-task performance, in H. Pashler (ed.), *Attention*. Hove: Psychology Press: 155–189

Pêcher, C., Lemercier, C., and Cellier, J.-M. 2009. Emotions drive attention: Effects on driver's behaviour. *Safety Science* 47(9): 1254–9

Poloter, M. R., Nadel, L., and Schacter, D. L. 2007. Cognitive neuroscience analyses of memory: A historical perspective, *Journal of Cognitive Neuroscience* 3(2): 95–116

Posner, M. I. 1982. Cumulative development of attention theory, *American Psychologist* 37: 168–79

   1994. Attention: The mechanisms of consciousness, *Proceedings of the National Academy of Sciences of the United States of America* 91(16): 7398–403

Posner, M. I., and Fan, J. 2007. Attention as an organ system, in J. Pomerantz (ed.), *Neurobiology of Perception and Communication: From Synapse to Society. The IVth De Lange Conference*. Cambridge, UK: Cambridge University Press

Posner, M. I., and Rothbart, M. K. 2007. Research on attention networks as a model for the integration of psychological science, *Annual Review of Psychology* 58(1): 1–23

Postle, B. R. 2006. Working memory as an emergent property of the mind and brain, *Neuroscience* 139(1): 23–38

Raskin, J. 2000. *The Humane Interface: New Directions for Designing Interactive Systems*. New York: Addison-Wesley

Ratwani, R. M., Andrews, A. E., Sousk, J. D., and Trafton, J. G. 2008. The effect of interruption modality on primary task resumption, *Human Factors and Ergonomics Society Annual Meeting Proceedings* 52: 393–7

Rensink, R. A. 2007. The modeling and control of visual perception, in W. Gray (ed.), *Integrated Models of Cognitive Systems*. New York: Oxford University Press: 132–48

Robertson, T. J., Prabhakararao, S., Burnett, M., Cook, C., Ruthruff, J. R., Beckwith, L., *et al.* 2004. Impact of interruption style on end-user debugging. Paper presented at the SIGCHI Conference on Human Factors in Computing Systems. Vienna: 287–94

Roda, C., and Nabeth, T. 2007. Supporting attention in learning environments: Attention support services and information management. Paper presented at

Creating New Experiences on a Global Scale. Second European Conference on Technology Enhanced Learning, EC-TEL 2007, Crete: 277–91

Roda, C., Stojanov, G., and Clauzel, D. 2006. Mind-prosthesis metaphor for design of human–computer interfaces that support better attention management. Paper presented at the AAAI 2006 Fall Symposium on 'Interaction and Emergent Phenomena in Societies of Agents', Arlington, VA: 52–9

Roda, C., and Thomas, J. 2006. Attention aware systems: Theories, applications, and research agenda, *Computers in Human Behavior* 22(4): 557–87

Rogers, R., and Monsell, S. 1995. Costs of a predictable switch between simple cognitive tasks, *Journal of Experimental Psychology: General* 124(2): 207–31

Sarter, N. 2005. Graded and multimodal interruption cueing in support of preattentive reference and attention management, *Human Factors and Ergonomics Society Annual Meeting Proceedings* 49: 478–81

   2006. Multiple-resource theory as a basis for multimodal interface design: Success stories, qualifications, and research needs, in A. F. Kramer, D. A. Wiegmann and A. Kirlik (eds.), *Attention: From Theory to Practice*. Oxford: Oxford University Press: 187–93

Schacter, D. L. 1987. Implicit memory: History and current status, *Journal of Experimental Psychology: Learning, Memory, and Cognition* 13(3): 501–18

Schill, K., Zetzsche, C., and Hois, J. 2009. A belief-based architecture for scene analysis: From sensorimotor features to knowledge and ontology, *Fuzzy Sets and Systems* 160(10): 1507–16

Scholl, B. J. 2001. Objects and attention: The state of the art, *Cognition* 80(1–2): 1–46

Sellen, A. J., Louie, G., Harris, J. E., and Wilkins, A. J. 1997. What brings intentions to mind? An in situ study of prospective memory, *Memory* 5(4): 483–507

Simons, D. J. Visual cognition lab – demos and stimuli. Retrieved June 2009 from: http://viscog.beckman.illinois.edu/djs_lab/demos.html.

Simons, D. J., and Chabris, C. F. 1999. Gorillas in our midst: Sustained inattentional blindness for dynamic events, *Perception* 28(9): 1059–74

Simons, D. J., and Rensink, R. A. 2005. Change blindness: past, present, and future, *Trends in Cognitive Sciences* 9(1): 16–20

Somervell, J., McCrickard, D. S., North, C., and Shukla, M. 2002. An evaluation of information visualization in attention-limited environments. Paper presented at the Symposium on Data Visualisation 2002, Barcelona

Speier, C., Vessey, I., and Valacich, J. S. 2003. The effects of interruptions, task complexity, and information presentation on computer-supported decision-making performance, *Decision Sciences* 34(4): 771–97

Spence, R. 2002. Rapid, serial and visual: A presentation technique with potential, *Information Visualization* 1(1): 13–19

Stinson, C. 2009. Searching for the source of executive attention, *Psyche* 15(1): 137–54

Takegata, R., Brattico, E., Tervaniemi, M., Varyagina, O., Näätänen, R., and Winkler, I. N. 2005. Preattentive representation of feature conjunctions for concurrent spatially distributed auditory objects, *Cognitive Brain Research* 25(1): 169–79

Thorpe, S., Fize, D., and Marlot, C. 1996. Speed of processing in the human visual system, *Nature* (381): 520–2

Toet, A. 2006. Gaze directed displays as an enabling technology for attention aware systems, *Computers in Human Behavior* 22(4): 615–47

Treisman, A. 1960. Contextual cues in selective listening, *Quarterly Journal of Experimental Psychology* 12: 242–8

1985. Preattentive processing in vision, *Computer Vision, Graphics and Image Processing* 31(2): 156–77

Treisman, A., and Gelade, G. 1980. A feature-integration theory of attention, *Cognitive Psychology* 12: 97–136

Treisman, A., Vieira, A., and Hayes, A. 1992. Automaticity and preattentive processing, *American Journal of Psychology* 105(2): 341–62

Tulving, E. 1972. Episodic and semantic memory, in E. Tulving and W. Donaldson (eds.), *Organization of Memory*. New York: Academic Press: 382–402

Unsworth, N., and Engle, R. W. 2007. On the division of short-term and working memory: An examination of simple and complex span and their relation to higher order abilities, *Psychological Bulletin* 133(6): 1038–66

Velichkovsky, D. M 1995. Communicating attention: Gaze position transfer in cooperative problem solving, *Pragmatics and Cognition* 3(2): 199–222

Vemuri, S., and Bender, W. 2004. Next-generation personal memory aids, *BT Technology Journal* 22(4): 125–38

Ware, C. 2000. *Information Visualization: Perception for Design* San Francisco: Morgan Kaufmann

Welford, A. T. 1952. The 'psychological refractory period' and the timing of high-speed performance: A review and a theory, *British Journal of Psychology* 43: 2–19

Wickens, C. D. 2002. Multiple resources and performance prediction, *Theoretical Issues in Ergonomics Science* 3(2): 159–77

Wilson, B. A., Evans, J. J., Emslie, H., Alderman, N., and Burgess, P. 1998. The development of an ecologically valid test for assessing patients with a dysexecutive syndrome, *Neuropsychological Rehabilitation* 8(3): 213–28

Winkler, I. N., Czigler, I. N., Sussman, E., Horváth, J. N., and Balázs, L. S. 2005. Preattentive binding of auditory and visual stimulus features, *Journal of Cognitive Neuroscience* 17(2): 320–39

Wixted, J. T. 2004. The psychology and neuroscience of forgetting, *Annual Review of Psychology* 55(1): 235–69

Wolfe, J. M. 2001. The level of attention: Mediating between the stimulus and perception, in L. Harris and M. Jenkin (eds.), *Levels of Perception: A Festschrift for Ian Howard*. New York: Springer Verlag; draft of 8/2/01, 12:06 p.m. retrieved 15 February 2005 from http://search.bwh.harvard.edu/pdf/ Festschrift.pdf

Woods, D. D. 1995. The alarm problem and directed attention in dynamic fault management, *Ergonomics* 38(11): 2371–93

Wright, R. D. 1998. *Visual Attention*. New York: Oxford University Press

Yantis, S. 2000. Goal-directed and stimulus-driven determinants of attentional control, *Attention and Performance* 18: 73–103

Zijlstra, F. R. H., Roe, R. A., Leonova, A. B., and Krediet, I. 1999. Temporal factors in mental work: Effects of interrupted activities, *Journal of Occupational and Organizational Psychology* 72: 163–85

Zimmermann, T. D., and Meier, B. 2010. The effect of implementation intentions on prospective memory performance across the lifespan, *Applied Cognitive Psychology* 24(5): 645–58

3   The management of visual attention in graphic displays

Ronald A. Rensink

This chapter presents an overview of several recent developments in vision science and outlines some of their implications for the management of visual attention in graphic displays. These include ways of sending attention to the right item at the right time, techniques to improve attentional efficiency, and possibilities for offloading some of the processing typically done by attention onto nonattentional mechanisms. In addition it is argued that such techniques not only allow more effective use to be made of visual attention but also open up new possibilities for human–machine interaction.

3.1   Introduction

Graphic displays such as maps, diagram and visual interfaces have long been used to present information in a form intended to be easy to comprehend (e.g., Massironi 2002; Tufte 2001; Ware 2008). While it is clear that such a goal is important, it is not so clear that it has always been achieved. Are current displays for the most part *effective* – do they enable user performance to be rapid, easy and accurate? Are they optimally so? Or are better designs possible?

These concerns are discussed here in the context of how to manage visual attention in graphic displays (including *visual* displays).[1] This chapter is not directly concerned with the design of displays that respond effectively to the user (e.g., Roda and Thomas 2006; Vertegaal 2003). Rather, it focuses on the complementary perspective: how to design a display so that the user responds effectively to *it*. Results here apply equally well to static, dynamic and interactive displays. For interactive displays the separation of the two perspectives need not be absolute: management of attention could depend on what the user does (e.g., the particular items

---

[1] As used here, 'graphic' denotes displays that employ graphic elements, without reference to any perceptual processing. In contrast, 'visual' displays involve extensive use of visual intelligence for their operation, and thus depend strongly on the involvement of a viewer. In a way, the distinction is primarily one of emphasis: means (graphics) vs. ends (vision). For the issues discussed here, this distinction is not a critical one.

highlighted could depend on where the user is looking). Indeed, designs that address both sets of issues – how the machine might effectively respond to the user *and* the user to the machine – will ultimately form the complete basis for effective interaction. But before tackling this, the best course is first to understand the individual perspectives separately. As such, discussion here will be limited to the ways that graphic displays can support the management of attention in a user.

Another restriction is that this chapter will focus exclusively on *visual* attention – i.e., those attentional processes that allow us to see. It will not be greatly concerned with many issues associated with 'attention' in general, e.g., task switching, or keeping attention on a particular task. The topic of attention is a highly complex one, with a great deal of associated literature; it cannot be covered in depth in a single chapter (for further information, see, e.g., Itti, Rees and Tsotsos 2005; Parasuraman 2000; Pashler 1998). However, as 'attention' is a term covering a set of processes that are largely independent of each other (Allport 1993), it is possible to focus on those particular processes that pertain to the visual 'picture' we experience. This includes not only eye movements, but also other, less visible processes. These processes often align in their operation, allowing 'attention' to be treated as a single process. But occasionally the characteristics of individual components become relevant, requiring descriptions that are more specific.

With these caveats in place, the stage is set. Discussion begins with a brief overview of recent findings concerning the role played by attention in visual perception. The subsequent sections outline three general approaches to managing it. The first involves ways to send attention where it is needed when it is needed. The second focuses on techniques for improving the efficiency of attention itself, so that it 'locks on' to information with minimal time and effort. The third involves the possibility of offloading of attention to other, nonattentional mechanisms that carry out operations of considerable sophistication, and that may form the basis of new possibilities for human–machine interaction.

3.2   Visual perception

To design displays that effectively manage visual attention, it is important to have some idea of its nature: what it does, what it does not do, and how it is controlled in 'normal' viewing. Four groups of processes are relevant here: (1) those that act prior to attention, providing the 'raw materials' on which it operates; (2) the mechanisms constituting attention itself; (3) the mechanisms that operate concurrently with – and independently of – attention; and (4) the processes that coordinate these to create the picture we have of our surroundings. These processes are only part of what is involved in visual perception; for further details see, for example, Palmer 1999. For discussion of how perceptual considerations in general can influence the design of graphic displays see, for example, Few 2004, 92–130; MacEachren 1995; and Ware 2008.

3.2.1   Early vision

When discussing how we see, a natural place to begin is with *rapid* visual processes – those that take place within the first few hundred milliseconds of viewing. These require little attention and are not greatly influenced by observer expectations; they are typically carried out automatically and without conscious awareness. An alternative starting point is the set of processes that act directly on inputs from the eye. These *low-level* processes are also highly automatic, and are highly parallel, operating concurrently in all parts of the visual field. The set of processes that are both rapid and low-level constitutes what is known as *early vision* (see, e.g., Marr 1982; Rensink and Enns 1998).

Early vision creates an array of elements upon which all subsequent processing – both attentional and nonattentional – is based. These *features* include colour, motion, contrast, curvature and orientation in the plane. Importantly, features are not just the basic 'building blocks' of visual perception, but are also involved in the control of attention: a unique feature is generally *salient*, automatically drawing attention to itself, and thus 'popping out' to a viewer almost immediately (see, e.g., Treisman 1988; Wolfe 2000). Since these features are largely determined before attention has had a chance to act, this level of processing is sometimes referred to as *pre-attentive* vision.

Although most features are simple, the structures they describe can be complex. For example, the length of a partially occluded figure is deter-mined via the extent of the completed figure, and not just the visible parts (Rensink and Enns 1998). This indicates a degree of *visual intelligence* at early levels   relatively sophisticated processing even in the absence of attention. Indeed, the output of the early visual system may be best char-acterized in terms of *proto-objects* (localized precursors of objects) rather than simple measurements (Rensink and Enns 1998; Rensink 2000). Other structures also exist at this level. For example, arrays of items sharing similar features often form groups that extend over large regions of space (see, e.g., Pylyshyn 2003, ch. 3; Wolfe 2000).

Early processes can recover several scene-based properties, such as three-dimensional orientation, direction of lighting, surface convex-ity/concavity and shadows. Such estimates are formed on the basis of 'quick and dirty' assumptions about the environment that are true most of the time (Rensink and Cavanagh 2004), in accordance with the proposal that early vision produces a viewer-centred description of the world that is represented in a fragmented fashion (Marr 1982).

3.2.2   Visual attention

A key factor in much of vision (including the conscious picture we experience) is visual attention. Although at the subjective level we generally have no problem understanding what it means, attention has proven surprisingly resistant to an objective formulation. It has sometimes been viewed as a 'filter' or 'fuel' (see, e.g., Wickens and McCarley 2008). But it can also be usefully characterized simply as selective control, carried out in different ways by different processes (Rensink 2003). There appear to be several types of visual attention – including eye movements as well as several covert processes – which may or may not be directly related to each other. (For a set of current perspectives, see Itti, Rees and Tsotsos 2005.) In all cases, these processes appear to be extremely limited in capacity, with only a few items attended at any time, and only a few properties of those items (see e.g., Hayhoe, Bensinger and Ballard 1998). Some of the more commonly encountered types are as follows:

3.2.2.1 Selective integration   One important type of attention is *selective integration*: the binding of selected parts or properties into a more complex structure. For example, searching for a single L-shaped item among several T-shaped items often takes a while; the distinguishing property – the arrangement of the horizontal and vertical segments – is evidently not salient. It likewise takes time to detect unique combinations of orientation and colour, or more generally, combinations of most features. It has been proposed that the detection of such combinations is via a *spotlight of attention* that selectively integrates the features at each location into an *object file* at a rate of about 50 milliseconds per item (Treisman 1988; Wolfe 2000). Thus, if a target element has a salient feature, it will automatically pop out (section 3.2.1); otherwise attention must travel around the display on an item-by-item basis until the target is integrated, and seen.

3.2.2.2 Selective coherence   Figure 3.1 shows an example of the *flicker paradigm*, where an original image A continually alternates with a modified image A', with brief blank fields between successive images. Under these conditions, observers usually have great difficulty noticing changes, even when the changes are large, repeatedly made, and expected by the

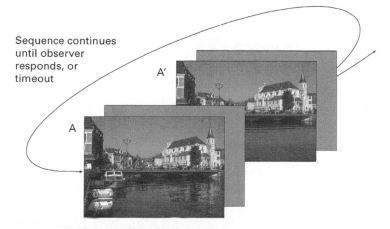

Sequence continues
until observer
responds, or
timeout

A'

A

Figure 3.1 Flicker paradigm. Original image A (harbour with reflection of castle) and modified image A' (harbour with reflection gone) are displayed in the sequence A, A', A, A',... with grey fields between successive images. Observers typically require several seconds to see such a change, even though it is large and easily seen once noticed.

observer. Indeed, this *change blindness* can exist for long stretches of time – up to 50 seconds under some conditions (Rensink, O'Regan and Clark 1997).

Change blindness can be accounted for by the proposal that attention is needed to consciously see change – i.e., it selectively integrates structures across time as well as space (cf. section 3.2.2.1). A change will be difficult to notice if its accompanying motion transients do not draw attention to its location – e.g., if they are swamped by other motion signals in the image. More generally, change blindness occurs whenever such swamping takes place, such as if the change is made during an eye movement, eyeblink or occlusion by some other object (Rensink 2002a).

The perception of change can be explained by *coherence theory* (Rensink 2000). Prior to attention, proto-objects are continually formed in parallel across the visual field (figure 3.2). Attention selects a few of these for entry into a *coherence field*, a circuit between the attended items and a single, higher-level *nexus*; this can be viewed as the holding of information in visual short-term memory. The proto-objects are thus 'knit' into a representation with spatio-temporal coherence, corresponding to a single coherent object. Attention is released by breaking this circuit, with the object dissolving back into its constituent proto-objects. There is little after-effect of having been attended, with no accumulation of items in conscious visual experience (see also Wolfe 1999).

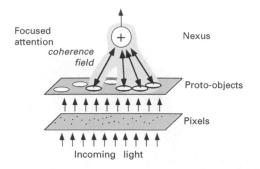

Figure 3.2 Coherence theory. Early vision continually creates proto-objects across the visual field. These are volatile, lasting only a short time; if a new item appears at the location of an existing item, its representation simply overwrites the old one. Attention can select a few proto-objects and set up reciprocal connections between them and an attentional nexus, resulting in a coherence field. (The '+' is purely symbolic, simply indicating that some form of pooling is used.) As long as the proto-objects are held in this field, they form a single object with both temporal and spatial coherence (Rensink 2000).

In this view, attended items are not entirely independent, but rather are parts of a coordinated complex: information is pooled into a single nexus, perhaps by taking the sum or the maximum of all inputs. It is therefore difficult for the nexus to differentiate between receiving a single change signal or multiple change signals, since the non-linear nature of the pooling leads to largely the same result in both cases. Consequently, observers can never distinguish two changes at a time from one, no matter how hard they try (Rensink 2001; 2002a).

3.2.2.3 Selective experience   Recent studies also indicate that attention is needed not just to see change, but even simply to *see* (i.e., to have a conscious picture of an element). For example, Mack and Rock (1998) asked observers to view an overlapping pair of lines (one horizontal and one vertical), and judge which was longer. After several such trials, a display was presented containing an unexpected test item (figure 3.3). Observers often failed to see the test item, even when they looked at it directly. Such *inattentional blindness* can occur even for objects that are highly visible, such as a person in a gorilla suit walking across a scene (Simons and Chabris 1999).

Interestingly, objects that are not consciously seen (and thus, are not attended) can still influence perception. For example, unseen lines surrounding a test item have been found to induce a length illusion in that

Figure 3.3 Inattentional blindness. Observers are shown a sequence of images, and asked to determine which line (horizontal or vertical) is longest in each. After several presentations, an image is presented containing an unexpected test stimulus. Observers often do not see this, even when looking directly at it (Mack and Rock 1998).

item (Moore and Egeth 1997). This reinforces the findings from early vision, which point towards a form of visual intelligence that involves neither conscious awareness nor attention.

3.2.3   Nonattentional processing

A common intuition about vision is that it exists entirely to produce a sensory experience of some kind (i.e., a picture) and that attention is the 'central gateway' for doing this. However, there is increasing evidence that several kinds of sophisticated processing can be done without attention, and that some of these processes have nothing directly to do with visual experience (see, e.g., Rensink 2007). These processes are believed to be based on early vision and operate concurrently with attentional processes, but independently of them.

3.2.3.1 Statistical summaries   An interesting form of visual intelligence is the ability to rapidly form *statistical summaries* of sets of briefly presented items. For example, when observers are briefly presented with a group of discs, they can match the mean size of these to an individual disc as accurately as they can match two individual discs (Ariely 2001). This can be done using exposures of as little as 50 milliseconds (Chong and Treisman 2003), indicating that attention is not central to the creation of such summaries. This ability may also extend to other statistical measures, such as range or variance, although this has not yet been confirmed.

3.2.3.2 Scene gist   Evidence is also accumulating that several aspects of scene composition can be determined rapidly and without attention. One of these is its abstract meaning (or *gist*) – e.g., whether it is a city, kitchen or farm. Gist can be determined within 150 milliseconds, a time insufficient for attending to more than a few items (Thorpe, Fize and Marlot 1996). It can be reliably extracted from blurred images, indicating that details are not important. Interestingly, the representation of two different gists can be activated simultaneously (Oliva 2005).

It also appears possible to determine several related properties this way. For example, observers can also rapidly determine how open or crowded a scene is (see, e.g., Oliva 2005). All these are likely based on the distribution of early-level features in the image (e.g., line orientations or colours), possibly by relying on rapid statistical summaries. They do not appear to involve coherent object representations.

3.2.3.3 Scene layout   Another possible nonattentional process is memory for *layout* – the spatial arrangement of objects in the scene (Hochberg 1978, 158–211). This may also contain a small amount of featural information, such as coarse descriptions of their size, colour and orientation. Some layout information may be extracted within several seconds of viewing – likely via eye movements or attentional shifts – and can be maintained over intervals of several seconds without the need for attention (Tatler 2002). Interestingly, memory for repeated layouts can be formed in the absence of awareness that such patterns are being repeated (Chun and Jiang 1998).

3.2.3.4 Visuomotor guidance   It has been proposed (Milner and Goodale 1995) that vision involves two largely separate systems: a fast, nonattentional *online* stream concerned with the guidance of visually guided actions such as reaching and eye movement, and a slower *offline* stream concerned with conscious perception and the recognition of objects. Evidence for this *two-systems theory* is largely based on patients with brain damage: some can see objects but have great difficulty grasping them, while others cannot see objects, but (when asked to) can nevertheless grasp them easily and accurately.

3.2.4   Scene perception

The discovery that attention is needed for conscious visual experience has several counterintuitive implications. For example, since attention has a limited capacity (e.g., Pylyshyn and Storm 1988), only a few objects can be consciously seen at any time. But if this were the case, why do we not notice such limitations? Why do we believe we see all objects and all events, and each of these in great detail?

The answer to these involves a shift in our view of how information is integrated to perceive a scene. Originally, it was believed that such integration involved the creation of a dense, static representation, in accordance with our impressions as observers. But more recent work is beginning to view integration in terms of dynamic rather than static processes – in terms of *coordination* rather than *construction* (see Ballard *et al.* 1997; Rensink 2007).

3.2.4.1 Virtual representation   The seeming contradiction between our impression of virtually unlimited perceptual content and the existence of severe attentional limitations can be accounted for by the idea of a *virtual representation*: instead of forming a coherent, detailed representation of all the objects in our surroundings, the visual system only creates a coherent representation of the items needed for the task at hand (Rensink 2000). If attention can be managed such that a coherent representation of an object can be created whenever needed, the scene representation will appear to higher levels as if all objects and events are represented simultaneously. Such a representation would have all the power of a 'real' one, while using much less in the way of processing and memory resources.

In this view, the conscious seeing of a display relies on a relatively sparse, dynamic just-in-time system that creates coherent representations whenever those are needed. Among other things, this implies that there is little or no general-purpose representation in vision: whatever is used at any moment is coupled to the task at hand and would likely be suboptimal for other purposes. Different people will literally see a scene in different ways, depending on their individual knowledge and expectations (Rensink 2007).

3.2.4.2 Triadic architecture   The successful use of virtual representation requires that attentional shifts be made to the appropriate items at the appropriate times. How might this be implemented in the human visual system? One possibility is a *triadic* architecture (Rensink 2000), sketched in figure 3.4. As its name implies, this architecture is based on three interacting subsystems:

1. *Early visual system.*   This rapidly creates proto-objects in parallel across the visual field; these are volatile, and must be continually regenerated. This system operates automatically and continually, without the awareness of the viewer.

2. *Attentional system.*   This can form a set of selected proto-objects (no more than three to four) into a coherent object representation. This is the basis of the conscious perception of change, and possibly, conscious perception in general.

3. *Setting system.*   This provides a coarse description of the scene to help guide attention to appropriate items. It is largely based on properties such as gist and layout, which can be obtained – or at least maintained – without attention. These can invoke knowledge in long-term memory,

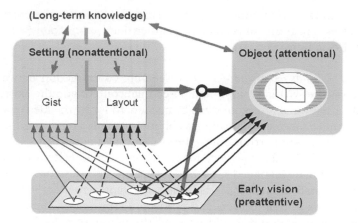

Figure 3.4 Triadic architecture (Rensink 2000). Perception is carried out via three interacting systems. (1) Early-level processes create volatile proto-objects. (2) Visual attention 'grabs' selected structures and forms them into an object with both temporal and spatial coherence. (3) Setting information (obtained via nonattentional processes) guides the allocation of visual attention on the basis of long-term knowledge. Control is based on the combination of this with the automatic drawing of attention based on physical properties at early levels.

which in turn constrains expectations as to likely objects, likely actions, etc. Although some information can be accumulated in the setting system, it is used for guidance only, and does not form part of the picture that is experienced.

These largely correspond to the groupings described in previous sections – early vision, visual attention and nonattentional processing – except that the setting system contains only those nonattentional processes that control attention. (Those that guide visuomotor actions, for example, belong to a separate group.) The connection to long-term knowledge helps inform attentional control, likely by acting through the layout system, and perhaps also by affecting attentional content directly. Most of long-term memory is not in play at any instant, and so is not considered part of here-and-now visual perception.

In this view, then, the perception of a scene (or a display) occurs via the constant allocation of visual attention, which is largely controlled by two mechanisms: (1) bottom-up drawing of attention to salient items on the basis of their low-level physical properties, and (2) top-down guidance to important items on the basis of high-level knowledge about the objects and the scene. Thus, what is seen reflects a sophisticated balance between the immediate, ever-changing information from the world, and the longer-term, more stable knowledge of the viewer.

3.3   Attentional coercion

The view of perception emerging from recent work in vision science is based on a just-in-time coordination of several subsystems, one of which is visual attention (section 3.2). A critical part of this coordination is the effective allocation of attention, so that it arrives at the right place at the right time.

Given that the visual experience of an observer depends on the coordination of attention, and given that this coordination is strongly affected by what is shown to the eyes, the possibility arises of *coercive graphics*: displays that coerce[2] attention to make the observer see (or not see) a particular part of a display in a natural way (Rensink 2002b, 2007). In essence, the mechanisms that manage attention in everyday seeing are 'hijacked' to control the viewing experience of the user. Such coercion has long been used by magicians and filmmakers to achieve a variety of striking effects, most of which are incorporated seamlessly into the experience of the viewer (e.g., Kuhn, Amlani and Rensink 2008). Given machines with 'superhuman' control over what is displayed, the potential exists for coercive displays that are even more powerful than these.

In any event, successful coercion could result in an observer always attending to whatever was needed by the task at hand. Apart from a general improvement of performance, such coercion might also be useful for specialized populations. For example, it might assist those users who have difficulty sending their attention to the right item at the right time; among these might be new users of a system, who often do not know what to attend, or when. Another potential application would be *soft alerts* that would not disturb existing attentional control (Rensink 2002b; 2007). Such alerts would be particularly useful for situations where the arrival of a new event does not require immediate attention – e.g., the arrival of email while the operator is monitoring some unrelated task (e.g., McCrickard and Chewar 2003).

Several different types of attentional coercion appear to be possible. Each of these involves a different set of mechanisms and has its own strengths and weaknesses.

---

[2] As used here, 'control' refers to the management of attention in everyday seeing (including all relevant mechanisms), while 'coercion' refers to the management of these control mechanisms via particular contents of the display (essentially a second-order form of control). Control is done internally; coercion is done by external means (i.e., via the display), ideally to improve the management of attention for the task at hand.

3.3.1   Low-level saliency

In everyday seeing, attention is automatically – and usually involuntarily – *drawn* to particular items or locations based on their physical properties (section 3.2.1). Much of this is based on *saliency*, a quantity that governs the priority of attentional allocation: the higher the saliency, the more likely attention is to be drawn. Such control is thought to be largely independent of the beliefs and goals of the viewer, although some aspects may be affected by the task and instruction set (Egeth and Yantis 1997; Theeuwes and Godijn 2002). Thus a considerable amount of coercion can be achieved simply by *highlighting* the target item (or region) to enhance its saliency. At least five possible ways of doing this exist.

3.3.1.1 Featural cues   Saliency is largely based on differences in the density of features in a region, with large differences creating the highest levels of saliency. Thus, attention can be coerced by the use of *featural cues* in a display: if a unique feature exists in an area, saliency will be high, and the corresponding item will simply 'pop out'. Even if its saliency is somewhat lower (e.g., if the difference in features from its surround is not that great), an item will still be attended relatively quickly (Itti 2005). Properties that can be used for this include:
- brightness (contrast)
- colour (hue)
- length
- width
- orientation (2D)
- curvature (2D)
- convexity/concavity (3D)
- motion
- blinking

Importantly, only simple properties appear to exert such control. For most of these (e.g., brightness, length), the absolute level of the features is important, with high levels more effective than low ones; for others (e.g., orientation), the degree of difference is also a factor (figure 3.5). For details, see, e.g., Ware (2004, ch. 5), Wickens and McCarley (2008) and Wolfe (2005).

It is important to note that saliency is based upon the properties of relatively complex proto-objects, and not simply pixels in the image (section 3.2.1). For example, a graphical element with a distinctive size or orientation will not be salient if it is part of a proto-object that is itself undistinguished (figure 3.6).

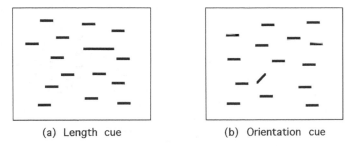

(a) Length cue   (b) Orientation cue

Figure 3.5 Featural cues. Attention is drawn to items with features differing from those of their neighbours. (a) Unique length. Attention is drawn to the item that is longer than its neighbours; a shorter item among longer ones would not be as salient (see, e.g., Wolfe 2000). (b) Unique orientation. Attention is drawn to the item for which orientation is different. While there may be a difference in the categories, the degree of the orientation difference is also important.

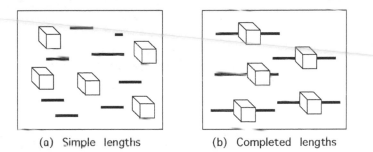

(a) Simple lengths   (b) Completed lengths

Figure 3.6 Proto-object structure (Rensink and Enns 1998). (a) A unique simple length pops out if distinct from others in the region. (b) When it is incorporated into a proto-object (here, the completed bar), it becomes unavailable, even though the same pixels are in the image as before. The proto-objects (bars) are not distinct, and so attention is not drawn to them automatically.

3.3.1.2 Lighting level Low-level coercion can also be achieved by a literal highlighting of an item in the depicted scene, with a more brightly lit region drawing attention (Khan *et al.* 2005; Seif El-Nasr 2005). It is likely that the absolute luminance of the region is not important here; rather the key factor may be the perceived level of illumination. Although this has not yet been verified in controlled experiments, it is known that lighting can be rapidly separated from surface brightness at early levels (section 3.2.1).

Conversely, it might also be possible to use lighting to divert attention away from a particular region or object. For example, given that shadows

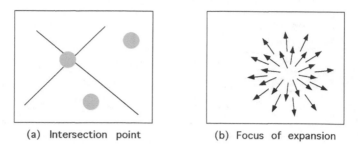

(a) Intersection point   (b) Focus of expansion

Figure 3.7 Drawing of attention by configural focus. (a) Intersection point of a pair of extended lines. Attention is automatically drawn to this point (or any items at that location), possibly because of its similarity to a vanishing point. (b) Focus of expansion over an extended area. Attention is automatically drawn to the point from which random dots move (motion represented by arrows), but only if their movement is outward, corresponding to an object travelling towards the viewer. In some ways, this could be considered the dynamic analogue to the intersection point.

are a natural opposite to highlights, and given that they can also be identified at early levels (Rensink and Cavanagh 2004), it might be possible to keep attention away from items or regions perceived as being in the shadows.

3.3.1.3 Level of detail Another approach to highlighting involves the *level of detail* in an item or region. Here, coercion is based on the fact that saliency is high for items with high levels of detail, which contain relatively high spatial frequencies (Itti 2005). Attention can therefore be coerced to a given item by using (selective) blurring to remove high-frequency components or features in the rest of the image, which then increases the saliency of the target item without affecting its appearance (Kosara, Miksch and Hauser 2002; Su, Durand and Agrawala 2005). Possibly related to this is the finding that viewers prefer items and regions with a greater level of detail, even when the differences in detail are not consciously noticed (Halper *et al.* 2003; see also DeCarlo and Santella 2002).

3.3.1.4 Configural focus Attention can also be drawn to a focus of a configuration that extends over a region of space (figure 3.7). For example, attention is automatically drawn to the intersection point of two or more lines that are sufficiently long (Ward 1996, 45–68); this does not occur if the lines are short (Wolfe and DiMase 2003). Attention is also drawn to the vanishing point of lines in one-point perspective (Ward 1996, 45–68). Both effects may be based on the fact that such a vanishing point corresponds to the viewer's direction of gaze.

Interestingly, the movement of random dots away from a single point – its *focus of expansion* – over a large area attracts attention; no other motion patterns induce such behaviour (von Mühlenen and Lleras 2007). This is likely because the expansion corresponds to the looming of an object travelling directly towards the viewer, which requires immediate response (figure 3.7). Expansion of an item over a small area does not appear to exhibit such an effect (Bartram, Ware and Calvert 2001), again indicating the importance of extended structure.

Such configurations could highlight an item if placed in the background (ideally, at low contrast), with the item being at the 'focus'. The computation of such structure – both static and dynamic – likely involves processes that act rapidly over large areas (section 3.2.3). If so, such highlighting could take place rapidly, and without interfering with other aspects of perception.

3.3.1.5 Centres of gravity   An item attracts more attention when placed at the centre of a display – or more precisely, when at the centre of gravity of the elements that the display contains (Bang 2000, 62–3; Solso 1994, 149–50; Richards and Kaufman 1969). Such increased saliency might also exist for centres of gravity of individual objects or groups, given that these appear to be the bases of eye movements and other perceptual measures (Vishwanath and Kowler 2003). Consistent with this, when tracking an item, attention appears to be concentrated around its centre of gravity (Alvarez and Scholl 2005). Taken together, these results suggest the existence of a general strategy of attentional control based on centres of gravity, possibly applicable to all levels of organization, and carried out via rapid nonattentional processes (section 3.2.3).

3.3.2   High-level interest

A rather different set of techniques for attentional coercion involves the voluntary *direction* of attention to an item. This is governed by more abstract, higher-level factors such as the viewer's interest in a particular object; these factors are generally contingent, depending on the particular viewer and the particular task carried out. This form of control is slower and more effortful than low-level control, and involves different mechanisms. The exact way these two types of control interact has not yet been established. However, high-level control can override low-level considerations if the interest in a particular item is sufficiently high (see Egeth and Yantis 1997).

Although 'interest' has a reasonably clear subjective meaning (e.g., Rensink, O'Regan and Clark 1997), it is difficult to give it an objective formulation. Some aspects can be captured in terms of features that are unexpected in the context of the given scene (Bruce and Tsotsos 2006; Elazary and Itti 2008). But such a characterization is necessarily incomplete – if nothing else, there is always a possible dependence on the task. More generally, interest must involve a high-level awareness of the situation at hand, and the mechanisms of such awareness are only beginning to be understood (e.g., Endsley 1995). In the absence of a firm theoretical framework, it may be best to design displays based on practical considerations obtained from other domains. For example, interest in an item could be created via the techniques of showmanship used by magicians (Kuhn, Amlani and Rensink 2008; Sharpe 1988; Tognazzini 1993). The idea of computer interface as theatre (Laurel 1993) may also be relevant, with interactions viewed as parts of a larger-scale situation which emphasizes some aspects of an interface, and de-emphasizes others.

In any event, designs can be quantifiably tested via techniques such as the flicker paradigm (section 3.2.2). For example, given that attention is needed to see a change, objects that are seen to change relatively quickly under these conditions can be interpreted as more quickly attended, and thus, more interesting. Systematic testing might provide an ordering of the items in the display in terms of their interest for a given observer, or a given task. Indeed, such techniques could be used to determine which particular parts or structural levels are most interesting in an image (New, Cosmides and Tooby 2007; Rensink 2002b).

3.3.3   Learned associations

Another potentially useful set of controls is *learned associations*. These can be viewed as hybrids of low- and high-level mechanisms: simple words and shapes that control attention quickly and automatically (like low-level control) on the basis of their meaning (like high-level control). Since the formation of these associations depends on learning, there is a possibility (yet untested) that they may not be universally effective. Instead, they may depend on the cultural background – and perhaps even the individual history – of the viewer.

In any event, this kind of control can be quite powerful if used correctly (Kuhn, Amlani and Rensink 2008). Two different types can be distinguished, based on their function:

3.3.3.1 Attractors   These are shapes or words that draw attention to themselves on the basis of their significance or meaning (i.e., semantics). For example, it is believed that attention is drawn automatically to the eyes of a human face (Block 2001, 132). It is also drawn automatically to a person's name, or to any other emotionally laden word or symbol; the meaning of these can apparently be obtained without attention (Mack and Rock 1998, ch. 6).

3.3.3.2 Directives   These are shapes or words that automatically send attention to a location other than their own (Rensink 2002b). For example, if a viewer attends to an image (or depiction) of a person in a display, their attention will automatically follow that person's gaze. Likewise, an image of a pointing finger will direct a viewer's attention to the item being pointed at (see, e.g., Burton *et al.* 2009; Kuhn, Amlani and Rensink 2008).

All of these likely reflect learned responses to social cues, which are typically of great importance to humans. However, this kind of direction can also be induced by schematic figures such as arrows, although the effects of these are somewhat weaker (Ristic, Wright and Kingstone 2007).

3.3.4   Unseen coercion

A potentially important – although currently speculative – type of control is based on graphical elements that do not enter into the conscious experience of the user, but still keep their coercive power. This type of coercion could form the basis of 'magical' displays in which a viewer would be guaranteed to see (or not see) a selected item, while experiencing nothing out of the ordinary (Rensink 2002b).

Such coercion could be done – at least in theory – by elements that are unattended. These can remain unseen while still having significant effects on various aspects of perception, including attentional control (e.g., Mack and Rock 1998). The feasibility of this approach therefore depends on the extent to which this can be done. One possibility is to present elements so briefly that they are not consciously registered (e.g., Marcel 1983); another is to draw attention away by a distractor, with the coercing items appearing in some other location where attention is necessarily absent. Indeed, once the first unseen coercion is accomplished, a 'coercive cascade' might begin, with each coercive element providing enough attentional diversion to allow the subsequent coercive element to remain unseen.

3.4   Attentional efficiency

An important part of the management of attention is to ensure that it gets to the right place at the right time. But it is also important to ensure that minimal effort is expended in doing so, that few errors are made, and that good use is made of attention when it arrives at its destination. In other words, it is important that *attentional efficiency* be high.[3] Otherwise the user might be needlessly slowed down or fatigued. Indeed, in the extreme case, the user might be asked to do something that visual attention simply cannot carry out.

Given that attention is managed by a variety of systems (section 3.2.4), it follows that there exist various ways of improving its efficiency. Three of the more important ones are as follows.

3.4.1   Low saliency

Ideally, attention should arrive at the desired location as quickly as possible, with minimal expenditure of effort. In normal viewing, it is drawn automatically and involuntarily to locations of high saliency (sections 3.2.1, 3.3.1). But while saliency is often useful in attracting attention to an item or location, it also has a dark side in that salient locations will draw attention regardless of the situation at hand. If the saliency of an irrelevant item is sufficiently high, it will therefore cause distraction, drawing attention away from where it should go, and requiring the viewer to devote time and effort to overcoming these effects.

A useful way of achieving high efficiency of allocation is therefore to keep the saliency of nonessential graphical elements as low as possible. One way of doing this is to require that nonessential elements not vary greatly – or sharply – in the values of the features they use (for a partial list of such features, see section 3.3.1). While these features need not be absolutely uniform, unique values and sudden changes should be minimized. In particular, the use of motion in a display should be avoided whenever possible, since it is a particularly effective feature for attracting attention (e.g., Bartram, Ware and Calvert 2001; Ware 2004, ch. 5).

Because elements that are nonessential in one task may be essential in another, it is important to keep in mind that low saliency could be achieved for different elements at different times. Thus, for example,

---

[3] 'Efficiency' is sometimes used as a synonym for search rate (e.g., Wolfe 2000). In this chapter, however, it is used in its more basic comparative sense – a measure of how close performance corresponds to that of an optimal system (where attentional mechanisms are used in the best way possible). Such attentional efficiency can therefore be viewed – at least in principle – as a percentage that can range between 0 and 100.

displays could have the properties of their graphical elements depend on the particular mode of use, with only the essential elements being salient at any instant.

3.4.2   Perceptual organization

Another way of improving efficiency is via the use of perceptual organization. This can help in several ways, including limiting the number of items that attention can potentially act upon at any time, as well as organizing these into effective units of selection.

3.4.2.1 Reduced clutter   The efficiency of attention can be improved simply by reducing clutter: given that attention is moved around on an item-by-item basis (section 3.2.2), the fewer the items in a display, the faster and easier its allocation. Clutter has historically been associated with simple image-based properties, being expressed in measures such as the ratio of data to ink (Tufte 2001, chs. 4–6). In this view, the main route to reducing clutter is to minimize the number of irrelevant items in the display, and the saliency of the remainder (e.g., St John et al. 2005; Wickens and McCarley 2008, 76–7).

However, recent work in vision science shows that attention acts not on simple image properties but on more sophisticated early-level structures, such as proto-objects and extended groups (section 3.2.1). Perceptual organization carried out at early levels can therefore help reduce clutter further. For example, if the graphical elements in a display are positioned to form early-level groups, the number of effective items – and thus, the amount of clutter – is greatly reduced, even though the amount of 'ink' is the same (figure 3.8).

3.4.2.2 Improved selectivity   In addition to reducing clutter, grouping can also organize data to improve the ease and effectiveness of attentional selection. Early-level groups can be formed on the basis of several considerations, such as texture boundaries, alignment of elements and element similarity (see, e.g., Wolfe 2000). Once created, these become the effective operands of attentional allocation, with easy suppression of items in other groups (see MacEachren 1995; Ware 2004, ch. 6). Related to these are *surfaces* (Nakayama, He and Shimojo 1995), two-dimensional 'sheets' which facilitate the travel of attention between items (figure 3.9).

Indeed, perceptual organization can go even further, forming *layers*: overlapping groups or surfaces that remain separate in regard to

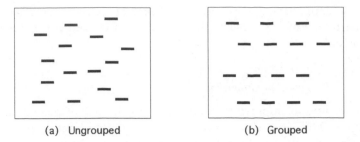

(a) Ungrouped   (b) Grouped

Figure 3.8 Reduction of clutter via grouping. (a) Ungrouped elements. Each element is a separate possibility for attentional allocation. The possibilities are numerous, and so the clutter is considerable. (b) Grouped elements. Elements are immediately grouped on the basis of common alignment. Since attention is initially allocated to such groups, the number of possible operands is low, thereby reducing clutter.

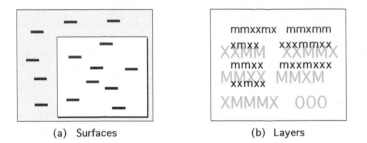

(a) Surfaces   (b) Layers

Figure 3.9 Organizational structures. (a) Surfaces. Attention travels easily between items on the same surface (i.e., bounded two-dimensional structure); it takes more time to travel between items on different ones. (b) Layers. Items are grouped on the basis of contrast and size to form two overlapping layers. When attention shifts among the items in a selected layer, there is relatively little interference from other items, even though they are in nearby locations.

attentional operations (Mullet and Sano 1995, 51–87; Tufte 1990, 53–65). This can be done via transparent surfaces, with the elements of each layer on a separate surface (Mullet and Sano 1995, 51–87; Ware 2004, ch. 6); elements with common contrast (colour) and scale, for example, can form such layers (figure 3.9). Because they are overlapping, layers are useful in facilitating the allocation of attention in small-screen displays (Kamba *et al.* 1996). They have also been found useful for minimizing interference from reference structures such as grids, labels and contour lines (Bartram and Stone 2007).

3.4.3   Compatibility with attentional mechanisms

Recent research on human vision has found that relatively little of a scene is attended to at any moment. Only a few items – and only a few properties of those items – can be attended at a given time (section 3.2.2). If attention is to be used efficiently, it is therefore important for display design to be compatible with the attentional mechanisms used. In particular, information should be presented such that the limited capacity of these mechanisms is not strained.

Attentional mechanisms can always extract information whenever the corresponding graphical properties are perceptually distinct. But if efficiency is to be high, the amount of processing must be minimized. If the process of extracting information from a display can avoid the need for several passes at an element, and the need for complex processing to encode the information contained in it, attention can 'lock on' to the displayed information with minimal time and effort. This can be achieved – at least in part – via careful restrictions on the design.

3.4.3.1 Restricted set of values   One way to achieve high efficiency is for the properties of the graphical elements to match the 'basic codes' of visual attention, so that distinct properties are represented by distinct mechanisms. This can be achieved by using a restricted set of values, which can – if carefully chosen – eliminate the need for sophisticated processing to make (and encode) any finer-grained distinctions that are unnecessary. Attentional pickup of information can then be as effortless as possible (see, e.g., Few 2004, 92–130; Ware 2004).

Although our understanding of this issue is far from complete, it appears that many of the features that attract attention are also basic encoding units (see Ware 2008; Wolfe 2005). In terms of commonly used properties, about four distinct values (or two bits) appear to exist for each spatial dimension (size, orientation, etc.), and about eight basic values (three bits) for colour (see Healey 1996; Shive and Francis 2008; Ware 2004, 182–3; Wolfe 2005). These could be used, for example, to represent particular ranges of size or particular categories. Finer-grained distinctions should be avoided, since these would require a greater number of bits, and thus, more complex computations (figure 3.10).

3.4.3.2 Restricted positioning   Another important approach to efficiency involves location – in particular, the distance between important graphical elements. If these are too close together (within 0.5E degrees of visual angle, where E is the distance from the centre of viewing), their locations will not correspond to separate position codes. The result is

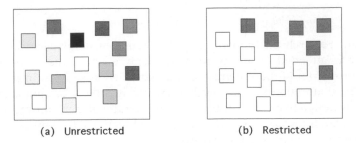

(a) Unrestricted   (b) Restricted

Figure 3.10 Effect of different sets of values. (a) Unrestricted set. Here, elements can take on a wide range of possible values. Distinguishing these from each other requires time and effort (attention). (b) Restricted set. Items now take on one of just a few possible values; the resultant display takes less time and effort to understand.

'crowding', where the properties of individual items are no longer easy to access (Intriligator and Cavanagh 2001; Wolfe 2005). For high efficiency, therefore, adjacent elements must be sufficiently separated. A restricted set of locations would be one way of achieving this.

A second source of restriction stems from the need to minimize change blindness (section 3.2.2). Change blindness can be induced by making the change during an eye movement (Grimes 1996). Since eye movements make up about 10 per cent of total viewing time on average, any transition will have at least a 10 per cent chance of being missed. One way to lower this probability is by minimizing the need for (or the size of) eye movements – e.g., by restricting the separation of important information sources so that they are always close together.

3.4.3.3 Restricted number of elements   Another important aspect of compatibility is to ensure that the number of items used at any time does not exceed attentional capacity. Otherwise, a considerable amount of processing may be required to compensate, if it can be compensated at all.

For example, only about four moving items can be tracked at the same time (Pylyshyn and Storm 1988; Pylyshyn 2003, ch. 5); attempting to track more will inevitably result in some being lost. Indeed, for most tasks, attentional capacity is about four items. The exact value differs for different observers, but is usually around three to five items. A limit of three is a reasonable restriction for displays intended for most users; if more items need to be attended to at any time, performance will tend to deteriorate.

An even more severe restriction applies to information that is conveyed dynamically (e.g., Albrecht-Buehler, Watson and Shamma 2005; Blok 2006). Since attended information is pooled in a single nexus (section 3.2.2), a user attending to two or more simultaneous changes will not be able to tell how many occurred, or which input was the source of a single change, even if given enough time (Rensink 2001; 2002b). In such a situation, therefore, displays should have only a single information source in operation at any time.

3.5   Offloading of attention

Among the more interesting possibilities opened up by new findings on human vision is the offloading of attentional processing onto nonattentional systems. A common intuition about visual perception is that it is 'attento-centric' – i.e., that attention is required for all the important aspects of its operation. However, it is becoming increasingly apparent that perception is based on several systems, many of which operate concurrently with attention, and even independently of it (section 3.2). Some of these have a high degree of visual intelligence, containing processes that – although limited in scope – show considerable sophistication (sections 3.2.1, 3.2.3). Thus, if a display can be appropriately designed, a task traditionally done by 'high-level', attention-intensive processes could be offloaded onto faster, less effortful, and perhaps even more capable nonattentional systems, freeing up attention for other things (Card, Mackinlay and Shneiderman 1999; Rensink 2002b).

Because current knowledge of nonattentional perception is still far from complete, the full extent to which offloading can be usefully applied is unclear. However, it appears applicable to at least three general kinds of task.

3.5.1   Pattern detection

Perhaps the best-developed example of offloading is the use of rapid nonattentional processes at early levels to detect patterns that would otherwise require conscious application of attention – i.e., 'using vision to think' (Card, Mackinlay and Shneiderman 1999). Here, numerical data is represented by simple graphical elements, with the properties of these elements coding the quantities of interest. Much of the focus of work in information visualization is on finding representations that allow the most suitable nonattentional mechanisms to be brought into play (e.g., Tufte 2001; Ware 2004). Important tasks here include detection of trends and detection of outliers. Both can be facilitated by rapid grouping at early visual levels (section 3.2.1): the shape and density of the groups provide a visual representation of trends, while the grouping itself causes non-grouped items (outliers) to become salient, and thus, easily seen.

This approach can be extended beyond the analysis of pure numerical quantities. For example, complex multidimensional data tied to particular spatial coordinates can be usefully analyzed via carefully designed maps (e.g., MacEachren 1995). And the emerging area of visual analytics is heavily based on the offloading of high-level, attention-demanding analysis processes onto faster, nonattentional visual mechanisms (e.g., Thomas and Cook 2005).

3.5.2   Statistical estimation

One of the more interesting forms of visual intelligence is the ability to rapidly estimate the mean size of a briefly presented set of items (section 3.2.3). The speed of this process (within 50 milliseconds) suggests that it is carried out in the absence of attention. This ability may also extend to other statistical measures – such as range or variance – although this has not yet been confirmed. Properties other than size might also be estimated this way; if so, the set of possible properties would likely include the features at early visual levels (section 3.2.1).

Possibly related to this is the finding that viewers can rapidly estimate percentages in large sets of items, based on the pre-attentive visual features of colour (hue) and orientation (Healey, Booth and Enns 1996). Estimates of absolute numbers can also be done rapidly, with speed depending only on the level of precision required, and not on the number of items in the display (Barth, Kanwisher and Spelke 2003).

3.5.3   Visuomotor control

Recent work in vision science suggests that vision involves two largely separate systems: a relatively slow system concerned with the conscious perception of objects, and a faster nonattentional (and nonconscious) system concerned with the online control of actions such as reaching, pointing and eye movements (Milner and Goodale 1995). As such, the possibility arises of displays designed expressly for this second system – i.e., displays that could control a visuomotor system without the involvement of visual attention or even conscious experience. Some support exists for this possibility. Visuomotor actions such as touch selection are faster and more accurate in the lower part of the visual field, where they apparently draw upon specialized representations for action (Po, Fisher and Booth 2004). And removing visual feedback can help a user to aim a laser pointer at a given location, an effect that is counterintuitive from the viewpoint of conscious perception (Po, Fisher and Booth 2003).

An interesting application of this would be displays that help a user move a mouse to a given location more quickly. In such a situation, there would not be any awareness of control: the user would simply 'do the right thing' (Rensink 2002b). An even more interesting – although highly speculative – possibility is that displays could be designed to coordinate visuomotor systems (and perhaps other processes) to allow the user to carry out highly sophisticated operations without their being aware of it, much like the 'auto-pilot' experience occasionally encountered by drivers, in which conscious control temporarily vanishes (see Norretranders 1999). If this kind of control could be achieved, it would be an important step towards the development of systems that enable highly effective interaction between humans and machines, forming a system that in many ways would be a hybrid of the two, capable of drawing on the strengths of each (Clark 2003; Rensink 2007).

3.6   Conclusions

This chapter has surveyed some of the recent advances in our understanding of human vision, and discussed their implications for the management of visual attention in graphic displays. Among these advances is the recognition that attention is not the 'central gateway' to visual perception, but is instead just one of several quasi-independent systems, each capable of sophisticated processing even in the absence of attention. It also appears that the experience of seeing is not supported by a dense, static representation that accumulates results in a task-indifferent way, but is instead supported by a dynamic coordination of attention that depends on the knowledge of the observer and the particular task being done. Other kinds of processes (such as motor control) are also carried out concurrently with this, even in the absence of conscious awareness.

Such a view has several important implications for the management of visual attention. To begin, it suggests that the ability to send attention to a particular item or location is not a secondary aspect of perception, but is fundamental to the creation of the picture we experience. By appropriate coercion of the control mechanisms used in everyday seeing, attention can be managed such that it minimally intrudes upon a viewer's experience. Meanwhile, the existence of nonattentional systems – each with its own form of visual intelligence – provides additional ways of achieving high attentional efficiency, e.g., by creating perceptual structures that help with attentional allocation and engagement. Finally, the possibility also arises of using nonattentional mechanisms to carry out some of the processing that would have been expected of attention.

Thus, the prospects for the effective management of attention extend beyond what would have been imagined had only our casual intuitions of visual perception been used. Among other things, the developments outlined here suggest that – if done effectively – the management of attention can enable humans and machines to combine their strengths seamlessly, resulting in systems with new levels of sophistication.

3.7   Acknowledgements

Many thanks to Minjung Kim and Lonnie Hastings for their comments on earlier drafts of this chapter. Much of the cited work done by the author was carried out at Cambridge Basic Research (CBR), a laboratory of Nissan Motor Company in Cambridge, MA, USA. Support for the writing of this chapter was provided by the Natural Sciences and Engineering Research Council of Canada (NSERC) and The Boeing Company.

3.8   References

Albrecht-Buehler, C., Watson, B., and Shamma, D. A. 2005. Visualizing live text streams using motion and temporal pooling, *IEEE Computer Graphics and Applications* 25: 52–9

Allport, D. A. 1993. Attention and control: Have we been asking the wrong questions? A critical review of twenty-five years, in D. E. Meyer and S. Kornblum (eds.), *Attention and Performance*. Cambridge, MA: MIT Press: vol. XIV: 183–218

Alvarez, G. A., and Scholl, B. J. 2005. How does attention select and track spatially extended objects? New effects of attentional concentration and amplification, *Journal of Experimental Psychology: General* 134: 461–76

Ariely, D. 2001. Seeing sets: Representation by statistical properties, *Psychological Science* 12: 157–62

Ballard, D. H., Hayhoe, M. M., Pook, P. K., and Rao, R. P. 1997. Deictic codes for the embodiment of cognition, *Behavioral and Brain Sciences* 20: 723–67

Bang, M. 2000. *Picture This: How Pictures Work*. New York: Seastar Books

Barth, H., Kanwisher, N., and Spelke, E. S. 2003. The construction of large number representations in adults, *Cognition* 86: 201–21

Bartram, L., and Stone, M. 2007. Whisper, don't scream: Characterizing subtle grids, in *Proceedings IEEE Visualization 2007*. Sacramento, CA

Bartram, L., Ware, C., and Calvert, T. 2001. Filtering and integrating visual information with motion, in *Proceedings on Information Visualization*. Los Alamitos, CA: IEEE: 66–79

Block, B. A. 2001. *The Visual Story: Seeing the Structure of Film, TV and New Media*. Boston: Focal Press

Blok, C. A. 2006. Interactive animation to visually explore time series of satellite imagery, in S. Bres and R. Laurini (eds.), *Visual Information and Information Systems*. Berlin: Springer: 71–82

Bruce, N., and Tsotsos, J. K. 2006. Saliency based on information maximization, *Advances in Neural Information Processing Systems* 18: 155–62

Burton, A. M., Bindemann, M., Langton, S. R., Schweinberger, S. R., and Jenkins, R. 2009. Gaze perception requires focused attention: Evidence from an interference task, *Journal of Experimental Psychology: Human Perception and Performance* 35: 108–18

Card, S. K., Mackinlay, J. D., and Shneiderman, B. 1999. Information visualization, in S. K. Card, J. D. Mackinlay, and B. Shneiderman (eds.), *Readings in Information Visualization: Using Vision to Think*. San Francisco: Morgan Kaufman: 1–34

Chong, S. C., and Treisman, A. 2003. Representation of statistical properties, *Vision Research* 43: 393–404

Chun, M., and Jiang, Y. 1998. Contextual cueing: Implicit learning and memory of visual context guides spatial attention, *Cognitive Psychology* 36: 28–71

Clark, A. J. 2003. *Natural-Born Cyborgs: Minds, Technologies, and the Future of Human Intelligence*. Cambridge, MA: MIT Press

DeCarlo, D., and Santella, A. 2002. Stylization and abstraction of photographs, in *Proceedings of SIGGRAPH 2002*, San Antonio, TX: 769–76

Egeth, H. E., and Yantis, S. 1997. Visual attention: Control, representation, and time course, *Annual Review of Psychology* 48: 269–97

Elazary, L., and Itti, L. 2008. Interesting objects are visually salient, *Journal of Vision* 8: 1–15

Endsley, M. R. 1995. Toward a theory of situation awareness in dynamic systems, *Human Factors* 37: 85–104

Few, S. C. 2004 *Show me the numbers: Designing tables and graphs to enlighten*. Oakland, CA: Analytics Press

Grimes, J. 1996. On the failure to detect changes in scenes across saccades, in K. Akins (ed.), *Perception*. New York: Oxford University Press: 89–110

Halper, N., Mellin, M., Herrmann, C. S., Linneweber, V., and Strothotte, T. 2003. Towards an understanding of the psychology of non-photorealistic rendering, *Workshop on Computational Visualistics, Media Informatics and Virtual Communities* (4–5 April, 2003), Wiesbaden: Deutscher Universitats-Verlag: 67–78

Hayhoe, M. M., Bensinger, D. G., and Ballard, D. H. 1998. Task constraints in visual working memory, *Vision Research* 38: 125–37

Healey, C. G. 1996. Choosing effective colors for data visualization, in *Proceedings of the 7th IEEE Conference on Visualization '96*. San Francisco: 263–70

Healey, C. G., Booth, K. S., and Enns, J. T. 1996. High-speed visual estimation using preattentive processing, *ACM Transactions on Computer–Human Interaction* 3: 107–35

Hochberg, J. E. 1978. *Perception* (2nd edn). Englewood Cliffs, NJ: Prentice-Hall

Intriligator, J., and Cavanagh, P. 2001. The spatial resolution of visual attention, *Cognitive Psychology* 43: 171–216

Itti, L. 2005. Models of bottom-up attention and saliency, in Itti, Rees and Tsotsos: 576–82

Itti, L., Rees, G., and Tsotsos, J. K. (eds.) 2005. *Neurobiology of Attention*. San Diego: Elsevier

Kamba, T., Elson, S. A., Harpold, T., Stamper, T., and Sukaviriya, P. 1996. Using small screen space more efficiently, in *Proceedings of ACM CHI 96*, Vancouver: 383–90

Khan, A., Matejka, J., Fitzmaurice, G., and Kurtenbach, G. 2005. Spotlight: Directing users' attention on large displays, in *Proceedings of ACM CHI 2005*, Portland, OR: 791–98

Kosara, R., Miksch, S., and Hauser, H. 2002. Focus and context taken literally, *IEEE Computer Graphics and its Applications* 22: 22–9

Kuhn, G., Amlani, A. A., and Rensink, R. A. 2008. Towards a science of magic, *Trends in Cognitive Sciences* 12: 349–54

Laurel, B. 1993. *Computers as Theatre*. Reading, MA: Addison-Wesley

MacEachren, A. M. 1995. *How Maps Work: Representation, Visualization, and Design*. New York: Guilford Press: 51–149

Mack, A., and Rock, I. 1998. *Inattentional Blindness*. Cambridge, MA: MIT Press

Marcel, A. J. 1983. Conscious and unconscious perception: Experiments on visual masking and word recognition, *Cognitive Psychology* 15: 197–237

Marr, D. 1982. *Vision: A Computational Investigation into the Human Representation and Processing of Visual Information*. San Francisco: Freeman

Massironi, M., 2002. *The Psychology of Graphic Images: Seeing, Drawing, Communicating*. Mahwah, NJ: Lawrence Erlbaum Associates

McCrickard, D. S., and Chewar, C. M. 2003. Attuning notification design to user goals and attention costs, *Communications of the ACM* 46: 67–72

Milner, A. D., and Goodale, M. A. 1995. *The Visual Brain in Action*. Oxford: Oxford University Press

Moore, C. M., and Egeth, H. 1997. Perception without attention: Evidence of grouping under conditions of inattention, *Journal of Experimental Psychology: Human Perception and Performance* 23: 339–52

Mühlenen, A. von, and Lleras, A. 2007. No-onset looming motion guides spatial attention, *Journal of Experimental Psychology: Human Perception and Performance* 33: 1297–1310

Mullet, K., and Sano, D. 1995. *Designing Visual Interfaces*. Englewood Cliffs, NJ: Prentice Hall

Nakayama, K., He, Z. J., and Shimojo, S. 1995. Visual surface representation: A critical link between lower-level and higher-level vision, in S. M. Kosslyn and D. N. Osherson (eds.), *Visual Cognition* (2nd edn). Cambridge, MA: MIT Press: 1–70

New, J., Cosmides, L., and Tooby, J. 2007. Category-specific attention for animals reflects ancestral priorities, not expertise, *Proceedings of the National Academy of Sciences* 104: 16598–603

Norretranders, T. 1999. *The User Illusion: Cutting Consciousness Down to Size*. New York: Penguin Books

Oliva, A. 2005. Gist of a scene, in Itti, Rees and Tsotsos: 251–6

Palmer, S. E. 1999. *Vision Science: Photons to Phenomenology*. Cambridge, MA: MIT Press

Parasuraman, R. (ed.) 2000. *The Attentive Brain*. Cambridge, MA: MIT Press

Pashler, H. 1998. *Attention*. San Diego: Psychology Press

Po, B. A., Fisher, B. D., and Booth, K. S. 2003. Pointing and visual feedback for spatial interaction in large-screen display environments, in *Proceedings of the 3rd International Symposium on Smart Graphics*, Heidelberg: 22–38

  2004. Mouse and touchscreen selection in the upper and lower visual fields, in *Proceedings of the SIGCHI Conference on Human Factors in Computing Systems*, Vienna: 359–66

Pylyshyn, Z. W. 2003. *Seeing and Visualizing: It's Not What You Think*. Cambridge, MA: MIT Press

Pylyshyn, Z. W., and Storm, R. W. 1988. Tracking multiple independent targets: Evidence for a parallel tracking mechanism, *Spatial Vision* 3: 179–97

Rensink, R. A. 2000. The dynamic representation of scenes, *Visual Cognition* 7: 17–42

  2001. Change blindness: Implications for the nature of attention, in M. Jenkin and L. Harris (eds.), *Vision and Attention*. New York: Springer: 169–88

  2002a. Change detection, *Annual Review of Psychology* 53: 245–77

  2002b. Internal vs. external information in visual perception, in *Proceedings of the 2nd International Symposium on Smart Graphics*, Hawthorne, NY: 63–70

  2003. Visual attention, in L. Nadel (ed.), *Encyclopedia of Cognitive Science*. London: Nature Publishing Group: 509–15

  2007. The modeling and control of visual perception, in W. D. Gray (ed.), *Integrated Models of Cognitive Systems*. New York: Oxford University Press: 132–48

Rensink, R. A., and Cavanagh, P. 2004. The influence of cast shadows on visual search, *Perception* 33: 1339–58

Rensink, R. A., and Enns, J. T. 1998. Early completion of occluded objects, *Vision Research* 38: 2489–505

Rensink, R. A., O'Regan, J. K., and Clark, J. J. 1997. To see or not to see: The need for attention to perceive changes in scenes, *Psychological Science* 8: 368–73

Richards, W., and Kaufman, L. 1969. 'Centre of-gravity' tendencies for fixations and flow patterns, *Perception and Psychophysics* 5: 81–4

Ristic, J., Wright, A., and Kingstone, A. 2007. Attentional control and reflexive orienting to gaze and arrow cues, *Psychonomic Bulletin and Review* 14: 964–9

Roda, C., and Thomas, J. (eds.) 2006. Attention aware systems, special issue of *Computers in Human Behavior* 22(4): Elsevier

Seif El-Nasr, M. 2005. Intelligent lighting for game environments, *Journal of Game Development* 1: 17–50

Sharpe, S. 1988. *Conjurers' Psychological Secrets*. Calgary: Hades Publications: 46–83

Shive, J., and Francis, G. 2008. Applying models of visual search to map display design, *International Journal of Human–Computer Studies* 66: 67–77

Simons, D. J., and Chabris, C. 1999. Gorillas in our midst: Sustained inattentional blindness for dynamic events, *Perception* 28: 1059–74

Solso, R. L. 1994. *Cognition and the Visual Arts.* Cambridge, MA: MIT Press

St John, M., Smallman, H. S., Manes, D. I., Feher, B. A., and Morrison, J. G. 2005. Heuristic automation for decluttering tactical displays, *Human Factors* 47: 509–25

Su, S. L., Durand, F., and Agrawala, M. 2005. De-emphasis of distracting image regions using texture power maps, in *Texture 2005: Proceedings of the 4th International Workshop on Texture Analysis and Synthesis*, Beijing: 119–24

Tatler, B. W. 2002. What information survives saccades in the real world? in J. Hyönä, D. Munoz, W. Heide, and R. Radach (eds.), *The Brain's Eye: Neurobiological and Clinical Aspects of Oculomotor Research.* Amsterdam: Elsevier: 149–63

Theeuwes, J., and Godijn, R. 2002. Irrelevant singletons capture attention: Evidence from inhibition of return, *Perception and Psychophysics* 64: 764–70

Thomas, J. J., and Cook, K. A. (eds.) 2005. *Illuminating the Path: The Research and Development Agenda for Visual Analytics.* Richland, WA: National Visualization and Analytics Center

Thorpe, S. J., Fize, D., and Marlot, C. 1996. Speed of processing in the human visual system, *Nature* 381: 520–2

Tognazzini, B. 1993. Principles, techniques, and ethics of stage magic and their application to human interface design, in *Proceedings of INTERCHI 96.* New York: ACM: 355–62

Treisman, A. 1988. Features and objects: The fourteenth Bartlett memorial lecture, *Quarterly Journal of Experimental Psychology* 40A: 201–37

Tufte, E. R. 1990. *Envisioning Information.* Cheshire, CT: Graphics Press
   2001. *The Visual Display of Quantitative Information* (2nd edn). Cheshire, CT: Graphics Press

Vertegaal, R. (ed.) 2003. Attentive user interfaces, special issue of *Communications of the ACM* 46

Vishwanath, D., and Kowler, E. 2003. Localization of shapes: Eye movements and perception compared, *Vision Research* 43: 1637–53

Ward, P. 1996. *Picture Composition for Film and Television.* Oxford: Butterworth-Heinemann

Ware, C. 2004. *Information Visualization: Perception for Design* (2nd edn). San Francisco: Morgan Kaufmann
   2008. *Visual Thinking for Design.* San Francisco: Morgan Kaufmann

Wickens, C. D., and McCarley, J. S. 2008. *Applied Attention Theory.* Boca Raton, FL: CRC Press

Wolfe, J. M. 1999. Inattentional amnesia, in V. Coltheart (ed.), *Fleeting Memories.* Cambridge, MA: MIT Press: 71–94
   2000. Visual attention, in K. K. De Valois (ed.), *Seeing* (2nd edn). San Diego: Academic Press: 335–86
   2005. How might the rules that govern visual search constrain the design of visual displays? *Society for Information Display.* Boston, MA

Wolfe, J. M., and DiMase, J. S. 2003. Do intersections serve as basic features in visual search? *Perception* 32: 645–56

4 Cognitive load theory, attentional processes and optimized learning outcomes in a digital environment

Renae Low, Putai Jin and John Sweller

The interactive relation and equivalence between working memory and attentional processes has been demonstrated by experimental, developmental, educational and clinical studies on preschoolers, schoolchildren, adolescents, younger adults and the elderly. It is important to understand the features of working memory from the ground theory of human cognitive architecture and its derived evolutionary educational psychology, which argue that the constraints of working memory are virtually necessary for both human survival and learning. Based on our knowledge of cognitive architecture and empirical research on effective instruction design that is in accordance with the functioning of working memory and related cognitive structures, cognitive load theory has been developed during recent decades to provide a number of principles for teaching and learning in a variety of settings. Much of this work has been carried out in a digital supported environment. In this chapter, recommendations based on cognitive load perspectives are presented along with further explorations of the potential for constructing digital supporting systems and tools.

4.1 Introduction

Digital technologies bring many capabilities to the teaching and learning environment. Anyone with access to the Internet can easily and quickly locate multimedia information. Text, images, sound and video can be accessed with the movement of a mouse or at the stroke of a key. Synchronous (e.g., video teleconferencing, chat sessions) and asynchronous (via bulletin boards, emails and the like) collaboration is possible. Indeed, the rapid development of new digital technology which has made possible the integration of text, images, narration, animation and virtual reality has enabled the widespread use of multimedia as a common learning format in schools and other instructional settings. The educational application of digital technologies is extensive, ranging from a young child reading picture story books in digitized format on CD-ROM, DVD or video to a soldier learning to use maps and descriptive details to plan an operation.

It is indisputable that digital technologies have enabled multimedia to represent a potentially powerful learning technology by presenting information in a wide variety of different formats (written or spoken text, pictures consisting of static objects, graphs, manipulated objects or animations). What is debatable is whether such a powerful learning technology translates to effective, meaningful learning. It is generally assumed that the use of a multimedia instructional format is effective. However, human learning, with or without educational aids, is subject to the constraints imposed by the human information-processing system, and in particular, working-memory capacity. The interactive relation and equivalence between working memory and attentional processes has been demonstrated by experimental, developmental, educational and clinical studies on preschoolers, schoolchildren, adolescents, younger adults and the elderly (see Bays and Husain 2008; Berninger *et al.* 2008; Engelhardt *et al.* 2008; Garon, Bryson and Smith 2008; Kim, Bayles and Beeson 2008; Oka and Miura 2008; Parks and Hopfinger 2008; Van Gerven *et al.* 2003).

There are several similar cognition-based theories of multimedia learning: for example, cognitive load theory (Sweller 2005a), cognitive theory of multimedia learning (Mayer 2005), integrative model of text and picture comprehension (Schnotz 2005) and four-component instructional design model for multimedia learning (van Merriënboer and Kester 2005; van Merriënboer and Kirschner 2007). The common core concept underlying these four theories is the limited capacity of working memory that can explain many of the effects found with multimedia learning materials. In this chapter, we focus on cognitive load theory, an instructional theory based on our knowledge of human cognitive architecture that specifically addresses the limitations of working memory. We begin with features of working memory from the ground theory of human cognitive architecture based on evolutionary educational psychology. Next, the empirical evidence for effective instruction design that is in accordance with the functioning of working memory and related cognitive structures is discussed within the framework of cognitive load theory. Lastly, recommendations based on cognitive load perspectives are presented along with further explorations of the potential for constructing digital supporting systems and tools.

4.2   Human cognitive architecture: an evolutionary perspective

Geary (2002, 2005, 2007, 2008) distinguishes between biologically primary and biologically secondary information. Biologically primary information is knowledge we have evolved to acquire, while biologically secondary knowledge is taught in educational institutions. Learners are strongly motivated to acquire biologically primary information which can be acquired easily, rapidly and unconsciously just by immersion in a social context. Examples of such knowledge are oral/aural language acquisition, simple tool usage, and the reading of facial expression and body language. In contrast, biologically secondary information, such as written language and mathematics, requires considerable conscious effort and external motivation to acquire. It is this category of biologically secondary knowledge for which schools and other education institutions were invented.

The cognitive architecture required to allow the acquisition of biologically secondary knowledge mirrors the processes and structures of evolution by natural selection. Both are examples of natural information-processing systems. Sweller and Sweller (2006) describe the analogy between human cognitive architecture and biological evolution using five basic principles.

4.2.1   Information store principle

In order to function in a natural environment, natural information processing systems must include a large information store to deal with the various contingencies with which they will be faced. In the case of evolutionary biology, that store is provided by a genome, while long-term memory provides a similar cognitive function. Evidence for the central importance of long-term memory in human learning, thinking and problem solving comes from the well-known studies demonstrating the role of long-term memory in the development of problem-solving expertise (Chase and Simon 1973; De Groot 1965). Highly skilled chess players normally defeat weaker opponents because they have stored tens of thousands of board configurations (Simon and Gilmartin 1973) and the best moves associated with those configurations in long-term memory.

4.2.2   Borrowing and reorganizing principle

Mechanisms are required to rapidly build a large information store. Natural information-processing systems build their stores primarily by borrowing information from other stores. Asexual reproduction provides an exact transmission of information, apart from mutations, from one store to another. Sexual reproduction ensures that borrowed information is first transmitted and then reorganized. Indeed, the reorganization that is characteristic of sexual reproduction provides its primary function, ensuring that descendants differ from their ancestors and their siblings, apart from monozygotic siblings.

The bulk of biologically secondary information held in long-term memory also is borrowed. Most of it is obtained from other people. We imitate what others do (Bandura 1986), listen to what they say and read what they write. The cognitive load theory effects discussed below all depend directly on the borrowing and reorganizing principle.

4.2.3   The randomness as genesis principle

While most information held in long-term memory is borrowed, that information has to be created in the first instance. Random generate and test during problem solving is the only known mechanism for generating creativity. In the case of biology, random mutation is the ultimate source of all biological novelty. Similarly, during problem solving, when knowledge is created, we virtually always use a combination of previously known information and random generate and test. Whether we are attempting to find a problem-solving move or searching for an analogue, to the extent that information is not available in long-term memory, we have no choice but to engage in random generation followed by a test for effectiveness. Without sufficient information in long-term memory, we cannot know the outcome of a problem-solving move until we have made that move, either mentally or physically. Analogously, the consequences of a mutation cannot be assessed biologically until after it has occurred.

4.2.4   The narrow limits of change principle

The randomness as genesis principle has structural consequences. If randomness is a part of the creation of novel structures and functions, change must be small and incremental because a large, random change will almost certainly be dysfunctional. In biology, the epigenetic system (Jablonka and Lamb 2005; West-Eberhard 2003) mediates the manner in which outside influences affect the genetic system. Working memory has the same function in human cognition (Sweller and Sweller 2006) when it deals with novel information from the senses. That information must be organized by working memory and the organization tested for effectiveness before being stored in long-term memory. To ensure that the number of randomly generated, possible alternative organizational patterns is not overwhelming, working memory has well-known temporal (Peterson and Peterson 1959) and capacity (Miller 1956) limits.

4.2.5   The environmental organizing and linking principle

This principle provides the ultimate aim of natural information-processing systems. Not only must the system assimilate information from the external world, it must also simultaneously use the information store to organize the external world and generate appropriate action. The epigenetic system can marshal huge amounts of genetic information from the same genome to determine vastly different biological structures and functions. For example, vastly different cells such as skin cells and liver cells have the same genetic code in their nuclei. Similarly, working memory can use massive amounts of organized information from long-term memory to determine action. The vast amounts of information from long-term memory that can be processed over extended periods by working memory indicate that there are no temporal or capacity limitations of working memory when dealing with familiar information from long-term memory (Ericsson and Kintsch 1995).

4.3   Working-memory characteristics and instructional implications

As indicated by the narrow limits of change principle, a limited working memory is an outcome of natural information-processing systems. It is necessarily limited, so that it only allows essential information to be sent to the long-term information store. That information is randomly generated but tested for effectiveness. Large amounts of randomly generated, untested and so probably dysfunctional information is not sent to the long-term store. In this way, the cognitive system maintains its relative stability and achieves its incremental progress.

Theoretically, the concept of working memory is a system with limited capacity for temporary maintenance (including storage) and manipulation of information in complex cognitive tasks (Allen, Baddeley and Hitch 2006; Cowan 2005) through a focus of attention (Oberauer and Bialkova 2009). It serves as the cognitive structure in which we consciously process information. The structure is notable for its severe capacity and duration limits when dealing with new information. Initial evidence for the limited capacity comes from the classic work of Miller (1956) while early evidence for its limited duration comes from Peterson and Peterson (1959). Miller (1956) indicated that working memory is only able to hold about five to nine chunks of information. It can probably process no more than two to four chunks (Cowan 2005). Peterson and Peterson (1959) found that almost all the contents of working memory are lost within about 20 seconds without rehearsal. Given these figures, the capacity of working memory is severely constrained when dealing with new information. In learning terms, new information must be processed by a structure that is very small in capacity and that retains the information for no more than a third of a minute. For instruction to be effective, these limitations should be a central consideration.

Not only is the working-memory system in its natural state severely limited in capacity and duration, it is also susceptible to distraction and interference. Daily life provides numerous examples: an attractive billboard may distract a driver, a fly hovering about may distract you from reading this chapter, someone talking while you are listening to a lecture may affect your concentration on the content and flow. In the laboratory, distractor processing has been extensively studied within a framework that integrates attention research with executive function yielding behavioural and neuroimaging data to demonstrate that attention is continuously needed to maintain information in working memory (see, for example, Lavie 2005; Moores and Maxwell 2008; San Miguel, Corral and Escera 2008; Zhang, Du and Zhang 2008). In a recent study, Makovski, Sussman and Jiang (2008) further demonstrated that if attention is divided so that memory of several items is simultaneously held in working memory, then memory for the items is vulnerable to interference from the test display. As distraction and interference is an additional memory load, its impact on the limited working-memory system has to be taken into consideration in a multimedia context where the different formats of words and pictures allow for many possible ways of presenting information.

4.4   Working-memory limitations and multimedia learning

Working memory was initially treated as a unitary structure. Current models assume that working memory consists of multiple processors. These multiple processors are frequently associated with the separate processing of visual-spatial and language-based material. For example, Baddeley and Hitch's (1974) three-component model of working memory consists of a control system of limited attentional capacity, referred to as the central executive, and two subsidiary storage systems: the phonological loop, responsible for sound and language, and the visuospatial sketchpad, responsible for two- and three-dimensional objects. In general, the phonological loop deals with auditory material while the visuospatial sketchpad deals with vision. These two independent subsystems are complementary to Paivio's (1986) dual coding system.

Low and Sweller (2005) have provided a discussion of the research evidence indicating strong support for the relative independence of the visuospatial sketchpad and the phonological loop in that they process different types of information. If the two systems are relatively independent, the total amount of information that can be processed in working memory may be determined by the mode of presentation (i.e., visual or auditory). Theoretically, it is possible to increase effective working-memory capacity by presenting information in a mixed visual and auditory mode rather than a single mode. Penney (1989) provided two lines of evidence demonstrating an increase in effective working-memory capacity with the use of both visual and auditory processors, rather than a single processor: improved ability in performing two concurrent tasks when information was presented in a partly auditory, partly visual format, rather than in either single format, and improved memory when information was presented to two sensory modalities (visual and auditory) rather than one.

4.5   Cognitive load theory and instructional consequences

The human cognitive architecture on which cognitive load theory is based assumes that most cognitive activities are driven by a large store of information held in long term memory (the information store principle). This knowledge acts as a central executive for working memory, directing the manner in which information is processed (the environmental organizing and linking principle). The ultimate goal of instruction is the alteration of long-term memory via the borrowing and reorganizing principle. In other words, for learning to occur, novel material must be organized and incorporated into long-term memory via a limited working memory. For instruction to be effective, it has to be designed in ways in which the limitations of the working memory are overcome. Many instructional materials and techniques may be ineffective because they ignore the limitations of human working memory and impose a heavy extraneous cognitive load. Cognitive load theory distinguishes between three kinds of cognitive load: intrinsic, germane and extraneous load.

Intrinsic cognitive load is related to task difficulty and is due to the complexity of the information that must be processed. It is determined by the levels of element interactivity inherent in the learning material. If element interactivity is low, so is working-memory load. For example, in learning to translate nouns of a foreign language, each translation can be learned independently of every other translation; learning to translate the word *potato* does not depend on learning to translate the word *egg*. In contrast, some material consist of elements that interact in the sense that one element cannot be meaningfully learned without learning many other elements simultaneously. For example, in learning the English word order for the phrase *inside the old building*, it is not sufficient to attend to individual words to decide that *the inside old building* is not appropriate. All the words in the phrase and the relations among them must be considered simultaneously because they interact. Element interactivity in this case is high, resulting in a high intrinsic cognitive load. Processing high-element-interactivity material imposes a high working-memory load. Because intrinsic load is inherent in the learning material, it cannot be manipulated without compromising understanding.

Germane load (Paas and van Merriënboer 1993) is the cognitive load caused by effortful learning due to attentional (working-memory) resources being directed to intrinsic cognitive load. For instance, giving learners lots of examples to demonstrate a point increases germane cognitive load although it is likely to assist in learning.

Extraneous cognitive load is caused by inappropriate instructional designs that fail to take into consideration the limitation of working-memory resources that are necessary for learning. This cognitive load is important in multimedia learning because of the cognitive effort required to process different sources of information. Theoretically, extraneous cognitive load can be alleviated by overcoming the limitations of working memory in two ways. First, instructional procedures can alleviate extraneous cognitive load by formatting instructional material in such a way as to minimize cognitive activities that are unnecessary to learning so that cognitive resources can be freed to concentrate on activities essential to dealing with intrinsic cognitive load. Second, working memory can be increased in capacity by taking the advantage that is offered by dual modality presentations.

Intrinsic, germane and extraneous cognitive load are additive. In any instructional situation, the aim is to reduce extraneous cognitive load imposed by an inappropriate presentation format. Reducing extraneous cognitive load frees working-memory capacity, permitting an increase in germane cognitive load which is necessary when dealing with complex material that imposes a high intrinsic cognitive load.

In the following sections, we focus on three cognitive load effects concerned with aspects of multimedia presentation of information: the split-attention effect, the redundancy effect and the modality effect.

4.5.1   The split-attention effect

Split attention occurs when learners are required to integrate multiple sources of information that are physically or temporally separate from each other where each source is essential for understanding the material. The working-memory load imposed by the need to mentally integrate disparate sources of information may interfere with learning. The first

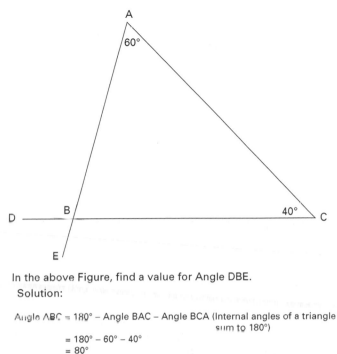

In the above Figure, find a value for Angle DBE.

Solution:

Angle ABC = 180° – Angle BAC – Angle BCA (Internal angles of a triangle
                                                            sum to 180°)
       = 180° – 60° – 40°
       = 80°
Angle DBE = Angle ABC (Vertically opposite angles are equal)
       = 80°

Figure 4.1 A conventional, split-attention geometry example

study on split attention was reported by Tarmizi and Sweller (1988), who
used geometry worked examples in their attempt to replicate the effectiveness of worked examples in algebra learning (Cooper and Sweller 1987;
Sweller and Cooper 1985) and in other mathematical-related domains
(Zhu and Simon 1987). Surprisingly, using worked examples did not produce better learning outcomes than using conventional problem-solving
strategies in their initial geometry experiment. They argued that the
requirement to mentally integrate the two sources of information (diagram and textual solutions) due to the conventionally structured format
of the worked examples (see figure 4.1) must have imposed an increase
in cognitive load that prevented cognitive resources being used for
learning.

When diagrams and the statements required to understand the diagrams are physically separate, as normally occurs in conventionally structured geometry worked examples, working-memory resources must be
expended to mentally integrate the two sources of information, reducing

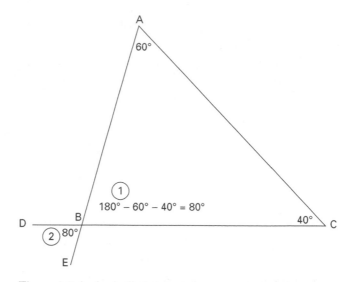

Figure 4.2 A physically integrated geometry example

the effectiveness of worked examples. In subsequent experiments, when the format of presenting geometry worked examples was altered to an integrated version in which statements were physically integrated with the diagram (see figure 4.2), studying worked examples proved more effective than a conventional problem-solving strategy. The integrated format alleviated the extraneous cognitive load imposed by the requirement to split attention between diagrams and text, freeing working-memory resources to attend to processes that facilitate learning.

Tarmizi and Sweller's (1988) findings have led to a number of studies that have extended the split-attention effect to the learning of coordinate geometry (Sweller *et al.* 1990), physics (Ward and Sweller 1990), material designed for training of electrical apprentices (Sweller and Chandler 1991) and learning in a computer environment (Sweller and Chandler 1994; Chandler and Sweller 1996). Similarly, Mayer and his research associates have demonstrated that split attention could also occur with temporal separation, thus leading to unnecessary extraneous cognitive load (Mayer and Anderson 1991, 1992; Mayer and Sims 1994; Moreno and Mayer 1999). In the area of language learning, Yeung, Jin and Sweller (1998) found that the integrated format, which combined explanatory notes with reading passages, was helpful in reducing the cognitive load related to vocabulary search and facilitating the process of reading comprehension for young native speakers as well as inexperienced English as a second language (ESL) learners. More recently, Hung (2007) found that reducing split attention facilitated learning by undergraduate geography students studying ESL.

The split-attention effect has implications for instructional design in a multimedia context where there will inevitably be at least two sources of information. Research suggests that multiple sources of information need to be integrated into an optimal format to minimize extraneous cognitive load. However, those sources of information must be complementary to each other rather than mere repetition of the same information (see next section on the redundancy effect). In addition, as pointed out by Sweller (1994), an integrated format is only effective when the learning material has high-element interactivity (i.e., the elements in the learning content must be simultaneously processed because they interact). Under this condition, the intrinsic cognitive load is relatively high and the employment of an integrated method can be helpful. On the other hand, if the learning material has low-element interactivity (i.e., elements in the learning content have little interaction and thus can be processed individually), there is a low intrinsic cognitive load. In this case, using an integrated format is unlikely to lead to a noticeable impact on learning outcomes. A further factor to consider when integrating different sources of information is learner characteristics that interact with material characteristics. Material that is not intelligible in isolation and is high in element interactivity for low-knowledge learners may be intelligible in isolation and low in element interactivity for learners with more knowledge. For high-knowledge individuals, physical integration may be harmful because of the redundancy effect (Kalyuga, Chandler and Sweller 1998; Yeung, Jin and Sweller 1998), discussed next.

4.5.2   The redundancy effect

The redundancy effect occurs when additional information presented to learners results in negative rather than positive effects on learning. In multimedia learning, it is not unusual for an instructor or a web-based course designer to consider providing the same information in different formats or presenting additional detailed information for the topic to enhance learning. Intuitively, it is easy to assume that such additional information will not produce negative learning outcomes. However, cognitive load theory suggests the possibility of negative effects due to redundancy. Because working memory is extremely limited in terms of its capacity and duration, when the learners are exposed to material containing the same information in multiple forms or some unnecessary elaborations, their cognitive functioning can be inhibited and their learning process may be negatively affected. For instance, to teach pupils to learn a noun, say, the name of an animal (horse), a teacher can write the word on a flashcard or on the whiteboard and read it (presenting essential information via both visual and audio channels). One may further assume that it is a good idea to show pupils a flashcard containing both the word and picture and at the same time provide the pronunciation. Such a type of instruction sounds more 'interesting' and more 'informative', and can be easily accomplished using modern information technology. However, controlled experiments designed to test the effect of adding pictures to words when learning to read have indicated that reading outcomes are superior using written words plus sounds rather than presenting written words, pictures and sounds simultaneously (Miller 1937; Solman, Singh and Kehoe 1992; Torcasio and Sweller 2010). This phenomenon can be explained by assuming that adding pictures to the presentation of written words and sounds is redundant, and that redundancy can have a negative impact on the effective use of limited working memory to process and transfer information to long-term memory. Redundancy imposes an extraneous cognitive load.

In a multimedia learning context, the redundancy effect has been demonstrated in a number of studies (Mayer 2001; Sweller 2005b). In one study, a series of experiments were carried out to test the redundancy effect in a computer course (Sweller and Chandler 1994; Chandler and Sweller 1996). The learners were divided into two groups: participants in one group worked on a computer with the assistance of a computer manual that combined text with diagrams; participants in the other group simply learned using the computer manual either on a screen or in hardcopy but did not actually work on a computer. Because the act of working on the computer was largely irrelevant to the real task of understanding the program, participants in the first group who had to work on a computer could not use working memory efficiently to transfer the knowledge of programming into their long-term memory. In other words, the computer work was redundant and occupied working-memory resources that otherwise could be used by learners to assimilate the appropriate information. In another series of experiments on the use of computer manuals, researchers reported that computer manuals with minimized explanatory text were more effective and user-friendly than conventional manuals (Carroll 1990; Carroll et al. 1987). Similarly, researchers have found that a reduced or summarized text was superior to a full text (in which some parts may be redundant) in terms of learning outcomes such as lower error rates, higher retention rates and shorter acquisition times (Mayer et al. 1996; Reder and Anderson 1980, 1982).

In research on learning English as a foreign language (EFL), Hirai (1999) noticed that, for less proficient Japanese EFL learners, their listening rate was far behind their reading rate. Diao and Sweller (2007) and Diao, Chandler and Sweller (2007) thus proposed that, if novice EFL learners were exposed to both auditory and visual information for reading comprehension, such an audio-visual presentation might result in a redundancy effect. They tested this hypothesis and found that the Chinese ESL learners who were exposed to simultaneous presentations of spoken and written text had a higher mental load and produced lower test scores in both word decoding and reading comprehension in comparison with those who were given written information only. In a similar vein, Kalyuga, Chandler and Sweller (2004) found that the simultaneous presentation of written and spoken text during a presentation imposes an extraneous cognitive load. Learning is enhanced by presenting in one modality only.

As is the case with the split-attention effect, the redundancy effect has been demonstrated in a variety of contexts. It is not just diagrams and redundant text that can be used to demonstrate the redundancy effect. While diagrams are frequently more intelligible than the equivalent text, there are instances where any one of diagrams, the presence of equipment or auditory information have been found to be redundant (see Sweller 2005b for experimental evidence). In other words, what is redundant depends on what is being taught. The redundancy effect provides a simple guideline for instructional design in practice: eliminate any redundant material in whatever form presented to learners and any redundant activity that instruction may encourage learners to engage in. However, this guideline alone does not indicate exactly what material may or may not be redundant. This guiding principle needs to be considered in conjunction with cognitive load theory. The theory can be used to provide guidance concerning the conditions that determine redundancy and hence what material is likely to be redundant. For instance, in deciding whether text should be added to a diagram, the instructional designer needs to consider several factors. Is the diagram intelligible on its own? If so, the text may be redundant. Does the text provide essential information? If so, it is not likely to be redundant and should be retained. Is there a high level of element interactivity within the text, that is, to understand one element, must one consider many other elements at the same time? If so, as far as possible, diagrams should not be presented with the text to avoid the risk of overloading working memory. Another factor to consider is learner expertise. Whether information is high in element interactivity and whether it is intelligible on its own depends largely on the learner. Information that is intelligible for more expert learners may not make sense to novices who require additional explanatory material. In short, whether or not additional material is redundant can be determined by considering the cognitive load implications of that material in the context of learner expertise.

4.5.3   The modality effect

It was noted earlier that the limitations of working memory can be overcome either by formatting instructional materials in a manner that minimizes extraneous cognitive load so that cognitive resources can be released to attend to processes useful for learning or by expanding effective working-memory capacity. While both the split-attention effect and the redundancy effect fall into the first category of minimizing extraneous cognitive load, the modality effect falls into the latter category of expanding working-memory capacity. The modality effect occurs when information presented in a mixed mode (partly visual and partly auditory) is more effective than when the same information is presented in a single mode (either visually or in auditory form alone). Mousavi, Low and Sweller (1995) tested this hypothesis in educational settings, in which geometry problems and related instructions were used. There were two data presentation conditions: audio-visual and visual-visual. In the audio-visual presentation, diagrams were given as visual information and the related text was provided as audio input, whereas in the visual-visual presentation, both diagrams and associated text were in a visual format. The data obtained from this series of experiments demonstrated that learners in the audio-visual group performed much better than did those in the visual-visual group.

From a cognitive load theory perspective, the modality effect can be explained by assuming the memory load due to a picture with written text presentation induces a high load in the visual working-memory system because both sources of information are processed in this system. In contrast, the diagram and narration version induces a lower load in visual working memory because auditory and visual information are each processed in their respective systems. Therefore, the total load induced by this version is spread between the visual and the auditory components in the working-memory system. In other words, the use of audio and visual information may not overload working memory if its capacity is effectively expanded by using a dual-mode presentation as opposed to a single-mode presentation.

This basic modality effect was confirmed in a number of subsequent studies. For instance, Tindall-Ford, Chandler and Sweller (1997) reported increased effective working memory and improved learning outcomes under audio-visual conditions in comparison with visual-visual conditions in electrical engineering courses in which the learning material was high in element interactivity. Adopting the scale recommended by Paas and van Merriënboer (1993), Tindall-Ford and colleagues found that the cognitive load was lower under audio-visual conditions than visual-visual conditions for learning such material. Applying the modality principle, Jeung, Chandler and Sweller (1997) reported improved learning outcomes by using visual indicators to highlight the most complex parts of information in the spoken text. In an industrial training course, beginners' learning experience was enhanced by dual-mode presentations delivered by the instructor (Kalyuga, Chandler and Sweller 2000).

The modality effect is especially important in the context of multimedia learning because the instructional medium involves different presentation modes and sensory modalities. Multimedia instruction is becoming increasingly popular and findings associated with the modality effect that can be interpreted within a cognitive load framework can provide a coherent theoretical base for multimedia investigations and applications. Using web-based or computer-aided instructional design, Mayer and his colleagues (Mayer and Moreno 1998; Moreno and Mayer 1999; Moreno et al. 2001) tested the modality effect in a number of courses. In general, they found that students learned more when scientific explanations were given as pictures plus narration (or spoken text) than under the condition of pictures together with on-screen text. According to Mayer's (2005) interpretation, when learners are dealing with pictures and related on-screen text, their visual channel may become overloaded while their auditory channel is unused. When words are narrated or the spoken text is provided, the learners can use their auditory channel to process such information, and the visual channel will deal with the pictures only. The redistribution of information flow can lead to enhanced multimedia learning. When the information contained in a picture is too complex, simultaneous presentation of corresponding auditory information may still be beyond the capacity of working memory. In this case, a sequencing method can be used to reduce cognitive load (Schnotz 2005). For instance, the picture can be presented before its related text (Kulhavy, Stock and Caterino 1994).

In line with cognitive load theory, Brünken et al. (2002) replicated the modality effect in two different multimedia learning environments. In this study, they used a dual-task approach to measure cognitive load where performance on a visual secondary reaction time task was taken as a direct measure of the cognitive load induced by multimedia instruction. Brünken and associates found that the differences in learning outcome demonstrated by the modality effect were related to different levels of cognitive load induced by the different presentation formats of the learning material. Specifically, they found that an emphasis on visual presentation of material resulted in a decrement on a visual secondary task, indicating an overload of the visual processor. In a subsequent study, Brünken, Plass and Leutner (2004) again reproduced the modality effect while measuring cognitive load using a dual-task methodology. In this study, the secondary task was auditory instead of visual and there was a decrement in performance on the auditory secondary task when the primary task placed an emphasis on the auditory processor.

The distinction between the conditions under which the modality and split-attention effects will be obtained and the conditions under which the redundancy effect will be obtained need to be carefully noted. The three effects depend heavily on the logical relation between the various sources of information. The split-attention and modality effects can only be obtained when the various sources of information are unintelligible in isolation and must be integrated before they can be understood. Thus, a diagram and text such as a geometry diagram and an explanation (see figure 4.1) can be used to demonstrate the split-attention or modality effects because a statement such as 'Angle ABC' is unintelligible without reference to a diagram. In contrast, if diagrams or text are intelligible in their own right and simply redescribe each other, physical integration or the use of dual-modality presentations will not be of benefit. Elimination of redundancy is called for under such conditions.

4.6   Implications for multimedia instruction and conclusions

The split-attention, redundancy and modality effects have both theoretical and practical implications. From a theoretical perspective, while experimental results demonstrating split-attention and redundancy effects provide evidence that the limitation of working memory can be overcome by formatting instructional materials in a manner that minimizes extraneous cognitive load, the experimental results indicating the modality effect demonstrate that working-memory capacity can be effectively expanded. From a practical perspective, the three cognitive load effects provide guidelines for effective instructional procedures. In constructing digital support systems and tools, the educational effectiveness of instructions that require learners to split their attention unnecessarily between multiple sources of information is likely to be compromised. Eliminating split attention has the potential to improve multimedia instruction substantially. One way to eliminate split attention is to integrate different sources of information physically (see figure 4.2). The modality principle suggests that under split-attention conditions, learning can also be enhanced by presenting a written source of information in auditory mode. However, it is important to ensure that the auditory material is essential and not redundant and that the instructional material is complex enough to necessitate the use of a cognitive load reducing technique.

Modern information technology has provided a variety of platforms and vehicles for the design and delivery of multimedia learning material. However, simply providing access to multimedia does not guarantee useful learning. The entire teaching and learning process must take into account the limitations of human working memory. Cognitive load theory specifically addresses the limitations of working memory. The split-attention, redundancy and modality effects discussed in this chapter can be explained by cognitive load theory. In turn, these effects provide a theoretical base for practical applications in multimedia presentations.

4.7   References

Allen, R. J., Baddeley, A. D., Hitch, G. 2006. Is the binding of visual features in working memory resource-demanding? *Journal of Experimental Psychology: General* 135(2): 298–313

Baddeley, A., and Hitch, G. 1974. Working memory, in G. A. Bower (ed.), *The Psychology of Learning and Motivation.* New York: Academic Press: vol. VIII: 47–89

Bandura, A. 1986. *Social Foundations of Thought and Action: A Social Cognitive Theory.* Englewood Cliffs, NJ: Prentice Hall

Bays, P. M., and Husain, M. 2008. Dynamic shifts of limited working memory resources in human vision, *Science* 321: 851–4

Berninger, V. W., Raskind, W., Richards, T., Abbott, R., and Stock, P. 2008. A multidisplinary approach to understanding developmental dyslexia within working-memory architecture: Genotypes, phenotypes, brain, and instruction, *Developmental Neuropsychology* 33(6): 707–44

Brünken, R., Plass, J. L., and Leutner, D. 2004. Assessment of cognitive load in multimedia learning with dual-task methodology: Auditory load and modality effects, *Instructional Science* 32: 115–32

Brünken, R., Steinbacher, S., Plass, J. L., and Leutner, D. 2002. Assessment of cognitive load in multimedia learning using dual-task methodology, *Experimental Psychology* 49: 109–19

Carroll, J. M. 1990. *The Nurnberg Funnel: Designing Minimalist Instruction for Practical Computer Skill.* Cambridge, MA: MIT Press

Carroll, J. M., Smith-Kerker, P., Ford, J., and Mazur-Rimetz, S. 1987. The minimal manual, *Human–Computer Interaction* 3: 123–53

Chandler, P., and Sweller, J. 1996. Cognitive load while learning to use a computer program, *Applied Cognitive Psychology* 10: 151–70

Chase, W. G., and Simon, H. A. 1973. Perception in chess, *Cognitive Psychology* 4: 55–81

Cooper, G., and Sweller, J. 1987. The effects of schema acquisition and rule automation on mathematical problem-solving transfer, *Journal of Educational Psychology* 79: 347–62

Cowan, N. 2005. *Working Memory Capacity*. New York: Psychology Press

De Groot, A. 1965. *Thought and Choice in Chess*. The Hague: Mouton (original work published 1946)

Diao, Y., Chandler, P., and Sweller, J. 2007. The effect of written text on learning to comprehend spoken English as a foreign language, *American Journal of Psychology* 120: 237–261

Diao, Y., and Sweller, J. 2007. Redundancy in foreign language reading comprehension instruction: Concurrent written and spoken presentations, *Learning and Instruction* 17: 78–88

Engelhardt, P. E., Nigg, J. T., Carr, L. A., and Ferreira, F. 2008. Cognitive inhibition and working memory in attention-deficit/hyperactivity disorder, *Journal of Abnormal Psychology* 117(3): 591–604

Ericsson, K. A., and Kintsch, W. 1995. Long-term working memory, *Psychological Review* 102: 211–45

Garon, N., Bryson, S. E., and Smith, I. M. 2008. Executive function in preschoolers: A review using an integrative framework, *Psychological Bulletin* 134(1): 31–60

Geary, D. 2002. Principles of evolutionary educational psychology, *Learning and Individual Differences* 12: 317–45

    2005. *The Origin of Mind: Evolution of Brain, Cognition, and General Intelligence*. Washington, DC: American Psychological Association

    2007. Educating the evolved mind: Conceptual foundations for an evolutionary educational psychology, in J. S. Carlson and J. R. Levin (eds.), *Psychological Perspectives on Contemporary Educational Issues*. Greenwich, CT: Information Age Publishing: 1–99

    2008. An evolutionarily informed education science, *Educational Psychologist* 43: 179–95

Hirai, A. 1999. The relationship between listening and reading rates of Japanese EFL learners, *Modern Language Journal* 83: 367–84

Hung, H. C. M. 2007. 'Split attention in reading comprehension: A case of English as a foreign/second language', unpublished masters thesis, University of New South Wales, Australia

Jablonka, E., and Lamb, M. J. 2005. *Evolution in Four Dimensions: Genetic, Epigenetic, Behavioral, and Symbolic Variation in the History of Life*. Cambridge, MA: MIT Press

Jeung, H., Chandler, P., and Sweller, J. 1997. The role of visual indicators in dual sensory mode instruction, *Educational Psychology* 17: 329–43

Kalyuga, S., Chandler, P., and Sweller, J. 1998. Levels of expertise and instructional design, *Human Factors* 40: 1–17

    2000. Incorporating learner experience into the design of multimedia instruction, *Journal of Educational Psychology* 92: 126–36

    2004. When redundant on-screen text in multimedia technical instruction can interfere with learning, *Human Factors* 46: 567–81

Kim, E. S., Bayles, K. A., and Beeson, P. M. 2008. Instruction processing in young and older adults: Contributions of memory span, *Aphasiology* 22(7): 753–62

Kulhavy, R. W., Stock, W. A., and Caterino, L. C. 1994. Reference maps as a framework for remembering text, in W. Schnotz and R. W. Kulhavy (eds.), *Comprehension of Graphics*. Amsterdam: Elsevier Science: 153–62

Lavie, N. 2005. Distracted and confused? Selective attention under load, *TRENDS in Cognitive Sciences* 9(2): 75–82

Low, R., and Sweller, J. 2005. The modality principle in multimedia learning, in R. E. Mayer (ed.), *The Cambridge Handbook of Multimedia Learning*. New York: Cambridge University Press: 147–58

Makovski, T., Sussman, R., and Jiang, Y. V. 2008. Orienting attention in visual working memory reduces interference from memory probes, *Journal of Experimental Psychology: Learning, Memory, and Cognition* 34(2): 369–80

Mayer, R. E. 2001. *Multimedia Learning*. New York: Cambridge University Press
    2005. Cognitive theory of multimedia learning, in R. E. Mayer (ed.), *The Cambridge Handbook of Multimedia Learning*. New York: Cambridge University Press: 31–48

Mayer, R. E., and Anderson, R. 1991. Animations need narrations: An experimental test of a dual-coding hypothesis, *Journal of Educational Psychology* 83: 484–90
    1992. The instructive animation: Helping students build connections between words and pictures in multimedia learning, *Journal of Educational Psychology* 84: 444–52

Mayer, R. E., Bove, W., Bryman, A., Mars, R., and Tapangco, L. 1996. When less is more: Meaningful learning from visual and verbal summaries of science textbook lessons, *Journal of Educational Psychology* 88: 64–73

Mayer, R. E., and Moreno, R. 1998. A split-attention effect in multimedia learning: Evidence for dual processing systems in working memory, *Journal of Educational Psychology* 90: 312–20

Mayer, R. E., and Sims, V. K. 1994. For whom is a picture worth a thousand words? Extensions of a dual-coding theory of multimedia learning, *Journal of Educational Psychology* 86: 389–401

Miller, G. A. 1956. The magical number seven, plus or minus two: Some limits on our capacity for processing information, *Psychological Review* 63: 81–97

Miller, W. 1937. The picture clutch in reading, *Elementary English Review* 14: 263–4

Moores, E., and Maxwell, J. 2008. The role of prior exposure in the capture of attention by items in working memory, *Visual Cognition* 16(5): 675–95

Moreno, R., and Mayer, R. E. 1999. Cognitive principles of multimedia learning: The role of modality and contiguity, *Journal of Educational Psychology* 91: 358–68

Moreno, R., Mayer, R. E., Spires, H. A., and Lester, J. C. 2001. The case for social agency in computer-based multimedia learning: Do students learn more deeply when they interact with animated pedagogical agents? *Cognition and Instruction* 19: 177–214

Mousavi, S., Low, R., and Sweller, J. 1995. Reducing cognitive load by mixing auditory and visual presentation modes, *Journal of Educational Psychology* 87: 319–34

Oberauer, K., and Bialkova, S. 2009. Accessing information in working memory: Can the focus of attention grasp two elements at the same time? *Journal of Experimental Psychology: General* 138(1): 64–87

Oka, K., and Miura, T. 2008. Allocation of attention and effect of practice on persons with and without mental retardation, *Research in Developmental Disabilities* 29(2): 165–75

Paas, F., and van Merriënboer, J. 1993. The efficiency of instructional conditions: An approach to combine mental-effort and performance measures, *Human Factors* 35: 737–43

Paivio, A. 1986. *Mental Representations: A Dual Coding Approach.* New York: Oxford University Press

Parks, E. L., and Hopfinger, J. B. 2008. Hold it! Memory affects attentional dwell time, *Psychonomic Bulletin and Review* 15(6): 1128–34

Penney, C. G. 1989. Modality effects and the structure of short-term verbal memory, *Memory and Cognition* 17: 398–422

Peterson, L., and Peterson, M. J. 1959. Short-term retention of individual verbal items, *Journal of Experimental Psychology* 58: 193–8

Reder, L., and Anderson, J. R. 1980. A comparison of texts and their summaries: Memorial consequences, *Journal of Verbal Learning and Verbal Behaviour* 19: 121–34

   1982. Effects of spacing and embellishment on memory for main points of a text, *Memory and Cognition* 10: 97–102

San Miguel, I., Corral, M., and Escera, C. 2008. When loading working memory reduces distraction: Behavioral and electrophysiological evidence from an auditory-visual distraction paradigm, *Journal of Cognitive Neuroscience* 20(7): 1131–45

Schnotz, W. 2005. An integrated model of text and picture comprehension, in R. E. Mayer (ed.), *The Cambridge Handbook of Multimedia Learning.* New York: Cambridge University Press: 49–66

Simon, H., and Gilmartin, K. 1973. A simulation of memory for chess positions, *Cognitive Psychology* 5: 29–46

Solman, R., Singh, N., and Kehoe, E. J. 1992. Pictures block the learning of sight words, *Educational Psychology* 12: 143–53

Sweller, J. 1994. Cognitive load theory, learning difficulty, and instructional design, *Learning and Instruction* 4: 295–312

   2005a. Implications of cognitive load theory for multimedia learning, in R. E. Mayer (ed.), *The Cambridge Handbook of Multimedia Learning.* New York: Cambridge University Press: 19–30

   2005b. The redundancy principle, in R. E. Mayer (ed.), *The Cambridge Handbook of Multimedia Learning.* New York: Cambridge University Press: 159–67

Sweller, J., and Chandler, P. 1991. Evidence for cognitive load theory, *Cognition and Instruction* 8: 351–62

   1994. Why some material is difficult to learn, *Cognition and Instruction* 12: 185–233

Sweller, J., Chandler, P., Tierney, P., and Cooper, M. 1990. Cognitive load as a factor in the structuring of technical material, *Journal of Experimental Psychology: General* 119: 176–92

Sweller, J., and Cooper, G. 1985. The use of worked examples as a substitute for problem solving in learning algebra, *Cognition and Instruction* 2: 59–89

Sweller, J., and Sweller, S. 2006. Natural information processing systems, *Evolutionary Psychology* 4: 434–58

Tarmizi, R., and Sweller, J. 1988. Guidance during mathematical problem solving, *Journal of Educational Psychology* 80: 424–36

Tindall-Ford, S., Chandler, P., and Sweller, J. 1997. When two sensory modes are better than one, *Journal of Experimental Psychology: Applied* 3: 257–87

Torcasio, S. and Sweller, J. 2010. The use of illustrations when learning to read: A cognitive load theory approach, *Applied Cognitive Psychology* 24(5): 659–72

Van Gerven, P. W., Paas, F., van Merriënboer, J., Hendriks, M., and Schmidt, H. G. 2003. The efficienty of multimedia learning into old age, *British Journal of Educational Psychology* 73(4): 489–505

van Merriënboer, J., and Kester, L. 2005. The four-component instructional design model: Multimedia principles in environments for complex learning, in R. E. Mayer (ed.), *The Cambridge Handbook of Multimedia Learning*. New York: Cambridge University Press: 71–93

van Merriënboer, J., and Kirschner, P. 2007. *Ten Steps to Complex Learning: A Systematic Approach to Four-Component Instructional Design* New York: Routledge

Ward, M., and Sweller, J. 1990. Structuring effective worked examples, *Cognition and Instruction* 7: 1–39

West-Eberhard, M. 2003. *Developmental Plasticity and Evolution*. New York: Oxford University Press

Yeung, A. S., Jin, P., and Sweller, J. 1998. Cognitive load and learner expertise: Split attention and redundancy effects in reading with explanatory notes, *Contemporary Educational Psychology* 23. 1 21

Zhang, Y., Du, Y., and Zhang, J X. 2008. Working memory selection and competition between target and distractor representations, *Psychological Reports* 102(1): 194–212

Zhu, X., and Simon, H. 1987. Learning mathematics from examples and by doing, *Cognition and Instruction* 4: 137–66

5   Salience sensitive control, temporal attention and stimulus-rich reactive interfaces

Howard Bowman, Li Su, Brad Wyble and Phil J. Barnard

This chapter reviews the results of the Salience Project, a cross-disciplinary research project focused on understanding how humans direct attention to salient stimuli. The first objective of the project was theoretical: that is, to understand behaviourally and electrophysiologically how humans direct attention through time to semantically and emotionally salient visual stimuli. Accordingly, we describe the glance-look model of the attentional blink. Notably, this model incorporates two levels of meaning, both of which are based upon latent semantic analysis, and, in addition, it incorporates an explicit body-state subsystem in which emotional experience manifests. Our second major objective has been to apply the same glance-look model to performance analysis of human–computer interaction. Specifically, we have considered a class of system which we call stimulus-rich reactive interfaces (SRRIs). Such systems are characterized by demanding (typically) visual environments, in which multiple stimuli compete for the user's attention, and a variety of physiological measures are employed to assess the user's cognitive state. In this context, we have particularly focused on electroencephalogram (EEG) feedback of stimulus perception. Moreover, we demonstrate how the glance-look model can be used to assess the performance of a variety of such reactive computer interfaces. Thus, the chapter contributes to the study of attentional support and adaptive interfaces associated with digital environments.

5.1   Introduction

Humans are very good at prioritizing competing processing demands. In particular, perception of a salient environmental event can interrupt ongoing processing, causing attention, and accompanying processing resources, to be redirected to the new event. A classic example of this is the well-known *cocktail party effect* (Cherry 1953). Not only are we easily able to follow just one conversation when several people are speaking, but the occurrence of a salient phrase in a peripheral conversation stream, such as somebody mentioning our name, causes auditory attention to be redirected. It is also clear that emotions, motivation and physiological state in general play a key role in such prioritization. For example, Oatley and Johnson-Laird suggest that:

the functions of emotion modes are both to enable one priority to be exchanged for another ... and to maintain this priority until it is satisfied or abandoned. (Oatley and Johnson-Laird 1987)

However, in an agent with multiple goals (such as a human) that is subject to continual environmental input, a compromise needs to be struck between, on the one hand, responding optimally to priority events and, on the other hand, maintaining efficient processing. In the extreme, a system could fail to complete the processing of any attended streams in circumstances where interruption is the norm. The heart of the conflict lies in balancing the need to respond in a timely fashion with the need to respond optimally given the salience of environmental stimuli. The problem is complicated by the fact that salience itself is highly context dependent. Hearing a lion roar may be extremely salient if you are on foot in the African savanna, but it would be much less salient if you were walking around a zoo. Our capacity to correctly attribute salience to stimuli in a context-dependent manner and interrupt or adjust ongoing processing accordingly has obvious adaptive benefits when viewed from an evolutionary perspective.

Current artificial systems clearly do less well. This manifests itself in two ways. First, they are often deficient at adjusting processing in ways that are appropriate to the situational context and on the basis of the salience of novel events. They may fail to respond appropriately to highly salient events or they may interrupt processing unnecessarily in response to low-salience events. Second, when interacting with humans, artificial systems can fail to utilize salience fully. In pursuit of a particular goal, interactive systems typically unreel sequences of what amount to ballistic steps, only being receptive at specific breakpoints to a restricted set of anticipated cues. In contrast, a salience-sensitive interface would adapt its behaviour according to the attentional and affective state of the user (Picard 1998).

A major barrier to constructing artificial systems that are appropriately salience sensitive is our relatively poorly developed grasp of how humans adapt their behaviour according to salience. While it is clear that humans do it well, the actual mechanisms are not well understood. Our knowledge of these mechanisms is improving, however, aided by the combination of behavioural experimentation and recent advances in brain imaging and EEG (Corbetta and Shulman 2002; Corbetta, Patel and Shulman 2008). In particular, a number of experimental paradigms which fall broadly within the study of human attention have started to reveal how real-time constraints and sensitivity to salient events are resolved in humans. Three such experimental paradigms are the attentional blink (AB) task (Raymond, Shapiro and Arnell 1992), the psychological refractory period (Pashler 1994) and emotional interference within Stroop experiments (McKenna and Sharma 2004).

In order to capitalize on the potential of these empirical advances, explicit computational models of salience-sensitive control need to be developed. These would provide concrete realizations of the *mechanisms* being revealed and also enable the construction of artificial systems that are appropriately sensitive to salience. The Salience Project, www.cs.kent. ac.uk/~hb5/attention.html, was undertaken at the University of Kent at Canterbury (in collaboration with the Medical Research Council's Cognition and Brain Sciences Unit, www.mrc-cbu.cam.ac.uk) to fulfil this need.

A major theme of the Salience Project was temporal attention, which concerns the capacity of humans to deal with a sequence of attentional episodes. The project explored questions such as how long attention is allocated to one event before it is free to be allocated to a second; how an incoming salient item interrupts processing of an earlier item and causes attention to be redirected; and, most importantly, what actually determines salience in this context, where obvious candidates include relevance to long-term goals and emotional significance. The AB task (Raymond, Shapiro and Arnell 1992) is one of the key paradigms that has been used to address these questions. Specifically, this paradigm has explored the temporal constraints and other parameters governing when salient stimuli are missed as a consequence of attention being directed at preceding stimuli. In addition, we now have some hard evidence of how both semantic and emotional salience regulate the allocation of temporal attention (Anderson and Phelps 2001; Barnard *et al.* 2004; Barnard *et al.* 2005).

The Salience Project, summarized in this chapter, concentrated on the development of computational models, validation of these models through behavioural and electrophysiological experimentation and exploration of the implications of these models for the development of computer interfaces. Our modelling of semantic and emotional effects in temporal attention will be discussed in the next section, the implications for construction of reactive human–computer interfaces will be addressed in section 5.3, followed, in a final section, by some concluding remarks and issues for further investigation.

5.2   Modelling of semantic and emotional effects in temporal attention

5.2.1   The attentional blink and meaning

We pay attention to information that matters to us, and this relevance is a result of the cognitive task we are engaged in, that information's personal salience and our motivational and emotional state. For example, anxious people preferentially pay attention to external threat (MacLeod, Mathews and Tata 1986), and the ways in which humans interact with computers are modulated by the emotional qualities of the interface (Walker, Sproull and Subramasi 1994). In all these domains, the key questions concern the dynamic redeployment of attention over time, as investigated in the AB (Raymond, Shapiro and Arnell 1992). A typical AB task is Chun and Potter's letters in-digits task (Chun and Potter 1995). In this task, a stream of items is presented one after the other at fixation,[1] with each replacing the previous item. Thus, items are presented in Rapid Serial Visual Presentation (RSVP), at around ten items per second. The majority of items presented are digits, although two letters are placed at different positions within the stream. The participant's task is simply to identify the two targets and then report them when the RSVP stream has ended. The second letter target (T2) is positioned with a number of intervening digits (referred to as the lag) between it and the first target (T1). Report of T2 is impaired dependent upon the position in which T2 follows T1. Specifically, if T2 occurs immediately after T1, then its presence is accurately reported (so-called lag 1 sparing). T2 accuracy is lower for slightly longer lags and then recovers back to baseline when T1 and T2 are separated by about half a second or more (generally this is at lags 5–8). This is the basic attentional blink which we abbreviate as AB (see figure 5 1). The empirical literature and theoretical accounts of the AB have all assumed that allocating attention to T1 leaves fewer attentional resources for processing T2.

As research on the blink has progressed, not only using letters but also words and pictures, it has become clear that the AB is affected by both the semantic and personal salience of items. Similar blink effects are readily obtained when words are used as list items (and subjects are required to report items from a particular category, e.g., job words). There is also evidence of specific effects of affective variables. Holmes

---

[1] A fixation mark probes where the subsequent stimuli will be presented on the screen; and during the experiment, participants fixate on a single spatial location.

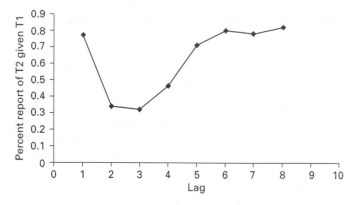

Figure 5.1 The basic AB effect for letter stimuli. Here, the blink curve is the percentage report of T2 conditional on T1 report, reflecting the effect on T2 report of successfully attending to T1 (adapted with permission from Chun and Potter 1995)

and Richard report differences in target detection in the AB paradigm for high and low anxious people (Holmes and Richard 1999). More dramatically, Anderson has shown that the blink effect is markedly attenuated when the second target is an aversive word, such as 'rape' or 'torture' (Anderson 2005). This suggests that perception of (high priority) emotionally salient (T2) stimuli can overcome the blink impairment. There is also evidence that patients with damage to specific emotional centres in the brain (namely unilateral damage to the left amygdala) show no attenuated blink effect to aversive words (Anderson and Phelps 2001). The implication is that this region plays a central role in the pathway by which affect-driven salience is assessed. Cumulative evidence from the AB paradigm is revealing how humans redeploy attentional resources when processing semantically, personally and emotionally salient stimuli and, moreover, it is clarifying the time course at which such mechanisms operate.

In order to examine semantic effects, Barnard *et al.* used a variant of the AB paradigm in which words were presented at fixation in RSVP format, at around ten items per second (Barnard *et al.* 2004). Targets were only distinguishable from background items in terms of their meaning. Participants were simply asked to report a word if it refers to a job or profession for which people get paid, such as waitress, and these targets were embedded in a list of background words that all belonged to the same category, e.g., nature words: see figure 5.2. However, streams also contained a key-distractor item, which, although not in the target

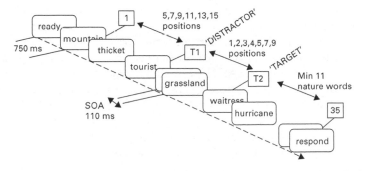

Figure 5.2 Task schema for the key-distractor blink (adapted from Barnard *et al.* 2004 with permission of John Wiley and Sons). SOA denotes Stimulus Onset Asynchrony

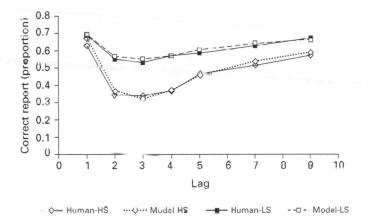

Figure 5.3 Proportion of correct responses from both humans and model simulations. HS and LS denote high and low salient condition respectively (Su, Bowman and Barnard 2007)

category, was semantically related to that category, e.g., tourist, vegetarian and so on: see figure 5.2 (Barnard *et al.* 2004). The serial-position at which the target appeared after the key-distractor was varied. The effect of attentional capture by meaning is encapsulated in the serial-position curve (denoted Human-HS) in figure 5.3. That is, the key-distractor drew attention away from the target with a clear temporal profile.

Barnard *et al.* used Latent Semantic Analysis (LSA) (Landauer and Dumais 1997; Landauer, Foltz and Laham 1998; Landauer, McNamara and Dennis 2007) to assess similarities between key-distractors and job targets (Barnard *et al.* 2004). LSA is a statistical learning method which inductively uses the co-occurrence of words in texts and principal component analysis to build a (compact) multidimensional representation of word meaning. In particular, an 'objective' measure of the semantic distance between a pair of words or between a word and a pool of words can be extracted from LSA. The critical finding of Barnard *et al.* was that the depth of the blink induced by a key-distractor was modulated by the semantic salience of that key-distractor, i.e., its proximity in LSA space to the target category.

When key-distractors were household items, a different category from both background and target words, there was little influence on target report. However, key-distractors that referenced a property of a human agent, but not one for which they were paid, like tourist or husband, gave rise to a classic and deep blink: see Human-HS in figure 5.3. We call household items low salient key-distractors and human items high salient key-distractors.

These AB experiments have counterparts in real life. For instance, when an anaesthetist monitors a patient during surgery, they have to consider a range of patient vital signs, as they monitor several physiological metrics, e.g., heart rate, blood pressure, breathing and skin colour. In this environment, events follow one another rapidly as do stimuli in RSVP streams. When a critical event occurs, e.g., a spike in one of the vital signs, the doctor allocates attention to this high-salient stimulus in a manner similar to a participant attending to a target/key-distractor in an RSVP stream. The AB phenomenon suggests that attending to such events could potentially divert the anaethetist's attention for about 500 ms and leave the doctor prone to missing a second critical stimulus. In this respect, the AB paradigm can be taken as generalizable to practical settings. Semantic salience is particularly relevant, because most real-world tasks relate to the significance or meaning of events.

5.2.2   The 'glance-look' model

Elsewhere, we have presented a detailed account of attentional capture by meaning and the temporal dynamics of that process (Su, Bowman and Barnard 2007). Key principles that underlie this account are sequential processing, two-stages and serial allocation of attention. We discuss these principles in turn.

5.2.2.1 Sequential processing With any RSVP task, items arrive in sequence and need to be correspondingly processed. We require a basic method for representing this sequential arrival and processing of items. At such a cognitive level, our approach can be viewed as implementing

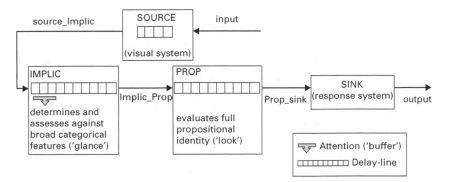

Figure 5.4 Top-level structure of the 'glance-look' model with implicational subsystem attended. Only data pathways are shown here; see Bowman, Su and Barnard 2006; Su *et al.* (2009) for more details

a pipeline. (At the level of the brain, how this mechanism is realized remains an interesting, as yet open, research question.) New items enter the front of the pipeline from the visual system; they are then fed through until they reach the back of the pipeline, where they enter the response system, as shown in figure 5.4. The key data structure that implements this pipeline metaphor is a delay-line. This is a simple means for representing time-constrained serial order. One can think of a delay-line as an abstraction for items passing (in turn) through a series of processing levels. On every cycle, a new constituent representation enters the pipeline and all constituent representations currently in transit are pushed along one place.

5.2.2.2 Two stages   Like Chun and Potter (1995) and Bowman and Wyble (2007), we have argued elsewhere for a two-stage model (Barnard *et al.* 2004; Barnard and Bowman 2004), but this time recast to focus exclusively on semantic analysis and executive processing. In particular, Barnard and Bowman modelled the key-distractor blink task using a two-stage model (Barnard and Bowman 2004). In the context of modelling distributed control, we implemented the two-stage model as a dialogue between two levels of meaning: see figure 5.4. At the first stage, a generic level of semantic representation is monitored and initially used to determine if an incoming item is likely to be salient in the context of the specified task. If it is found to be so, then, at the second stage, the specific referential meaning of the word is subjected to detailed semantic scrutiny. At this stage, a word's meaning is actively evaluated in relation to the required referential properties of the target category. If this reveals a match, then the target is encoded for later report. The first of these stages is akin to first taking a 'glance' at generic meaning, with the second rather like taking a closer 'look' at the relationship between the meaning of the incoming item and the target category. These two stages are implemented in two distinct semantic subsystems proposed within a multi-level model of cognition and emotion (the Interacting Cognitive Subsystems or ICS architecture). The implicational subsystem supports the first stage and the propositional subsystem supports the second (Barnard 1999). In this chapter, we refer to this theoretical account as the 'glance-look' model.

These two subsystems process qualitatively distinct types of meaning. One of these, implicational meaning, is holistic, abstract and schematic, and includes the representation and experience of affect (Barnard 1999). The other is classically 'rational', being based upon propositional representation, and captures referentially specific semantic properties and relationships. In the context of the task being considered here, these subsystems can be distinguished as follows:

- Implicational (or Implic). This subsystem performs the broad 'categorical' analysis of items, which might be related to Chun and Potter's first stage of processing, by detecting the likely presence of targets according to their broad categorical features.
- Propositional (or Prop). This subsystem builds upon the implicational representation generated from the glance in order to construct a full (propositional) identification of the item under consideration, which is sufficient to test whether the meaning of the incoming item meets the task specification and should therefore be reported.

The implicational and propositional subsystems perform their corresponding salience assessments as items pass through them in the pipeline.

5.2.2.3 Serial allocation of attention   Our third principle is a mechanism of attentional engagement. It is only when attention is engaged at a subsystem that it can assess the salience of items passing through it. Furthermore, attention can only be engaged at one subsystem at a time. Consequently, semantic processes cannot glance at an incoming item to assess its salience, while looking at and scrutinizing another. When attention is engaged at a subsystem, we say that it is buffered (Barnard 1999), which does not have the usual computer science meaning here. In this respect, salience assignment can only be performed if the subsystem is buffered and only one subsystem can be buffered at a time, as shown in figure 5.4.

As previously mentioned, the model presented here can be placed within the context of ICS; both the delay-line and buffering concepts that we use have their roots in ICS. However, most significantly, the implicational–propositional distinction reflects ICS' dual-subsystem central engine, which implements executive functions for controlling attention in a distributed manner (Teasdale and Barnard 1993).

5.2.2.4 How the model blinks   In many real life situations, stimuli do not arrive as rapidly as in AB experiments, so Implic and Prop will normally interpret the representation of the same item or event over an extended period. However, in demanding situations, such as RSVP, items may fail to be implicationally processed as the buffer moves between subsystems. The buffer movement dynamic, thus, provides the underlying mechanism for the blink, i.e.:

- When the key-distractor is found to be implicationally salient, the buffer moves from Implic to Prop, and salience assessment cannot be performed on those words (i.e., a portion of the RSVP stream) entering Implic following the key-distractor. Hence, when these implicationally uninterpreted words are passed to Prop, propositional meaning, which builds upon coherent detection of implicational meaning, cannot be accessed. If a target word falls within this window, it will not be detected as implicationally salient and thus will not be reported.
- When faced with an implicationally uninterpreted item, Prop is no longer able to assign salience and the buffer has to return to Implic to assess implicational meaning. Then, Implic is in a position to assign salience to its constituent representations once again. After this, targets entering the system will be detected as both implicationally and propositionally salient and will be reported. Hence, the blink recovers.

The results of the simulation were compared to human performance in order to verify our theories of temporal attention (Su, Bowman and Barnard 2007): see figure 5.3.

5.2.2.5 Semantic salience   Our model also reflects gradations in semantic salience. We assume that the human cognitive system has a space of semantic similarity available to it similar to that derived from Latent Semantic Analysis (Landauer and Dumais 1997). The link between principal component analysis (which is at the heart of LSA) and Hebbian learning (O'Reilly and Munakata 2000), which remains the most biologically plausible learning algorithm, provides support for this hypothesis. Accordingly, we have characterized the assessment of semantic salience in terms of LSA.

To encapsulate the target category in LSA space, we identified five pools of words, for, respectively, human relatedness, occupation relatedness, payment relatedness, household relatedness and nature relatedness. Then, we calculated the centre of each pool in LSA space. We reasoned

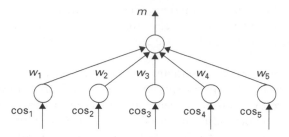

Figure 5.5 A neural network that integrates five LSA cosines to classify words as targets

that the target category could be identified relative to these five semantic meanings (i.e., pool centres). This process can be seen as part of a more general categorization mechanism that works on all LSA dimensions. In the context of this experiment, it focuses on the five most strongly related components, as discussed above.

Next, we needed to determine the significance that the human system placed on proximity to each of these five meanings when making target category judgements. To do this, we trained a two-layer neural network to make what amounts to a 'targetness' judgement from LSA distances (i.e., cosines) to each of the five meanings: see figure 5.5. Specifically, we trained a single response node using the Delta rule (O'Reilly and Munakata 2000) to classify words as targets. The words used in Barnard *et al.*'s experiment were used as the training patterns (Barnard *et al.* 2004). During training, for each target word, the five corresponding LSA distances (i.e., cosines) were paired with an output (i.e., response node activation) of one, while the LSA distances for non-target words were paired with an output of zero. This analysis generated five weights: one for each LSA distance. These weights effectively characterize the significance that the target salience check ascribes to each of the five constituent meanings, thereby skewing LSA space as required by implicational salience assessment.

Activation of our neural network response unit (denoted m in figure 5.5) became the Implic salience assessment decision axis in our model. Thus, words that generate response unit activation above a prescribed threshold were interpreted as implicationally salient, while words generating an activation below the threshold were interpreted as unsalient.

Importantly, high-salience key-distractors were much more likely to generate above-threshold response unit activation than low-salience items. This in turn ensured that high salient items were more often judged to be implicationally salient, which ensured that the buffer moved from Implic to Prop more often for high salient items. Since the blink

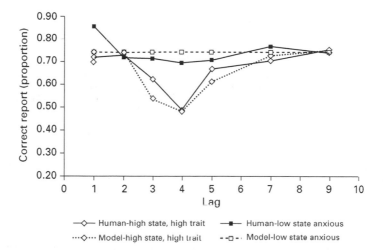

Figure 5.6 Target report accuracy by serial position comparing human data (Barnard *et al.* 2005) and model simulations for high state and high trait anxious and low state anxious

deficit is caused by such buffer movement, targets following high salient items were more likely to be blinked: see figure 5.3.

In this way, we demonstrated how key-distractors can capture attention through time, causing semantically prescribed targets to be missed. In addition, our model interfaces with statistical learning theories of meaning (i.e., LSA) to demonstrate how attentional capture over time is modulated by the semantic salience of the eliciting distractor.

5.2.2.6 Emotional blink

As previously discussed, emotions have a major influence on salience sensitive control and the interaction between emotional salience and temporal attention is being actively investigated in the AB literature. Consequently, we have incorporated emotional salience into the 'glance-look' model. We have particularly focused on modelling the effect of threatening stimuli in Barnard's key-distractor AB tasks (Barnard *et al.* 2005). In these tasks, participants search an RSVP stream of words for a word in a target category, e.g., jobs. Again, performance on the target identification task is investigated as a function of the lag that the target item appears relative to a key-distractor. However, rather than being semantically salient, in this task, the key-distractor is a threatening word. The main finding in this study was that the threatening key-distractor only captured attention with participants that were both high state and high trait anxious and the attentional capture was late and short: see figure 5.6 solid lines (where it is only at Lag 4 that human high

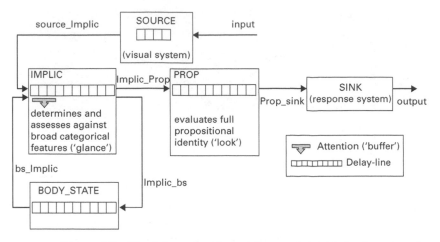

Figure 5.7   The 'glance-look' model extended with body-state sub-system

state and high trait anxious differs significantly from human low state anxious). State anxiety is defined as transitory anxiety experienced at a particular time (often in the recent past or during the experiment). On the other hand, trait anxiety refers to a more general and long-term experience of anxiety; and it often reflects individual differences in reaction to threat (Spielberger 1972; Spielberger 1983).

Consistent with the ICS framework, this attentional capture by threat was modelled through the addition of a body-state subsystem: see figure 5.7. It is assumed that the body-state subsystem responds to the glance at meaning, i.e., to implicational meaning. A bodily evaluation of salience is then fed back to Implic, thereby enriching the representation. In effect, the body state feeds back information in the form of a 'somatic marker' (Damasio 1994; Bechara, Tranel and Damasio 2000), which, in the context of the task being considered here, would be a threat marker. Furthermore, it is assumed that high anxiety levels (both state and trait) are required before this body-state feedback has sufficient strength to have a major effect on implicational salience. Thus, for high state and high trait anxious individuals, threatening key-distractors are implicationally interpreted as highly salient when body-state feedback enhances their implicational representation. This enhanced representation precipitates a detailed 'look' at the meaning of these items by initiating a buffer move to Prop. Any new items, in particular targets, that arrive at Implic while the buffer is at Prop will be missed. However, since threatening key-distractors are not semantically salient, the buffer will move swiftly back to Implic and the blink is restricted in its length and depth: see figure 5.6 dashed lines.

5.3   Implications for construction of reactive human–computer interfaces

Our theoretical findings are relevant to a number of different application areas, e.g., robotics and HCI. However, we have focused on a specific class of human–computer interfaces, which we call *stimulus-rich reactive interfaces*. This class of system has the following characteristics: (1) stimuli arrive rapidly; (2) there is typically a central task, from which the rapidly arriving peripheral stimuli can capture attention; (3) safety is critical, e.g., a high degree of certainty is required that the user/operator perceives certain stimuli; and (4) physiological feedback of the cognitive state of the user is available, enabling the system to adapt its behaviour in order to optimize operator performance. Examples of stimulus-rich reactive interfaces include flying a plane, driving a car, monitoring a patient, or even viewing web pages. To take the first of these as a case in point, flying, or particularly landing, a plane would be the central task; incoming sensory data (e.g., the presence of other planes or turbulence) would yield streams of rapidly arriving peripheral stimuli; safety is clearly critical; and a spectrum of physiological feedback, e.g., eye trackers, EEG electrodes in helmets, heart and skin conductance monitors, could be built into the cockpit.

We have investigated stimulus-rich reactive interfaces in a number of ways, as elaborated in the following sections. First, we have developed a prototype test system, which we have used to evaluate attentional capture from a central task (Wyble, Craston and Bowman 2006). Second, we have explored the feasibility of extracting online EEG measures of attentional engagement and perception (Wyble, Craston and Bowman 2006). And third, we have applied the 'glance-look' model of the human salience detection system to evaluating the feasibility of stimulus-rich reactive interfaces (Su, Bowman and Barnard 2008).

5.3.1   Attentional capture in HCIs

Theoretical work has identified a set of attentional mechanisms (Bowman and Wyble 2007). We have also explored the practical implications of these mechanisms. Two findings that have particularly inspired our practical explorations are the existence of a very rapid (first) phase of attention, called transient attentional enhancement, which acts within 150 ms of stimulus presentation; and a finding that even such rapid attentional deployment is modulated by task set, e.g., it could be initi-ated by detection of an item in a target category (Bowman and Wyble 2007). Such mechanisms have great relevance for the development of stimulus-rich human–computer interfaces. In particular, in interfaces with rapidly arriving streams of information, it is important to under-stand how stimuli capture attention, in order both to prevent distraction from a central task and to ensure critical stimuli are not missed.

To explore this issue, we developed a prototype test interface that contains a central task involving driving through a virtual maze and the presentation of an intermittent stream of competing stimuli of varying levels of salience. Centrally presented arrows are followed in the driving task and, as a reflection of the presentation methods typically used in this setting, the stream of competing stimuli is presented via a head-mounted display. The colour relationship between the central arrows and stimuli in the competing stream is varied. How this 'task prescribed' colour relationship impinges upon attentional capture by stimuli in the competing stream is investigated.

Previous studies, in particular by Most *et al.*, suggest that the task set from a central (driving) task interacts with speed of response to infrequent obstacles (Most *et al.* 2007). Our findings suggest though that, as long as the competing stimuli task is independent of the central task, the human cognitive system can isolate the two, allocating separate task sets to each, with little inter-task interference (Wyble, Craston and Bowman 2006).

5.3.2   *EEG and reactive interfaces*

We have also explored the feasibility of using EEG in reactive/adaptive computer interfaces as a source of feedback on the cognitive state of the user. This has involved running experiments to evaluate the utility of two potential EEG measures. We have investigated whether modulations in EEG power in the alpha band (around 10 Hz) at posterior areas (partic-ularly the occipital cortex) can be used as a measure of attentional readi-ness in the visual modality. We have also considered whether a positive deflection in the P3 region (around 350 ms post-stimulus presentation) could be used as a measure of whether a stimulus was perceived.

Both these measures are of potential value, but they are somewhat dif-ferent in their character and utility. Alpha band information is proactive, in the sense that it predicts whether the subject *will* perceive a later stim-ulus. In contrast, P3 information is reactive, in the sense that it predicts whether a stimulus *has been* perceived. These measures open up the pos-sibility of withholding presentation of a critical stimulus until the user is ready, and potentially enable re-presentation of a critical stimulus that has been missed. P3 information would have particular value if it were combined with eye-tracking to determine which stimuli are being fixated when a perceptual event is detected.

In the context of stimulus-rich reactive interfaces, the key question to answer is whether these measures can be reliably extracted online, i.e., in real time. Thus, we have investigated the extent to which online extraction of these measures predicts target report. Our research suggests that, with current methods, the approach based on alpha band power is not feasible. However, an approach based on P3 detection is feasible; it forms a relatively reliable online measure of whether an item has been perceived and can be extracted (Wyble, Craston and Bowman 2006).

5.3.2.1 P3 detection When one records EEG from the human scalp, the signal measured is deflected by ongoing cognitive operations. In the EEG literature, these deflections are referred to as components, which are observed in the Event Related Potential (ERP) that emerges from averaging together a large number of trials time-locked to the onset of a salient stimulus.

ERP components occur at specific temporal intervals following a stimulus and can be manipulated experimentally; hence, they have been associated with particular cognitive processes. Whereas the early components in an ERP waveform are particularly associated with sensory processing of target stimuli, the later components are associated with high-level processing of a stimulus. A key late component is the P3 (i.e., the third positive peak of the ERP, also referred to as the P300 due to its typical latency of 300 ms post-stimulus). Although some researchers have identified a frontally located P3a component, which is elicited by infrequent but task-irrelevant stimuli, we focus on the P3b, which has its maximum over parietal electrode sites. The P3b (called P3 from here on) is present for stimuli that are both infrequent and relevant to the task (Squires, Squires and Hillyard 1975). As the P3 is only observed for target stimuli that are detected by the subject (Vogel, Luck and Shapiro 1998), it can be assumed to be an indication of an item being encoded into working memory (Donchin 1981).

Depending on the amount of noise in the signal, one normally has to average across a considerable number of trials to obtain a clean ERP waveform. However, the P3 component is often large enough to be detected even in the raw EEG. Of course, one cannot draw conclusions about P3 latency and shape from raw P3s; however, they are often clear enough to be detected on a trial-by-trial basis. The algorithm used in our approach focuses on these raw P3s.

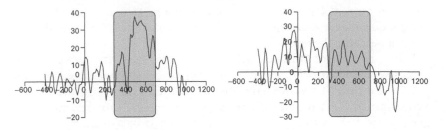

Figure 5.8 Examples of raw P3s recorded from human participants (targets were presented at time 0, the y-axis units are uV (relative to a reference electrode), and the x-axis denotes time in milliseconds) (Su *et al.* 2009). Note that EEG is often plotted with the y-axis reversed, e.g., negative up and positive down; we have avoided this convention for reasons of presentational clarity. The shaded areas represent the P3 regions. These raw EEG signals are very noisy, so the P3 is the only visible deflection and other earlier components, such as the P1 and the P2, are not visible. They can only be seen when an average is taken across a large number of runs, as in ERP data (Su *et al.* 2009)

Two examples of raw P3s recorded from human participants are shown in figure 5.8. In this experiment, participants viewed an RSVP stream containing digits as background items and a single letter target. The task was to report the identity of the single letter included in the stream. Items were presented at fixation, with each replacing the previous item at a rate of twenty items per second. EEG was recorded from multiple electrodes while subjects performed this task. The following P3 analyses were restricted to the three parietal electrodes *P3*, *Pz* and *P4*. The diagram on the left-hand side shows a clear P3, while the P3 in the diagram on the right-hand side is less obvious. The shape and time course of the P3s can be influenced by many factors, and (as is evident here) there are often substantial individual differences. Some P3s are more readily detectable than others.

For each trial, an algorithm determined whether subjects did or did not see a target based on the EEG data after the time of the target presentation. A measure of total area under the curve was computed for each participant (figure 5.8), centred around the time of maximal P3 amplitude. This time window was selected within 300–700 ms after the target, but varied for each individual subject. This measure was taken for both target-seen and target-missed trials. A threshold value for each participant was set at 50 per cent of the area under the curve from the average of all target-seen trials. Then, for each trial, we determined if the P3 exceeded this value. If a target-seen trial had a P3 of larger

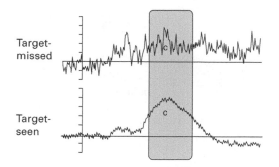

Figure 5.9 ERPs of a participant for target-seen and target-missed trials. The shaded region represents the time points chosen to detect a P3 for this subject

area than the threshold, the value was counted as a hit; otherwise the trial was scored as a miss. On target-missed trials, if the P3 area was larger than the threshold, the trial was scored as a false alarm; otherwise it was a correct rejection. With these measurements of percentage hits and percentage false alarms, we were able to compute a d′ score of algorithm sensitivity individually for each subject (McNichol 1972). d′ is the difference between the z-transforms of hit rate and false-alarm rate.

For the twelve participants, the d′ ranged from 0.39 to 1.69 per participant. For the participant with the highest d′ score, hits were 62 per cent, with only 8 per cent false alarms. The average d′ across all subjects was 0.82. This represents a substantial extraction of information (note that chance performance would correspond to a d′ of zero). Figure 5.9 illustrates the ERP for participant 5 for both target-seen and target-missed trials, with the temporal window used to discriminate between them marked in grey.

5.3.2.2 Building an interface device   As mentioned above, a common method of ensuring that a critical piece of information is perceived by the user is to use a salient visual or auditory cue to capture attention. However, if an environment is particularly rich in such critical signals, the user can be faced with an overwhelming number of such alerts, forcing some alerts to be ignored. Information overload thus renders all of the inputs at the same level of salience relatively less informative.

The brainwave-based receipt acknowledgement device would attempt to use brainwaves generated by a user to provide the computer controlling the interface with feedback about whether the user did or did not see a particular piece of information. This sort of device should allow the

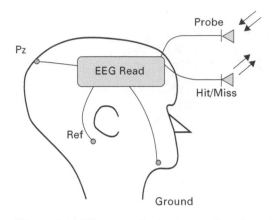

Figure 5.10 Diagram of a brainwave-based receipt acknowledgement device. The probe input is a light sensor, which will trigger a detection event

computer to avoid the use of frequent alarm signals in information-rich environments, by simply re-presenting stimuli until they have been successfully noticed, much as packets are retransmitted over a noisy communications network.

The brainwave-based receipt acknowledgement signal must operate quickly to be useful in a time-critical environment, such as a pilot cockpit. Therefore, the acknowledgement must be present almost immediately after the occurrence of a cognitive event in the mind of the user. The algorithm described is ideal for this sort of application. It is simple enough to be executable on minimal hardware platforms in real time, using off-the-shelf IC components with minimal power requirements.

The system we describe (figure 5.10) is intended to fit within a head-mounted system. It requires three electrodes held against the scalp with an elastic headband, a small circuit-board (perhaps 6 by 6 cm in size) with components powered by a battery pack. The system communicates with the outside world by infrared, thus isolating the user from any electric currents or ground loops, and allowing for free movement.

When presenting a target to the user, the computer interface device sends a stimulus time-locked probe (e.g., an infrared input) to the input port of the brainwave-based receipt acknowledgement system, triggering the detection of P3 correlates of receipt acknowledgement. The system replies to the interface with a single flash of its LED if it has determined that the target was seen. The detection algorithm described above would be used, as depicted in figure 5.10.

5.3.3   Performance analysis of reactive computer interfaces

A major benefit of computational modelling is that it provides a concrete 'executable' realization of a theory. As a result, hypothetical explorations can be run, e.g., the consequences of degrading or even removing a component can be investigated or the implications for a variety of design and parameter choices can be examined in simulation. The latter of these options is our particular focus here.

We have applied our simulations of the human salience detection system to evaluating the feasibility of a variety of stimulus-rich reactive interfaces. As previously discussed, we have developed a (cognitive-level) model of the ICS central engine, the 'glance-look' model, with which we have simulated attentional capture in the context of Barnard's key-distractor AB task. The same core system would be at work when human operators interact with stimulus-rich reactive interfaces. Thus, we have used this model to evaluate the performance trade-offs that would arise from varying key parameters in such systems.

Examples of the types of questions we have investigated include the following. How effective does prediction of the operator's attentional and perceptual state have to be for performance to benefit from the use of a stimulus-rich reactive interface? How are these performance benefits affected by the temporal profile of stimulus arrival, e.g., whether it is fast or slow, regular or bursty?

5.3.3.1 Modelling P3s   In order to explore the effectiveness of the brainwave-based receipt acknowledgement system, it is important to consider how the 'glance-look' model could be extended to generate P3s. The full details of our P3 modelling can be found in Su et al. (2009). Here, we simply summarize that work.

There is good evidence (Donchin 1981; Vogel, Luck and Shapiro 1998) that the P3 indexes working-memory update. Accordingly, we view update of referential working memory as the main generator of the P3 in our model. Although the model does not explicitly simulate such an update process, we can assume that it would be engaged while an item is processed propositionally. Specifically, the length of the P3 is determined by the length of time the buffer stays at Prop, while the amplitude of the P3 at any moment is proportional to the number of propositionally salient elements in transit through Prop.

Perhaps the major difficulty with EEG research is the presence of what, in the context of a particular experiment, can be viewed as extraneous noise. In order to reflect this particular complexity, we extracted segments of noise from our EEG experiments that were not contaminated by

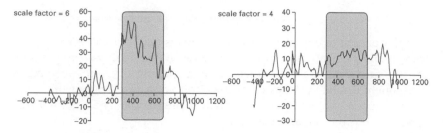

Figure 5.11 Examples of virtual P3s generated from model simulations (targets were presented at time 0, the unit for the y-axis is μV and for the x-axis is ms). Note that the simulation only models the P3, and so other components of a typical EEG, such as the N1 and the N2, are absent. As a result, the virtual EEGs generated here do not necessarily look like real EEGs other than in respect of the presence of a large positive deflection at around 300–700 ms, i.e., the shaded regions (Su *et al.* 2009)

target processing. This noise was then added on top of the pure P3 signal generated from the model. However, in order to reflect individual differences in P3 size, we included a multiplicative constant, called the scale factor, which modulated the size of the pure model-generated P3. Thus, a scale factor of zero yields a noise-only trace, while P3 component size increases with the scale factor. Figure 5.11 shows two model-generated P3s, one with a large scale factor and the other with a small scale factor.

5.3.3.2 Event traffic   Our objective was to explore in simulation the performance of the salience assessment system during interaction with a variety of interface presentation methods. Specifically, we explored the effectiveness of an AB-aware presentation system that attempts to avoid presenting salient stimuli during the blink window. In addition, we considered how effective a brainwave-based receipt acknowledgement system would be at improving performance.

In order to investigate these issues, we needed a method for simulating event traffic from a computer interface. We explored event sequences with three varieties of event, corresponding to the presentation of high-salience items, low-salience items and background items. We simulated the uncoordinated occurrence of such items at an interface using the *b*-model (Wang *et al.* 2002). This approach enabled us to vary three key parameters: burstiness, number of events and aggregation level. The first two concepts are familiar, while the last controls the density of stimuli across the entire simulation window. In this way, our simulations

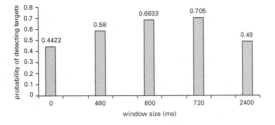

Figure 5.12 Performance (measured as probability of detecting targets) of AB-unaware and AB-aware systems by varying the window sizes of the stimuli. The AB-unaware system is a special case of the AB-aware system with a window size of 0 (Su *et al.* 2009)

explored how accurate detection of high salient events varies as a function of burstiness and aggregation across presentation methods.

5.3.3.3 Performance of constructive interface   The existence of the attentional blink deficit can be responded to by spacing out the presentation of salient stimuli through time. We call such an approach constructive. The key parameter that can be varied is window size, i.e., the fixed interval that is placed between consecutive high salient items. Su *et al.* (2009) explored how performance, in this case report of high salient items, varied according to burstiness, aggregation level and number of high salient items presented. These simulations demonstrated the generally improved performance offered by the AB-aware system (with 600 ms window size) when compared with the AB-unaware system.

With this constructive approach, there is a clear trade-off between the probability of correct report and urgency. That is, as the window size is increased, at least when increased up to around 720 ms, performance improves, while the average delay enforced on each item increases. This is shown in figure 5.12, where the probability of an item being seen increases as window size increases until a size of 2400 ms, where performance drops again. The reason for this decline at the biggest window size is because the simulation has a fixed time period in which to complete the presentation, and with a window size of 2.4 seconds, a proportion of items fail to be presented in the allotted time.

One simple observation that emerges from these simulations is that this constructive approach never does much better than a 70% chance of reporting the high-salience item, while it never does worse than a 40% chance of correct report. (Here, we use slightly different parameters for event traffic than in Su *et al.* (2009).) This is easily explained though, since the highest performance on the blink experiment (see figure 5.3)

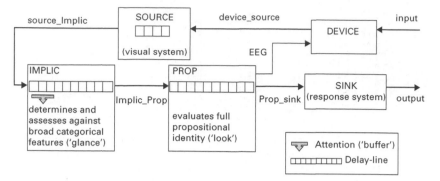

Figure 5.13 Top-level structure of the 'glance-look' model with computer interaction (through device) and implicational subsystem attended (Su *et al.* 2009)

is never much greater than 70%, while the worst performance does not fall much below 40%. Thus, the model's performance limits on these constructive interfaces is inherited from the blink experiments that the model was originally devised to simulate. In the next section, we describe how a reactive approach can be used to improve on this performance.

5.3.3.4 Reactive approach   The main reactive approach is the brainwave-based receipt acknowledgement system; so called since it reacts to the user's cognitive state. Thus, here we consider the effectiveness of such an approach in simulation. Accordingly, we have extended the 'glance-look' model of salience sensitive control with EEG feedback, as discussed in subsection 5.3.3.1. This system is depicted in figure 5.13, where the component labelled device compares the Prop-generated P3 with a criterion/threshold and re-presents the stimulus if the threshold is not met. There is an analogy here with *stop-and-wait* protocols from computer communication networks (Tanenbaum 2002), since, for each stimulus presented, the device waits for a successful acknowledgement (i.e., P3 detection) before it presents the next stimulus. Furthermore, this waiting period may involve multiple negative acknowledgements (i.e., below criterion P3s) and re-presentation cycles.

We first explored how P3 detection sensitivity varies with the scale factor. We work within a signal detection framework (Snodgrass and Corwin 1988) and measure sensitivity in terms of d'. This reflects the difference in hit and false-alarm rates. Hits correspond to simulation runs in which the brainwave-based receipt acknowledgement system detects the presence of a P3 (i.e., above criterion activation) when the target was indeed

Table 5.1 *Comparison of experimental results across twelve human participants with model simulations. The table is ordered by human d' scores. Participants 2, 6, 7 and 8 can only be matched by model simulation using real-number scale factors (Su et al. 2009).*

Participants	Human d'	Model d'	Scale factor
11	0.39	0.44	3
1	0.48	0.44	3
7	0.53		
6	0.56		
2	0.59		
3	0.61	0.65	4
12	0.73	0.85	5
10	0.93	0.85	5
9	1.07	1.02	6
4	1.09	1.02	6
8	1.21		
5	1.69	1.7	10

detected by the model, while false alarms correspond to situations in which the brainwave-based receipt acknowledgement registers the presence of a P3 erroneously, i.e., when no target was detected by the model. Unsurprisingly, d' sensitivity increases as the scale factor increases. This can be easily observed in table 5.1, where we explore the match between natural number scale factors and participant d's. (Note that allowing scale factors to range over the real numbers and employing a simple search algorithm would enable us to match the d' of all participants to any level of accuracy.)

The overall effectiveness though of the reactive approach needs to be assessed in terms of the model's report accuracy when configured with a brainwave-based receipt acknowledgement system. That is, we need to consider the probability of correctly detecting high salient items in the presence of P3 detection and re-presentation. We also wish to compare this reactive approach with the earlier constructive approach with different window sizes. Such a comparison is made in figure 5.14, where the proportion correct report is presented for the brainwave-based receipt acknowledgement system with different scale factors and different P3 threshold criteria. The parameters of these simulations are that repeated items are only counted once, the aggregation level is set to 6, the number of high salient items is set to 20, the b value, which controls

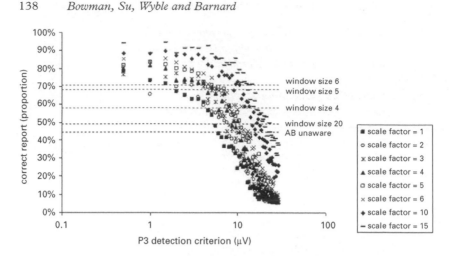

Figure 5.14 Performance (measured as probability of detecting the targets) of the reactive approach using EEG feedback with variability in the P3 detection criterion. Each set of data has a different scale factor, which captures differences in discrimination. For comparison, absolute performance of constructive approach is shown for different window sizes (Su *et al.* 2009)

burstiness, was chosen randomly between 0 and 0.5, and correct report is the proportion of high-salience items reported within a bounded time period.

Figure 5.14 demonstrates that the reactive interface can outperform the hard performance upper limit for the constructive approach. To show this, we include horizontal lines indicating performance of the constructive approach for various window sizes. Furthermore, as anticipated, the reactive approach performance improves as the scale factor increases. This is because sensitivity (i.e., d') increases with an increasing scale factor. In addition, the diagram also reflects the interaction between accuracy and urgency. The latter of these shows up in generally reduced performance with large P3 detection criterion values. This is because with large P3 criteria, the miss rate becomes very large, since the criterion for responding hit becomes extremely strict. Consequently, the system enters a cycle of repeatedly failing to obtain an acknowledgement and re-presenting the target. Continuing the analogy with computer communication protocols, this situation is similar to a stop-and-wait protocol with an extremely lossy acknowledgement channel. In our simulation, this continued re-presentation manifests as a decline in accuracy, since the full quota of high salient items fails to be presented within the allotted time period.

One potential benefit of the type of analysis discussed here is that it could serve as a feasibility check; that is, the clarity of an individual's P3 could be used to derive a scale factor for that individual. Then, in simulation, a feasibility analysis could be performed to determine the effectiveness of implementing a brainwave-based receipt acknowledgement system for that individual.

5.4   Discussion

There are a number of ways in which our work can inform the construction of human–computer interfaces that adapt their behaviour according to the attentional/emotional state of the user. One area is affective computing (Picard 1998), which has a great potential to create 'human-centred' systems, having been made possible by a number of emotion recognition technologies, e.g., recognition of facial expressions, voice intonation, EEG and galvanic skin response. Many applications of these technologies have been proposed, e.g., systems which learn user preferences or help humans (such as autistic children) to recognize emotions. A typical example of affective computing would be an intelligent tutoring system that modulates its tuition according to the student's emotional state, e.g., curious, fascinated, puzzled, frustrated or anxious. For example, the system might regulate demands on the student according to their level of anxiety; it might make subtle (affect-related) changes to the interface in response to user frustration; or it might present emotionally sympathetic responses, e.g., via an avatar (see Morel and Ach, chapter 6 of this volume).

However, in order to reap the full benefits of affective computing, not only is it important to understand emotions, it is also critical to understand the executive processes (in particular attention) within which emotions function. For example, knowing how an (affective) tutoring system should respond to the anxiety level of the student is dependent upon how anxiety modulates human attention. In addition, knowing when to present emotionally sympathetic responses requires an understanding of how emotional stimuli (e.g., emotional expressions) modulate attention and the timeframes over which this modulation functions. These are exactly the kinds of questions that are being answered by empirical phenomena such as the AB (Raymond, Shapiro and Arnell 1992) and affective variants of the task (Barnard et al. 2005). The Salience Project has attempted to act as a bridge between these studies and HCI.

The issue of context is also an area that invites further investigation, and is particularly important in HCI domains where situational awareness is critical. For example, pilots or anaesthetists need rapidly to create an accurate representation of their current situation, by detecting, integrating and interpreting data gathered from a noisy environment. However, for reasons such as task overload, fatigue, etc., human operators often miss salient events and thus build an incorrect picture of the situational context in which they are operating. A major goal of HCI research is to build devices that help humans to attend to salient events, to correctly prioritize environmental stimuli and thus to operate with situational awareness. Once again, in order to construct such systems, we need to understand how attentional resources are deployed, the time-course of this deployment and how priority levels are assigned to competing stimuli. This is a central objective of our research programme.

In order to make such a link between theory and practice, the Salience Project has made a number of contributions. First, we have developed computational models crossing abstraction levels. For example, we have developed neural models of the basic attentional blink (which is not semantic in nature) (Bowman and Wyble 2007) and we have developed 'cognitive-level' symbolic models of semantic and emotional attentional blink effects, as discussed earlier. Second, we have verified predictions arising from these models, both behaviourally (Bowman and Wyble 2007; Wyble, Bowman and Potter 2009) and electrophysiologically (Craston et al. 2009). Third, we have explored the implications of our modelling and experimental work for the development of computer interfaces. This has involved behavioural experiments focused on how peripheral distractors can or cannot capture attention away from a central driving task; considering how effective the EEG P3 component could be as an HCI acknowledgement signal; and using the 'glance-look' model of salience sensitive control to assess the efficacy of a variety of computer interfaces, including a P3 acknowledgement system.

Our research also suggests a number of avenues for future work. For example, it would be revealing to undertake further behavioural experiments focused on attentional capture in more realistic HCI interfaces. These might particularly consider the distracting effects of semantically and emotionally salient stimuli. In addition, there is much room for research exploring the practicality of the brainwave-based receipt acknowledgement system proposed here. For example, it would be interesting to integrate such a P3 detection system with eye-tracking. This would enable a spatial measure of attentional focus to be integrated with a measure of the presence or absence of conscious perception. Thus, one could determine both whether a stimulus is perceived and what that stimulus might be in a display. Indeed, spatial aspects of attention have been largely ignored in our research to date. Thus, there is considerable room to explore rapidly arising stimuli across a number of spatial locations.

More widely, we have argued that many of the goals of IICI research require us to understand human executive processes. Such an understanding will greatly inform interface construction. However, it also prompts the question of mechanisms that should be used to construct such systems. Techniques such as user modelling and task analysis have made important contributions to interface construction (Schraagen, Chipman and Shalin 2000; Diaper and Stanton 2004). However, it is unlikely that they will be sufficient in a domain in which dynamic sensitivity to salience and timing is critical. We believe our computational modelling activities can also help here by providing an abstract specification of user behaviour, which can be placed at the centre of interface usability analysis.

5.5   Acknowledgements

The UK Engineering and Physical Sciences Research Council supported this research (grant number GR/S15075/01). The participation of Philip Barnard in this project was supported by the Medical Research Council (project code U.1055.02.003.00001.01). We thank Patrick Craston, Srivas Chennu and Dell Green for their contribution to the collection and analysis of the EEG data.

5.6   References

Anderson, A. K. 2005. Affective influences on the attentional dynamics supporting awareness, *Journal of Experimental Psychology: General* 134: 258–81

Anderson, A. K., and Phelps, E. A. 2001. Lesions of the human amygdala impair enhanced perception of emotionally salient events, *Nature* 411: 305–9

Barnard, P. J. 1999. Interacting cognitive subsystems: Modelling working memory phenomena within a multi-processor architecture, in A. Miyake and P. Shah (eds.), *Models of Working Memory: Mechanisms of Active Maintenance and Executive Control*. Cambridge, UK: Cambridge University Press: 298–339

Barnard, P. J., and Bowman, H. 2004. Rendering information processing models of cognition and affect computationally explicit: Distributed executive control and the deployment of attention, *Cognitive Science Quarterly* 3: 297–328

Barnard, P. J., Ramponi, C., Battye, G., and Mackintosh, B. 2005. Anxiety and the deployment of visual attention over time, *Visual Cognition* 12: 181–211

Barnard, P. J., Scott, S., Taylor, J., May, J., and Knightley, W. 2004. Paying attention to meaning, *Psychological Science* 15: 179–86

Bechara, A., Tranel, D., and Damasio, H. 2000. Characterization of the decision-making deficit of patients with ventromedial prefrontal cortex lesions, *Brain* 123(11): 2189–202

Bowman, H., Su, L., and Barnard, P. J. 2006. *Semantic Modulation of Temporal Attention: Distributed Control and Levels of Abstraction in Computational Modelling* (Technical Report 9-06): Computing Laboratory, University of Kent at Canterbury

Bowman, H., and Wyble, B. 2007. The simultaneous type, serial token model of temporal attention and working memory, *Psychological Review* 114: 38–70

Cherry, E. C. 1953. Some experiments on the recognition of speech, with one and with two ears, *Journal of Acoustical Society of America* 25: 975–9

Chun, M. M., and Potter, M. C. 1995. A two-stage model for multiple target detection in rapid serial visual presentation, *Journal of Experimental Psychology: Human Perception and Performance* 21: 109–27

Corbetta, M., Patel, G., and Shulman, G. L. 2008. The reorienting system of the human brain: From environment to theory of mind, *Neuron* 58: 306–24

Corbetta, M., and Shulman, G. L. 2002. Control of goal-directed and stimulus-driven attention in the brain, *Nature Reviews* 3: 201–15

Craston, P., Wyble, B., Chennu, S., and Bowman, H. 2009. The attentional blink reveals serial working memory encoding: Evidence from virtual and human event-related potentials, *Journal of Cognitive Neuroscience* 21: 550–66

Damasio, A. 1994. *Descartes' Error*. New York: G. P. Putnam

Diaper, D., and Stanton, N. (eds.) 2004. *The Handbook of Task Analysis for Human–Computer Interaction*. Mahwah, NJ: Lawrence Erlbaum Associates

Donchin, E. 1981. Presidential address, 1980. Surprise! . . . Surprise? *Psychophysiology* 18: 493–513

Holmes, A., and Richard, A. 1999. Attentional bias to threat related material in anxiety: A resource allocation or a practice effect? Poster presentation at September conference, Cognitive Section of the British Psychological Society

Landauer, T. K., and Dumais, S. T. 1997. A solution to Plato's problem: The latent semantic analysis theory of the acquisition, induction and representation of knowledge, *Psychological Review* 104: 211–40

Landauer, T. K., Foltz, P. W., and Laham, D. 1998. An introduction to latent semantic analysis, *Discourse Processes* 25: 259–84

Landauer, T. K., McNamara, D. S., and Dennis, S. (eds.) 2007. *Handbook of Latent Semantic Analysis*. Mahwah, NJ: Lawrence Erlbaum Associates

MacLeod, C., Mathews, A., and Tata, P. 1986. Attentional bias in emotional disorders, *Journal of Abnormal Psychology* 95: 15–20

McKenna, F. P., and Sharma, D. 2004. Reversing the emotional Stroop effect reveals that it is not what it seems: The role of fast and slow components, *Journal of Experimental Psychology: Learning, Memory and Cognition* 30: 382–92

McNichol, D. 1972. *A Primer of Signal Detection Theory*. London: George Allen & Unwin

Most, S. B., Smith, S. D., Cooter, A. B., Levy, B. N., and Zald, D. H. 2007. The naked truth: Positive, arousing distractors impair rapid target perception, *Cognition and Emotion* 21: 964–81

Oatley, K., and Johnson-Laird, P. 1987. Towards a cognitive theory of emotion, *Cognition and Emotion* 1: 29–50

O'Reilly, R. C., and Munakata, Y. 2000. *Computational Explorations in Cognitive Neuroscience: Understanding the Mind by Simulating the Brain.* Cambridge, MA: MIT Press

Pashler, H. 1994. Dual-task interference in simple tasks: Data and theory, *Psychological Bulletin* 116: 220–44

Picard, R. W. 1998. *Affective Computing.* Cambridge, MA: MIT Press

Raymond, J. E., Shapiro, K. L., and Arnell, K. M. 1992. Temporary suppression of visual processing in an RSVP task: An attentional blink, *Journal of Experimental Psychology: Human Perception and Performance* 18: 849–60

Schraagen, J. M., Chipman, S. F., and Shalin, V. L. (eds.) 2000. *Cognitive Task Analysis.* Mahwah, NJ: Lawrence Erlbaum Associates

Snodgrass, J. G., and Corwin, J. 1988. Pragmatics of measuring recognition memory: Applications to dementia and amnesia, *Journal of Experimental Psychology: General* 117: 34–50

Spielberger, C. D. 1972. *Anxiety: Current Trends in Theory and Research: I.* New York: Academic Press

1983. *Manual for the State-Trait Anxiety Inventory (STAI).* Palo Alto, CA: Consulting Psychologists Press

Squires, N. K., Squires, K. C., and Hillyard, S. A. 1975. Two varieties of long latency positive waves evoked by unpredictable auditory stimuli in man, *Electroencephalography and Clinical Neurophysiology* 38: 387–401

Su, L., Bowman, H., and Barnard, P. J. 2007. Attentional capture by meaning: A multi-level modelling study, in *Proceedings of 29th Annual Meeting of the Cognitive Science Society.* Nashville, TN

2008. Performance of reactive interfaces in stimulus rich environments, applying formal methods and cognitive frameworks, *Electronic Notes in Theoretical Computer Science* 208: 95–111

Su, L., Bowman, H., and Barnard, P. J. and Wyble, B. 2009. Process algebraic modelling of attentional capture and human electrophysiology in reactive systems, *Formal Aspects of Computing* 21(6): 513–39

Tanenbaum, A. S. 2002. *Computer Networks.* Upper Saddle River, NJ: Prentice Hall

Teasdale, J. D., and Barnard, P. J. 1993. *Affect, Cognition and Change: Re-modelling Depressive Thought.* Hove: Lawrence Erlbaum Associates

Vogel, E. K., Luck, S. J., and Shapiro, K. L. 1998. Electrophysiological evidence for a postperceptual locus of suppression during the attentional blink, *Journal of Experimental Psychology: Human Perception and Performance* 24: 1656–74

Walker, J. H., Sproull, L., and Subramasi, R. 1994. Using a human face in an interface, in *Proceedings CHI'94* ACM: 85–91

Wang, M., Madhyastha, T., Chan, N. H., Papadimitriou, S., and Faloutsos, C. 2002. Data mining meets performance evaluation: Fast algorithms for modeling bursty traffic, in *Proceedings of the 18th International Conference on Data Engineering*, San Jose, CA

Wyble, B., Bowman, H., and Potter, M. 2009. Categorically defined targets trigger spatiotemporal attention, *Journal of Experimental Psychology: Human Perception and Performance* 35(2): 324–37

Wyble, B., Craston, P., and Bowman, H. 2006. *Electrophysiological Feedback in Adaptive Human–Computer Interfaces* (Technical Report 8-06): Computing Laboratory, University of Kent at Canterbury

Part II

Theoretical and software tools

6   Attention-aware intelligent embodied agents

Benoît Morel and Laurent Ach

This chapter describes how intelligent embodied agents may react according to end-users' attention states and how these agents may adapt their interventions to encourage end users to participate actively in virtual environments such as collaboration platforms or e-learning modules. Attention-related data are taken into account by adapting generically defined interventions (templates) to particular contexts through the use of scripting and markup languages. This chapter introduces the Living Actor[TM] *technology, whose main purpose is to provide end users with high-quality adaptive embodied agents, or avatars. Living Actor*[TM] *technology receives input from software components' reasoning on users' attention states and adjusts the actions of its embodied agents. The result is the creation of embodied agents, or avatars, that are capable of natural, intuitive, autonomous and adaptive behaviours that account for variations in emotion, gesture, mood, voice, culture and personality.*

6.1   Introduction

According to Gartner (April 2007), by the end of 2011, 80 per cent of active Internet users (and Fortune 500 enterprises) will have a 'second life', not necessarily *in* the virtual world, called *Second Life*. Users' virtual lives will be represented by embodied agents in the form of avatars, or virtual representations of the self which allow users to express themselves with a personalized identity of their own creation. In the present chapter the authors define agents as 'soft- and/or hardware that is intended to represent a complete person, animal, or personality' (Sengers 2004: 4). Although agents may also be non-visualized code, we are primarily concerned with agents that are capable of verbal and nonverbal communication and take the form of embodied, conversational and interactive avatars. The authors define an embodied agent, or avatar, as the representation of an entity, such as a company or a single person, that interacts with the user and the environment. Thus, they refer to the virtual characters and avatars discussed in this chapter as embodied agents.

Sustaining users' attention while they interact with digital information is not only the subject of this book but also an important endeavour that can directly impact learning (Clauzel *et al.* 2007) or a company's bottom line. In the battle for human attention, designers of virtual environments use a variety of persuasive strategies involving the use of text, audio, colours and visual images. Thus, information can be represented in a user interface as words, icons and sounds or any combination thereof. Information is stored in both verbal and visual memory. According to Montigneaux (2002), artists and designers of memorable company mascots create characters that play off our perceptions and emotions for maximum appeal and memory recall. Montigneaux indicates that the great richness of visual memory compensates for a lack of vocabulary when one is asked to recall a mascot. He adds that even when attention is not sustained and one's memory is poor, some visual elements are still preserved, which is not the case with semantic elements.

It has also been observed that pictures and images are recalled more easily than both abstract and concrete words, and real objects are recalled even more easily than pictures (Madigan 1983). For example, desktops utilize visual icons to represent file folders, applications and trash bins. These icons enhance memory recall. A humanized interface with interactive embodied agents represented by geometric 3D models is more memorable than one with static pictures or icons. These embodied agents can be instantiated in the image of the user, further humanizing and personalizing an interface. Thus these avatars can employ several interactive strategies to sustain attention and enhance their memorability. As opposed to simple, static pictures, an embodied agent is given habits, attitudes and general behaviours on physical and psychological levels which strongly influence users and capture their attention. Interactions among human beings are made of emotions and memories, and it is interesting to see how these emotions can be modelled in computer applications, as Rosalind Picard (1995) discusses in *Affective Computing*. She and others argue that the humanization of the interface is of great value since research has shown that 'the way people interact with technology is the way they interact with each other' (Picard 2004). As a result, there is a growing demand for interactivity and 'dialogue' with computer applications. Recent research has shown that embodied agents and avatars in attention-aware technologies or systems can improve task attention and memory recall.

In this chapter, the authors explain how they have created embodied agents that successfully sustain users' engagement. This chapter addresses the following central question: What are some important features of embodied agents that maintain the attention of the users, and what is the underlying agent management technology that brings the agent actor to life? The authors address this question in two parts: first they discuss the physical features or attributes an avatar may possess to better capture user attention, and second they describe the attention-management agent technology that underlies the embodied agent interface. In the first part of this chapter the authors identify four general features which are important in attention research: the embodied agent's representation, behaviour and voice, and interaction between the agent and application. Next, the authors focus on a detailed description of the attention-management technology, including controlling embodied agents with graphs of states, attention-management scenarios and moving beyond scripting. Throughout the discussions in this chapter, state-of-the-art examples are provided using Cantoche Living Actor^{TM} embodied agents. Cantoche is the inventor of the patent-pending Living Actor^{TM} technology for creating and animating avatars and embodied agents. Based on the authors' real-world experience using attention-aware intelligent embodied agents for a number of applications, they offer an in-depth explanation of the Living Actor^{TM} technology that has been applied successfully to humanize interfaces for commercial, mobile, e-learning and research applications.

The subsequent sections present research findings and introduce the technology underlying the examples used in order to address the first part of the central question, 'What are some important features of embodied agents that maintain the attention of the users?'

6.2   Embodied agent features that maintain user attention

The authors have identified four important embodied agent features that are integral to maintaining users' attention: the embodied agent's representation, behaviour, voice and the interaction between the agent and application. These features are discussed in more detail below.

6.2.1   Embodied agent representation

Users' first impressions of avatars, or embodied agents, usually depend on their ability to quickly 'sum up' the agent's purpose or functionality. Many lasting impressions are formed from the embodied agent's visual appeal. Thus, the mission of these embodied agents is to show added value and retain the users' attention quickly. In video games, for example, Gard (2000) indicates that the players' first impression of an avatar often determines the way players will interact with the game. This first impression, then, is a matter of importance that has lasting effects for the player and often even involves some subtle form of 'seduction' to win players' acceptance and approval.

Fogg (2003) demonstrates how the recognizable names Disk Doctor and Win Doctor, associated with the Symantec Norton Utilities products, were not chosen by chance. In these examples, the use of the word 'doctor' calls to mind associations with intelligence, knowledge and expertise and therefore engenders user confidence. Disk Doctor and Win Doctor are more persuasive word choices than 'Disk Helper' or 'Disk Assistant' because a diagnosis made by an experienced doctor is more credible and comforting than the same one made by a junior doctor or assistant. When examples of expertise are represented visually in an embodied agent, these notions could be conveyed through the visible age of the character, accessories such as glasses, posture, gait and purposeful gestures. Finally, the voice or name (or nickname) associated with the embodied agent also provides meaningful cues. The name 'Living Actor^{TM}' was chosen with the intended purpose of representing the embodied agent. The use of the word 'living' suggests an entity that is real, intuitive and autonomous. The use of the word 'actor' suggests an ability to convey emotions, gestures, mood, voice and personality naturally and expertly. Thus the name Living Actor^{TM} is meant to remind the user of genuine, human interaction. Therefore the representation of the agent will be the means by which designers initially capture users' attention. Depending on the audience, the embodied agent's mission and the goal of the application or platform that will be the environment in which the avatar resides, embodied agents can take many forms. For example, they can be realistic or cartoonish, consist of a talking head, upper body or full body, be human, animal, take on an abstract form or be an object. Embodied agents don't necessarily have to be human characters in order to capture one's attention successfully. Even very early applications of embodied agents were concerned with these aspects of visual representation. For instance, Microsoft launched a genie character in 1996 which De Rosis, De Carolis and Pizzutilo (1999) defined as an extraverted agent with a dominant personality. Its physical appearance was intended to be powerful, and its blue colour was intended to be calming. As in the examples above, representative features are often chosen to encourage users to trust the interface functionality.

While modern embodied agents come in a variety of forms, as shown in figure 6.1 (see plate), the authors have found that whether the embodied agents are realistic, anthropomorphized or cartoonish, users expect a high-quality human-like connection. Embodied agents build rapport and connect with users when their behaviours, gestures and interactions are *genuine*. Humans thrive on social interaction that is genuine and often seek to identify or find commonalities with interlocutors on several different levels (Raybourn 2004).

An embodied agent can also exhibit different personalities or call to mind visual representations that may be familiar from childhood, teenage years or any happy times in one's life. An example is the embodied agent Numix which was developed by Cantoche in 2003 for the new intranet of the French national TV station, France 2. The purpose and mission of the Numix character was to assist France 2 employees with the transition from traditional work practices to the adoption of new processes and digital technologies. Maintaining attention was necessary not only to train users on new processes, but also to ease users' anxieties about change. As this sort of change is often painful for established, older employees, Cantoche needed to address the following question: What is the best design for an embodied agent whose purpose is to help diverse users (of different ages, educations, genders, ethnicities, etc.) adapt to a new technology and accept cultural change more easily?

Cantoche solved the problem for France 2 by creating an embodied agent whose representation encouraged creativity, light-heartedness and openness. Numix was not too 'high tech' and unapproachable but rather resembled well-known characters that appeal to most French people of all ages and was reminiscent of the smart, funny and widely popular French cartoon series of the early 1970s, Shadoks (Rouxel 2006). The Shadoks, created by Jacques Rouxel, are drawn with simple lines and feature characters that are neither human nor animal, but an amalgamation of interesting shapes. The Numix embodied agent is represented through round shapes and soft, natural colours that contrast with the technical images and content of intranet. The spiral body and antennae of Numix pulsate as if he were breathing, thus communicating that he is a living, organic entity that inhabits a technical environment. By purposefully controlling Numix's breathing in idle and other states, the embodied agent communicated to the user that he was alive and that the user was not alone in his exploration of new technical content.

By choosing to create a countercultural embodied agent that would be familiar to all users and a welcomed contrast to the very unfamiliar content of the intranet, Cantoche brought the user closer to foreign materials and processes (Raybourn 2004). Numix served as the interactional glue needed to ease the cultural change that the organization was undergoing. As discussed above, the ability of the embodied agent to capture and sustain users' attention is a result of a number of interaction strategies, such as the graphical aesthetic, technical quality, relevant behaviour and overall perceived added value. When executed correctly, a caricature of a dog can even be perceived as more intelligent than a caricature of a human (Koda and Maes 1996). Numix is a real-world example of an embodied agent that captured the attention of users as a result of these interaction strategies.

6.2.2   Behaviour

Albert Mehrabian (1971) demonstrated that body movement comprises 55 per cent of nonverbal communication. Body gestures are especially important when helping users navigate complex content and contexts. Living Actor™ embodied agents are most often full-body avatars that leverage the full range of human capabilities for interpreting nonverbal communication by providing movement with purposeful intent, while the reinforcement of verbal communication improves retention. As shown in figure 6.2 (see plate), the full body can engage users by demonstrating posture, movement, emotion and personality.

Living Actor™ avatar behaviours represent a complete departure from existing solutions due to a significant and unique innovation. Living Actor™ uses a behavioural intelligence engine which endows the avatar with an autonomous existence, thereby allowing it to adjust its interaction to each user. This technology provides the intelligent virtual agent with unsurpassed automatic behaviours and expressiveness that enables it to engage in high-quality nonverbal communication that is essential to effective communication. The resulting automation also makes it possible to reduce the cost and production time of developing the embodied agent's behaviours and interactions significantly.

As a Living Actor™ avatar can be embedded directly in the application, the agent can gesture and point to specific content, as shown in figure 6.2. The avatar also orients the attention of the user to specific points and can keep users engaged throughout the dialogue process.

Now let us distinguish between two physical parts of the embodied agent, the face and the body. Humans feel an innate, genuine connection to other human faces. The embodied agent's face is no exception to facilitating a genuine connection. The avatars use expressions to convey emotions, produce emotions within the user, draw attention to something or retain users' attention. The avatar's body actions, behaviours and gestures strongly contribute to the agent's ability to be understood and correctly contextualized. The full-body actions complement the speech and create a holistic experience.

A person's behaviours are as important in conveying language as his verbal communication. Embodied agents are understood by reading their body language or behaviour which gives them the characteristics needed to perform a mission credibly. Hogan (1996) discusses two strategies for becoming a more convincing and persuasive interlocutor: make people like you, and make people believe you. He says the best way to be believed is to have coherent or congruent verbal and nonverbal communication. Therefore, many researchers consider behaviour to be very important in all types of communication. Attention, for example, significantly benefits from nonverbal communication.

Years of research pertaining to eye movements has produced an abundance of literature on this subject. Early research was carried out by Dr Ernest Hildegard in the fifties. Gaze is a very important part of attention in terms of retaining one's focus on a specific graphical area, but eye movements are also meaningful when observed in waiting phases. Research results indicate that people are likely to move their eyes temporarily to specific positions when remembering events, answering questions, talking to themselves, feeling something or visualizing future events. Eye motion is therefore the basis of various interpretations, and we must be careful when making use of it. Hogan is very precise in his research and defines six key positions or movements of the human eyes. For instance, he shows that looking at an upper right location is a sign of image visualization of a previously unknown situation. Hogan concludes that the knowledge we gain from the information provided by eye movements is a powerful communication tool. It is so powerful, in fact, that eye movements alone can contribute to and influence other people's decisions. Appropriate eye movement signals confidence and attentiveness. A sustained look from the agent shows the user that an action is expected (Hogan 1996).

With their experiment, *The solar system*, Cassell and Thorisson (1999) show that an embodied agent's nonverbal behaviour, while improving the structure of conversation, can also make the actions of the system better understood. The study demonstrates that an embodied agent's active or passive behaviours, without dialogue, allow people to understand that the system is waiting for an action.

However, embodied agent behaviours executed without purposeful intent might also hamper user understanding and appropriate attention allocation. For instance, distracting movements may unintentionally let users think that the system expects something from them. In addition, users may wonder what they have done right or wrong when they see an embodied agent blinking at them or performing automatic actions that cannot be understood. Consequently, programmers must ensure that embodied agents' behaviours correspond to their purpose and the context of the situation. As Picard (2001) indicates, an animated paper clip which blinks any time you click on it is perceived as a person who protests by blinking when asked to leave your desktop.

Body language also provides rich information for human communication. Human beings have an unlimited range of emotions that are easily understood through body language. In her book, *Reading People*, Dimitrius (1998) describes many human states and traits that can be easily identified through body language.

Body motion also allows an embodied agent to occupy the space or environment completely and draw in users' attention. Embodied agents can point to elements using their hands, move, disappear and reappear.

The rhythm of the embodied agents' movements is also a key factor in nonverbal communication. To persuade the user to execute an action, embodied agents can show that they are listening or waiting through slight movements and gaze. These subtle behaviours contrast with more active behaviours executed by embodied agents. By orienting the embodied agents' body behaviours towards the user, moving a hand in the user's direction or indicating intent with specific nonverbal emblems, embodied agents can prompt users to interact.

Many additional factors contribute to the extent to which we identify with others through communication. These include nonverbal visual cues that encode meaning, such as clothing, colours, gestures, behaviours and accessories. As embodied agents become more mainstream, users will want their personal avatars to reflect aspects of who they are or who they wish to be. Research has demonstrated that young persons and adults desire greater flexibility in designing and authoring avatars. Cantoche Living Actor^{TM} allows users to encode specific meanings in embodied agents' behaviours and visual features by endowing them with personalities unique to each individual character.

6.2.3   Voice

When the voice is involved the user memorizes the message better and is more receptive to information communicated confidently by the embodied agent. Hogan (1996) studied the confidence exhibited by a person according to vocal attributes. He demonstrates that significant features associated with different kinds of people can be transposed to embodied agents. For example, if the agent is a female, Hogan recommends lowering the frequency of her voice by one octave in order for the voice to be perceived as more professional. According to research, women with high-frequency voices are considered as weak and boring. If the agent is a male, Hogan recommends making him more powerful and respectable by lowering his vocal frequency by half an octave.

Other vocal parameters, such as the rhythm of speech and changes in intonation, give the user confidence in the embodied agent and therefore give the embodied agent persuasive power. A dominating character, for instance, uses a faster vocal rhythm than a submissive character.

'It's not what you say, it's how you say it' (Dimitrius 1998). Dimitrius shows how our everyday attitudes are not revealed by words but by the way we say them. According to her, two different dialogues take place in any conversation: the first uses words, and the second uses intonation. When you ask somebody 'how are you?' and you hear 'very well', you do not automatically trust the answer. The tone of voice is pre-eminent in indicating whether the interlocutor is depressed, anxious, excited or something else. When you listen to the tone, the volume, the pace and other vocal features, you enter a nonverbal conversation where you can actually find the truth. These features are obviously less emphasized when using synthetic voices. Emotion in text-to-speech (TTS) is not as powerful as emotion in recorded speech (Nass, Foehr and Somoza 2000). However, even with the lack of emotion carried by synthetic voices compared with recorded voices, both may be productive.

Audio is enabled in the majority of modern computers, though it is not always possible to play it as desired in workplaces such as open-space offices; that is why the embodied agent's speech may occasionally be written in a speech bubble like a comic strip's dialogue balloon. In this case, the user's gaze is distracted by the text in the balloon, and this lowers the impact of the agent's behavioural language. However, this is still an interesting solution. Users are more attentive to an image of a human face with the mouth animated in synchrony with speech than to simple text (Sproull et al. 1996).

6.2.4   Interaction between agent and application

Living Actor™ avatars can be displayed in different formats or reside on different platforms (from PCs and mobile phones to set-top boxes for interactive television). These avatars are represented via superior graphics, and they can be distributed throughout various types of interfaces and devices depending on the technological specifications of the end-user. Therefore there are a number of possible interactions between the agent and application that can be used to direct the user's attention. Embodied agents inhabit the application, and as such designers must make a number of decisions regarding size and position within the space. It is interesting to experiment with the size and attitudes of embodied agents. The Living Actor™ avatar for the Louvre, described below and shown in figure 6.3 (see plate), provides a resizeable embodied agent which can be moved over the interface and disappears when asked to. The agent Dominique-Vivant Denon helps both children and adults explore the Louvre website. Dominique has specific attitudes and sizes that are purposefully varied to capture the internaut's attention.

An interesting technique to capture users' attention is the position of the embodied agent within the application. The first and simplest rule in filmmaking relates to the position of the subject within the frame. It is more harmonious and dynamic not to place the subject systematically right in the centre of the frame (Couchouron 2004). All classical techniques of photography and cinematography, including viewing angles, may be applied to embodied agent visualization. A high angle shot tends to squeeze the character, whereas a low angle shot will have the opposite effect, strengthening a dominating personality.

All of these features are used in movies and cartoons. An excellent example that shows all the important features used to capture users' attention is the cartoon *Duck Amuck*, directed by Chuck Jones in 1953 and selected as number two of 'The 50 Greatest Cartoons: As Selected by 1,000 Animation Professionals'. In this cartoon, the star, Daffy Duck, is tormented by a sadistic, unseen animator (later revealed to be his friend and rival Bugs Bunny) who constantly changes Daffy's location, clothing, voice, physical appearance and even shape.

In the example in figure 6.3 the embodied agent interacts with the application by calling users' attention to details in the website content that the user would have otherwise missed or ignored. Dominique-Vivant Denon leans forward and whispers to the user as if sharing privileged information. The embodied agent's gestures, behaviours and position within the application interact with the content to maintain the user's attention.

In the sections above, the authors have discussed four general features important in attention research: the embodied agent's representation, behaviour, voice and interaction between the agent and application. The subsequent discussion will focus on a detailed description of the attention-management technology and will include controlling embodied agents with graphs of states, attention-management scenarios and, finally, moving beyond scripting.

6.3   Special status of embodied agents in user interface

An attention-management agent that is embodied in a virtual character facilitates a human-like interaction with software users to bring their attention to a particular focus. It is different from usual user interfaces, as it introduces a new channel of communication through dialogues, gestures and facial expressions. Its special status is also apparent from the way an embodied agent is integrated in software programs, usually on top of all other visual elements or inserted in a dedicated area. Its specificities bring more capabilities but also more complexity.

As a special component between the man–machine interface and users, the agent constitutes a good intermediate object between the basis of a working environment and some overlay system dedicated to attention management. It is indeed possible to coordinate the actions of any type of agent with an attention-management system and to infer intervention factors from attention metadata, but if the agent is a virtual character that uses body language in addition to speech and text, it is helpful in transmitting recommendations and pulling the user out of his immediate tasks to suggest a new attention focus.

Using an embodied agent implies communicating by means of text and speech as well as gestures and expressions. The embodied agents' activities must also remain connected with the working environment to be able to play a role in attention management inside the specific context of the application. Inside web pages, for instance, data and instructions may be exchanged with any code snippet to be executed in a page where the embodied agent appears. A triangle of interactions is formed by the user, the embodied agent and the software. Interactions between the embodied agent and users can be detached from the rest of the interface during some interactions, but the embodied agent often acts as a mediator between the user and the software.

By bringing life to user interfaces and staying connected with other graphical and textual components, embodied agents are in a good position to capture users' attention through new dimensions of communication and more humanized messages than buttons and hypertext content. They allow for new paradigms of interactions that overcome the limitations of common increasingly complex graphical user interfaces such as websites where too many items are proposed to visitors in menus, submenus and various sub-windows. Exaggeration of the number of images, colours and font sizes as a means of capturing users' attention can be efficiently replaced by the intervention of a human-like character. These new ways of capturing and managing user attention also introduce new complexity in interactions since embodied agents obviously cannot be manipulated as easily as a graphical tool. However, they do share certain principles with simpler user interface objects.

6.4   Technical design principles

The Living Actor™ technology was developed by Cantoche and launched in January 2002 for the major accounts market which includes external and internal communication and e-learning. Their embodied agents also serve as cross-platform ambassadors for large multinational organizations. The avatars express social behaviours and emotions, and have organized personalities that complement company brands and address audience and end-user needs. Since 1999, more than 500 virtual characters and avatars have been created and animated by Cantoche using the Living Actor™ technology. Cantoche provides easy-to-use software to end-users so that they can create and customize their own avatar solutions. After two years, Living Actor™ was established at every level in the B-to-B (business-to-business) market as the technology of reference for multimedia, interactive virtual agent solutions. Beginning in 2005, Cantoche stepped up its growth in the user-generated content market. Cantoche created an innovative real-time technology for emotion-rich avatars driven solely by the user's voice that allows end-users and companies to generate advanced personalized video calls and video content on mobile and chat-based services. This novel technology is discussed further in subsequent sections.

Besides general principles shared with other components, embodied agents demonstrate special characteristics of expert direction such as human actors receive when performing in a film and that is unlike anything related to software objects. Therefore, instructions sent to embodied agents should be defined at the right level of detail, without specifying too many details of the gestures and facial expressions but carrying enough information to angle their intervention for a particular purpose. Embodied agents should be able to act according to directives just as real actors do.

To reduce the complexity of directing embodied agents, the set of instructions determining their behaviour must be restricted to a small number of commands. However, in order to ensure efficient communication, the agent's behaviour must be well adapted to the context. Therefore, there is a need to introduce alternatives in the way similar simple orders are completed depending on the context. Defining several levels of directives is a good solution to this problem that allows variations in the sequence of actions at different stages: (1) choosing an intervention script; (2) using scripting language commands; (3) implementing actions corresponding to a command. This layered structure simplifies the control of embodied agents and distinguishes the artistic task of creating character animations (stage 3) and the scripting tasks that build interactive scenarios (stages 1 and 2).

In building the agent's behaviour, special consideration must be given to how agent intervention will be perceived by the user. The feeling produced by an external intervention inside a multimedia environment depends on the type of application. In graphical user interfaces, actions are directed from the user to the machine, whereas games and software interactive scenarios set up conditions where both directions of communication are present. When embodied agent interventions take place where users want to control the machine, considered as a working or learning tool, a new human-like interaction may have a negative impact, especially when its goal is to change users' attention focus. Just like any user interface component, embodied agent interventions must be accepted by users, who should not consider them an intrusion in a software environment they are used to. However, the risk of irritation is higher than with standardized elements that are more easily adjusted for consistency with the rest of the environment.

The previous considerations about embodied agents' specific constraints as a user interface component lead to a set of requirements that must be complied with for managing users' attention: high level of interaction, adaptation to the context and acceptance by users. The technical features embedded in an embodied agent implementation must be sufficient to let computer graphics artists and scriptwriters work on the content for maximum efficiency of agent interventions with respect to those constraints.

6.4.1   Controlling an embodied agent using a graph of states

The similarity between real actors and embodied agents can be applied only if the latter are autonomous to a certain extent so that they are able to follow the script of an interactive scenario. Unlike real actors, able freely to explore human interpretive potential, our embodied agents' actions are restricted to a limited set of movements, gestures and expressions. So we organize all possible actions in fixed sequences, each one making a transition between two states of the actor. A state corresponds to a pose or attitude of the actor but is not necessarily static; there may be low-range activity around a central position associated with one graph state without having to switch to another state. A transition between two states is mainly a sequence and combination of gestures and facial expressions. In 3D they include skeletal animation, geometry morphing or any other type of animation. In 2D transitions are defined by sequences of pictures. For instance, a transition from the main pose to a happy state could be an animation where the character raises his hands and smiles widely.

The graph of states represents all the main poses the embodied agent can assume and the ways to move from one to the other. Even the special case of the appearance and disappearance of the embodied agent can be handled using the graph of states by defining some *hide* and *show* states used as start and end points of a scenario. The graph of states approach ensures the continuity of animations by providing the means to move from one state to the other with a proper transition and by preventing abrupt shifts if there is no transition available. To change the current state, we must follow a direct link to another state or find a path through several links and states towards a final target state.

The graph of states is a good structure to delimit a set of animations sufficient to cover a list of anticipated generic situations such as speaking, explaining, arguing, suggesting, declining, greeting and other actions more specific to particular scenarios such as opening a book or typing on a computer (see level 2 in figure 6.4 (see plate)). A flat list of commands corresponding to all the possible states can be derived from the graph so that the behaviour of an embodied agent may be managed using simple commands. After a command is sent, a corresponding target node is chosen as a goal to be reached through some path in the graph. The existence of such a path ensures a continuity of actions and smooth transitions towards the target state that can thus be chosen safely as long as the graph is not so complex as to contain unreachable nodes. We end up with a powerful yet simple tool that ensures the continuity of animations while letting us control the embodied agent through a limited set of instructions.

On top of the behaviour defined by the graph of states, autonomous animations may be added in new tracks or blended with transition animations in order to synchronize the actor with events that do not depend on the graph. A primary example is the *lip-synch* that animates the mouth according to speech data. Another example would be facial expressions denoting a general mood throughout the different sequences of actions. Other types of actions such as external programs affecting the background application or changes in interface customization may be part of an interactive scenario without being directly related to the virtual character animation and without dependence at all on the graph of states. All these types of actions have to be managed in the same process to ensure synchronization.

6.4.2   Scripting attention-management scenarios

The combination of target states, speech commands and connections to external events becomes the basis for writing attention-management scenarios where, depending on the situation, proper interventions of the embodied agent are triggered. A global set of scripting commands is defined to describe these actions in a scripting language based on XML format, which provides the high level of control needed to implement attention scenarios (see level 3 in figure 6.4). XML intervention scripts consist of a list of actions with their associated conditions. An action may be related to the virtual character, such as a sequence of animations towards a target state, audio or textual speech commands, or it can be any function running in the background application, such as some JavaScript code in a web page.

The availability of a scripting language at this level makes it easy to write scenarios according to schemes of interventions deduced from attention models. An attention-management system may detect the suitable conditions to call the agent and match them with patterns of intervention implemented using the scripting language. Template scripts may be defined for generic interventions, and different parameters can introduce variations in the behaviour of the embodied agent to match both user-specific factors and the applicative context. A template intervention script is attached to a situation where an action must be taken to manage users' attention using some type of agent intervention, such as proposing to switch to a new task or notifying the user about a significant event. The form of such interventions must be chosen according to the type of missions assigned to the embodied agent from the perspective of attention management in a certain type of situation. Thus, writing these scripts is a collaborative task for attention-management systems designers and writers of embodied agent scripts.

The parameters for introducing variations in the template scripts can be related to the application context, attention system variables or users' characteristics. This technique was used in the system described by Molenaar *et al.* in chapter 11 of this book, where parameters related to users' specific tasks allowed changing the strength of the embodied agent's intervention and his mood as conveyed by non-verbal expression. The three-level model combined with an attention-management system was an efficient tool in this context.

Textual information or audio speech can be directly transmitted from the attention system by the embodied agent and bring factual information to the user just as a pop-up message can do, but some other types of information based on more sensitive perception may also be transmitted. The gestures, facial expressions and speech conveyed by the embodied agent express emotions that accentuate the speech if they are properly chosen; on the contrary, if they are not properly chosen, they contradict what is said. To this regard, a special consideration should be given to the way emotions are expressed by the embodied agent and what emotions are recognized by the users. Emotions may be perceived differently by people of diverse cultures and different user profiles.

Having a scripting language is useful to describe embodied agent interventions and to connect them with an attention-management system, as it allows the transformation of a model of intervention into an appropriate embodied agent behaviour and maps attention variables and other context data with script parameters. This provides the means to start the main effort, which consists of choosing and implementing the best behaviour for the agent and creating the animation data. These other tasks concern the tools used to create and animate the living actor and compose the character production line.

6.4.3   *Character production line*

Acceptance is more easily achieved when the embodied agent reminds us of characters that can be found in the real world, even if the embodied agent shows exaggerated gestures or expressions. Animating such a virtual character is thus a creative task that may conflict with the quest for productivity: automating gestures and expressions is difficult without sacrificing artistic animations that would better match expectations about a humanized assistant. A balance has to be found between a fully automated system where the gestures appear too artificial and the limited but lifelike animations created by computer graphics artists that would prevent re-use in different contexts and dialogues. Between these two extremes there are some useful techniques to preserve animation quality while allowing for automatic procedures and variations in scenarios. They have been used for years in the gaming industry and computer animation, although they are seldom seen in software environments where more serious business is involved.

After several years of experimentation with character animation to create virtual guides and virtual assistants for companies, Cantoche has settled some principles in its Living Actor™ technology, such as the distribution of tasks according to a division between that which belongs to artistic animations and that which belongs to the creation of behaviours or the scripting of interventions. They ensure that the animation quality is not compromised by automatic procedures. Thanks to the animation graph, a certain amount of autonomy is ensured while preserving animation data and providing means to control the living actor at a high level.

These principles are put into practice by the Living Actor™ character production line. At the first stage, computer graphics artists create 3D or 2D animations using standard commercial software intended for the gaming and film industries. In case of a 3D embodied agent, a mesh surface is usually created for the skin and clothes along with a skeleton and animated bones plus material attributes and textures for final image rendering. The result is a 3D model that can be directly used for shooting images and creating films. Since our goal is to have real-time interactions, another step is needed to create a virtual actor even though the basis of all gestures and facial expressions is already built.

This method preserves the work of character animators who build gestures and expressions according to a personality given to the embodied agent. When this work is carried out well, emotions are transmitted by the embodied agent to the user and this is what makes its intervention powerful compared with a simpler manner of conveying information such as displaying text and icons. Emotions are understood or misunderstood depending on the shared cultural background of computer graphics artists and future users. Thus, this part of embodied agent creation cannot be replaced by any automatic procedures using existing technologies.

At the second stage we import the 3D model into a Living Actor^{TM} tool called Avatar Maker which provides the functionalities needed to transform 3D data into a virtual actor able to participate in any interactive scenario. This step of the production process consists of building a graph of animations as previously described and takes place between graphical creation and scenario scripting. It is an intermediate task that brings life to the embodied agent by completely defining his possible behaviours for attention management or for other missions he is now ready to carry out.

What follows depends on the type of environment we plan to use and for which the Living Actor^{TM} character will be stored in a suitable format such as Adobe Flash-based data for web pages or a different image-based format for video applications. However, the initial steps of character production are common to all formats; it is the same virtual actor that will appear on a web page, in a film or during a video call session between mobile phone users. Whatever execution environment is used, the same animations will be triggered from the same high-level instructions. The behaviours implemented through the graph of states are managed automatically, but the underlying gestures, postures and expressions result from the artistic character animation work carried out at the first stage of the production line. A balance between automatic behaviour and artistic quality is thus realized while allowing emotions and personality to emerge from the embodied agent's activities.

6.4.4   Beyond scripting: real-time control from the user's voice

Control over the embodied agent can be achieved by scripting scenarios of interventions, but types of input other than manually writing instructions can be envisioned. Since each general behaviour is implemented along with a set of high-level instructions, it can be connected to an automatic system that chooses the best actions to be performed by the embodied agent from features detected in a user's voice or in a webcam video stream. This combination of audio analysis and automatic behaviours creates a system that is able to control an embodied agent vocally. In the future we plan to recognize emotions in the voice of the user and match them with the emotions conveyed by the virtual actor to demonstrate his personality. By synchronizing the user and agent and adding real-time lip-synch, the user's avatar will speak with his own voice and convey the same emotions as the user. Such a system has been developed by Cantoche and is called Living Actor^{TM} SpeechToVideo. It takes into account the periods of speech and other basic features from audio signal analysis in order to choose the best target state in animation graph at each moment. Furthermore, current research focuses on detecting emotions in the voice. This approach could be applied to attention management by replacing intervention scripts with a human directly controlling the embodied agent through his voice.

6.5   Conclusions

This chapter addressed a central question: What are some important features of embodied agents that maintain the attention of the users, and what is the underlying agent-management technology that brings the agent actor to life? The authors addressed this question in two parts – first by discussing the physical features or attributes an avatar may possess to capture user attention better, and second by describing the attention-management agent technology that underlies the embodied agent interface. Throughout the chapter, examples were provided using Cantoche Living Actor^{TM} embodied agents that have been created for commercial applications to maintain attention. Social science research that motivates embodied agent development was presented, and an in-depth explanation of the Living Actor^{TM} technology that has been used successfully to 'humanize' interfaces for commercial, learning and research applications was provided. Research regarding what embodied agents and associated technologies will bring future generations to help maintain user's attention in e-learning systems and other applications is in the early stages.

6.6   Acknowledgements

We thank Dr Elaine Raybourn for her feedback in preparing this chapter.

6.7   References

Cassell, J., and Thorisson, K. R. 1999. The power of a nod and a glance: Envelope vs. emotional feedback in animated conversational agents, *Applied Artificial Intelligence* 13: 519–38

Clauzel, D., Roda, C., Ach, L., and Morel, B. 2007. Attention based, naive strategies for guiding intelligent virtual agents, in *Proceedings of the IVA2007 7th International Conference on Intelligent Virtual Agents (Poster section)*. 17–19 September, Paris: 369–70

Couchouron, S. M. 2004. Continuité visuelle et narrative. Retrieved in 2008 from: dvfr.com/guide-pratique/tournage/58-continuite-visuelle-et-narrative.html

De Rosis, F., De Carolis, B., and Pizzutilo, S. 1999. Software documentation with animated agents. Department of Informatics, University of Bari, Italy

Dimitrius, J.-E. 1998. *Reading People: How to Understand People and Predict Their Behavior – Anytime, Anyplace*. New York: Ballantine Books

Fogg, B. J. 2003. *Persuasive Technology: Using Computers to Change What We Think and Do*. San Francisco: Morgan Kaufmann

Gard, T. 2000. Building character 2004. Gama Network: Gamasutra.com. Retrieved 5 March 2004 from: www.gamasutra.com/features/20000720/gard_pfv.htm

Hogan, K. 1996. *The Psychology of Persuasion: How to Persuade Others to Your Way of Thinking*. Gretna, LA: Pelican Publishing Company

Koda, T., and Maes, P. 1996. Agents with Faces: The effects of personification of agents, in *Proceedings of HCI '96*, London

Madigan, S. 1983. Picture memory, in J. C. Yuille (ed.), *Imagery, Memory and Cognition*. Hillsdale, NJ: Lawrence Erlbaum Associates: 65–89

Mehrabian, A. 1971. *Silent Messages*. Belmont, CA: Wadsworth

Montigneaux, N. 2002. *Les marques parlent aux enfants grâce aux personnages imaginaires*. Paris: Éditions d'Organisation

Nass, C., Foehr, U., and Somoza, M. 2000. The effect of emotion of voice in synthesized and recorded speech. Stanford University

Picard, R. 1995. *Affective Computing* (Technical report): MIT Media Laboratory, Cambridge, MA

2001. *Affective Computing: Challenges*. MIT Media Laboratory, Cambridge, MA

2004. Human responses to technology scrutinized, by Shankar Vedantam, *Washington Post*, 7 June 2004, page A14, www.washingtonpost.com/wp-dyn/articles/A20688-2004Jun6.html

Raybourn, E. M. 2004. Designing intercultural agents for multicultural interactions, in S. Payr and R. Trappl (eds.), *Agent Culture: Designing Virtual Characters for a Multi-Cultural World*. New York: Lawrence Erlbaum Associates: 267–85

Rouxel, J. 2006. Les Shadoks: Édition intégrale, 9 November, *Archives Ina – TF1 Vidéo*

Sengers, P. 2004. The agents of McDonaldization, in S. Payr and R. Trappl (eds.), *Agent Culture: Designing Virtual Characters for a Multi-Cultural World*. New York: Lawrence Erlbaum Associates: 3–19

Sproull, L., Subramani, M., Kiesler, S., Walker, J. H., and Waters, K. 1996. When the interface is a face, *Human–Computer Interaction* 11: 97–124

7 Tracking of visual attention and adaptive applications

Kari-Jouko Räihä, Aulikki Hyrskykari and Päivi Majaranta

This chapter presents a number of software applications that make use of an eye tracker. It builds on the knowledge of visual attention and its control mechanisms as presented in chapters 3 and 5. It provides a tour through the years, showing how the use of eye gaze as indicator of visual attention has developed from being an additional input modality, supporting the disambiguation of fuzzy signals, to an interaction enhancement technique that allows software systems to work proactively and retrieve information without the user giving explicit commands.

7.1 Introduction

Our environment provides far more perceptual information than can be effectively processed. Hence, the ability to focus our attention on the essential is a crucial skill in a world full of visual stimuli. *What we see is determined by what we attend to*: the direction of our eye gaze, the focus of our *visual attention*, has a close relationship with the focus of our attention.

Eye trackers, which are used to measure the point of gaze, have developed rapidly during recent years. The history of eye-tracking equipment is long. For decades, eye trackers have been used as diagnostic equipment in medical laboratories and to enable and help communication with severely disabled people (see, e.g., Majaranta and Räihä 2007). Only recently have eye trackers reached the level of development where they can be considered as input devices for commonly used computing systems.

The most common form of eye trackers are video-based and desk-mounted. The camera is either on the desk beside or under the screen, or integrated with the screen. In figure 7.1 (see plate) we can see examples of how the eye-tracking technology has evolved over time. In the ASL 4250R eye-tracking system (purchased in 1995) the camera optics needed for tracking the eye are housed in the black box below the screen. In the iViewX tracking system (purchased in 2001) the camera resides on the table beside the screen. Both of these tracking systems need an additional computer (not visible in the figures) dedicated to processing the video image of the eye. The Tobii T60 eye tracker (purchased in 2008) does not look much different from a traditional screen. Both the needed optics and embedded firmware are integrated into the screen.

Today's eye trackers are able to report the point of gaze on screen in real time with high accuracy. However, irrespective of the evolving tracker technology, the potential error of the reported focus of visual attention will always stay in the order of 1° of visual angle because of the biological structure of the eye. At any one time we are able to see sharply about a 2° wide area but the exact point of attention within that area cannot be determined for certain. This means that at a viewing distance of 70 cm (about an arm's length) the visual focus can be concluded with an accuracy of 2–2.5 cm. So, we are able to track the focus of gaze: How can we make use of this information in applications?

In this chapter, we first briefly review the psychological foundation of visual attention (section 7.2): What is its relation to attention and to the point of gaze? Section 7.3 asks if information about the point of gaze can be used for making applications adaptive. After that, we survey (sections 7.4–7.8) the applications that have made use of visual attention.

7.2   Visual attention

Is the focus of visual attention the same as the focus of attention? No: the focus of attention may vary independently of where the eyes are looking. When we attend to a task, like reading this text, our attention may be drawn (voluntarily or, in many cases, involuntarily) to other issues, even though we still keep our eyes on the text. For example, the concept 'visual attention' used in the text may remind us of some previously read article and covertly lead our attention to think back to that article. As another example, the ongoing discussion in the room may suddenly attract our attention since we hear someone speaking our name, and we overtly shift our attention to the speaker. Thus, re-orienting attention may sometimes happen totally independently of visual attention, having no effect on eye movements.

The two types of mechanisms controlling our shift of attention are called *bottom-up* and *top-down processing* (e.g., Wolfe 1998; Pashler, Johnston and Ruthruff 2001; Ware 2008). Bottom-up shifts of attention are driven by the perceived stimulus; when vision is the best stirring sense, the visual information pattern falling on the retina drives the shift of attention. Top-down shifts of attention are driven by the demands of attention, determined by the needs of the task. The first example in the previous paragraph is an example of a top-down shift of attention. The attention is driven by the internal goal of understanding the concept, i.e., the stimulus is related to the ongoing task. In the other example, hearing our name is a distinct stimulus that catches our attention, unrelated to the current task, and is hence an example of a bottom-up shift of attention.

While these two coarse mechanisms are widely recognized, there are several more detailed theories on how the filtering of irrelevant information takes place. However, common to most theories is the idea that the entire visual field of information is 'preprocessed' in a pre-attentive stage where parallel processes segment visual information into clusters to form separate objects. Gestalt laws, such as proximity, closure, similarity and good continuation, are applied during this stage. After that, conscious, active attention is paid to the objects sequentially, one at a time (Duncan 1984). Some distinct features in the visual field, like colour, shape and size (Wolfe 1998), or objects with abrupt onset (Yantis and Jonides 1990), have been shown to increase the probability of passing the preattended target to conscious attention. Motion has been found to be an especially powerful attribute for activating the focus of attention (see, e.g., Abrams and Christ 2003; Bartram, Ware and Calvert 2003; Franconeri and Simons 2003).

If we are able to focus our active attention on only one object at a time, how can we explain the everyday situations where we can execute many tasks simultaneously? We are, for example, able to drink coffee and still fully focus on reading a newspaper, or we can walk on a path along the pavement of a city and constantly monitor for bumps and stones that may trip us and detect anything that may be on the trajectory to cross our path. Raskin (2000: 18–20) explains that this is enabled by habit development, or *automaticity* in the language of cognitive scientists. Repeatedly performed tasks gradually become automatic, the kind of habitual reactions we are often unable to avoid. When we perform several simultaneous tasks, all but one of them are automatic. Ware (2008: 4) explains our ability to perform simultaneous complex tasks (like seeing while walking) by our structured and direct seeing processes, of which we are often unaware. For example, in face-to-face conversation with someone, we unconsciously supplement the verbal information by monitoring facial expressions, gestures and gaze direction.

More details on visual attention and its control mechanisms can be found in other chapters of this book, especially chapters 3 and 5.

7.3   Can applications benefit from knowing the focus of visual attention?

In human–human interaction, a common way of utilizing eye gaze is to use it as an indicator of attention for mediating the conversation. Conversation partners can adapt their behaviour based on cues signalling whether they have the attention of the people they are trying to address. If two people compete for attention, the one that does not get visual attention is more likely to let the other one take the first turn. Attention is a powerful mediator in communication (Horvitz *et al.* 2003; Roda and Thomas 2006b).

In computer-based tracking, such attentive user interfaces are a much newer phenomenon than command-and-control applications. Recently, the general increase in interest in attentive, non-command interfaces (Lieberman and Selker 2000) has boosted the development of applications that make use of eye gaze for detecting visual attention, and for adapting the application based on this information. A number of reviews and special issues of journals that focus on this theme have been published (Maglio *et al.* 2000; Porta 2002; Duchowski 2002; Baudisch *et al.* 2003; Vertegaal 2003; Zhai 2003; Selker 2004; Hyrskykari, Majaranta and Räihä 2005; Roda and Thomas 2006a).

By monitoring the user's behaviour, we are able to get information that helps the application predict what the user's needs are at a particular point in time. An adaptive (or 'attentive', Vertegaal 2003) application tries to serve the user by adapting the way the application responds, by providing the most relevant information the user needs to proceed with the ongoing task. We can use several different sensing mechanisms to collect information on the behaviour of a user interacting with a system. These may include microphones for capturing acoustic information, cameras enabling the monitoring of the user's gaze or body gestures, or even electronic sensors recording muscle or brain activity.

However, monitoring the user's gaze behaviour is the only one of these approaches that is able to provide reliable information on the actual focus of the user's attention. Even though it reflects only the overt attention – meaning that the user may be engaged with some cognitive processes not related to the focus of visual attention – the correlation between focus of attention and focus of visual attention is acknowledged to be strong (e.g., Posner 1980: 5). Although attention may shift without redirection of the focus of visual attention, there is some evidence that saccadic eye movements always produce a concurrent shift of attention (Groner and Groner 1989), which makes the correlation even stronger.

Next, we will survey the example applications that have been developed to make use of visual attention. Starting with the early examples where gaze has been used as one modality in multimodal interaction, we will gradually move towards more attentive systems and applications. We will survey the role of attention in controlling home appliances, in interacting with computer displays and in computer-mediated communication.

7.4   Early examples of gaze as indicator of visual attention

A classic example of multimodal interaction is the Put-That-There application (figure 7.2: see plate) by Bolt (1980). It was installed in a 'media room' with a wall-sized display. The user was seated in a chair that was surrounded by position-sensing equipment, to facilitate gesture tracking: the user could point at items displayed on the screen. The second modality supported was speech. Thus, the name of the system: users could issue spoken commands like 'put that there' while first pointing at one object on the screen, and then pointing at the target position.

Eye gaze was not among the modalities initially supported in Put-That-There, but it was soon added (Bolt 1982) as an alternative to the pointing gesture.

In Put-That-There gaze is not primarily an indicator of attention, but rather an explicitly controlled means to provide a parameter for the command. It was soon used in yet another way: gesturing and gaze indicated the same target while the spoken command was uttered (Bolt 1984). Much later experiments (Maglio *et al.* 2000; Oh *et al.* 2002) have shown that it is very natural to look at the target before issuing a spoken command, so this was a step in the direction of attentive interfaces. Yet the primary purpose was still issuing commands, but more reliably. Since both gesture recognition and eye tracking are inaccurate technologies, and were so particularly in the early days of Put-That-There, fusing information from the two sources helps to disambiguate commands that could be inaccurate with the use of just one modality (Thorisson, Koons and Bolt 1992).

Another experimental system developed at the same time by the same group, for the same media room, was called 'Gaze-Orchestrated Dynamic Windows' (Bolt 1981). There the display was filled with a large number of windows, each showing visual information. Some would replay a continuous video stream, others would show a still image. Looking at the video stream made it freeze briefly in order to provide feedback to the user that the gaze had been registered. A subsequent look at a still image would launch a video stream in that window. Each video stream had an accompanying soundtrack, and when several videos were being simultaneously replayed, the sound scene was noisy. Bolt contemplated various options for using gaze. The window under focus could have its soundtrack turned markedly louder than the soundtrack of the other windows, which would in turn be muted or attenuated. The window under focus could be zoomed in. But then the question arises of how to zoom out or interrupt the zoom operation. Perhaps another modality used in combination with eye gaze, such as the joystick embedded in the chair in the media room, would provide more natural control. This problem of finding a natural way to use eye gaze for communicating with computers has since been the focus of much research in the field.

In their basic form, Gaze-Orchestrated Dynamic Windows are unimodal systems, with gaze as the only input modality. They are probably the first example of a truly attentive, gaze-aware, adaptive system that makes use of the natural property of eye gaze as indicator of visual attention.

7.5   From the media room to real-world applications

The media room was demolished to make room for new experiments in the late 1980s, but similar ideas have later been implemented in more natural environments. The eyePliances of Roel Vertegaal's lab at Queen's University (Ontario) are a well-known example (Shell, Selker and Vertegaal 2003; Shell, Vertegaal and Skaburskis 2003). For instance, an attentive television (see figure 7.3, top (see plate)) can pause a movie when nobody is watching, and continue when there is eye contact again. In a multimodal context, an attentive light can be turned on and off by speaking the 'on' and 'off' commands. They only affect the device that the user is looking at, which is crucial for this scenario to work – a typical environment has numerous devices that could be switched on and off, and having them all react to spoken commands would render the speech modality unusable in this context. Eye gaze has been used in a similar manner for lighting control by Kembel (2003), but with gesture commands instead of speech.

Such applications are made possible by advancements in eye-tracking technology. Bolt's experiments were made with a tracking device attached in eye glasses and with a Polhemus system to track the head position. Obviously, a remote tracking system would be more desirable. Traditional eye-tracking systems are expensive and it is not feasible to assume that household appliances could be equipped with such technology. Instead, a new brand of trackers called 'eye contact sensors' has emerged. The technique was originally developed by Morimoto et al. (2000). It uses several light sources around the camera lens to produce both bright and dark pupil images; this makes it possible to detect the eyes of several people simultaneously. The commercially available product, eyebox2 by Xuuk, Inc., is shown in figure 7.3, bottom. It is small, provides tracking accuracy of 8° up to 3 metres, and further on an accuracy of 12° up to 8 metres. This is not sufficient for fine-grained target selection on a display, but it works fine for detecting whether a user is looking in the direction of a real-world object equipped with such a device.

7.6   Gaze in desktop interaction

The basic idea of Bolt's Gaze-Orchestrated Dynamic Windows has also been applied in the normal desktop environment. Fono and Vertegaal (2005) presented EyeWindows, an application where eye gaze is used to indicate the active window. The user could look at the window, and focus would move to that window either automatically (as soon as the user looks there) or after pressing a dedicated trigger key on the keyboard. As in Bolt's system, so too in EyeWindows would the window being focused on increase zoom. EyeWindows is particularly useful in that no mouse activity is needed to achieve the focus change, and hands can remain on the keyboard for the primary task. It does, however, assume a system of non-overlapping windows; obviously, it would be impossible to use gaze to focus on a window that is completely hidden.

In user tests carried out by Fono and Vertegaal (2005), automatic gaze-activated window switching proved to be more than 20 per cent faster than key-based activation. Both techniques clearly outperformed the use of the mouse or function keys (F1–F12) for window switching. However, users found key-based activation much easier to use than automatic switching: they felt that it was annoying when they could not look around while typing text – a glance at another window would have brought that in focus and directed the input stream incorrectly. In particular, non-touch typists could not easily look at the keyboard while typing, since moving the gaze from the active window to the keyboard could easily pass through another window. This made the users feel fatigued. Thus, Fono and Vertegaal conclude that using eyes to indicate the focus but letting the user perform the actual selection by a manual key press works considerably better than using the gaze alone.

The idea of combining the use of gaze as attention indicator and the use of special trigger keys was taken a step further in the EyePoint system developed in the GUIDe (Gaze-enhanced User Interface Design) project by Kumar, Paepcke and Winograd (2007). The basic operation in EyePoint is a look-press-look-release action: the user looks at the target, presses one of the many trigger keys (each with a different effect), the area of the screen being looked at is zoomed in on, and the action is carried out when the key is released. There are separate buttons for left and right click, for starting and ending click and drag, for double click, and for mouse over. The selected action affects the object being gazed at in the zoomed window at the time of release. Zooming was introduced to overcome the common inaccuracy of eye trackers that makes it hard to pinpoint small targets on the screen.

In the user study they carried out, Kumar, Paepcke and Winograd (2007) found that the speed of pointing and selection by EyePoint is on the same level as that of the mouse. The mouse has the benefit that as users are highly experienced with it, they can look at the target and move the pointer to it at the same time. This compensates for the motor movement time that is bound to be longer than the time needed for gaze movement. The biggest advantage for the mouse, however, was that it was more accurate than EyePoint. Nevertheless, EyePoint is a tempting option for users with such motor disabilities that the use of the mouse is out of the question.

Pointing and clicking is the most common operation with GUIs (Graphical User Interfaces). A special technique called manual and gaze input cascaded (MAGIC) pointing was developed for this task by Zhai, Morimoto and Ihde (1999). If the point of gaze is less than a given threshold away from a selectable object, MAGIC pointing automatically warps the mouse cursor close to the object. The remaining fine grain positioning is then carried out by the mouse as usual. The intended advantage is that the motor movement required by the mouse becomes smaller. MAGIC pointing came in two versions: conservative and liberal. In the first, a small mouse movement was required to initiate the warp, whereas in the liberal version the cursor would always warp when the gaze hit a suitable target.

A small user study indicated that MAGIC pointing was liked by users. The liberal technique was slightly faster than standard selection with the mouse, whereas the conservative version was slightly slower. The speed difference between MAGIC pointing and standard mouse pointing was not big enough to lead to commercialization of the idea. However, the situation may change with the recent growth in display size. This may reinforce the advantages gained by shortening the mouse movement. The same rationale motivated a recent study by Räihä and Špakov (2009). In their gaze-disambiguated Ninja cursors, several cursors can be used in a multi-monitor setting, and the cursor that is looked at is the active one. Again, this shortens the mouse movement, since one of the many cursors usually is closer to the target point than a single cursor would be. A user study showed that the technique did speed up target acquisition over long ranges (when the target was on a different monitor than the current focus) but not on short ranges. Some users preferred to have just one cursor per monitor, some preferred more cursors, but almost all preferred multiple cursors to the current standard of having just one cursor shared by all monitors.

7.7   Gaze as conversation aid

So far we have discussed applications of gaze for initiating or modifying an action. Sometimes the best use of gaze as attention indicator is simply to relay that information to other partners in a virtual conversation, just as we focus visually on the conversation partner in the real world.

The first example of the use of gaze for this purpose is the GAZE groupware system (Vertegaal 1999). GAZE supports video conferences of four persons, each sitting in front of their workstation equipped with an eye tracker. The screen of a participant in the conference shows pictures of the other three participants in pseudo-3D panes. The orientation of the pane indicates which of the other participants the person is looking at. This conveys much of the feeling of the focus of attention in a co-located meeting. In addition, a document window is displayed on the screen, and the part of the text focused on by each user is relayed to the other participants as coloured spots in the corresponding window on their screen. This helps in creating a frame of reference for the discussion without tedious explanation of which part of the text is currently under discussion.

The original GAZE system used still images of participants in the panes. This saved bandwidth but still conveyed the illusion of the participants' focus of attention. In a follow-up version, GAZE-2 (Vertegaal, Weevers and Sohn 2002), the still images were replaced by live video streams to increase the experience of a co-located conference further.

A similar idea has been applied in the context of a remote tourist consulting service (Qvarfordt, Beymer and Zhai 2005). In the first experiment, the RealTourist system facilitated communication between a customer and a consultant who were connected over the Internet. They saw the same map on their screens and could hear each other, but in addition the consultant could see the customer's eye movements replayed on her screen. This helped in the communication: if the consultant was explaining details about a target that the customer was not paying attention to, discussion could move on faster to targets of interest. The experience gathered through the use of RealTourist gave support in many ways to the usefulness of displaying the gaze information. (1) Eye gaze carries deictic and spatial reference information; hence, displaying it may reduce effort of frequent referencing. (2) Eye gaze reflects a listener's interest and can be used to judge whether to continue on the current conversation topic. (3) Eye gaze supports common focus coordination and topic switching. (4) Eye gaze reduces ambiguity and increases redundancy in communication.

As a follow-up to RealTourist, a fully computerized consulting system, iTourist, was built (Qvarfordt and Zhai 2005). The live remote consultant was replaced by a computer program that made use of recorded speech and images in providing tourist information. The feedback in a qualitative study with twelve participants was overwhelmingly positive: the participants liked the system, it very rarely talked about targets the participants were not interested in, and provided information on the targets that the participants were interested in fairly well.

Another way of using eye gaze for touristic information was introduced in the EyeGuide system (Eaddy et al. 2004). It used a wearable eye tracker that could detect the user's point of gaze on a map displayed on the wall (or, in the real-world scenario, in information displays around the city). When the user looked at a target destination, the system would whisper instructions on how to get to that destination in the earphone of the user. Furthermore, when the user visually traced the route on the map, the system would guide the user if they were distracted from the intended path. The non-audible interaction makes the approach useful when sensitive information is being transmitted.

Our final example of using eye gaze in conversation support comes from human–robot interaction. In human–human communication, gaze is an integral element of the dialogue. Speaking to a person who avoids eye contact is awkward, because a critical element of the feedback channel is missing. Similarly, maintaining eye contact with a robot, and being able to observe that the robot tries to maintain eye contact with you, makes human–robot contact much more like in the real world.

Perhaps the best-known example of a robot that can engage in social interaction is Kismet (see, e.g., Breazel 2003). It provides fine-grained control of the robot's eyes (eye balls, eyelids and eyebrows) to support social interaction with the human. Another early example of a robot providing such capability is PONG (Koons and Flickner 2003). PONG uses eye contact sensors like the ones used in eyePliances (see section 7.5) to detect eye contact. It has servomotors that can move the eye balls, eyebrows and lips to create truly expressive faces with simple, small adjustments (figure 7.4: see plate). Quoting Koons and Flickner: 'PONG expresses happiness on seeing the user and sadness when the user leaves. PONG engages by looking directly at the user and maintaining eye contact during conversation . . . A camera system finds the user's eyes so PONG can establish eye contact. Automatic speech recognition enables PONG to have a conversation. PONG knows its name and age, is very good at arithmetic, and can spell.'

Maintaining eye contact with a robot is one of the many research efforts being pursued in the rapidly expanding human–robot interaction community. Figure 7.5 shows one recent example by Yonezawa *et al.* (2007) (see plates). A remote eye tracker can detect where a person is looking and direct the robot to look at the same target to create a feeling of joint attention. Alternatively, when the person is looking at the robot, it can maintain eye contact. A user study showed that joint attention combined with the ability to maintain eye contact created in the user favourable feelings towards the robot.

7.8   Attentive and adaptive systems

We have seen many ways of making use of gaze as attention indicator in human–computer and human–robot interaction. Mostly, however, gaze information has been used to aid in interaction or communication. In this section we will take a look at applications where the knowledge of the user's attention changes the behaviour of the application or at least the information content on the display.

A classic example of this type of gaze-aware system is the ship database by Jacob (1991). The idea is simple and attractive: the main display (figure 7.6, top (see plates)) shows the locations of a collection of ships. To get information on a particular ship, all the user needs to do is look at the ship (EF-15 in the example) and then look at the information panel on the left. Gazing at the ship has caused the system to fetch and display the data about that ship. Thus, the system supports the task of the user without the need to issue explicit commands for retrieving the information.

Our iDict system (Hyrskykari 2006; figure 7.6, bottom) builds on the idea of the two panes in the ship database. iDict is a reading aid that helps non-native speakers in reading English text. The text of the document is shown in the left window frame. Eye tracking is used to detect when readers have difficulties with an unknown word or phrase. A gloss (short translation) is then displayed above the word. If this help is not sufficient, the reader can look at the frame on the right. Just like in the ship database, more information on the word has been fetched in the background and is displayed without any explicit commands. In this case the information consists of a full dictionary entry, including alternative translations for different meanings, and examples.

While this sounds easy on the surface, implementing the system so that it leads to a useful application with an enjoyable user experience required solving a number of problems. On a general level, the main questions were (1) when to display the additional information, (2) what to display, and (3) where and how to display it (Hyrskykari, Majaranta and Räihä 2003). The first question was particularly challenging: how does gaze behaviour indicate that the reader is struggling with a word? There are various alternatives: trouble in reading a word may lead to longer fixations, increased regressions back to the word, a higher number of fixations on the word, or an increased total dwell time on the word (the sum of the durations of all fixations landing on the word). After experimenting with these options, the last alternative was chosen, since it was the best predictor for when the reader really wanted to get help. After the total duration exceeded a threshold, the gloss was displayed. The threshold was dependent on the frequency of the word, so that for rare words the gloss was triggered sooner.

Before this approach works reliably, gaze points have to be mapped to the words and phrases. We applied a parser to break the text into lexical units to facilitate this. The inaccuracy of eye trackers was an additional difficulty that had to be solved when text was displayed with fairly normal line spacing (see figure 7.6, bottom). It was not uncommon for the reported gaze points to drift from one line to another while the reader was, in fact, progressing normally on one and the same line. For this, a more tolerant adaptive algorithm was implemented that allowed more variation in the vertical coordinates towards the end of the line.

A detailed discussion of this and the other design problems is given by Hyrskykari (2006). She also reports on a user study that was carried out. Three conditions were compared: gaze-triggered translations, mouse-triggered translations, and a combination of gaze and a dedicated trigger key (like the one used in EyeWindows and EyePoint: see section 7.6). Surprisingly, the last of these three options was the least liked by the participants in the experiment. Most of them wanted to have the translations triggered by gaze alone, or by the mouse alone, but not by a combination of two modalities.

For iDict it is important that the dictionary information is correct. If it is given for a word that the reader was not having trouble with, the reader's trust in the system could quickly decline. We found, however, that this only holds true for the information in the separate dictionary frame. Giving glosses for words that readers did not have trouble with often went unnoticed by the readers and did not disturb the reading experience. In different domains the relevance of the information may be less crucial. Maglio and Campbell (2003) present the SUITOR system that monitors the user who is reading a web page. The topic of the text being read is analysed automatically, and news items related to the topic are fetched from a newsfeed in the background. They are displayed in a news ticker at the bottom of the screen. The user may glance there at will, but since the linkage between the triggering text and the displayed text is weak, irrelevant news items could easily be ignored, just as irrelevant advertisements are routinely ignored by seasoned web users.

All the preceding examples in this section provide additional textual information based on attention. Some examples exist that make use of other modalities. Starker and Bolt (1990) developed a 3D world inspired by Antoine de Saint-Exupéry's book *The Little Prince*. It showed an imaginary planet that revolved slowly. A narrator gave spoken information about either the general scene or the whole planet depending on the user's gaze path, in a style that resembles the adaptation much later in iTourist (Qvarfordt and Zhai 2005) (see section 7.7). *The Little Prince* also inspired the winner of the COGAIN student competition in 2007 (COGAIN 2007), Ralf Biedert, who had implemented an electronic version of *The Little Prince*. When the user was reading a paragraph of text on the screen, the illustration related to that paragraph would appear next to it. This provided an engaging reading experience: the reader was tempted to read along, not only because of the interesting story, but also to see what illustrations would be revealed further along. This concept of augmenting the text based on the point of gaze has since been applied to other books too (Biedert *et al.* 2010).

The level of feedback that it is appropriate to show in an attentive system depends on the application. For example, gaze-guided interactive films can adapt to the user's interest based on either implicit or explicit use of gaze. Vesterby *et al.* (2005) conducted an experiment where half of the participants were aware that gaze could be used to control the narrative and the other half were unaware of the use of the control. In both groups participants' visual interest affected the story but in the latter the viewers were not aware of the implicit control. No explicit feedback was shown. Participants who were aware of the possibility of control were looking for confirmations of gaze selections, but some completely forgot it and concentrated on what was happening in the film. Vesterby *et al.* concluded that non-intrusive feedback seems to be crucial for successful gaze-interactive media but the feedback should not disturb immersion and concentration on the storyline.

In some applications, the user can greatly benefit from feedback based on gaze behaviour even if the actual gaze tracking happens in the background and the user is not expected to change his or her viewing behaviour. Ohno (2004) introduced EyePrint, an application that tracks the user's gaze while browsing digital documents (e.g., web pages). It supports later visits on the same documents by providing visual cues on the previously visited items. For example, it can provide different levels of highlighting on areas that have received a lot of attention from the user; the intensity of the highlight represents the greater level of activation (e.g., casual scanning vs. intensive reading). Another way to support the user is to use levels of zoom based on the user's interest: important areas and text get more space while low activation areas are decreased in size. This can make returning to important information easier. Furthermore, EyePrint supports searching by providing a restricted keyword search that only takes into account highly activated areas.

By keeping track of the user's gaze behaviour while viewing electronic content, it is possible to enhance interaction in various ways. Buscher and Dengel (2008) applied attention-based term extraction to personalized document classifying. They gave labels to documents based on the text and keywords the user paid most attention to, which might help the user in finding the information again later. Buscher, Dengel, and van Elst (2008) used gaze tracking to enhance personalized searches and to improve search result accuracy. They kept track of the parts the user had read and gave interest scores on parts that received more attention. Based on such 'gaze-filtering' of documents, they were able to expand and re-rank the queries so that they better matched the user's personal preferences and interests. Similarly, knowledge of the user's visual interest can result in better quality of personalized recommendations, as shown by Xu, Jiang and Lau (2008). Their system tracks the user's attention time over a collection of online documents, videos and images, and can predict the attention time for new materials based on prior behaviour. Results from an experiment show that their attention-based system can produce more accurate recommendations that better reflect the user expectations and preferences than current recommendation systems.

Finally, eye tracking can also bring benefits to educational applications. Wang, Chignell and Ishizuka (2006) propose empathic tutoring agents that are able to react to users' eye movements and pupil dilation. The data from pupil dilation is used to make assumptions on the user's emotional state and gaze direction indicates where the user's focus of attention is targeted at. With the extra information on the user's interest and emotions, combined with knowledge of the learner's (past) actions, the agents are able to respond with appropriate feedback. For example, the agents can remind the users of the current topic if they seem to lose concentration, or they can give more detailed information on a topic which seems to interest the student intensely. The agents also show emotions that reflect the user's stage. The agent appears happy if the learner is concentrating or empathetic if the learner gives a wrong reply. In addition, the system could react to natural eye movements as a more explicit input to the system. If the user nods or shakes their head, it is interpreted as 'yes' or 'no', and a long dwell on a target causes it to be selected and more information to be shown on it. Results from a preliminary test indicate that users appreciated the feedback given by the system on their eye movements, for example, when the system zoomed in and gave more information on a picture they looked at. However, some users did not like it when the agent gave them warning messages when the learner seemed to lose interest in the topic.

7.9   Discussion and conclusions

Advances in eye-tracking technology have led to numerous new ways to apply the attention information available in gaze data to human–human and human–computer interaction. The recent miniaturization of the technology, especially, can open new commercial opportunities. Imagine, for instance, a TV equipped with an eye-contact sensor. While it may be questionable whether one would want the replay of a DVD film always to stop when the watcher's visual attention is diverted, the set-up can find other uses. For instance, TV show audience ratings are currently based solely on the number of devices that are turned on and tuned-in to a particular station. If, in addition, the TV could automatically take into account the number of people watching that particular set, the numbers would be more reliable. As another example, billboards that collect information on how many people watch them, and for how long, could be valuable for advertisers.

The development of attentive interfaces is still in its early phases. Drawing a clear line between command-and-control interfaces and attentive interfaces is not easy – in fact, it may be impossible. iDict was designed to be a fully attentive system. However, when users realized how the system functioned, they learned to control it deliberately by staring at a word long enough to have the gloss pop up. Such behaviour is neither avoidable nor undesirable. After all, the goal of attentive, adaptive systems is to help the users unobtrusively in their task, and if the user finds a good way to help the system in this, all the better.

Although gaze direction is currently the best indicator of visual attention that one can imagine, equally important is the attention of the user on the cognitive level – and it may be different. One can stare at the display without really perceiving it, if the mind is occupied with something else. Rudmann, McConkie and Zheng (2003) carried out an experiment in which participants were presented with a gear-assembly problem on the screen. When the image of the gear arrangement was turned off suddenly, 73 per cent of participants reported thinking of a particular region of the screen, but gaze data showed that actually only 46 per cent had looked at it when, or just before, the display was turned off. Thus, whether gaze direction reflects the cognitive state of a person depends a lot on the task with which the person is occupied. Some results in eye-movement analysis (Velichkovsky *et al.* 2002) suggest that it may be possible to distinguish between 'ambient' viewing (when the viewer's attention is not focused on the area reflected in the fovea) and 'focal' viewing by analysing the lengths of fixations and the amplitudes of saccades together. If the results can be operationalized reliably, attentive interfaces can be built more robustly to help in adapting the interface so that it better matches the cognitive state of the user.

Research on gaze-based attentive interfaces is still relatively new, but new applications appear at an increasing rate. Many factors (eye trackers getting cheaper and less obtrusive, better understanding of how to interpret eye-movement data, and proven benefits of the adaptation and engagement) lead us to believe that it will not take long before such features can be found as elements of commodity software.

7.10   Acknowledgements

This work was partially supported by two projects funded by the European Commission (COGAIN, IST-2003-511598 (NoE), and EYE-to-IT, FET-2005-517590) and by the Academy of Finland (project 1111658).

7.11   References

Abrams, R. A., and Christ, S. E. 2003. Motion onset captures attention, *Psychological Science* 14: 427–32

Bartram, L., Ware, C., and Calvert, T. 2003. Moticons: Detection, distraction and task, *International Journal of Human–Computer Studies* 58: 515–45

Baudisch, P., DeCarlo, D., Duchowski, A. T., and Geisler, W. S. 2003. Focusing on the essential: Considering attention in display design, *Communications of the ACM* 46(3): 60–66, http://doi.acm.org/10.1145/636772.636799

Biedert, R., Buscher, G., Schwarz, S., Hees, J., and Dengel, A. 2010. Text 2.0, in *Proceedings Extended Abstracts of Conference on Human Factors in Computing Systems (CHI EA '10)*, Atlanta, GA: ACM Press: 4003–8, http://doi.acm.org/10.1145/1753846.1754093

Bolt, R. A. 1980. 'Put-That-There': Voice and gesture at the graphics interface, in *Proceedings of the 7th Annual Conference on Computer Graphics and Interactive Techniques (SIGGRAPH'80)*, Seattle, WA: ACM Press: 262–70, http://doi.acm.org/10.1145/800250.807503

1981. Gaze-orchestrated dynamic windows, in *Proceedings of the 8th Annual Conference on Computer Graphics and Interactive Techniques (SIGGRAPH'81)*, Dallas, TX: ACM Press: 109–19, http://doi.acm.org/10.1145/800224. 806796

1982. Eyes at the interface, in *Proceedings of the 1982 Conference on Human Factors in Computing Systems (CHI'82)*, Gaithersburg, MD: ACM Press: 360–2, http://doi.acm.org/10.1145/800049.801811

1984. *The Human Interface*. New York: Van Nostrand Reinhold

Breazel, C. 2003. Emotion and sociable humanoid robots, *International Journal of Human–Computer Studies* 59(1–2): 119–55

Buscher, G., and Dengel, A. 2008. Attention-based document classifier learning, in *Proceedings of the 8th IAPR Workshop on Document Analysis Systems (DAS'08)*, Nara, Japan: IEEE Xplore: 87–94

Buscher, G., Dengel, A., and van Elst, L. 2008. Query expansion using gaze-based feedback on the subdocument level, in *Proceedings of the 31st Annual International ACM SIGIR Conference on Research and Development in Information Retrieval (SIGIR'08)*, Singapore: ACM Press: 387–94, http://doi.acm. org/10.1145/1390334.1390401

COGAIN 2007. COGAIN Student Competition Results. European Network of Excellence on Communication by Gaze Interaction. Retrieved 13 July 2010 from: www.cogain.org/node/41

Duchowski, A. T. 2002. A breadth-first survey of eye tracking applications, *Behavior Research Methods, Instruments, and Computers (BRMIC)* 34: 455–70

Duncan, J. 1984. Selective attention and the organization of visual information, *Journal of Experimental Psychology* 113: 501–17

Eaddy, M., Blasko, G., Babcock, J., and Feiner, S. 2004. My own private kiosk: Privacy-preserving public displays, in *Proceedings 8th International Symposium on Wearable Computers (ISWC'04)*, Arlington, WA: IEEE Computer Society: 132–5

Fono, D., and Vertegaal, R. 2005. EyeWindows: Evaluation of eye-controlled zooming windows for focus selection, in *Proceedings SIGCHI Conference on Human Factors in Computing Systems (CHI'05)*, Portland, OR: ACM Press: 151–60, http://doi.acm.org/10.1145/1054972.1054994

Franconeri, S. L., and Simons, D. J. 2003. Moving and looming stimuli capture attention, *Perception and Psychophysics* 65(7): 999–1010

Groner, R., and Groner, M. T. 1989. Attention and eye movement control: An overview, *European Archives of Psychiatry and Neurological Sciences* 239(1): 9–16

Horvitz, E., Kadie, C., Paek, T., and Hovel, D. 2003. Models of attention in computing and communication: From principles to applications, *Communications of the ACM* 46(3): 52–9, http://doi.acm.org/10.1145/636772. 636798

Hyrskykari, A. 2006. Eyes in attentive interfaces: Experiences from creating iDict, a gaze-aware reading aid. Dissertations in Interactive Technology 4, Department of Computer Sciences, University of Tampere. Retrieved 13 July 2010 from: http://acta.uta.fi/pdf/951-44-6643-8.pdf

Hyrskykari, A., Majaranta, P., and Räihä, K.-J. 2003. Proactive response to eye movements, in *Proceedings of INTERACT 2003*, M. Rauterberg, M. Menozzi and J. Wesson (eds.), Zurich: IOS Press: 129–36

2005. From gaze control to attentive interfaces, in *Proceedings of the HCII 2005*, Las Vegas

Jacob, R. J. K. 1991. The use of eye movements in human–computer interaction techniques: What you look at is what you get, *ACM Transactions on Information Systems* 9(2): 152–69, http://doi.acm.org/10.1145/123078.128728

Kembel, J. A. 2003. Reciprocal eye contact as an interaction technique, in *Extended Abstracts of SIGCHI Conference on Human Factors in Computing Systems (CHI'03)*, Ft Lauderdale, FL: ACM Press: 952–3, http://doi.acm.org/10.1145/765891.766089

Koons, D., and Flickner, M. 2003. PONG: The attentive robot, *Communication of the ACM* 46(3): 50 (sidebar), http://doi.acm.org/10.1145/636772.636797

Kumar, M., Paepcke, A., and Winograd, T. 2007. EyePoint: Practical pointing and selection using gaze and keyboard, in *Proceedings of the SIGCHI Conference on Human Factors in Computing Systems (CHI'07)*, San Jose, CA: ACM Press: 421–30, http://doi.acm.org/10.1145/1240624.1240692

Lieberman, H. A., and Selker, T. 2000. Out of context: Computer systems that adapt to, and learn from, context, *IBM Systems Journal* 39: 617–31

Maglio, P. P., and Campbell, C. S. 2003. Attentive agents, *Communication of the ACM* 46(3): 47–51, http://doi.acm.org/10.1145/636772.636797

Maglio, P. P., Matlock, T., Campbell, C. S., Zhai, S., and Smith, B. A. 2000. Gaze and speech in attentive user interfaces, in *Proceedings of the 3rd International Conference on Advances in Multimodal Interfaces (ICMI 2000)*, Beijing 1–7

Majaranta, P., and Räihä, K.-J. 2007. Text entry by gaze: Utilizing eye-tracking, in I. S. MacKenzie and K. Tanaka-Ishii (eds.), *Text Entry Systems: Mobility, Accessibility, Universality*. San Francisco: Morgan Kaufmann: 175–87

Morimoto, C. H., Koons, D., Amir, A., and Flickner, M. 2000. Pupil detection and tracking using multiple light sources, *Image and Vision Computing* 18(4): 331–5

Oh, A., Fox, H., Van Kleek, M., Adler, A., Gajos, K., Morency, L.-P., and Darrell, T. 2002. Evaluating Look-to-Talk: A gaze-aware interface in a collaborative environment, in *Extended Abstracts of SIGCHI Conference on Human Factors in Computing Systems (CHI'02)*, Minneapolis: ACM Press: 650–1, http://doi.acm.org/10.1145/506443.506528

Ohno, T. 2004. EyePrint: Support of document browsing with eye gaze trace, in *Proceedings of the 6th International Conference on Multimodal Interfaces (ICMI'04)*, State College, PA: ACM Press: 16–23, http://doi.acm.org/10.1145/1027933.1027937

Pashler, H., Johnston, J. C., and Ruthruff, E. 2001. Attention and performance, *Annual Review of Psychology* 52: 629–51

Porta, M. 2002. Vision-based user interfaces: Methods and applications, *International Journal of Human–Computer Studies* 57: 27–73

Posner, M. I. 1980. Orienting of attention, *Quarterly Journal of Experimental Psychology* 32: 3–25

Qvarfordt, P., Beymer, D., and Zhai, S. 2005. RealTourist: A study of augmenting human–human and human–computer dialogue with eye-gaze overlay, in M. F. Costabile and F. Paternò (eds.), *Proceedings of INTERACT 2005*, Rome: Springer: 767–80

Qvarfordt, P., and Zhai, S. 2005. Conversing with the user based on eye-gaze patterns, in *Proceedings SIGCHI Conference on Human Factors in Computing Systems (CHI'05)*, Portland, OR: ACM Press: 221–30, http://doi.acm.org/10.1145/1054972.1055004

Räihä, K.-J., and Špakov, O. 2009. Disambiguating Ninja cursors with eyegaze, in *Proceedings of the 27th International Conference on Human Factors in Computing Systems (CHI'09)*, Boston: ACM Press, http://doi.acm.org/10.1145/1518701.1518913

Raskin, J. 2000. *The Humane Interface*. Reading, MA: Addison-Wesley

Roda, C., and Thomas, J. 2006a. Attention aware systems: Introduction to special issue, *Computers in Human Behavior* 22(4): 555–6

    2006b. Attention aware systems: Theories, applications, and research agenda. *Computers in Human Behavior* 22(4): 557–87

Rudmann, D. S., McConkie, G. W., and Zheng, X. S. 2003. Eyetracking in cognitive state detection for HCI, in *Proceedings of the 5th International Conference on Multimodal Interfaces (ICMI'03)*, Vancouver: ACM Press: 159–63, http://doi.acm.org/10.1145/958432.958464

Selker, T. 2004. Visual attentive interfaces, *BT Technology Journal* 22: 146–50

Shell, J. S., Selker, T., and Vertegaal, R. 2003. Interacting with groups of computers, *Communications of the ACM* 46(3): 40–6, http://doi.acm.org/10.1145/636772.636796

Shell, J. S., Vertegaal, R., and Skaburskis, A. W. 2003. EyePliances: Attention-seeking devices that respond to visual attention, in *Extended Abstracts of SIGCHI Conference on Human Factors in Computing Systems (CHI'03)*, Fort Lauderdale, FL: ACM Press: 770–1, http://doi.acm.org/10.1145/765891.765981

Sibert, L. E., and Jacob, R. J. K. 2000. Evaluation of eye gaze interaction, in *Proceedings of the SIGCHI Conference on Human Factors in Computing Systems (CHI 2000)*, The Hague: ACM Press: 281–8, http://doi.acm.org/10.1145/332040.332445

Starker, I., and Bolt, R. A. 1990. A gaze-responsive self-disclosing display, in *Proceedings of the SIGCHI Conference on Human Factors in Computing Systems (CHI'90)*, Seattle: ACM Press: 3–10, http://doi.acm.org/10.1145/97243.97245

Thorisson, K. R., Koons, D. B., and Bolt, R. A. 1992. Multi-modal natural dialogue, in *Proceedings of the SIGCHI Conference on Human Factors in Computing Systems (CHI'92)*, Monterey, CA: ACM Press: 653–4, http://doi.acm.org/10.1145/142750.150714

Velichkovsky, B. M., Rothert, A., Kopf, M., Dornhoefer, S. M., and Joos, M. 2002. Towards an express diagnostics for level of processing and hazard perception, *Transportation Research, Part F*, 5(2): 145–56

Vertegaal, R. 1999. The GAZE groupware system: Mediating joint attention in multiparty communication and collaboration, in *Proceedings of the SIGCHI*

Conference on Human Factors in Computing Systems (CHI'99), Pittsburgh: ACM Press: 294–301, http://doi.acm.org/10.1145/302979.303065

2003. Introduction to special issue on 'Attentive user interfaces', *Communications of the ACM* 46(3): 30–3, http://doi.acm.org/10.1145/636772.636794

Vertegaal, R., Weevers, I., and Sohn, C. 2002. GAZE-2: An attentive video conferencing system, in *Extended Abstracts of SIGCHI Conference on Human Factors in Computing Systems (CHI'02)*, Minneapolis: ACM Press: 736–7, http://doi.acm.org/10.1145/506443.506572

Vesterby, T., Voss, J. C., Hansen, J. P., Glenstrup, A. J., Hansen, D. W., and Rudolph, M. 2005. Gaze-guided viewing of interactive movies, *Digital Creativity* 16(4): 193–204

Wang, H., Chignell, M., and Ishizuka, M. 2006. Empathic tutoring software agents using real-time eye tracking, in *Proceedings of the 2006 Symposium on Eye Tracking Research and Applications (ETRA'06)*, San Diego: ACM Press: 73–8, http://doi.acm.org/10.1145/1117309.1117346

Ware, C. 2008. *Visual Thinking for Design*. Burlington, MA: Morgan Kaufmann

Wolfe, J. M. 1998. Visual search, in H. Pashler (ed.), *Attention* (5th edn). Hove: Psychology Press: 13–73

Xu, S., Jiang, H., and Lau, F. C. 2008. Personalized online document, image and video recommendation via commodity eye-tracking, in *Proceedings of the 2008 ACM Conference on Recommender Systems (RecSys'08)*, Lausanne, Switzerland: ACM Press: 83–90, http://doi.acm.org/10.1145/1454008.1454023

Yantis, S., and Jonides, J. 1990. Abrupt visual onsets and selective attention: Voluntary versus automatic allocation, *Journal of Experimental Psychology* 16(1): 121–34

Yonezawa, T., Yamazoe, H., Utsumi, A., and Abe, S. 2007. Gaze-communicative behavior of stuffed-toy robot with joint attention and eye contact based on ambient gaze-tracking, in *Proceedings of the 9th International Conference on Multimodal Interfaces (ICMI'07)*, Nagoya, Japan: 140–5, http://doi.acm.org/10.1145/1322192.1322218

Zhai, S. 2003. What's in the eyes for attentive input? *Communications of the ACM* 46(3): 34–9, http://doi.acm.org/10.1145/636772.636795

Zhai, S., Morimoto, C., and Ihde, S. 1999. Manual and gaze input cascaded (MAGIC) pointing, in *Proceedings of the SIGCHI Conference on Human Factors in Computing Systems (CHI'99)*, Pittsburgh, PA: ACM Press: 246–53, http://doi.acm.org/10.1145/302979.303053

8   Contextualized attention metadata

Hans-Christian Schmitz, Martin Wolpers,
Uwe Kirschenmann and Katja Niemann

We describe and justify the use of a schema for contextualized attention meta-
data (CAM) and a framework for capturing and exploiting such data. CAM
are data about computer-related activities and the foci of attention for computer
users. As such, they are a prerequisite for the personalization of both infor-
mation and task environments. We outline the possibilities of utilizing CAM,
with a focus on technology-enhanced learning (TEL) scenarios, presenting the
MACE system for architecture education as a CAM test bed.

8.1   Introduction

8.1.1   Contextualized attention metadata

The contextualized attention metadata (CAM) format, defined by an
XML schema, is a format for data about the foci of attention and activities of computer users. Contextualized attention metadata describe which
data objects attract the users' attention, which actions users perform
with these objects and what the use contexts are. As such, they are a
prerequisite for generating context-specific user profiles that help to personalize and optimize task and information environments. They can be
employed for annotating data objects with information about their users
and usages, thereby rendering possible object classifications according
to use frequency, use contexts and user groups. Moreover, they can be
crucial for supporting cooperative work: they may be utilized for monitoring distributed task processing, for identifying and sharing knowledge
of critical information, and for bringing together working groups (Schuff
et al. 2007; Hauser *et al.* 2009; Adomavicius and Tuzhilin 2005, among
others).

8.1.2   Example application scenario

The following is a scenario for an attention-aware system that exploits
contextualized attention metadata (Wolpers *et al.* 2007; Rapp 2006): a

lecturer begins the design of an online course, but interrupts her work on the course before returning to it again. In previous interactions the system in question generated a task profile, but on this occasion it recognizes the ongoing task of designing the online course and recovers the working environment accordingly. The system presents a task history and opens unfinished documents with the appropriate tools. (We call this *task recovery*.) While the lecturer works on the course material, the system accommodates itself to the lecturer's preferences, tasks and activities. It automatically generates search queries and acquires relevant information in order to provide the lecturer with new learning material that is suitable with respect both to the course she is designing and to her activity profile, which was generated during previous sessions. The lecturer prefers to receive only information related to the course; consequently, the system, for instance, temporarily hides emails not relevant to the current task. (We call this *task support* and *personalization*.)

Let us assume that a similar online course has been held before. The learning objects used in this course have been annotated with contextualized attention metadata captured from the students who were enrolled on the course. The lecturer analyses the metadata and finds out how the students used the course and which kinds of learning objects attracted their attention. She derives the students' learning strategies, compares the learning strategies of students who finished the course with a high grade with the strategies of students who finished with a low grade, and infers which learning strategies were most effective and should therefore be supported. She uses this information in order to tailor the new course according to the students' needs and preferences (We call this *course evaluation*.)

When the design of the new course is finished and the course is online, the students' actual usages are monitored. The learning system advises the students of important material that they have not found and used so far. It suggests other students who may be able to help with specific problems, and it helps to set up effective working groups. It actively supports a collaborative learning process. (We call this *task support* and *personalization*.)

In examples like the scenario just described, we capture contextualized attention metadata from the students' interactions with the online course and from the lecturer's usage of application programs for designing the course. We merge the metadata for generating user profiles, which in turn we use for course optimization (through the evaluation of individual learning strategies) and information retrieval (by the use of an automatic search for material with respect to the students' and the lecturer's profiles), among other tasks. Moreover, we use the metadata for describing and classifying documents, in particular learning objects. Also, a task profile serves to adapt the lecturer's working environment.

8.1.3   Outline of the chapter

In this chapter, we first define our basic terminology (in particular our usages of the terms 'attention' and 'attention metadata') and the purposes attention metadata serve. Then we describe CAM (contextualized attention metadata) as a formalized digital representation of user attention. We describe the format's essential structure and the directions in which it is being developed. We continue by defining a general framework for capturing, storing and analysing CAM, by developing an infrastructure for the generation and exploitation of CAM. Following this, we discuss possible ways of exploiting CAM, and we outline applications and a test bed.

8.2   Basic terminology and objectives

8.2.1   Attention and attention metadata

Let us first define our basic terminology: the theoretical term 'attention' can refer both to cognitive mechanisms of data selection and to actual data selection behaviour, that is, the *attending-to* behaviour of agents (Mole 2009). We will use the term 'attention' as referring to *attending-to* behaviour. Agents can attend to things of diverse types. They can attend to objects (e.g., *Katja attends to the email that she has just received*), to properties (e.g., *Uwe attends to the style and orthography of a particular paper*) and to propositions (e.g., *Martin attends to the fact that he has exceeded his disk quota*), among others. By attending to something, an agent focuses on this 'thing' (object, property or proposition) and thereby selects it for further cognitive processing. Agents do not always attend to the same thing; their foci of attention change. Therefore, attention is dynamic.

If we want to detect an agent's attention, we have to observe her. We cannot observe her attention directly, but we can observe her activities. From her activities we infer which things she attends to. To this end, we presume that certain activities require attention. For example, we presume that an agent who opens a web page and, after a while, clicks on a link, attends to this page. Thus, from the observations of the agent's activities we conclude that she is (or has been) in a particular attentional state. This conclusion is reliable, although in principle defeasible, since the possibility remains that the agent opens the web page and clicks on the link by accident while attending to something entirely different. Furthermore, from our observations we can conclude that the agent attends to the particular web page but we cannot conclude that she attends to its content, style or orthography. Thus, our observations fail to determine the agent's attention in this respect. In order to infer that she attended to a particular property of the page, we have to include and interpret further observations. For example, it seems reliable to infer that she attended to the content of the web page from the observation that she copied some part of the page and pasted it into another document. That is, we presuppose that there are strong correlations of observable actions and attention.

Attention is selection (see above). An act of selecting something (like a focus of attention) is not fully defined by the things being selected, but also by the set from which these things are being selected. Thus, the actual attention of an agent is defined both by the things the agent currently focuses on and by the set of available things upon which the agent might have chosen to focus, but has not. In laboratory situations, it can be possible to determine the set of available things. Suppose that a test subject has to focus her attention on the colour of a particular triangle displayed on a screen. The set of available things comprises all objects on the screen, including their forms (triangle, square, etc.), sizes and colours; the focused-on colour of the chosen triangle belongs to this set of available things. In real-world situations, however, it might be (and mostly will be) impossible to determine the set of available things. First, the boundary between availability and unavailability is vague. Consider the case that Uwe is attending to a web page. What are the available things from which Uwe can select? All the pages of the particular website? All the pages related by links to the website? Or even the entire World Wide Web? Do parts and properties of web pages also belong to the available things? These questions cannot be easily answered because we are not provided with a definite criterion for defining the boundary between availability and unavailability. Second, the number of available things can be just too large to enumerate them practically. Therefore, in real-world situations we are mostly unable to define the attention of an agent exhaustively.

An expression (or a sequence of expressions) that specifies an agent's attention is an *attention representation*. Attention representations serve purposes: they can form the basis for a theory of the cognitive mechanisms of data selection; in market research, they can be used for analysing which products have raised a customer's interest (Hauser *et al.* 2009); they can form the basis for detecting the tasks and goals of an agent, for analysing her learning strategies, and so on. There are purposes that do not require exhaustive attention representations (including enumerations of all available objects). For some purposes – e.g., for a product recommender system – it can be sufficient to evaluate only the objects that an agent attends to without taking the alternatives into account. It may also be that information on how often she attends to a certain object and on the chronological order of this attention can be ignored. Thus, it might be sufficient to represent her attention by merely naming the set of objects to which she attends. However, some purposes require more than pure attention representations. Additional information on the agent, on the activities correlated with her attention (for instance, whether attending to a text document involved changing it) and on further contextual parameters might be required. The cognitive mechanisms of data selection, for example, are most probably context-sensitive; therefore, if these mechanisms are to be explored, information on the contexts of actual attending-to behaviour is required.

To conclude so far: there are interesting attention-aware systems that do not require exhaustively specified attention representations. The lack of determinacy of attention therefore need not be a problem for the design of an attention-aware system. However, for some purposes pure attention representations are not sufficient. To meet these purposes, attention representations have to be enriched, for instance, with further information on the observed agent's activities and the context in which she is acting.

8.2.2   Objectives

Our aim is to observe computer users, to record their attentions and to use these recordings for diverse purposes like the detection of their tasks and goals, the generation of attention-based user- and object-profiles, and so on. We record a user's attention on a macro-level rather than on a micro-level. In our terms, 'micro-level attention' refers to highly dynamic, short-term *attending-to* behaviour like, for instance, focusing on single words while reading a text. In contrast, 'macro-level attention' refers to a more stable, long-term *attending-to* behaviour like, for instance, attending to a text in its entirety by reading or writing it.[1] For recording user attention, we need tools for capturing observations. Moreover, we need a formalized digital representation to be able to describe, merge, store and process streams of observations; that is, we need an attention metadata[2]

---

[1] For capturing activities indicating micro- and macro-level attention see Atterer (2006).

[2] Metadata are data about data; attention metadata are data about attention, not about data in the narrower sense. Is there a good reason for speaking of attention *meta*data instead of attention data? One reason to call these data metadata is that they have been

format. We want user-observation to be non-obtrusive; we ensure non-obtrusiveness by capturing attention metadata only from the computer applications being used. Consequently, attention metadata (as we define them) are at the least underspecified representations of the attending-to behaviour of computer users engaged in interaction with application programs. They can also contain further information on the agent's actions, the contexts of action and on the data objects in question.

8.2.3   Stock-taking

Let us take stock: (1) We understand *attention* as *attending-to* behaviour. (2) *Attention metadata* are *representations of attention*. (3) *Attention metadata schemata* are representation formats. (4) Our aim is to observe computer users and record their attentions. We observe activities in which a computer user carries out an action on a data object like a file or an email message. We call these activities *events*. An example of an event is 'user x opens file y'. (5) Our *observations* depend on our observation instruments. Thus, our observations are restricted. (6) Our observations are represented as attention metadata. Records of attention metadata – for short, *attention records* – need not represent everything that is observed. For example, we might observe that a user opens, changes, saves and closes a document, but instead we record only that she attends to the document. In this case, the attention record does not entail the user's actions. However, it can also be that attention records are more than pure attention representations: aside from a user's attention, they can represent her actions and action contexts, among other things. (7) Only in exceptional cases will an attention record be a complete representation of an attentional state or a sequence of attentional states. Mostly, attention records will contain the objects that have been in the focus of attention but not the particular aspects or properties that have been attended to, nor the available alternatives that the user did not attend to. Therefore, attention records are in this respect incomplete. This, however, need not be a crucial problem for the design of an attention-aware system.

---

called metadata in the literature – we do not want to change an established terminology. Moreover, as we will see, attention metadata are not only data describing actions and attentional states of users. They can also be focused on data objects, thereby describing how much attention has been spent on certain objects and what has been done with these objects. That is, attention metadata can be interpreted as data about data objects, that is, as metadata.

8.3   From Attention.XML to contextualized attention metadata (CAM)

8.3.1   Attention metadata

A format for attention metadata must fulfil two preconditions. First, it must be a format for data that can be captured without disturbing the user in her everyday work. That is, capturing these data must not require obtrusive sensors like eye-trackers and so on. As a consequence, attention metadata as we understand them describe user behaviour rather on a macro- than on a micro-level (see above). We account for the granularity level in the format specification. Second, attention metadata must provide rich sets of information on user attention, which can be related to descriptions of use context, at the same time avoiding as much data noise as possible. For this reason, we observe the user at the level of application, rather than monitoring such things as keystrokes and mouse movements (see Wolpers *et al.* 2007).

Attention.XML (Attention.XML 2004; Çelik 2005) is an early approach to capturing and storing attention metadata that meets these preconditions. Its conception is based on three premises. First, attention metadata are recorded for single users. Second, attention records are bags of data objects that have been in the user's focus (contrary to sets, bags can contain the same element twice; contrary to lists, bags are not ordered). These objects can be ordered according to the time when they have been in the focus of attention. Third, users receive data objects through diverse channels; the objects are sorted according to these channels. For instance, when a user receives messages through a newsfeed channel and accesses web pages with her browser, then her attention record comprises two bags of objects, one for the newsfeed and one for the browser. Attention.XML records are stored as XML files. The root element *group* comprises the respective user's name (*title*) and a set of channels (*blog*, *feed*, *site*). The channel elements contain *item* elements that refer to the data objects that have been in the user's focus. *Item*s have several sub-elements for specifying properties like the respective item's *title*, *type* and *GUID* and information on its usage like *lastRead*, *duration* and *followedLinks*.

Attention.XML has been criticized for not being able to record a user's attention in sufficient detail. First, Attention.XML records data objects but not what the user does with those objects. This is a crucial drawback when complex interactions – for instance, updating a text or manipulating a spreadsheet – are to be recorded or when joint activities of multiple users are to be analysed. Second, Attention.XML does not describe use

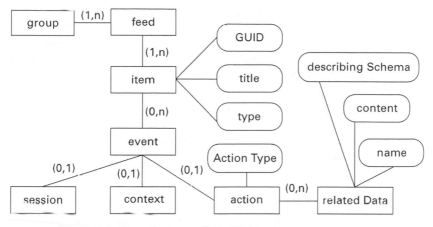

Figure 8.1 Core elements of the CAM schema

contexts. It neither specifies the sets of objects from which the user selects her foci nor further circumstances of her selection. Therefore, attention metadata cannot be evaluated with respect to specific contexts.

8.3.2   Contextualized attention metadata

As a consequence, the CAM schema (*contextualized attention metadata* schema) has been defined as an extension of Attention.XML (Wolpers *et al.* 2007). The most important extensions focus CAM on actions that occur on data objects. To this end, the following elements are added to a slightly modified version of Attention.XML: each *item* (that is, each data object) may be involved in several *events*. Events are associated with a timestamp (*datetime*) and a *description*, among others. An event can be associated with an *action* of a certain *type*, including action-*related data*. For instance, when an email message is sent, the message is an *item* (data object) involved in an *event* with a *send-action*. Events occur in *contexts*, and they are part of technical *sessions*, e.g., a browser session. The CAM schema is only partially specified for *context*-elements: *context*-elements can contain arbitrary *value*- and *value type*-elements. Within the *session*-element a session ID, the IP address of the user's computer and further information on the involved users are collected. A complete description of the CAM schema is given by Wolpers and colleagues (2007). The core elements – not the entire CAM schema – are depicted in figure 8.1.

CAM is developed to describe as many types of attention metadata as possible. CAM follows the Attention.XML approach that attention records contain bags in which *items* represent data objects (actually,

CAM records contain sets instead of bags of items); for each data object, *action-*, *context-* and *session-related data* via *event*s are added. CAM records of a user, therefore, do not merely describe the user's foci of attention, but rather her entire computer usage behaviour. The CAM schema is essentially a unified schema for usage metadata: all metadata related to usage behaviour are stored within one structure.

Collections of CAM records can be exploited for generating diverse kinds of profiles like user profiles and object profiles (*item* profiles). CAM records represent a user's computer-related foci of attention and actions. As such, they instantly constitute profiles of individual users' computer usage behaviour. These user action profiles can be augmented with other information on the users which is, for instance, extracted from a learning management system as in our example above. Moreover, CAM records of different users can be exploited for generating attention- and usage-based object profiles. Object profiles make content relationships, usage relationships and social relationships explicit, taking into account advanced social information like information on the role a user has when using the object, with whom the user is collaborating on the object, etc. User and object profiles are entailed by CAM collections; they can be derived by simple data transformations.

8.3.3   Further development

The CAM schema is a very rich attention metadata schema and provides powerful means for describing, storing, merging and processing streams of user observation. However, it is still under development. The following issues lead to a revision. First, tasks are not explicitly specified within the original CAM schema. Suppose that we want to transform CAM records of several users into object profiles: every object that occurs within the CAM records will be annotated with usage-related information about both the users of the object and the circumstances under which it was used. We generate object profiles by mere transformations of CAM datasets. It would be an advantage if we were able to relate the objects to the tasks that the users were carrying out when they used the objects and thus to augment the object profiles with task-related information. Moreover, it would be an advantage if we were able to transform CAM records into generic task profiles, as suggested in the example given in the introductory section. To this end, we need information on the particular tasks. Either CAM records contain this information directly or they contain pointers to external task representations. Currently, the CAM schema provides neither an element for a direct task representation nor a pointer to such a representation. One way to solve the problem is to introduce a *task*-element as a further sub-element of *event*. The *task*-element has to contain a *title*-, an *ID*-, a *description*- and a *type*-element by which a task can be named, identified, described and categorized with respect to a task ontology. Note that at this stage it does not matter from where the task-related information is retrieved. Task-related information might be determined by analysing CAM records; it is then added as a supplement to already existing records. Alternatively, the information might be captured from tools like TaskTracer (Dragunov *et al.* 2005) which allow users to specify the tasks they are currently working on themselves; it is then inserted into CAM records before further analysis is carried out.

The second issue in the revision of CAM is the semi-structured nature of elements like *context*-, *session*- and *action-related data*. These elements serve as containers for diverse kinds of data. The *related data* sub-element of *action* can, for instance, contain content data (like keywords) or lists of email recipients, among other things. On the one hand, this is an advantage, since it makes CAM flexible and allows the integration of different kinds of metadata. On the other hand, it forms an obstacle for data exchange and automatic evaluation. A possible solution is to import different metadata schemata for structuring different kinds of metadata. Contents of elements like *context*-, *session*- and *action-related data* are then provided with links to their format definitions.

The third issue is the redundancy of sets of CAM records. Sets of CAM records are redundant, for instance, when semantic information on data objects (like keyword lists) is stored as *action-related data*. When a data object is involved in several events, the semantic information is stored for each event even if the event does not affect the object's semantic properties. For example, Katja opens an email message and then moves it to a particular folder. The keyword list of the email message is stored twice, namely within the *related data* sub-element of the *open-action* and within the *related data* sub-element of the *move-action*. A solution is to separate event descriptions and object descriptions so that different event descriptions can be related to the same object descriptions without replicating the object descriptions.

A tentative approach to address the above-mentioned problems is to redefine the CAM schema as a distributed metadata schema with a flat hierarchy. Core CAM instances are defined as pairs consisting of a label and a triple $<s,p,o>$, where $<s,p,o>$- triples describe events like 'user x opens file y'. That is, s is a user who performs an action p on a data object o. The elements s, p and o point to other metadata repositories that contain information on the user, the action and the object, respectively. The subject s, for instance, can be a pointer to an FOAF-document (www.foaf-project.org), the predicate p can point to metadata denoting the application by which the action was carried out and the time when the action was carried out, and the object o can, for instance, be a pointer to a Dublin Core record of that object (www.dublincore.org). According to this tentative approach, we solve the problem of redundancy, since semantic information on objects is stored independently of event descriptions. Moreover, the semi-structured nature of some elements and the missing *task*-element are no longer problems of the CAM schema. We separate these elements from the CAM core; to define them we refer to other existing metadata standards.

8.4   A general framework for capturing, storing and analysing CAM

In the previous section we described the CAM schema as a general metadata format for merging, storing and processing user observations. In this section, we outline a general framework and infrastructure for collecting and processing CAM records. Such a framework has to meet the objective that attention and usage metadata are generated from as many applications as possible. Together, the metadata captured from these applications represent a user's actual computer usage. They are generated continuously as long as the user operates her computer. The data have to be integrated and transformed into a unified representation for which we propose the CAM schema as an adequate format. CAM records are to be stored locally and, possibly, on remote servers or in peer-to-peer networks. Storage must be reliable in order to ensure a most accurate analysis. Furthermore, the metadata represent highly personal data. Therefore, storage and provision of contextualized attention metadata must ensure privacy and security; access should be restricted to parties licensed by the owner (who is the observed user).

  We can foresee neither which software will be used to store contextualized attention metadata in the long run, nor which network infrastructure will be used – the choice is between client-server and peer-to-peer infrastructures. Moreover, we cannot foresee which application programs will be used. Therefore, it must be possible to integrate new applications that generate CAM records into the CAM framework. The CAM framework needs to be extensible in terms of metadata-providing applications, as well as storage and analysis software. The underlying infrastructure must enable client-server features in parallel with peer-to-peer features; it has to be set up as a hybrid infrastructure. For sustainability – that is, for rendering the adaptation to new use cases, tools and protocols possible – the hybrid infrastructure will make use of standardized protocols

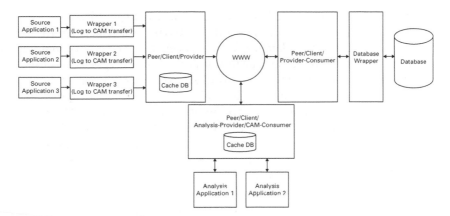

Figure 8.2 CAM infrastructure

that enable its easy extension while reducing limits on newly added soft-ware as much as possible. Abstracting the actual storage and transport of metadata away from the metadata wrappers enables third parties easily to provide software that captures attention metadata. The abstraction also enables the development of analysis tools that are unaware of the underlying infrastructure, and therefore simplifies the development and adaptation of such tools.

The CAM framework is depicted in figure 8.2.[3] The framework provides the ability to collect, transfer, provide and store observation-based attention metadata. Metadata are collected and transferred into the CAM schema by wrappers for application programs that run on the computer (wrappers serve as observation providers). The metadata are stored locally on the client side and/or – depending on the user's approval – remotely in databases of various types (databases are observation consumers and providers). Using a hybrid network infrastructure, attention metadata are accessed from respective analysis tools (these are observation consumers) that run either locally or remotely. The following paragraphs will briefly explain the conceptual structure of the framework by outlining its structure and composition.

8.4.1 Conceptual structure of the framework

Observations: Observation data are generated by all applications with which the user works on her computer. Most application programs

[3] Where is the user within this diagram? The source applications are the interface to the user; her interactions with these applications are monitored.

provide some sort of usage history, either directly as log files or stored in databases. The communication software Skype (www.skype.com), for instance, uses an internal database to store all chat conversations. In order to enable the domain and application-independent processing of observation data, these data have to be transferred into a unifying schema, namely the CAM schema. To this end, we use existing wrappers for the file system and application programs – e.g., the ALCOM framework (Verbert *et al.* 2005) and the *User Activity Logger* developed at L3S (pas.kbs.uni-hannover.de, Chernov *et al.* 2007) – and we develop new wrappers for diverse applications that are able to provide observation data. Wrappers already exist for the file system, the Firefox browser, the Thunderbird email client, the Skype communication tool, Microsoft Office, Microsoft Outlook, the Winamp music player, etc.

Storage and provision: All wrappers running on a computer deliver CAM records to a peer application. The peer abstracts the underlying storage and network infrastructure away from the wrappers. It therefore provides an open and extensible framework for the development of wrappers. The peer is responsible for transportation and storage of the CAM streams. It stores all CAM records in a local database. Based on the access rights provided by the user, it can also store observation data on a remote server or make them accessible within a peer-to-peer infrastructure.

A peer is also able to receive observation data from other peers in order to store them in a local database. Simple encryption mechanisms within the network (like PGP) ensure the security of transferring data. In order to ensure privacy, and in addition to the respective access restriction mechanisms, observation data are anonymized (unless otherwise explicitly specified by the user) using mechanisms like K-anonymization (Sweeney 2002).

Analysis tools can access the observation data depending on where and by whom they are run. Tools that are run locally by the observed user have full access to all observation data of this user. Furthermore, using the peer application and respective access rights, they can access all observation data stored remotely on a server or within the respective peer-to-peer network.

We have not yet dealt with the issue of the controlled exchange of usage and attention metadata. One such technique might be APML (attention profiling mark-up language, www.apml.org), which is designed as a format for exchanging attention profiles. APML profiles can be automatically generated, but they can also be edited by their owners. That is, users can add information or delete information from their profiles before distribution. We will investigate this open issue later.

8.5   Exploitation of CAM

8.5.1   Research areas

The contents of a CAM database describe in detail the computer-related behaviour of one or several users. The entries in the database contain – or, at least, can be related to – additional information on the users (age, profession, etc.), the data objects being used (their semantic properties, modalities, etc.) and the contexts of action (time, location, working time/leisure time, etc.). Therefore, by querying a CAM database, precise behaviour-oriented user profiles can be generated: What did a particular user do under specific contextual conditions? Which kinds of data objects did she use? Usage-based object profiles can be generated as well: By whom has a particular object been used? In what kinds of contexts has the object been used? What has been done with the object? A CAM database gives rise to diverse user and object classifications: Which users performed certain actions with an above-average frequency? Which users attended to objects with certain semantic properties? Which objects have been in the focus of a certain user group? Finally, since communication behaviour can also be observed, it is possible to deduce propositions about social relationships: Who has been in contact with whom about what? A CAM database is a dynamic representation of computer usage. Therefore, user and object profiles and classifications have a temporal dimension and reflect the evolutions of usages and attentions.

Research is carried out in the further evaluation and interpretation of contextualized attention metadata. First, by classifying the objects a user (repeatedly) refers to, her general preferences regarding contents, modalities, etc. can be inferred. A simple, but quite plausible, presumption for such a defeasible inference is that a user prefers those kinds of objects that she uses with a high frequency. For instance, from the fact that she often attends to learning videos when texts are also available we infer that she prefers video presentations to plain texts. Since CAM records contain the contexts of attention, preferences can be relativized with respect to specific contexts – the user's video preference need not be true for all contexts. Inferences on preferences can be improved and made more reliable when explicit information – like object recommendations by the respective user – is taken into account. Since recommending-actions can be recorded, this information can be entailed in a CAM database.

Second, CAM records can be used for the detection of competencies. Assuming that the learning objects of an e-learning system are annotated with information regarding their complexity, these annotations indicate the previous knowledge that is required to use and understand the learning objects. Thus, the user's attention to objects indicates her (previous) knowledge. Moreover, knowledge and skills are proven not only by the ability to give answers but also by asking the right questions (Ram 1991). Thus, a user's information search behaviour (which search queries does she pose in which contexts?) seems to be a promising clue to her actual competencies (Hölscher and Strube 2000).

Third, research is going on in the area of cognitive and emotional state recognition. Research so far has concentrated on the analysis of speech acts. Systems have been implemented following Weintraub's (1964) studies in psychological states expressed via language (Shaw 2008) and the Linguistic Category Model (Fiedler 2008; Semin 2008).[4] The systems basically depend on keyword vectors for their analysis: word tokens of different categories are counted, and from the word frequencies conclusions regarding the author's cognitive and emotional state are drawn. The analysis is to be extended to non-verbal symbols like emoticons and, furthermore, from speech acts to other kinds of acts in order to detect significant frequencies of attention shifts and repetitions, among others. Results from the analysis of email and chat messages are used to enrich social network data, thereby generating fully fledged diachronic sociograms that can be used for socially aware systems (Pentland 2005).

Fourth, we derive action patterns from CAM records, which are used for the automatic recognition of users' tasks, goals and intentions both in single-user and multi-user environments. For task recognition, approaches from algorithmic learning of formal languages are applied. Atomic actions are treated as symbols over an alphabet; tasks are considered to be sequences of actions. Therefore, the aim is to construct a task grammar that generates tasks as sequences of actions from a given action-alphabet. For the detection of goals and intentions, outcome states and their evaluations are taken into consideration as well.

Research in the interpretation of CAM records can be carried out by using the CAM framework as a research instrument. The framework provides the means for observing users in controlled settings and for analysing observation data. We can apply the framework as a tool for investigating the correlations of users' actions with their preferences, competencies, tasks, and so on. However, the CAM framework is not a research instrument in the first place. Analysis tools are extended to real application programs for task and learning support and efficient information retrieval, among others. These programs are designed not

---

[4] See, for instance, the 'Linguistic Inquiry and Word Count' software: www.liwc.net (retrieved 25 November 2006).

only for the controlled, experimental environment but, first and foremost, for real-world application.

8.5.2 Applications and test beds: reporting tool

One application that makes the individual installation of the CAM framework attractive is a reporting tool that summarizes the user's actions and gives her an overview of what she did and which data objects she worked with during the day, the previous week or the past month. Taking the results of analyses into account, she can assess her preferences, competencies and completed (as well as ongoing) tasks. She can gain an overview of which data she sent to whom (maybe without being aware of it) and conclude what others might know about her. For example, she can record which data were sent to Google as search queries, gmail-messages, etc. and thereby appraise her Google-profile. This can be regarded as a type of early warning defence system in terms of privacy: becoming aware of personal data distribution might lead to a more cautious behaviour in web-based environments.

As a prototype, we have implemented a tool for observing, analysing and reporting on a user's email- and chat-communication. With this tool, we can analyse emails that are stored locally in mbox format (a file format used, for instance, by Thunderbird to store emails) or remotely on an imap server. We extract the sender, the receiver(s), the sent date, the subject and keywords from the email message. Keyword lists serve as shallow content representations; they are generated by the use of the Yahoo! term extractor[5] and tagthe.net (www.tagthe.net). We use a plug-in for Thunderbird, namely Adapted Dragontalk,[6] to generate information about the usage of the email tool; that is, to observe when (and how often) a user opens a particular email and when an email is forwarded, responded, moved or deleted. Moreover, we collect chat data from the Skype communication tool. The communication partners, times and keywords of conversations are extracted as metadata. All metadata are transformed into the CAM format and stored in a local, native XML eXist database (www.exist.org). We analyse both email contacts and chat conversations for creating and visualizing an egocentric social network of the user. The tool allows a user to explore her email and chat archive in

---

[5] Retrieved 24 November 2008 from: developer.yahoo.com/search/content/V1/term Extraction.html.

[6] The Dragontalk plug-in was developed by DFKI (German Research Centre for Artificial Intelligence): dragontalk.opendfki.de (retrieved 24 November 2008). The plug-in was developed further by the L3S Research Centre: pas.kbs.uni-hannover.de/download.html (retrieved 24 November 2008).

a new way: she generates an overview of who talked about what to whom and when, so that she can, for instance, recognize that a specific topic was discussed by different groups of her contacts, maybe at different times. She can evaluate her communication behaviour and recognize whose emails she read most often and answered quickly. Furthermore, the use of emoticons is analysed and depicted as a tentative clue to the evolution of social contacts. The user is provided with reports on the dynamics of her social relationships.

8.5.3   Applications and test beds: MACE

Another application area was described in the introduction to this chapter. We described a scenario involving an e-learning system in which usage and attention metadata are evaluated not only locally on the observed user's computer but also remotely on the server running the e-learning system. In this scenario, CAM records of all students using an online course are collected, stored and analysed with the aim of evaluating the learning system and supporting individual learning strategies and collaborative learning processes. In such a scenario, CAM records can come from two sources, namely from the individual users' computers and from server log files. The metadata coming from the different sources are integrated into a large CAM dataset.

A first test bed for the collection and exploitation of many users' contextualized attention metadata has been implemented within the MACE project (portal.mace-project.eu). The aim of MACE (Stefaner *et al.* 2007) is to improve access to digital architectural learning resources by setting up a federation of architectural learning repositories: large amounts of architectural contents from distributed sources are integrated and made accessible to architects, architecture students and lecturers. Applying an extension to LOM[7] (learning objects metadata), the metadata descriptions of architectural learning resources are harvested from a large number of European repositories into a central metadata repository. The harvested metadata are enriched with various types of additional metadata, including content metadata, competence[8] and learning process metadata (Koper and Tattersall 2005) and contextualized attention metadata. Within MACE, contextualized attention metadata are

[7] IEEE Standard for Learning Object Metadata: ltsc.ieee.org/wg12/par1484–12-1.html. Retrieved 25 November 2008.
[8] Directive 2005/36/EC of the European Parliament and of the Council on the Recognition of Professional Qualifications, 7 September 2005.

composed of individual usage-related metadata as described above, as well as of metadata acquired through social interaction – like recommendations by peer users and blog entries. Social interaction of MACE users relies on the ALOE system (aloe-project.de, Memmel, Kockler and Schirru 2008) which renders it possible to capture, store and allocate metadata on interactions like joint tagging of learning resources, exchange of bookmarks, object ratings and recommendations. Using the rich set of metadata, very expressive object profiles can be generated which make it possible to offer multiple perspectives on the architectural contents and diverse navigation paths through the contents. Users can find resources by simple keyword search but also with visual navigation tools for browsing through the different classifications of the MACE resources. In addition, MACE offers statistical data that are exploited, among others, for listing the most popular learning resources and for summarizing trend features within a *Zeitgeist*[9] application.

A prototype for the use of contextualized attention metadata within MACE has been set up. It is based on two major components, namely a usage metadata repository and a set of usage metadata services. The usage metadata repository stores CAM records captured from different sources. It uses the XML-enabled database IBM DB 2 system so that CAM instances are stored natively without pre-processing. For communication with the outside world, the usage metadata repository offers three interfaces: (1) the Simple Publishing Interface (SPI, Ternier et al. 2008) for inserting CAM instances into the database (SPI is used by CAM in providing sources like the MACE portal, the MACE infrastructure services and the ALOE system); (2) the Simple Query Interface (SQI, Simon et al. 2005) for querying the repository (SQI is used by the analytical services described below); and (3) the Open Archives Initiative Protocol (OAI-PMH) to expose CAM records to a harvester in order to enable processing off site by other parties. Currently, the usage metadata repository stores metadata on the following types of events captured from the MACE infrastructure services:

1. A user requesting the metadata of a learning resource.
2. A user searching for a learning resource using keyword search.
3. A user searching for a learning resource using the full text search feature of all repositories integrated into MACE.
4. A user searching for a learning resource using the 'browse classification' functionality.
5. A user updating a metadata instance within the MACE store.

[9] See www.google.com/intl/en/press/zeitgeist/index.html. Retrieved 25 November 2008.

6. A user logging into the MACE system via the MACE portal.
7. A user requesting a listing of all the users registered on the MACE system.
8. A user searching for a specific user.
9. A user requesting information on a specific user.
10. A new user ID being created within the MACE system.
11. A user account being activated after a verification process.
12. A user account being deactivated.

Moreover, we record interactions with the MACE repository via the ALOE system. That is, we capture activities such as: accessing, uploading, bookmarking, sharing and contributing to resources; tagging, rating and commenting on resources; creating collections of resources; associating metadata with resources; and joining and initiating user groups. The events are described according to the CAM schema. For each event, at least the user, the involved learning resources, the time and date of the event and the location of the user are recorded.

The prototypical MACE usage metadata service provides statistical analyses for ranking search queries and learning objects: Which search queries have been posed most often, and which learning objects have been requested most often? Ordered lists of learning resources are generated on demand: the user is enabled to define her own ranking criteria. She can ask for an ordered list of the objects that have been requested most often in general or of the objects that have been requested most often by herself, for example. So far, the following ranking metrics have been implemented:

1. Number of metadata instance views: a list of the top-k objects ranked according to the number of views in a defined period of time (e.g., day, week, month, year, since recorded history) is returned. The ranking metric generates two types of lists: one global list integrating the views of all users and learning resources and one that integrates only the learning resources of a particular user.
2. Number of metadata updates: a list of the top-k objects ranked according to the number of updates in a defined period of time (e.g., day, week, month, year, since recorded history) is returned. Again, the ranking metric generates two types of lists: one global list integrating the views of all users and learning resources and one that integrates only the learning resources per user.
3. Timeline of metadata instance usage: usage timelines are returned. This first *Zeitgeist* implementation shows when particular learning resources have been especially popular. Usage timelines can be used for ranking objects regarding particular time periods.

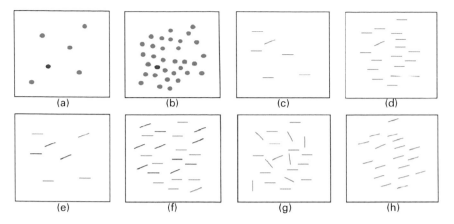

Figure 2.1 What makes visual search fast? Assessing the presence of the red spot in image (b) is as fast as retrieving it in image (a); the same holds for the only diagonal bar in (c) and (d). The number of distractors (the blue dots in (a) and (b), and the horizontal bars in (c) and (d)) has no influence on the search time; the search must be parallel and therefore pre-attentive. The situation is different when searching for targets defined by the conjunction of features such as the blue-diagonal of (e) and (f). In this case attention must be applied and the search time for (f) is significantly different from the search time for (e). When distractors are not homogenous (g) or very similar to the target (h), the search time is longer.

Figure 6.1 Examples of different types of Cantoche embodied agents (from realistic to cartoonish style). © 2009 Cantoche

Figure 6.2 The Cantoche Avatar Eva displays a series of behaviours that highlight the advantages of full-body avatars. © 2009 Cantoche

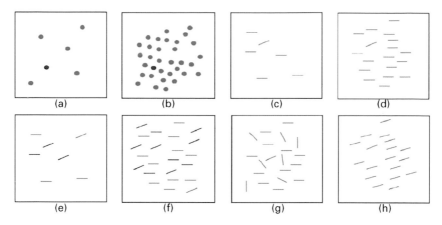

Figure 2.1 What makes visual search fast? Assessing the presence of the red spot in image (b) is as fast as retrieving it in image (a); the same holds for the only diagonal bar in (c) and (d). The number of distractors (the blue dots in (a) and (b), and the horizontal bars in (c) and (d)) has no influence on the search time; the search must be parallel and therefore pre-attentive. The situation is different when searching for targets defined by the conjunction of features such as the blue-diagonal of (e) and (f). In this case attention must be applied and the search time for (f) is significantly different from the search time for (e). When distractors are not homogenous (g) or very similar to the target (h), the search time is longer.

Figure 6.1 Examples of different types of Cantoche embodied agents (from realistic to cartoonish style). © 2009 Cantoche

Figure 6.2 The Cantoche Avatar Eva displays a series of behaviours that highlight the advantages of full-body avatars. © 2009 Cantoche

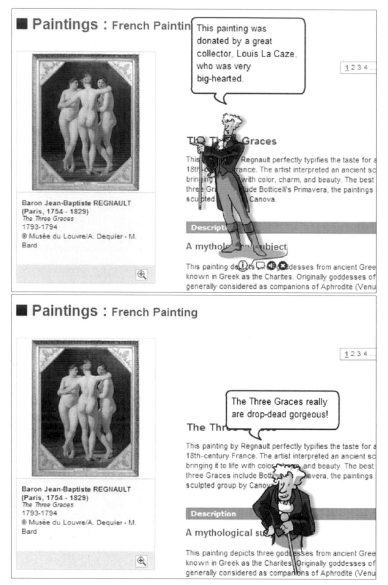

Figure 6.3 The Cantoche Avatar Dominique-Vivant Denon helps users explore the Louvre website. © 2007 François Place/Musée du Louvre

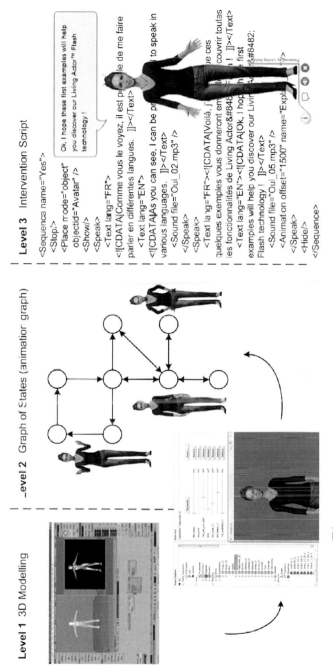

Figure 6.4 Living Actor™ technology: the three levels of control. © 2009 Cantoche

Figure 7.1 Desk-mounted video-based eye trackers: ASL 4250R at the top, SMI iViewX in the middle and Tobii T60 at the bottom

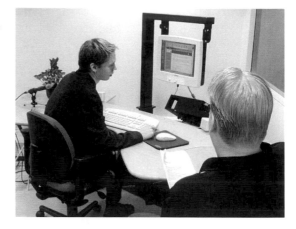

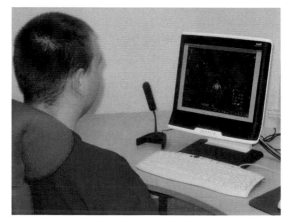

Figure 7.2 Put-That-There
(Bolt 1980) © 1980 ACM,
Inc. Reprinted with
permission

Figure 7.3 Top: attentive television (Shell,
Selker and Vertegaal 2003) © 2003 ACM,
Inc.; bottom: eyebox2 by Xuuk, Inc.,
www.xuuk.com. Both images reprinted with
permission

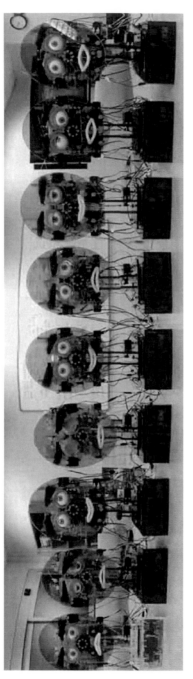

Figure 7.4 Nine instances of PONG, an attentive robot (Koons and Flickner 2003). © 2003 ACM, Inc. Reprinted with permission

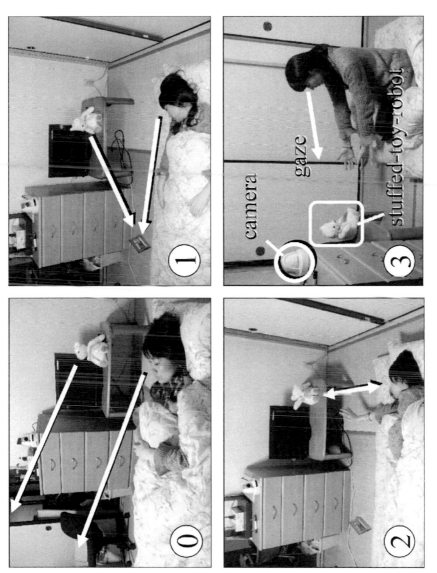

Figure 7.5 Joint attention and eye contact with a stuffed toy robot (Yonezawa et al. 2007). Picture reprinted courtesy of Tomoko Yonezawa

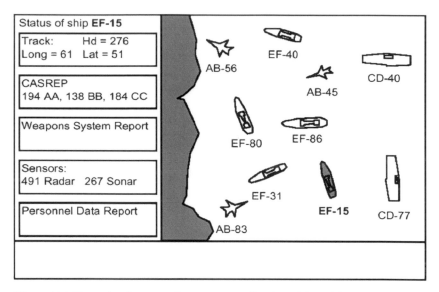

Figure 7.6 Two adaptive attention-aware applications. Top: ship database (Sibert and Jacob 2000) © 2000 ACM, Inc., reprinted with permission; bottom: iDict, a reading aid (Hyrskykari 2006)

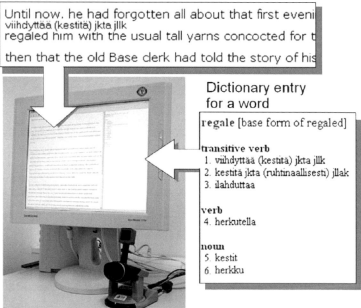

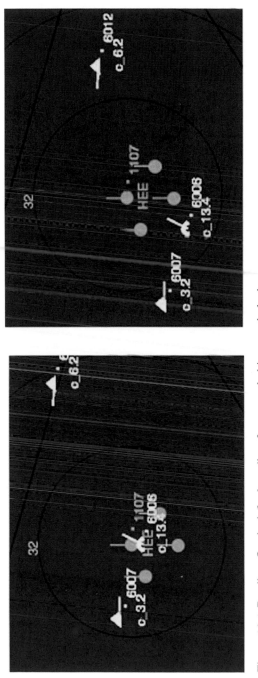

Figure 10.1 Parallax. On the left: the yellow foreground objects occlude the blue background objects. On the right: a (head) movement to the right and up makes all objects clearly visible, simulating the 'de-cluttering function' of parallax.

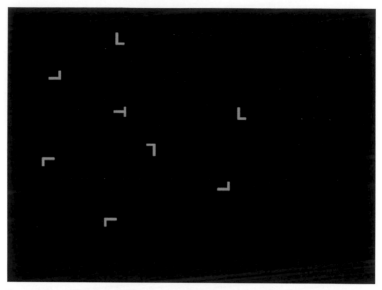

Front layer: A cockpit search task with a search set of seven distractors plus the target (T).

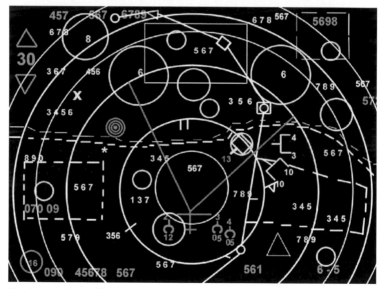

Rear layer: A cluttered background analogous to a Navigation Display.

Figure 10.2 In the experiment these two images were either separated in depth (Dual-layer) or not (Single-layer). The target and distractors shown at the top were each purposely positioned over the black background or purposely overlapped with one of the display symbols shown at the bottom. The symbols in the top image are all green while the symbols in the bottom figure are a combination of white, green, yellow and blue.

Figure 10.6 The dual-layer display implemented in the Grace flight simulator at NLR (www.hilas.info) has two layers separated by 15 mm: the Primary Flight Display in the front and synthetic terrain and tunnel in the rear. The depth difference visually separates the two images, allowing the pilot to focus on one or the other without special 3D glasses. The focus is not purely attentional but is also physiological (eye convergence and accommodation). The added value of splitting the Primary Flight Display into two layers in the manner shown here turned out to be of limited value; as a single-layer display, the amount of clutter was within reasonable bounds. The display content in figures 10.6 and 10.7 has been produced by NLR. Reprinted by permission (Zon and Roerdink 2007) © NLR and Springer-Verlag

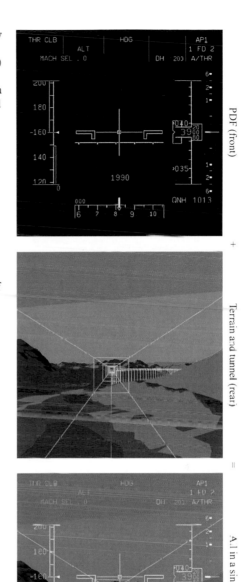

Figure 10.7 The Navigation
Display is split between a front
layer with the air-traffic and a
rear layer with other, less critical,
information. The HILAS test
pilots in the flight simulator
experiment consistently preferred
the Navigation Display split into
two layers. Reprinted by
permission © NLR

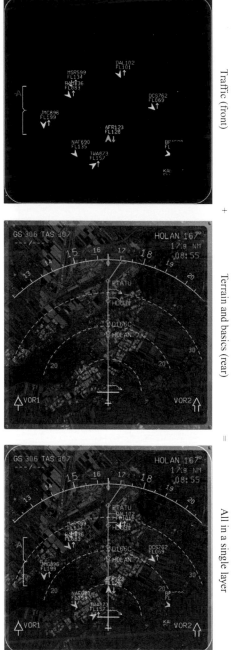

Traffic (front)

+

Terrain and basics (rear)

=

All in a single layer

Figure 11.1 Example of metacognitive planning intervention

Here you introduce yourself, for example, I am David, 15 years old and I like playing games and listening to music!

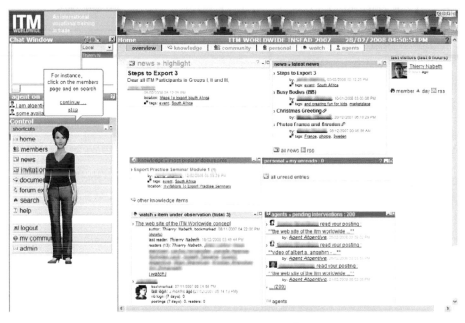

Figure 12.1 A snapshot of the AtGentNet platform[1]

[1] Other snapshots of the platform are available at www.calt.insead.edu/LivingLab/AtGentive/Wiki/?AtGentNet.

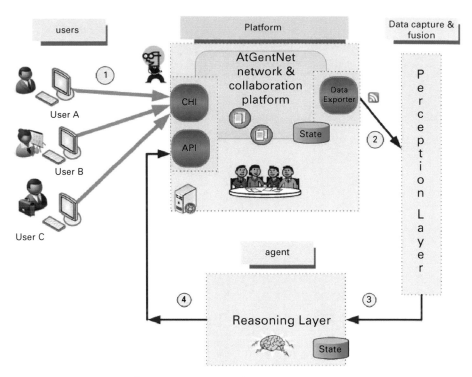

Figure 12.2 The AtGentNet overall architecture

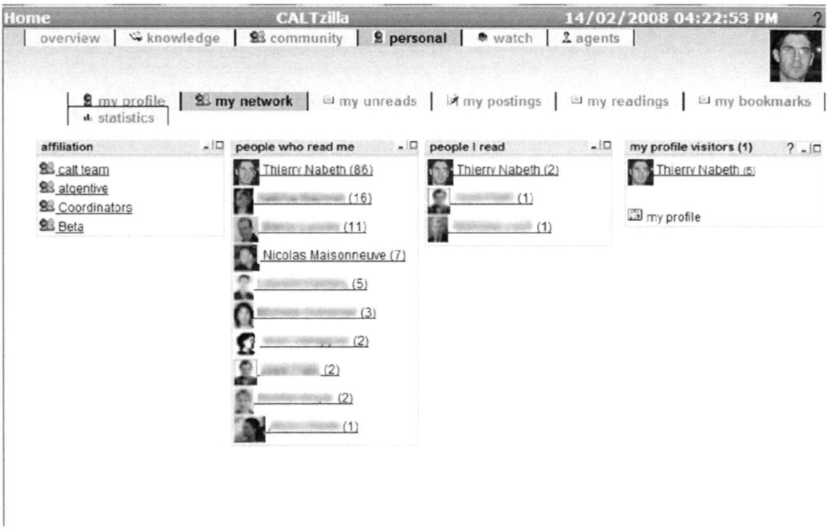

Figure 12.3 Who reads me? Who do I read?

Figure 12.4 Stated and observed competences and interests

The ranking service (as part of the usage metadata service) can be used by any authorized client application. For performance reasons, the ranking service internally uses two databases: a normal (non-embedded) database – in this case PostgreSQL – and a database which is embedded in the particular ranking application – for this implementation we use HSQLDB. The non-embedded database stores the same information on user activities as the usage metadata repository, but according to the relational paradigm. This database is also responsible for the support of statistical services that do not require long calculation times. The usage metadata service has an internal job scheduling system that manages the update of the non-embedded database. By using the OAI Protocol, this component can be configured to harvest automatically new CAM instances from the usage metadata repository and insert them into the non-embedded database.

The embedded database is used to store pre-calculated (complex) ranking metrics supported as service features. The database is pre-populated during the web application loading, by referring to the non-embedded database in order to obtain the necessary data for calculating ranking metrics. All calculations from the non-embedded database for a single ranking metric are stored in a single database table. If a ranking service is required, the usage metadata service uses this table and is thus able to respond to requests quickly. Finally, to keep the embedded database up to date, all rankings metrics are re-calculated after an automatic harvest has been done.

8.5.4   Outcomes and outlook

The application of CAM within the MACE project has two important outcomes. First, since the usage and attention of users is evaluated and visualized, individual users can reflect on which objects they have attended and to which objects significant numbers of other users have attended. Personal usage histories serve as reminders: users remember the objects that they have attended to and that might become relevant again. Statistical evaluations serve as recommendations: users are pointed to objects to which a significant number of other users attended. This makes it possible to recognize trends, to follow those trends or, conversely, to resist those trends and look for objects that have not been in the focus of 'the general public' so far. Second, we annotate data objects with usage- and attention-based metadata. Objects are classified and associated according to their actual usages. These associations can be used for improving information retrieval. (Google's original PageRank algorithm (Brin and Page 1998) takes explicit associations – that is, hard-wired hyperlinks – into account. We extend those links with dynamic, usage-based associations.) By making explicit when and by whom a particular object has been used for what, and which objects have been used together with this object, and by presuming that objects are *relevant* in their usage contexts, we specify the object's potential relevance. That is, we contribute to sharpening the concept of relevance and to making it operational for information retrieval.

Current Web2.0 approaches like Amazon, ALOE, Digg, YouTube and others already demonstrate that information access and retrieval can be personalized by exploiting usage metadata. The application of CAM within the MACE project shows how CAM can improve current person-alization efforts for information systems. For example, the annotation with attention metadata advances the possibilities of exploratory search and the creation of (individual and community-based) associative nets beyond mere link-based document graphs as in the former HTML-based web. Admittedly, this is work-in-progress.

We chose the MACE system as a test bed for CAM because it contains a large data repository (needed for generating object profiles), because it has a large number of users (needed for generating user profiles) and because it is used for e-learning in architectural courses at different uni-versities. Especially in architecture, it is important to structure, associate and remember large amounts of contents. Architects use colleagues' work as an inspirational source for both copying and extending. They require access to large amounts of highly diverse information, ranging from pictures of buildings, project sketches and reviews to governmen-tal regulations. They have to take diverse perspectives on this material and structure their views according to their actual individual interests. Therefore, the MACE system is ideal for testing and proving the benefits of CAM exploitation.

8.6   Conclusion

In this chapter, we have defined our current understanding of the nature of contextualized attention metadata (CAM) as describing the *attending-to* behaviour of agents, in particular the behaviour of users while using digital information on their computer. We have introduced the CAM schema as a general schema to represent contextualized attention meta-data computationally. Furthermore, we have described a framework for capturing, storing and analysing CAM records. The framework collects instances of CAM from application programs and stores them locally and possibly (depending on access rights, among others) on remote servers.

We have outlined different ways of exploiting CAM records and thus demonstrated various ways in which the analysis of CAM instances can be beneficial for users. Finally, we have introduced two demonstrators for the exploitation of CAM records, namely a tool for observing, analysing and reporting on a user's email- and chat-communication and the MACE system as a test bed for using CAM in a distributed environment. While the first application focuses on the single user, the e-learning scenario of MACE enables us to pursue research questions in multi-user CAM scenarios.

Technology-enhanced learning (TEL) scenarios are very promising for the application of CAM. On the one hand, TEL demands personalization and self-monitoring. Therefore attention and usage metadata have to be captured and analysed; there is a need for a framework like the one described in this chapter. On the other hand, TEL scenarios provide many possibilities for exploiting CAM. Thus, they allow CAM to show its full potential. Currently, new test beds and applications for CAM are designed within the European Integrated Project ROLE (www.role-project.eu) and other projects. We expect significant outcomes from these projects.

8.7   References

Adomavicius, G., and Tuzhilin, A. 2005. Toward the next generation of recommender systems: A survey of the state-of-the-art and possible extensions, *IEEE Transactions on Knowledge and Data Engineering* 17(6): 734–49

Attention.XML. 2004. *Attention.XML Draft Specification*. Retrieved 3 February 2007 from: http://developers.technorati.com/wiki/attentionxml

Atterer, R. 2006. Logging usage of AJAX applications with the 'UsaProxy' HTTP Proxy, in *Proceedings of the WWW 2006 Workshop on Logging Traces of Web Activity: The Mechanics of Data Collection*, Edinburgh

Brin, S., and Page, L. 1998. The anatomy of a large-scale hypertextual Web search engine, *Computer Networks and ISDN System* 30(1–7): 107 17

Çelik, T. 2005. Attention.xml technology overview. Retrieved 10 June 2008 from: http://tantek.com/presentations/2005/01/attentionxml.html

Chernov, S., Sergyukov, P., Chirita, P. A., Demartini, G., and Neijdl, W. 2007. Building a desktop search test-bed, in *Proceedings of the 29th European Conference on Information Retrieval (ECIR)*, Rome

Dragunov, A. N., Dietterich, T. G., Johnsrude, K., McLaughlin, M., Li, L., and Herlocker, J. L. 2005. TaskTracer: A desktop environment to support multitasking knowledge workers, in *Proceedings of the International Conference on Intelligent User Interfaces*, San Diego, 9–12 January 2005

Fiedler, K. 2008. The implicit meta-theory that has inspired and restricted LCM research, *Journal of Language and Social Psychology* 27(2): 182–96

Hauser, J. R., Urban, G. L., Liberali, G., and Braun, M. 2009. Website morphing, *Marketing Science* 28(2): 202–23

Hölscher, C., and Strube, G. 2000. Web search behavior of internet experts and newbies, *Computer Networks* 33(1–6): 337–46

Koper, R., and Tattersall, C. 2005. *Learning Design: A Handbook on Modeling and Delivering Networked Education and Training*. Heidelberg: Springer

Memmel, M., and Kockler, M., and Schirru, R. 2008. Providing multi-source tag recommendations in a social resource sharing platform, in *Proceedings of I-MEDIA '08*, Graz, Austria: 226–33

Mole, C. 2009. Attention, in J. Symons and P. Calvo (eds.), *The Routledge Companion to the Philosophy of Psychology*. Abingdon, Oxfordshire: Routledge: 499–508

Pentland, A. 2005. Socially aware computation and communication, *IEEE Computer*, 38(3): 33–40

Ram, A. 1991. Theory of questions and question asking, *Journal of the Learning Sciences* 1(3–4): 273–318

Rapp, D. N. 2006. The value of attention aware systems in educational settings, *Computers in Human Behavior* 22(4): 603–14

Schuff, D., Turetken, O., D'Arcy, J., and Croson, D. 2007. Managing e-mail overload: Solutions and future challenges, *Computer* 40(2): 31–6

Semin, G. R. 2008. Language puzzles. A prospective retrospective on the linguistic category model, *Journal of Language and Social Psychology* 27(2): 197–209

Shaw, E. D. 2008. System and method for computerized psychological content analysis for computer and media generated communications to produce communications management support, indications and warnings of dangerous behavior, assessment of media images, and personnel selection support, *United States Patent Application Publication*: Pub. No. US 2008/0109214 A1

Simon, B., Massart, D., van Assche, F., Ternier, S., Duval, E., Brantner, S., Olmedilla, D., and Miklos, Z. 2005. A Simple Query Interface for interoperable learning repositories, in *Proceedings of the 1st Workshop on Interoperability of Web-based Educational Systems*, Chiba, Japan: 11–18

Stefaner, M., Vecchia, E., Condotta, M., Wolpers, M., Sprecht, M., Apelt, S., and Ducal, E. 2007. MACE – Enriching architectural learning objects for experience multiplication, in E. Ducal, R. Klamma and M. Wolpers (eds.), *Creating New Learning Experiences on a Global Scale*. Heidelberg: Springer: 322–36

Sweeney, L. 2002. k-anonymity: A model for protecting privacy, *International Journal on Uncertainty, Fuzziness and Knowledge-based Systems* 10(5): 557–70

Ternier, S., Massart, D., Van Assche, F., Smith, N., Simon, B., and Duval, E. 2008. A simple publishing interface for learning object repositories, in *Proceedings of the World Conference on Educational Multimedia, Hypermedia and Telecommunications 2008*, Chesapeake, VA: 1840–5

Verbert, K., Jovanovic, J., Gasevic, D., and Duval, E. 2005. Repurposing learning object components, in *Proceedings of the OTM 2005 Workshop on Ontologies, Semantics and E-Learning*, Agia Napa, Cyprus: 1169–78

Weintraub, W. 1964. The application of verbal behavior analysis to the study of psychological defense mechanisms. II. Speech pattern associated with impulsive behavior, *Journal of Nervous and Mental Disease* 139: 75–82

Wolpers, M., Najjar, J., Verbert, K., and Duval, E. 2007. Tracking actual usage: The attention metadata approach, *Educational Technology and Society* 10(3): 106–21

9 Modelling attention within a complete cognitive architecture

Georgi Stojanov and Andrea Kulakov

Human attention is a complex phenomenon (or a set of related phenomena) that occurs at different levels of cognition (from low-level perceptual processes to higher perceptual and cognitive processes). Since the dawn of modern psychology through cognitive sciences to fields like Human–Computer Interaction (HCI), attention has been one of the most controversial research topics. Attempts to model attentional processes often show their authors' implicit construal of related cognitive phenomena and even their overall meta-theoretical stands about what cognition is. Moreover, the modelling of attention cannot be done in isolation from related cognitive phenomena like curiosity, motivation, anticipation and awareness, to mention but a few. For these reasons we believe that attention models are best presented within a complete cognitive architecture where most authors' assumptions will be made explicit.

In this chapter we first present several attempts to model attention within a complete cognitive architecture. Several known cognitive architectures (ACT-R, Fluid Concepts, LIDA, DUAL, Novamente AGI and MAMID) are reviewed from the point of view of their treatment of attentional processes. Before presenting our own take on attention modelling, we briefly present the meta-theoretical approach of interactivism as advocated by Mark Bickhard.

We then give a description of a cognitive architecture that we have been developing in the last ten years. We present some of the cognitive phenomena that we have modelled (expectations, routine behaviour, planning, curiosity and motivation) and what parts of the architecture can be seen as involved in the attentional processes. In the final part we will give more details about implementation of low-level video-processing modules which are a recent addition to the architecture. Finally, the chapter closes with general comments and a discussion of future work.

9.1 Introduction

Human attention is a complex mechanism and involves multiple components at both the physiological (brain and neural networks) level and the behavioural and functional levels. Multiple models offer a straightforward computational link between neural activities and cognitive behaviours (e.g., Wang and Fan 2007). We believe that the approach to cognition as information processing is still a dominant paradigm. Therefore attention is usually modelled at certain levels of abstraction along the information processing path followed inside a given cognitive architecture.

It can be said that attention influences micro-decisions at different perceptual levels, in the generation of expectations and goals as well as in the interactions with the modelled semantic, metacognitive and emotional processes. A brief review of the literature on attention modelling (e.g., Styles 2005) shows that *visual* attention has been by far the preferred topic of interest. Certain models of attention also partition attention into subsystems, describing it as a system that consists of three specialized networks, well defined in anatomical and functional terms (Posner and Petersen 1990): *alerting, orienting* and *executive control. Alerting* involves an adjustment in the internal state of the organism so that it may be more prepared for perceiving a stimulus. Alertness, or general preparatory attention, is crucial for optimal performance in various cognitive tasks. *Orienting* engages the selection of a subset of information available from the sensory input. *Executive control* of attention is a sort of cognitive selectivity which demands more complex mental operations for monitoring and resolving conflicts between computations occurring in different brain areas such as planning, decision making, error detection, novel responses and overcoming habitual actions.

We first briefly introduce the methodology of cognitive architectures and mention some of the most influential attention theories in this domain. In section 9.3 we describe several particular cognitive architectures and the role of attention within them. In section 9.4, before describing our own cognitive architecture, we lay out the basic assumptions of the interactivist approach. The section then continues with a sketch of the architecture itself and several of the cognitive phenomena that we have modelled. The relation of these phenomena to attention is then discussed. In section 9.5 we describe the most recent component which controls low-level attention in the incoming video stream. Finally, section 9.6 concludes the chapter with a general discussion and directions for future work.

9.2   Why cognitive architectures?

A cognitive architecture attempts to describe the infrastructure for an intelligent system (Newell 1990; Langley and Choi 2006). The author of the architecture thus commits to certain choices, such as what the main building blocks of the cognitive system are, how they interact, what types of knowledge representation are used and how learning happens (e.g., declarative and procedural memory, perception and reasoning modules, chunking mechanism, knowledge recompilation, and other types of learning and abstraction mechanisms). Apart from the conceptual model, cognitive architectures usually also comprise some partially implemented computational models.

The work on a cognitive architecture is incremental and usually lasts for years. In a way, it may define the authors' overall research careers. There have been series of conferences devoted to a single architecture (e.g., the Soar and ACT-R annual workshop series) or even commercial companies (e.g., Soar Technology Inc.).

The goals for proposing cognitive architectures are multifaceted. They embody a particular theory of cognition, offer a test bed for testing ideas about particular cognitive processes (e.g., memorization and retrieval of meaningless words) and provide various constraints that functional cognitive systems are subjected to.

Two very important and complementary aims of cognitive architectures are (1) to provide a framework for including new empirical findings about human cognition and (2) to provide empirical predictions and ideas for psychological experiments.

In the realm of applied science, cognitive architectures have been successfully used to model, evaluate and predict human user behaviour in HCI design (Anderson, Matessa and Labiere 1997).

9.3   Theories of attention used in cognitive architectures

As with many topics that recur in cognitive sciences research, such as learning, perception or consciousness, there is no widely agreed upon definition of attention. This is certainly to be expected, as any definition determines its author's overall construal of cognitive systems and hence his or her framework for research. Within that framework definitions of various terms will be interdependent. Dixon (1981) even argues that the legacy of behaviourism cast a long shadow over research in consciousness and, if attention is seen as a process that brings certain elements of the perceptual environment into the conscious realm, attention research was also affected by this shadow. Nevertheless, there are several recurring terms that come into play whenever there is an attempt to give a definition of attention.

Selection is probably one of the most frequent terms. The general idea starts with the fact that there is a huge quantity of perceptual input. Given the limited capacity of cognitive agents to attend to and/or process this input, cognitive systems need to be selective about what part of the input they will attend to. Thus, in what is probably one of the first attempts to formulate a theory of attention, Broadbent proposed the *filter theory of attention* (Broadbent 1958). Filters, according to this theory, represent early processing of the perceptual input and allow only certain percepts to go through (towards higher-level cognitive processing) on the basis of simple features such as colour, location and size. Cognitive agents are thus said to be selective while choosing what perceptual inputs will be attended to. A lot of empirical support for this category of theories of attention came from dichotic hearing experimental set-ups where the subject is given two different audio streams, one coming into each ear. It is virtually impossible to understand and report what is being said in one channel while attending the other. Nonetheless, subjects may be aware of some basic features of the non-attended channel, such as whether it represents a male or female voice, its pitch, volume, etc.

Another concept closely associated with attention is *awareness*: we may be looking at something and not be aware of what it is (i.e., not consciously recognize it). Treisman and Gelade (1980) see attention as 'glue' which integrates elementary features into objects. Thus, while observing a scene, we may be aware of only a few objects in front of us, but with our peripheral vision we can have only crude pre-attentive information about what is around us.

Finally, attention is said to *guide action*. Wolfe and Horowitz (2004) give an overview of the research on attention in the context of the visual search task. Subjects are asked whether a certain object is present or not on the screen and to answer 'yes' or 'no', and their reaction time is measured. According to their classification, if there is only a single object on the screen, the task is trivial. Things become far more interesting if other objects (*distractors*) are present. In this case, subject reaction time depends on the features of distractors and the target. Visual attention deployment is said to be guided by these features (or *attributes*, as Wolfe and Horowitz call them). Experiments suggest that colour, motion, orientation and size are likely to have the most important role in guiding visual attention. These are followed by luminance, curvature, shape, closure, etc. Much less importance is found for glossiness, expansion, number and aspect ratio.

To summarize, we could say that nowadays attention is understood as a set of processes that determine what portion of the perceptual input will be processed and how fast. They can be input-driven (bottom-up) and also affected by agents' goals, intentions, general internal state and immediate experience (top-down).

Within the literature of cognitive architecture, attention is sometimes listed as an entity or process on a par with thinking, memory and learning.

Other times it is given a rather specific interpretation as a metacognitive process that chooses what will be the current goal to be pursued given the goal's priority (Langley and Choi 2006). In the remainder of the chapter, we will see what theories have been most influential in the field of cognitive architectures and how attention has been conceptualized.

9.3.1   ACT-R

ACT-R is a cognitive architecture where the backbone of the cognitive agent is modelled as a production system (Anderson 1993). Cognition is essentially construed as information processing and the architecture itself is designed to predict human behaviour by processing information and generating intelligent behaviour.

ACT-R integrates theories of cognition, visual attention and motor movement. It has *a working memory* and two types of *long-term knowledge, declarative* and *procedural knowledge*. Declarative knowledge contains facts about the world represented by chunks which are schema-like structures organized in a prepositional network. Procedural knowledge encodes skills and is formed by production rules consisting of condition–action pairs. Production rules correspond to specific goals or sub-goals and mainly retrieve and change declarative knowledge.

As a parallel to this symbolic (procedural and declarative) aspect, the system also has a sub-symbolic feature that determines the history of usage and the general usefulness of the symbolic knowledge. Each symbolic structure (a chunk or a production rule) has sub-symbolic parameters associated with it that indicate their past use in terms of a probability. These parameters determine what information is currently available in the declarative memory module and what the likely outcomes are if certain rules fire.

Over time ACT-R has been extended to include explicitly a theory of visual attention and pattern recognition (Anderson, Matessa and Douglass 1995). Production rules can direct attention to the primitive visual features in the current view. Features distributed in some regions can be combined into declarative chunks only when attention is focused on that region. When comparing the results from a number of basic studies of visual attention, this model shows a certain degree of reliability, assuming a time to switch attention of about 200 ms.

In order to achieve a psychologically plausible theory of visual attention, ACT-R uses a mixture of the spotlight metaphor of Posner (1980), the feature-synthesis model of Treisman (Treisman and Sato 1990) and the attentional model of Wolfe (1994). These models of visual attention provide a set of constraints which are embedded within the ACT-R theory of higher-level cognition. The spotlight metaphor of visual attention is implemented in such a way that a variable-sized spotlight of attention can be moved across the visual field. When the spotlight fixates on an object, its features can be recognized. Once recognized, the objects are available as declarative structures (chunks) in ACT-R's working memory and can receive higher-level processing. Here is an example: if two bars (centre-vertical and horizontal) are present and the group is within the spotlight of attention, the following is a potential chunk encoding of the letter T:

```
object
     isa T
     centre-vertical    bar1
     horizontal         bar2
```

It is assumed that before the object is recognized, different features (the bars, in this example) are apparent as part of an object, but the object itself is not yet recognized. The system cannot respond to the coincidence of features that define a pattern until it has shifted its attention to that part of the visual field and actually recognized the pattern of features as such. Thus, in order for the ACT-R system to recognize what is in its environment, it must constantly move its attentional focus over the visual field. In ACT-R the requests for shift of attention are controlled by explicit triggering of production rules. Thus, it takes some time to encode visual information, a fact that emphasizes the limited capacity of visual attention.

Another such model of visual attention within ACT-R theory is EMMA (Eye Movements and Movement of Attention), which represents an integration of several existing eye-movement models for specific domains into a general model for any problem-solving domain. The model posits that eye movements are initiated by shifts of attention and are sometimes cancelled by subsequent shifts (Salvucci 2000).

Another aspect of modelling attention in ACT-R is the formulation of a general executive for multi-tasking (Salvucci, Kushleyeva and Lee 2004) that facilitates the integration of separate task models and subsequent prediction of the effects of multi-tasking and task interaction in the ACT-R cognitive architecture. The general executive manages a set of current goals and determines when each goal may proceed given ordering constraints based on desired initiation times for each goal. This general executive also tries to balance three parameters: (1) the individual goal's desire for unobstructed progress in each task; (2) the overall system's need for adequate resource allocation across tasks; and (3) the achievement of higher-level goals.

9.3.2   *Fluid concepts models: CopyCat and TableTop*

CopyCat and TableTop are both computational models of human analogy-making. Although CopyCat and TableTop are not usually considered as complete cognitive architectures, several parts of these models actually model advanced cognitive abilities. The key idea put forward by Hofstadter and his colleagues is that analogy is the heart of cognition. Most of these models are described in a collection of papers by Hofstadter's research group (Hofstadter 1996). In their paper, Chalmers, French and Hofstadter (1992: 185) discuss the vital function of high-level perception during the cognitive processing of stimuli:

High-level perception – the process of making sense of complex data at an abstract, conceptual level – is fundamental to human cognition. Through high-level perception, chaotic environmental stimuli are organized into the mental representations that are used throughout cognitive processing. Much work in traditional artificial intelligence has ignored the process of high-level perception, by starting with hand-coded representations.

The authors also claim that the 'perceptual processes cannot be separated from other cognitive processes even in principle, and therefore the traditional artificial-intelligence models cannot be defended by supposing the existence of a "representation module" that supplies ready-made representations' to the rest of the (reasoning) modules in the cognitive architecture.

High-level perception is flexible and it is influenced by prior beliefs or expectations, by goals and by the external context. Analogy is not separate from perception: analogy making *is* a perceptual process. Given these premises, Hofstadter's group has created several models of analogy making, such as CopyCat, TableTop, LetterSpirit and others, that integrate high-level perception with analogy making. They all deal with very simplistic low-level perception in a micro-domain such as letter analogy problems (*abc* to *abd* is like *ijk* to what?) or simple arrangements of kitchen utensils on a table (French 1992). A common characteristic of all these models is that they have highly parallel, non-deterministic architecture which builds its own representations and finds appropriate analogies by means of the continual interaction of perceptual structuring-agents with an associative concept network.

Even in their simplest architecture, CopyCat, attention is explicitly modelled as a process which controls the degree to which different objects in the problem at hand attract the computational processes conducted by a myriad of thin agents called *codelets*. There are two factors that contribute to an object's ability to attract the attention of the computational processes (codelets):

- An object is important to the extent that its descriptions are built out of highly activated concepts in the long-term conceptual memory. The more descriptions an object has and the more activated the corresponding nodes in the memory are, the more attention that object would seem to deserve.

- 'Unhappiness' is a measure of how integrated the description of an object is with the other objects. An unhappy object is one that has few or no connections (descriptions) to the rest of the objects in the working memory and thus seems to request more attention.

There are two types of codelets in the system, scout codelets and effector codelets. A scout merely looks at a potential action and tries to estimate its promise; the only effect it can have is to create one or more codelets – either scouts or effectors – to follow up on its findings ('a follow-up codelet'). By contrast, an effector codelet actually creates (or destroys) some relational structure (connections) in the working memory. Another distinction between codelets is between bottom-up and top-down codelets. Bottom-up codelets (or 'noticers') look around in an unfocused manner, open to whatever they find, whereas top-down codelets (or 'seekers') are on the lookout for a particular type of phenomenon (e.g., *successor* relations or *sameness* groups). Bottom-up codelets are continually being added into the working memory, while only active nodes in the long-term conceptual memory can add top-down codelets.

Another parameter that influences attention is the *urgency* of the codelets. Each new codelet's urgency is assigned by its creator as a function of the estimated promise of the task it is supposed to carry out. Thus, the urgency of a follow-up codelet is a function of the amount of progress made by the codelet that posted it, as estimated by that codelet itself, while the urgency of a top-down codelet is a function of the activation of the conceptual node that posted it. In that way, urgency of bottom-up codelets is context-independent.

In a different micro-domain, that of a TableTop set for a dinner, examples of codelets include agents that look for groups of objects on the table, agents that look for neighbours of a particular object, agents that, given a particular group of objects, look for the same type of group elsewhere on the table, and so on. These perceptual agents are low-level observers and builders of relations among objects in the sense that they do not have a global view of the table at any time.

All these models are extensively verified by psycho-physiological tests which show very accurate predictions of human behaviour in similar tasks. Generally, we can say that in this family of cognitive models, attention incorporates features of *attention as filter* and *attention as integrator* theories.

A very similar approach to attention is present in another cognitive architecture called LIDA (Franklin 2003, 2007). Here *attention codelets* bring relevant and important information to the *global workspace*, a concept taken from Baars' theory of consciousness and cognition (Baars 1988). Attention codelets have their own special interests, and they search the workspace for items of interest, such as objects, relations and situations. After successful matching, they create a coalition of codelets of these items in the global workspace, where there is another competition as a final filtering of input. 'The idea is to attend to filter the most relevant, the most important, the most urgent, the most insistent aspects of the current situation' (Franklin 2007).

9.3.3   DUAL

DUAL (Kokinov 1994, 1997; Kokinov and Petrov 2001) is a general cognitive architecture intended to give a foundation for modelling high-level context-sensitive cognitive processes, first of all for analogy making. The name DUAL is given to the architecture because its symbolic processing part is combined in parallel with neural-networks computations. At the lowest level DUAL consists of a large collection of units, called DUAL agents, reminiscent of Minsky's (Minsky 1986) 'society of mind'. DUAL agents are characterized by the symbols they represent and by their level of activation. Agents communicate with each other by passing symbolic messages. They also interact with each other by spreading activation via weighted links. Different events, situations and objects are represented by different *coalitions* of agents. These coalitions of DUAL agents are created dynamically, depending on their level of activation and on the strength of the links connecting a given subset of agents. The *working memory* of the system is defined as the set of all active units at a time, while DUAL's *long-term memory* is represented by the set of all units.

Within the cognitive architecture DUAL, attention is not modelled explicitly; rather, it is seen as a process which spreads activation to certain DUAL agents residing in the long-term memory and thus focuses on those parts which are deemed relevant in the current context. The same process activates some DUAL agents and brings them into the working memory, where more specific computation of the DUAL agents takes place. All DUAL agents require a certain level of *activation energy* in order to become active and start the symbolic processing for which they are predetermined.

The cognitive architecture DUAL has been extended with a model of visual attention and perception (Nestor and Kokinov 2004). In this version of DUAL a combination of massively parallel activation-based computations is used, combined with a serial attention-based symbolic processing mechanism instantiating in that way the principle of active vision.

The three main components of the model are the *Retinotopic Visual Array* (RVA), the *Visual Working Memory* (VWM) and DUAL's *semantic memory*. Attention is explicitly allocated to an area of the visual array by the object in VWM controlling attention, while scene and object categories corresponding to the contents of VWM are retrieved from the semantic memory.

RVA is essentially a set of DUAL agents arranged in the cells of an imaginary matrix. Presenting a stimulus to the RVA fixes the state of each agent in RVA to be either filled or empty depending on the stimulus. Each agent in the array communicates only with its immediate neighbours and is unaware of its absolute coordinates in the array, which makes the model more biologically plausible.

Simple parallel image-based processes are implemented at this level; they determine whether an agent is a termination (end of row or column) or a part of a bigger blob in the image. The model implements blob detection as a serial procedure in which neighbouring agents gather initially into small groups, then intersecting groups blend into larger ones, and the process repeats itself until a whole block of cells is recognized as a single unit. After detecting a whole block of cells as a single unit, it is stored in VWM as a pre-attentive object (see Wolfe and Bennett 1997). A scene layout is represented in VWM as a coalition of DUAL agents, representing the objects in the scene together with their spatial relations. Still, this mechanism of coalition forming may not find all possible relations in the input because some insufficiently activated agents may not be involved in the processing. In that way, if some object in VWM is not very active at a given moment, it may be left out of the scene coalition. This is also plausible because without giving attention to an object one may not even notice the presence of that object, a phenomenon called *inattentional blindness* or *inattentional amnesia* (Wolfe 1999).

This model of visual attention has been tested by comparing its performance with the performance of human subjects in order to check its adequacy as a cognitive model. One such test is the simulation of eye-movement data in an observation task with stimuli in a restricted micro-domain for text reading.

Table 9.1 *A coarse-grained view of the semantics of the attention values attached to Novamente AGI architecture atoms*

	Low long-term importance	High long-term importance
Low short-term importance	Useless	Remembered but not currently used (e.g., mother's phone number)
High short-term importance	Used then forgotten (e.g., most percepts)	Used and remembered

9.3.4   Novamente AGI architecture

This fairly new cognitive architecture has the ambition of achieving Artificial General Intelligence (AGI). Novamente AGI architecture (Goertzel and Pennachin 2007) can be described in terms of four different aspects: knowledge representation, cognitive architecture, cognitive processes and emergent structures. We will refer only to those aspects that are explicitly related to attention.

The knowledge representation used in Novamente AGI architecture consists of a declarative knowledge using weighted, labelled hyper-graphs. Nodes and links in the declarative knowledge hyper-graph are grouped together into the category of *atoms*. Our interest is in the quantification of the atoms with *attention values* (table 9.1) which have two components, short-term and long-term importance, representing the estimated value of the atom on immediate and long-term timescales.

Declarative knowledge representation is neither a neural net nor a semantic net, although it shares certain characteristics with both of these established knowledge representations. Attention values have certain resemblance to the time-averages of neural-net activations. Artificial economics is used for attention allocation, leading to novel forms of adaptive 'moving focus of attention'. Some of the main cognitive processes in this architecture are *focused processes* which begin by selecting a small set of estimated important or relevant atoms and then act on these to generate larger sets of atoms and iterate.

Attention allocation updates short- and long-term importance values associated with atoms and uses a 'simulated economy' approach with separate currencies for short- and long-term importance. Through the process of *importance propagation*, atoms pass some of their 'attentional currency' to atoms that they estimate could help them become important again in the future. This also applies to the case of *credit assignment* when, given a particular goal, the system tries to figure out which execution of procedures and which atoms' importance can be expected to lead to the goal's achievement.

This architecture is implemented and tested in virtual environments with the aim of producing intelligent behaviour by virtual characters.

9.3.5 MAMID architecture

Even though MAMID architecture (Hudlicka 2005) is mainly a model of interaction between metacognition and emotion in a cognitive architecture, the modelling of attention is inherent in the system. The stimuli from the environment are processed in a sequential manner through several subsystems for attention, situation assessment, expectation generation, affect appraisal, goal management and action selection. All of these subsystems are affected by different emotions which actually have a central role in the architecture. The *feeling of confidence* is also modelled in the architecture, and the aim of the metacognitive control of the architecture is to increase and stabilize that parameter, even projecting it into the future, to instil a feeling of confidence in the expectations. The feeling of confidence is added as a parameter to the modelled attention in the stimulus as confidence that attended cues properly reflect the stimulus.

9.3.6 Kismet

Although Kismet (Breazeal 2000) was meant to mimic human behaviour, the very endeavour of building such a complex system brings certain interesting ideas into realization and understanding. In order to promote human–robot interaction and social learning, it is assumed that both robots and humans find the same sorts of perceptual features interesting. This also assures that the stimuli and cues which humans usually use to direct robots' attention are indeed attended to by robots. The initial sets of perceptual cues which attract Kismet's attention were designed to imitate the way in which human infants find salient cues.

Kismet's architecture consists of six subsystems: the low-level feature extraction system, high-level perception system, attention system, motivation system, behaviour system and the motor system.

The attention system (almost a direct implementation of Wolfe's *guided search 2.0* (Wolfe 1994)) is organized in two stages: the first is a preattentive, massively parallel stage that processes information across the entire visual field about basic visual features such as colour (especially skin tone), motion, depth cues, etc.; the second stage performs other more complex operations such as facial expression recognition, eye detection or object identification over a localized region of the visual field.

These processes are deployed sequentially from location to location under attentional control which is guided by the properties of the visual stimuli.

Kismet operates in a continuous cycle of behaviour influencing what is attended/perceived, and perception influencing subsequent behaviours. Kismet does not incorporate any theory of learning and is instead used to analyse human behaviour during human–robot interaction.

9.4   Interactivist anticipative approach

Before presenting our cognitive architecture in the next subsection, we will briefly explain the meta-theoretical background that we have adopted, called *interactivism*. Interactivism is a vast and rather ambitious philosophical and theoretical system originally developed by Mark Bickhard (Bickhard 1980a, 1980b, 1993; Bickhard and Terveen 1995; Bickhard 1998) which covers a plethora of aspects related to the mind and person. Within interactivism, an agent is regarded as an *action system*, an autonomous, self-organizing, self-maintaining entity which can act and sense the effects of its actions in the environment it inhabits. *Process-based* ontology is adopted to treat various cognitive phenomena from low-level perception to representation and language. Embracing interactivism, we have developed several cognitive architectures (Stojanov 1997, 2001; Kulakov 1998). Elsewhere we have put forward an interactivist approach to knowledge representation (Stojanov and Kulakov 2003). Given the radical departure of interactivism from current *substance-based* approaches there have not been many systems implementing some of the interactivist ideas. In Stojanov, Trajkovski and Kulakov 2006 we gave an overview of interactivist ideas adopted in artificial intelligence and robotics.

For the purposes of this chapter, we will give a brief summary of our interactivist view on agency and the basis for our cognitive architecture which is dealt with later in the chapter. Agents (or action-systems) act to preserve their autonomy and to maintain the conditions for their further existence (i.e., they are *autopoietic*). Bickhard often puts forward the canonical example of a candle flame as an analogy for cognitive systems. The flame maintains itself above threshold combustion temperature, vaporizing wax into fuel, and in standard conditions induces convection (which brings in fresh oxygen and disposes of the waste products). He calls these systems *self-maintenant*. Furthermore, a system capable of maintaining its condition of being self-maintenant is called a *recursively* self-maintenant system. A candle flame certainly is not recursively self-maintenant because there is not much that the candle flame can do when it runs out of wax. However, a bacterium (Campbell 1990) may be able to swim as long as the sugar gradient rises and tumble if it senses that it is swimming down the gradient. In the above-mentioned sense, this bacterium is a primitive recursive self-maintenant system capable of switching between interactions that differentiate between a *good* and a *bad* direction to swim. In order to be recursively self-maintenant, an action-system has to be able to *discriminate* between various aspects of its environment and evaluate them within its *inner value system*. The *situation image* at a given moment should also include indicators of possibilities for interactions, which would guide the trajectories towards preferred (in the sense of the inner value system) interaction subspaces. For example, a representation of some physically manipulable object (for a particular agent) would include indicators for the *invariant patterns of interaction* with that object, based on past experiences. The situation image would also include indications of potential paths. These indications would include contextual information regarding the agent's goals, experience and the level of its ontological development.

Wrapping up this section of the chapter, we quote Bickhard (1980a) again:

There is no direct or total knowledge of the world, only fallible and partial knowledge of its interactive characteristics. Thus, the world image is constructed from the specific to the general, out of the basic elements of knowledge in the *procedures innate to the system*, while the situation image is differentiated within the world image from the general to the specific by the outcomes of various interactions. The world image is a *hierarchicalized network* of general interaction possibilities and dependencies, while the situation image is a scheme structure of current possibilities. (emphasis added)

An agent, i.e., a cognizing system, thus in the interactivist view is seen as a collection of processes which are endogenously active and result in the self-maintenance of the agent. The environment only modulates the ongoing activities of and within the agent. The agent's actions are interactions with the environment.

Generally, attention is seen as a mechanism that has evolved in order to maximize an agent's chances of survival by deploying resources to deal with unanticipated changes in a timely and resource-efficient manner.

9.4.1   *The basics of the Vygo cognitive architecture*

In this section we will highlight only those parts of our architecture which are relevant to attention.

Vygo is a cognitive architecture that models the process of *environment internalization*, i.e., the emergence of concepts from *sensory motor*

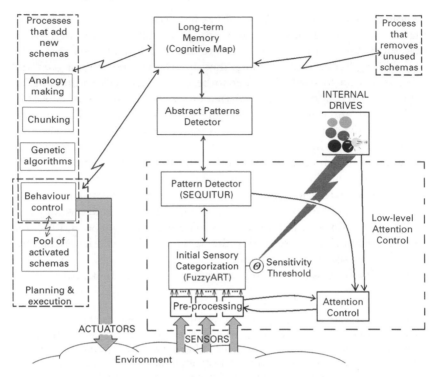

Figure 9.1 Main data structures and parallel processes incorporated into the Vygo architecture

interactions. These concepts are used to *predict* and *act* in an *efficient way* on the basis of the *motivational system.* The essential element of the architecture is the *sensory motor schema structure.* It is inspired by Piaget's notion of schema and is not unlike Drescher's implementation (Drescher 1991). More will be said below.

The architecture (figure 9.1) includes several distinct, independently running modules, which synchronize and communicate with each other to produce the complete, unified agent behaviour. The pre-processing of the sensory inputs and their initial classification in the FuzzyART module (Carpenter, Grossberg and Rosen 1991) into proto-categories are added in order to reduce sensory complexity. The *conceptual network* (also referred to as a *cognitive map*) serves as a long-term storage of knowledge structures, representing the environment by relations between sensors and motor actions grounded in experience. The *internal drives* are the value system of the agent, evaluating the percepts by their relevance to the agent's survival and wellbeing and motivating certain behaviours according to the current needs. The *behaviour module* provides an *adaptive, anticipative* and fault-tolerant behaviour construction in accordance with the current drives and goals of the agent.

There are several different types of pre-processing units depending on the sensory modality: wavelet transformation or pre-processing specialized for the visual input, frequency analysis for the auditory input and yet another type of neural network for the haptic system.

The central part of our cognitive architecture is the above-mentioned cognitive map, which consists of more or less abstract sensory-motor schemas and is implemented as a *directed graph*. It represents the *long-term memory* of the agent. The graph consists of nodes and links, where the outgoing node is a *condition* node, and the incoming node is an *expectation* node of a schema. Each schema has an associated *reliability* value which shows the degree of confidence in the results of the execution of that schema in the course of agent–environment interaction.

Several processes can add new schemas to the map: by *analogy making* among several existing schemas and transferring certain schemas to a new part of the cognitive map, i.e., into a new domain; by *chunking* the longest reliable chain of schemas with sufficient reliability into one super-schema (more abstract), making the smaller schemas in the chain just steps in the sequence of sub-schemas; and by *random combinations* of existing schemas according to a process (not unlike a genetic algorithm). These processes run in parallel. There is also a process that removes unused or very unreliable schemas, which can run during the periods of the agent's inactivity (i.e., when the agent is not engaged in interaction with the environment)

All the nodes in the cognitive map are accompanied by a connectionist part (activation, net input and accumulated activation) that gives a measure of each node's relevance to the current sensory inputs and preferences. The process of activation spreading is implemented as a parallel thread.

In our previous architectures, the similarity between pseudo-concepts was calculated as in classical theories about similarity with a scalar product between the percept and each category (Tversky and Gati 1978). In the latest version of the architecture we use FuzzyART networks for this task. FuzzyART networks, in their course of functioning, give a so-called *winning category* which is represented by the most activated node out of all remembered category prototype nodes. This activation actually shows the level of similarity between the current sensory input and the remembered category prototypes stored in nodes. Using this activation as information about the similarity of the current sensory input to each stored category prototype, we can further activate parts of the cognitive map which are relevant to the current situation. This represents the bottom-up influence on the process of perception.

The top-down influence on the perception is simulated by the overall prior activation of the nodes created by different mechanisms (*behavioural plans*, analogy making and the influence of the internal drives). In that way, the above-mentioned processes establish a starting advantage for certain categories of nodes or the initial perceptual *bias* of the system.

Several modules of the Vygo architecture (Pre-processing, Initial Sensory Categorization, Pattern Detector and Attention Control) essentially represent the *Low-level Attention Control*. In a way, these modules can be regarded as implementing *attention as initial selection*. Given the high dimensionality of the overall sensory input, the low-level attention control actually filters out the larger part of this information but attempts to direct attention to the important parts of sensory input according to the influence and control from the other modules.

Although there can be indirect influence from the overall cognitive map and the internal drives on the current attentional focus, nevertheless, this part of the architecture has certain autonomy in the selection of the sequences of centres of attention, and that is why we refer to it as the low-level control of attention. Different sensory modalities have different such subsystems for low-level attention control. One such subsystem for the visual sensory modality is presented later in this chapter. In the following subsections we present some of the cognitive phenomena that were modelled using the Vygo architecture.

9.4.2   Modelled cognitive phenomena

We have discussed various cognitive phenomena modelled in our architecture before (Kulakov, Stojanov and Davcev 2002; Kulakov and Stojanov 2002). Still, for the sake of easier understanding of the role of attention in the cognitive architecture, we will briefly overview Perceptional, Motivational and Behavioural modules where several cognitive phenomena are modelled.

9.4.3   Perception and categorization

The agent discerns between different sensory stimuli and clusters them into categories using the FuzzyART neural network as an initial classifier. The sensitivity threshold of FuzzyART is dynamically adjusted according to the current *desirability* of the perceived sensor vector, which accounts for different levels of attention depending on how interesting (desirable or undesirable) it finds the current sensory information.

9.4.4   Activation spreading

The activation-spreading mechanisms are often used as a way to define the degree of proximity between nodes in the conceptual graph, for example between a given referent node and every other node in the graph. In Vygo, they serve two distinct purposes. The first is to modulate and guide goal-directed behaviour by spreading activation from the goal nodes. Depending on the active motivational drive, those nodes in the network which are considered most important for satisfying the active drive are designated as goal nodes. Activation then begins to spread from the goal nodes through the schema links backwards. With each step in the activation spreading (i.e., each schema on the path), the activation of the nodes is decreased, thus making the nodes which are closer to the goal nodes more activated and the more distant ones less activated. This activation is used in the process of choosing schemas for execution in the behaviour system. This mechanism allows for the current desires and goals actually to influence attention through the determination of subsequent behaviour.

The second activation-spreading mechanism is used for determining the relevance of particular facets of knowledge according to the current situation or context. The activation is spread the same way as in goal activation, except that here it originates from the current executing schema and is spread in all directions through the schema nodes (backwards and forwards). The set of nodes that are activated in the surrounding area of the current schema is referred to as the *working memory*. It plays a major role in the top-down context-driven influence on perception. When the process of categorization is taking place, the percept nodes in the working memory are more likely to be selected as a winning category because their activity in the FuzzyART network increases depending on the degree of their context activation. This narrows the perception process to the concepts which are relevant for the current context.

9.4.5   Internal drives as a basic motivational subsystem

Every autonomous agent, either natural or artificial, which is going through the process of ontogenetic development must have some sort of built-in innate value system. The value system guides the process of learning such that the agent will acquire that type of knowledge which in turn will be the most beneficial for its 'survival' and 'well-being' in the environment. Vygo incorporates an internal drive system as an elementary value system and motivational force for behaviour. It includes the hunger, affect (pain/pleasure) and curiosity drives. The three drives that comprise the drive system are evolutionarily very plausible since they are strongly connected to the survival of the species and are inborn drives. More details about the curiosity drive and its relation to other cognitive phenomena like the feeling of understanding, analogy making and expectations are given elsewhere (Stojanov and Kulakov 2006).

A developmental system by definition is a system that continuously grows and organizes its knowledge, initially departing from some basic innate structures and schemas. Given the constrained 'storage and processing' resources of the agent, not all the data acquired through acting in the environment can be either memorized or processed, so there must be some subsystem that would judge the usefulness and the relevance of every new piece of knowledge and accordingly decide to store it or to discard it, to consider it or to ignore it. This is the function of the value system. The value system relates the sensorial and action data (and the more complex cognitive structures that emerge from them) to the agent's needs and goals, thus giving them subjective meaning and purpose in the context of the agent's existence.

Supplemental to the major function it has in the 'emotional' organization of knowledge, the value system also serves a role as a motivational system, or behaviour modulator. It discerns between good and bad actions in the acting process and keeps the agent on track in conformance with its goals. The value system marks the actions and percepts according to its current emotional and bodily state so that it can reinforce just the positive actions when Vygo encounters a similar situation, improving on the agent's overall behaviour. The same principle applies when, for example, in the visual system, the actions are the saccadic movements of the gaze direction.

9.4.6   Behaviour module

The behaviour module is the most active, real-time element of the architecture, for its main role is navigating Vygo through the environment by continuously generating a coherent stream of actions for the motor system to execute. This is accomplished through *selection* and *execution* of *action plans*, which are in fact sequences of abstract schemas from the conceptual network. In order to keep the generated behaviour in conformance with the accumulated knowledge through experience and also to utilize this knowledge maximally in pursuing the goals and desires of the agent, the behaviour module is strongly coupled with the pseudo-conceptual cognitive network and the internal drives system. In the process of plan construction, it selects from the conceptual network a set of the most appropriate and desirable schemas according to the current context and then probabilistically chooses one schema from this set to serve as a current plan. Likewise, the process of schema selection is influenced by the drives, since it uses the desirability and activation of schemas and their percepts as indicators, which among other factors are mainly determined by the state of the internal drives system. Furthermore, this coupling between the behaviour module on one side and the conceptual network and internal drives on the other is not only one-directional, since by generating new random behaviour sequences, the behaviour module continuously adds new schemas in the conceptual network, hence contributing to the process of knowledge accumulation. Additionally, by generating behaviour that achieves the established goals and wanders through desirable places, the behaviour module indirectly influences the state and values of the internal drive system, satisfying the agent's needs and preferences.

9.4.7   Plan execution

A plan in the behaviour module is defined as the current executing schema, being either abstract or concrete. There is a specific behaviour sequence associated with each concrete schema, represented by an ordered sequence of parallel action sets. The behavioural field usually comprises several independent actuator elements that can be manipulated simultaneously without conflict (for example, moving and gazing in different directions). Therefore, every step in the behaviour sequence specifies a set of actions that can be executed in parallel, operating on different parts of the motor system. So, supposing that the schema representing a plan is a concrete one, the behaviour module actually executes the plan by traversing the behaviour sequence of the schema step by step, and at every step it sends parallel action signals to the motor system of the agent. After the execution of the behaviour sequence is completed, the plan is considered finished, and it is judged to have been executed successfully or not according to the degree of matching between the current percept and the expectancy percept of the plan schema. Next, the procedure for generating a new plan is initiated, which employs a probabilistic pool mechanism to choose the next appropriate schema to be executed as a plan. This holds provided that the schema selected as a plan is a concrete one (abstract level 0). The abstract schemas, due to their composite hierarchical structure, are handled in a different way.

The action space in Vygo is formally defined as groups of actions, where every action can have a definite number of parameters (either real or integer). Each step in the behaviour sequence can only include

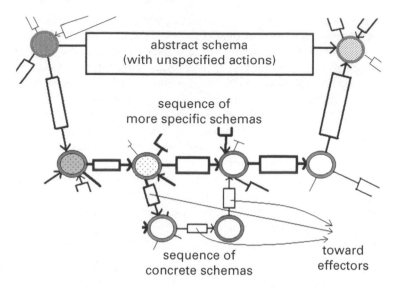

Figure 9.2 Expansion of an abstract schema up to concrete schemas

actions from different groups, i.e., actions from the same group cannot be executed in parallel.

If the schema selected through the pool mechanism turns out to be an abstract one, then it is expanded recursively up to concrete schemas and then executed in a pre-order fashion. Since an abstract schema consists of an ordered sequence of schemas, which may also be abstract schemas, when all the schemas are expanded up to their sub-schemas we get a tree structure, with abstract schemas in the internal nodes and concrete schemas as leaves of the tree (see figure 9.2). Execution of the plan then proceeds by traversing the tree with the pre-order method, going through the concrete schemas from left to right in the pre-order representation of the tree. After every abstract or concrete schema finishes its execution, a check is made as to whether Vygo is on track, that is, whether the current percept matches the expected percept of that schema. If the expectancy is confirmed, then the execution is successful, and the reliability of the finished schema is increased, otherwise the schema is considered to have failed and its reliability is decreased.

The failure of a given sub-schema doesn't imply that the whole plan immediately fails. There are adaptive recovery mechanisms which try to continue the execution of the plan in spite of the failure of some of its substeps. Only when these adaptive mechanisms, by trying alternative sub-schemas in the execution, don't succeed in recovering the plan execution does the whole plan finally admit failure, and a burst of activation is sent to that part of the cognitive map, invoking Vygo's attention.

9.4.8 *Expectancy and routine behaviour*

The design and the dynamics of the behaviour module are highly anticipative in nature. At every moment, depending on the current plan, Vygo anticipates several future percept encounters, and expects them to be met. As long as these expectations are true, it continues undistracted with its planned course of action, and nothing new is learned. Only when a surprise happens does it trigger learning procedures to accommodate (or assimilate) the newly discovered discrepancies between current knowledge and the environment.

After the schemas are sufficiently validated, i.e., after their reliability is increased to a certain threshold level, the concrete schemas can be combined into chunks, making abstract schemas, which can be thought of as more complex routine behaviours. These more complex routine behaviours further organize the interaction knowledge into meaningful behaviour structures and increase the situatedness of the agent in the environment.

Habituation and attention stand in an antagonistic relationship, and where a habit grows, attention disappears. William James (1890) noticed that a big part of our course of actions is performed purely automatically, or by habit. The process through which some behaviour is transformed into a habit (or a routine) is called *practice*. The forming of routines gives us more and more powerful mechanisms and allows us to set more and more distant goals, while at the same time it extends the prediction of future events. Together with the biological benefits of routine behaviour as a purposeful stereotypical reaction to uniform, consistent and more or less constant environmental stimuli, the nervous system is equipped with another, biologically not less important but perfectly antagonistic, mechanism – exhaustion, whose aim is to break down ongoing routine and facilitate the appearance of new reactions.

9.5   Sub-module for modelling attention at a lower perceptual level

This subsystem is the most recent addition to our architecture. It is intended to tackle the initial real-time processing of the incoming continuous video and sound input. Within our general cognitive architecture we have developed a general learning system capable of learning sequences or time-series of signal patterns.

The inputs from the sensors in the general scheme are first pre-processed in a few layers using either a Discrete Wavelet Transform or Fast Fourier Transform. Then the FuzzyART network classifies the analogue input data and the classification identification numbers (IDs) are used as symbol inputs to a modified version of the so-called SEQUITUR algorithm (Nevill-Manning and Witten 1997) which is used for analysis of a sequence of signal patterns. The SEQUITUR algorithm generates *rules* out of the reappearance of the symbol patterns in a sequence.

The modifications of the SEQUITUR algorithm include the calculation of an activation function for each symbol and rule obtained from the SEQUITUR algorithm, which is later used for correct recognition of the signal pattern over time, turning the whole SEQUITUR data structure into one big *evolving neural network*. For that purpose, for each rule, its level of abstractness is calculated and its length in number of symbols at the lowest level is updated constantly. To some selected rules we attach an *annotation label* which is sent over the communication channel whenever some rule is recognized from the signal input or whenever the level of activation of some rule exceeds a certain high threshold.

9.5.1   The general learning system

Most of the artificial neural networks are created for pattern recognition of static input. Exceptions are the so-called recurrent neural networks, where the current output is fed back to the input layer where it is combined with the future input. Generally, output is a function not only of current input, but also of all past input. Still, the number of recurrent neurons determines the memory capacity of the whole neural network.

As an alternative, we have used a FuzzyART neural network, which classifies the input signals with certain granularity of the input space and gives them certain classification IDs. Later these classification IDs are treated as symbols and are fed into the SEQUITUR algorithm, which is specialized for sequence analysis.

We have modified the original SEQUITUR algorithm by adding several new properties to rules and symbols, like the *level of abstractness* of the rule and the total *number of symbols* at the bottom level of the rule. We have also included *level of activation* for each rule, symbol and *activation-spreading mechanism*.

Since the number of different categories into which the FuzzyART module classifies the sensory inputs tends to saturate, it is a finite number that depends on the sensitivity threshold. The idea behind this architecture is that the classification IDs from the FuzzyART module can be treated as symbols and entered into the SEQUITUR algorithm in order

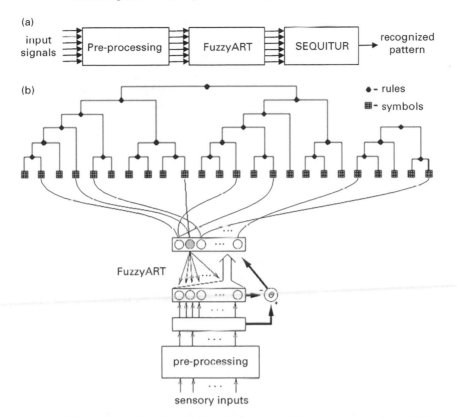

Figure 9.3 (a) a general learning system; (b) the category nodes of the FuzzyART module serve as input symbols to the SEQUITUR module in this unsupervised version of a general learning system

to analyse their pattern over time. With the activation-spreading mechanism added to the SEQUITUR rules and symbols, the SEQUITUR rules can be considered an ensemble of evolving neural networks specialized to be activated by certain sensory stimuli.

The winning category node from the FuzzyART module is added as the next symbol in the sequence of incoming symbols in the SEQUITUR module. The symbols at the bottom level of the hierarchy in SEQUITUR receive different levels of activation from the corresponding category nodes of the FuzzyART module – the winning category casts a maximal activation on the layer of symbols at SEQUITUR, but the rest of the FuzzyART categories also transmit some activation to the symbols at SEQUITUR (see figures 9.3(a) and 9.3(b)). This mechanism provides the necessary flexibility during the recognition process – which

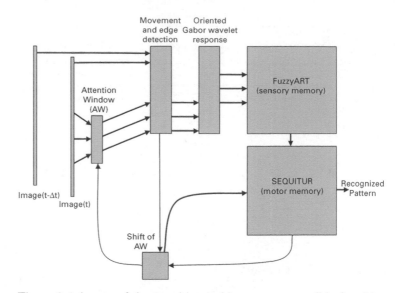

Figure 9.4 A part of the cognitive architecture, responsible for video processing, having the general learning system at its core

SEQUITUR rule has gained the maximum activation because similar categories are given similar activations in the FuzzyART module.

The purpose of spreading the activation is to determine the relevance of each particular piece of knowledge (in our case the rules), bringing relevant ones into the working memory. The associative mechanism used in our architecture is a modified version of the Grossberg activation function (Grossberg 1978).

We define a continuous sensing activity as the continuous group of saccades during which the expectations for the retinal image around the focus were met in a row.

The upper-level nodes in the SEQUITUR module are the starting levels of the conceptual graph nodes in the long-term memory (the cognitive map).

9.5.2   A system for video processing

We have adapted the Behavioural Model of Visual Perception (BMVP) (Rybak *et al.* 1998) where, among other things, we have replaced the sensory memory with a FuzzyART neural network instead of a Hopfield neural network. Also, instead of fixed motor memory we have used the SEQUITUR module (see figure 9.4). The BMVP develops representations of the visual objects based on the responses from a fixed number of edge-detecting sensors during saccadic movements of a small Attention Window (AW). Instead of using these edge-detecting sensors as inputs to the sensory memory as in the BMVP, we have experimentally deduced that using oriented Gabor wavelet responses yields better and faster results. The original BMVP was used for recognition of still images, whereas we have used the modified BMVP on live video sequences.

In figure 9.4, the thicker arrows denote the information flow, while the thinner arrows denote control flow. The movement detection also controls the shift of the AW and it has been modified so that, unlike in the BMVP, there is no need for human intervention to determine the so-called 'interesting' zones around the eyes in certain pictures, since the blinks and other movements of the head make them interesting by only including the movement detection to influence the decision about the shift of AW, i.e., about the position of the next focus of attention.

Figure 9.5, adapted from Rybak et al. (1998), explains the content of one AW. The relative orientation of each context point ϕ is calculated as a difference between the absolute angle of the edge at the centre of the AW and the absolute angle of the edge at that context point. This relative orientation is used to get the oriented Gabor wavelet response at that context point in a small window. This response is then used as an input to the FuzzyART neural network, which plays the role of a sensory memory.

The SEQUITUR is used as a motor memory by providing alternating inputs once from the sensory memory and once from the vector selector that determines the next focal point of the AW. As can be seen from figure 9.5, there are forty-eight different possible saccadic movements, at the intersections of sixteen radiating lines and three concentric circles. These are represented by forty-eight different symbols, which are entered as input symbols to the SEQUITUR module. The SEQUITUR rules are of form Percept–Saccade–Percept–Saccade–. . . –Percept, taken from the FuzzyART and from the 'Shift of AW' modules.

The relative calculation of the orientation of the edges at the next focal points, according to the orientation of the edge at the current focus of AW, gives rise to the possibility for recognition of objects independent of orientation. The relative calculation of the distance between the current and the next focal point allows recognition of objects independent of their size.

The estimated centre of the movement activity is used as an influence towards which the saccade jumps at each new video sequence and also when the saccades tend to exit the image frontiers.

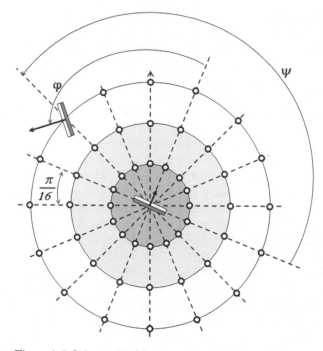

Figure 9.5 Schematic of the Attention Window (AW). The next possible focal points are located at the intersections of sixteen radiating lines and three concentric circles. The relative parameters, Φ and Ψ, of the edge at one possible next focal point are shown.

Even though the selection of the next saccade is relatively simply solved and could be further improved, the resulting saccadic movements demonstrate psychologically plausible patterns which pursue the most interesting parts of natural images (edges, eyes, mouth, face contours, etc.), as can be seen from figure 9.6, where two examples of the saccadic movements over two different images are shown.

9.6   Conclusions and future work

In this chapter we have tried to give an overview of the role given to attention in cognitive architectures research. We have reviewed some of the most popular cognitive architecture from the point of view of its treatment of attention.

Although attention is conceptualized in different manners, we can safely say that most follow some of the well-known attention models from psychology literature. The added value here is that attention models are

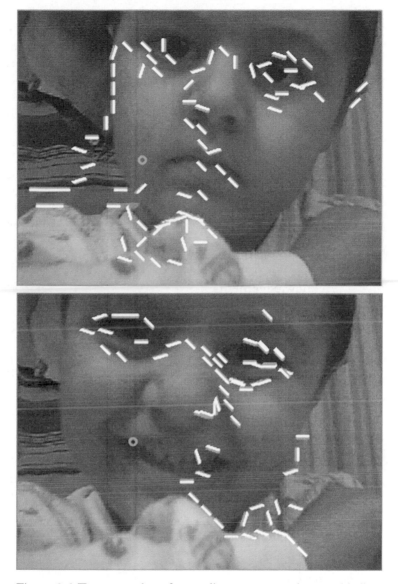

Figure 9.6 Two examples of saccadic movements shown with lines which are oriented to the approximately detected edges at these points. Eighty saccadic movements are made over one video sequence. The small circle in the middle shows the estimated centre of the movement activity.

implemented as well as embedded in a complete cognitive architecture. This forces researchers to be rather specific and spell out even those details that were not accounted for in the adopted stand-alone model. It also makes explicit the relation of attention to the other modules of the cognitive system, leading possibly to revisions and new insights.

In section 9.4 we briefly presented the overall design and the main parts of our cognitive architecture and discussed the role of high- and low-level attention processes.

In section 9.5 we described the most recent addition to the architecture: a sub-module dedicated to low-level processing of real-time video and audio input which also implements a low-level attention model that guides the visual perception. So far, our architecture has only been used within simulated environments, and the latest addition will enable experiments in real-world environments with a video camera as the main perceptual input.

9.7   Acknowledgements

The work described in this chapter has been partially funded by the European Commission's Sixth Framework Programme under contract no. 029427 as part of the Specific Targeted Research Project XPERO ('Robotic Learning by Experimentation'), partially by the Walter Karplus Fund of the IEEE Computational Intelligence Society and partially by the Ministry of Education and Science of Macedonia.

9.8   References

Anderson, J. R. 1993. *Rules of the Mind.* Hillsdale, NJ: Erlbaum
Anderson, J. R., Matessa, M., and Douglass, S. 1995. The ACT-R theory and visual attention, in *Proceedings of the 17th Annual Conference of the Cognitive Science Society,* Hillsdale, NJ: Lawrence Erlbaum Associates: 61–5
Anderson, J. R., Matessa, M., and Lebiere, C. 1997. ACT-R: A theory of higher level cognition and its relation to visual attention, *Human–Computer Interaction* 12(4): 439–62
Baars, B. J. 1988. *A Cognitive Theory of Consciousness.* Cambridge: Cambridge University Press
Bickhard, M. H. (1980a). *Cognition, Convention, and Communication.* New York: Praeger Publishers
   (1980b). A model of developmental and psychological processes, *Genetic Psychology Monographs* 102: 61–116
   1993. Representational content in humans and machines, *Journal of Experimental and Theoretical Artificial Intelligence* 5: 285–333

1998. Levels of representationality, *Journal of Experimental and Theoretical Artificial Intelligence* 10(2): 179–215

Bickhard, M. H., and Terveen, L. 1995. *Foundational Issues in Artificial Intelligence and Cognitive Science: Impasse and Solution*. Amsterdam: Elsevier

Breazeal, C. 2000. Sociable machines: Expressive social exchange between humans and robots. Sc.D. dissertation, Department of Electrical Engineering and Computer Science, Massachusetts Institute of Technology

Broadbent, D. 1958. *Perception and Communication*. London: Pergamon Press

Campbell, D. T. 1990. Levels of organization, downward causation, and the selection-theory approach to evolutionary epistemology. In G. Greenberg and E. Tobach (eds.), *Theories of the Evolution of Knowing*. Hillsdale, NJ: Lawrence Erlbaum Associates: 1–17

Carpenter, G. A., Grossberg, S., and Rosen, D. B. 1991. FuzzyART: Fast stable learning and categorization of analog patterns by an adaptive resonance system, *Neural Networks* 4: 759–71

Chalmers, D., French, R., and Hofstadter, D. 1992. High-level perception, representation, and analogy: A critique of artificial intelligence methodology, *Journal of Experimental and Theoretical Artificial Intelligence*: 4(3): 169–93

Dixon, N. 1981. *Preconscious Processing*. Chichester: Wiley

Drescher, G. 1991. *Made-up Minds: A Constructivist Approach to Artificial Intelligence*. Cambridge, MA: MIT Press

Franklin, S. 2003. IDA: A conscious artifact? *Journal of Consciousness Studies* 10: 47–66

2007. A foundational architecture for artificial general intelligence, in B. Goertzel and P. Wang (eds.), *Advances in Artificial General Intelligence: Concepts, Architectures and Algorithms, Proceedings of the AGI Workshop, 2006*, Amsterdam: IOS Press: 36–54

French, R. M. 1992, TableTop: An emergent, stochastic computer model of analogy-making. Ph.D. thesis, University of Michigan

Goertzel, B., and Pennachin, C. 2007. The Novamente artificial intelligence engine, in B. Goertzel and P. Wang (eds.), *Advances in Artificial General Intelligence: Concepts, Architectures and Algorithms, Proceedings of the AGI Workshop, 2006*, Amsterdam: IOS Press: 63–129

Grossberg, S. 1978. A theory of visual coding, memory, and development, in E. L. J. Leeuwenberg and H. F. J. M. Buffart (eds.), *Formal Theories of Visual Comparative Analysis*. New York: Wiley: 7–26

Hofstadter, D. 1996. *Fluid Concepts and Creative Analogies: Computer Models of the Fundamental Mechanisms of Thought*. New York: Basic Books

Hudlicka, E. 2005. Modeling interactions between metacognition and emotion in a cognitive architecture, in *Proceedings of the AAAI Spring Symposium on Metacognition in Computation*. AAAI Technical Report SS-05-04. Menlo Park, CA: AAAI Press: 55–61

James, W. 1890. *The Principles of Psychology*: 404–5. Retrieved 29 September 2009 from: http://psychclassics.asu.edu/James/Principles/prin11.htm

Kokinov, B. 1994. The DUAL cognitive architecture: A hybrid multi-agent approach, in A. G. Cohn (ed.), *Proceedings of the 11th European Conference on Artificial Intelligence (ECAI '94)*. London: Wiley: 203–7

1997. Micro-level hybridization in the cognitive architecture DUAL, in R. Sun and F. Alexander (eds.), *Connectionist-Symbolic Integration: From Unified to Hybrid Architectures*. Hillsdale, NJ: Lawrence Erlbaum Associates: 197–208

Kokinov, B., and Petrov, A. 2001. Integration of memory and reasoning in analogy-making: The AMBR model, in D. Gentner, K. J. Holyoak and B. N. Kokinov (eds.), *The Analogical Mind: Perspectives from Cognitive Science*. Cambridge, MA: MIT Press

Kulakov, A. 1998. Vygovorotsky: A model of an anticipative and analogy-making actor. M.Sc. thesis, New Bulgarian University, Sofia

Kulakov, A., and Stojanov, G. 2002. Structures, inner values, hierarchies and stages: Essentials for developmental robot architectures, in *Proceedings of the 2nd International Workshop on Epigenetic Robotics: Modelling Cognitive Development in Robotic Systems*, Edinburgh: 63–9

Kulakov, A., Stojanov, G., and Davcev, D. 2002. A model of an expectancy-driven and analogy-making actor, in *Proceedings of the 2nd International Conference on Development and Learning*, Cambridge, MA: 61–8

Langley, P., and Choi, D. 2006. A unified cognitive architecture for physical agents, in *Proceedings of the AAAI 2006*, Boston: 1469–74

Minsky, M. 1986. *The Society of Mind*. New York: Simon and Schuster

Nestor, A., and Kokinov, B. 2004. Towards active vision in the DUAL cognitive architecture, *International Journal of Information Theories and Applications* 11(1): 11

Nevill-Manning, C. G., and Witten, I. H. 1997. Identifying hierarchical structure in sequences: A linear-time algorithm, *Journal of Artificial Intelligence Research* 7: 67–82

Newell, A. 1990. *Unified Theories of Cognition*. Cambridge, MA: Harvard University Press

Posner, M. I. 1980. Orienting of attention, *Quarterly Journal of Experimental Psychology* 32: 3–25

Posner, M. I., and Petersen, S. E. 1990. The attention system of the human brain, *Annual Review of Neuroscience* 13: 25–42

Rybak, I. A., Gusakova, V. I., Golovan, A. V., Podladchikova, L. N., and Shevtsova, N. A. 1998. A model of attention-guided visual perception and recognition, *Vision Research* 38: 2387–400

Salvucci, D. D. 2000. A model of eye movements and visual attention, in *Proceedings of the International Conference on Cognitive Modeling*, Veenendaal, The Netherlands: Universal Press: 252–9

Salvucci, D. D., Kushleyeva, Y., and Lee, F. J. 2004. Toward an ACT-R general executive for human multitasking, in *Proceedings of the 6th International Conference on Cognitive Modeling*, Pittsburgh: 267–72

Stojanov, G. 1997. Expectancy theory and interpretation of the EXG curves in context of machine and biological intelligence, Ph.D. thesis, University Sts Cyril and Methodius, Skopje, Macedonia

2001. Petitagé: A case study in developmental robotics. *Proceedings of the 1st International Workshop on Epigenetic Robotics*, Lund University Cognitive Studies, 85

Stojanov, G., and Kulakov, A. 2003. Interactivist approach to representation in epigenetic agents, in *Proceedings of the 3rd International Workshop on Epigenetic Robotics*, Lund, Sweden: 123–30

2006. On curiosity in intelligent robotic systems, in *Proceedings of the 2006 AAAI Fall Symposia*, Arlington, VA, 12–15 October: 44–51

Stojanov, G., and Trajkovski, G., and Kulakov, A., 2006. Interactivism in artificial intelligence (AI) and intelligent robotics, *New Ideas in Psychology* 24(2): 163–85

Styles, E. A. 2005. *Attention, Perception, and Memory: An Integrated Introduction*. Hove: Psychology Press

Treisman, A. M., and Gelade, G. 1980. A feature-integration theory of attention, *Cognitive Psychology* 12: 97–136

Treisman, A. M., and Sato, S. 1990. Conjunction search revisited, *Journal of Experimental Psychology: Human Perception and Performance* 16: 459–78

Tversky, A., and Gati, I. 1978. Studies of similarity, in E. Rosch and B. B. Lloyd (eds.), *Cognition and Categorization*. Hillsdale, NJ: Lawrence Erlbaum Associates: 79–98

Wang, H., and Fan, J. 2007. Human attentional networks: A connectionist model, *Journal of Cognitive Neuroscience* 19(10): 1678–89

Wolfe, J. M. 1994. Guided search 2.0: A revised model of visual search, *Psychonomic Bulletin and Review* 1: 202–38

1999. In attentional amnesia. In V. Coltheart (ed.), *Fleeting Memories*. Cambridge, MA: MIT Press: 71–94

Wolfe, J. M., and Bennett, S. C. 1997. Preattentive object files. *Vision Research* 37: 25–44

Wolfe, J. M., and Horowitz, T. S. 2004. What attributes guide the deployment of visual attention and how do they do it? *Nature Reviews Neuroscience* 5(6): 495–501

Part III

Applications

10 A display with two depth layers: attentional segregation and declutter

Frank Kooi

Analogous to the introduction of colour displays, 3D displays hold the potential to expand the information that can be displayed without increasing clutter. This is in addition to the application of 3D technology to showing volumetric data. Going beyond colour, separation by depth has in the past been shown to enable very fast ('parallel') visual search (Nakayama and Silverman 1986), something that separation by colour alone does not do. The ability to focus attention exclusively on a depth plane provides a potentially powerful (and relatively practical) extension to command-and-control displays. Just one extra depth layer[1] can declutter the display. For this reason we have developed a 'Dual-layer' display with two physically separated layers. As expected, conjunction search times become parallel when information is split into two depth layers but only when the stimuli are simple and non-overlapping; complex and over-lapping imagery in the rear layer still interferes with visual search in the front layer. With the Dual-layer cockpit display, it is possible to increase information content significantly without substantially affecting ease-of-search. We show experimentally that the secondary depth cues (accommodation and parallax) boost this advantage.

We expect the primary 'declutter' market to lie in applications that do not tolerate the overlooking of crucial information, in environments that are space limited, and in mobile displays. Note that the use of 3D to declutter fundamentally differs from the use of 3D to show volumetric spatial relationships. The standard ways to prioritize attention increase the conspicuity of the highlighted symbols by adding colour, increasing luminance, or by setting the prioritized information apart. These declutter methods come with a reaction time cost; the first two increase overall clutter, and the last one requires extra eye movements to be made. The advantage of using real depth is that it only marginally affects the readability and searchability of the other, unhighlighted, information. Adding a layer therefore barely increases the search time in the already present layer, if at all. The experimental validation of the Dual-layer so far has focused on two cockpit displays, the Primary Flight Display and the Navigation Display. The

---

[1] Note that 'layer' in this chapter means 'physical layer' and not 'software layer'.

245

next step is to combine depth displays with dynamic attention allocation, which is of interest because of the spin-offs to, for example, free flight in the aviation domain and multiple applications in the civilian market.

10.1   Display clutter

The desire to view increasing amounts of information on small displays like PDAs has spurred research into smart and compact information presentations. The goal is to keep the display 'clutter free' by good ergonomic design of the visual content and by adding innovative methods to navigate through the information. These include context-aware designs (Olmos, Wickens and Chudy 2000; Streefkerk, van Esch-Bussemakers and Neerincx 2006), gestures like zooming in by moving two fingers closer together on a touch-screen (for an overview see Baudisch 2008), algorithms to minimize symbol overlap (Rosenholtz, Li and Nakano 2007; Fuchs and Schumann 2004) and gaze directed displays (Toet 2006). Decluttering through improved design is treated elsewhere, such as in chapter 3 of this book. The human–computer interface literature focuses on software solutions to clutter and the perception literature focuses on three-dimensional (3D) technology. This chapter primarily falls into the second category.

10.2   Potential of depth to declutter

One of the coming breakthroughs in display hardware is generally believed to be the introduction of '3D displays': displays with a true sense of depth. Though these types of displays already exist in a variety of forms, the commercial application of 3D to make displays more readable is currently limited. The two primary bottlenecks are a reduction in image quality and a lack of viewing comfort. We argue that the 'Dual-layer' display, consisting of just two physically separated layers, is an effective means of steering attention because it does not suffer from either of these two drawbacks. At present it is possible to construct prototypes, and the expectation is that in the near future (within five to seven years) technology will be sufficiently mature to market dual-layer attention support displays.

Virtual Environments (VEs) incorporate the ability to see the world in 3D, in depth. This is an entirely different use of 3D displays and requires multiple depth planes. To achieve *attentional segregation*, just one extra layer will do. In fact, according to Wheatley, Cook and Vidyasagar (2004), attentional segregation by depth works *best* with just one extra

Table 10.1 *The depth cues which are directly relevant to depth-displays. The right column contains the physical unit belonging to the depth cue.*

	Depth cue	Parameter unit
1	Stereopsis	Binocular or stereoscopic disparity (degrees)
2	Accommodation	Optical power (diopters)
3	(Motion) parallax	Relative position/motion (degrees / degrees/sec)
4	Monocular depth cues	Not relevant (no units)

depth layer because the distractors can best be discounted by the visual system when grouped in one (perceptual) layer.

10.3   The visual system: how 3D is perceived

In essence, the two eyes make two-dimensional images of the world, just like photographs do. The 3D structure of the world around us therefore needs to be interpreted using the left and right eye images as a starting point. This interpretation takes place in the visual part of the human brain, not in the eyes. 3D vision can therefore be disturbed by a problem with the eyes (flawed imagery) or by a problem in the brain (flawed interpretation).

10.4   The depth cues

The brain uses a number of *tricks* to make the 3D interpretation, commonly called 'depth cues'. Referring to the process in this way implies that the interpretation is not always correct. Indeed, many, if not most, visual illusions are the result of an erroneous 3D interpretation. To understand 3D technology, the depth cues shown in table 10.1 are directly relevant.

10.4.1   Stereoscopic convergence

Stereopsis is the result of viewing with two eyes rather than one.[2] When an object that is close by is viewed, the eyes turn inward to fuse the object. This is called convergence. Turning the eyes out is called divergence. Vergence and accommodation are neurologically coupled. When converging, the eyes accommodate; when diverging, the eyes relax the

---

[2] Up to 10 per cent of the population has a reduced or no stereo acuity.

accommodation. The reverse is also true: when the eyes accommodate, they also tend to converge. This coupling is very convenient because it helps to prevent double vision (diplopia) and blur. In 3D displays the importance of the coupling increases with the depth difference. A stereoscopic display that does not co-vary accommodation will invariably cause double vision at large enough depths. The application discussed in this chapter, clutter reduction by attentional segregation, does not require large depths and in fact does not want large depths, yet the blur threshold proposed by Pastoor (1993) is easily reached.

10.4.2   Accommodation

Accommodation is necessary in order to see a focused image because the eyes have a limited depth of focus. At any point in time only one distance is truly seen sharply; everything in front and everything behind is blurred to some extent. While at first this may seem unfortunate, it in fact greatly helps to prevent visual attention from wavering. When both foreground and background are seen sharply, both equally draw attention. This phenomenon is easily noticed when looking at a person's face; the background does not draw attention. Similarly a 3D display is easier to view without distractions when the undesired depth planes are (slightly) out of focus.

10.4.3   (Motion) parallax

Moving the head sideways or up/down has two effects: (1) it provides a depth percept during the motion from the optic flow; and (2) it provides different points of view, also after the head motion is stopped. The first effect is analogous to stereopsis. The second, static, effect is demonstrated in figure 10.1 (see plate), where some of the background objects can only be seen from certain points of view. Moving the head sideways is a natural behaviour that allows us to get a better view.

10.4.4   Monocular depth cues

The monocular depth cues, also called *pictorial depth cues*, provide depth perception when viewing the world with one eye closed and the other kept perfectly stationary. This type of depth is also called '$2\frac{1}{2}$D' (Marr 1982). The depth in photographs and on TV is based exclusively on these cues. Examples include perspective, occlusion and shading. While the pictorial depth cues in principle are also suited to segregating objects by depth (e.g., He and Nakayama 1992; Nakayama and Silverman 1986), they will by their more complex appearance inadvertently also increase clutter.

10.5   Auto-stereoscopic 3D displays

To avoid the constraints imposed by wearing optics, so-called *auto-stereoscopic 3D displays* are being developed. The word 'auto' signifies that the user does not need to wear an optical device. The optics are incorporated in the display, splitting the image into a left- and a right-eye component on the display.[3] An inherent feature of auto-stereoscopic displays is therefore that the head needs to be positioned correctly. If, for example, the right eye is shifted 6 cm to the left, it will then see the image meant for the left eye. Though solutions exist that allow some freedom of head movement (e.g., the Philips 9 view auto-stereoscopic display: www.research.philips.com/generalinfo/special/3dlcd/index.htm), a price is paid in terms of a decrease in resolution and an increase in cross-talk which reduces the viewing comfort. For a comparison of 3D methodologies on visual comfort see Kooi and Toet (2004) and Pastoor (1993).

A relatively simple way to include accommodation and parallax in the depth percept is to superimpose two or more images that are located at different distances. Such a *transparent display* presents 'true depth' in the sense that all depth cues are present.[4] Deep Video Imaging Ltd from New Zealand has a dual-layer display on the market (www.Deepvideo. com). The front layer only *subtracts* light and therefore can only show darker objects on a lighter background. This is a significant limitation to displaying objects that draw attention. The display does include the accommodation and parallax depth cues in addition to stereoscopic disparity. We have built on this concept with a Dual-layer display that *adds* light in the front layer. Our patent (Kooi 2003) describes a method to extend a subtractive transparent display to a subtractive and additive transparent display.

10.6   Depth and attention

The relationship between depth and attention has mostly been studied in the laboratory with stereopsis-only 3D displays. Experiments have shown

---

[3] These optics are typically called 'lenticular screens', and are glued to the flat-panel display. A lenticular screen consists of small lenses that bend the light from different display pixels in different directions.

[4] For additive transparent displays this statement is not completely correct because the *occlusion depth cue* is missing; the light coming from the two or more planes simply adds up. Objects therefore cannot 'hide' each other.

that stereoscopic depth is potentially more powerful than colour in helping to find an object (Nakayama and Silverman 1986; Kooi *et al.* 1994). These studies showed that when attention is focused on one layer the other layer virtually can be ignored, eliminating its influence on the search task. The reader may recognize this effect in the common experience of overlooking an object at the front of the refrigerator while searching for it at the back.

The Nakayama and Silverman (1986) conjunction search tasks are as follows:

COLOUR:	find a RED O	among	**RED Xs and GREEN Os**
DEPTH:	find an in-front O	among	in-front Xs and **in-back Os**

When the number of 'distractors' in the colour task increases, the search time rises proportionally. This is called serial search (Treisman and Gelade 1980). When the number of distractors in the depth task goes up, the search time stays roughly constant. This is called parallel search and indicates that people are able to search within one depth plane, ignoring the other. This ability provides a distinct advantage to an operator who knows where (in what depth plane) to find the desired information. Colour coding does not provide the same ease of target detection and is in this sense inferior to depth coding. Depth is therefore a powerful tool in steering attention and in principle is more powerful than colour. Colour coding, on the other hand, is superior to depth coding in the *number of categories* that can be distinguished. The human visual system is able to distinguish at least a few hundred colours in one view but far fewer depth planes. The experiment described above compares visual search for just one colour pair with search for just one depth pair. What happens with multiple colours and multiple depth planes is not fully understood. He and Nakayama (1995), for example, conclude that attention cannot be efficiently allocated to arbitrary depths and extents in space but instead must be linked to *perceived surfaces* which may be slanted in depth. Wagner and Hochstein (2000) confirm the strong relationship between attentional segregation and perceived depth, where 'perceived depth' explicitly is not the same as 'stereoscopic depth'. The science of the relationship between depth and attention therefore remains incomplete.

10.7   Applied and fundamental studies on 3D

No matter how elegantly designed, the stimuli of fundamental experiments tend to be rather far removed from the real world. For example, they typically do not contain overlapping symbols. Ellis and McGreevy (1987) tested a $2\frac{1}{2}$D traffic (navigation) display made of line drawings. The experiment showed that it leads to faster reaction times for uncluttered air traffic situations due to the improved situation awareness. The design is less suited for cluttered air traffic given that $2\frac{1}{2}$D line drawings require more lines than 1D line drawings.

We desire to find an alternative to the $2\frac{1}{2}$D approach making use of true 3D technology. One of our laboratory stimuli is a cockpit display (figure 10.2: see plate) which also served in a flight simulator experiment with experienced pilots (figure 10.5).

In the HILAS European Union project (www.hilas.info)[5] we have effectively extended visual search experiments to real-world situations, in particular the cockpit, by mounting the 'Dual-layer' displays consisting of two physically separated depth layers. Besides stereoscopic disparity, the depth sensation is also created by accommodation and parallax. Here we report part of the laboratory results from the same Dual-layer display; the simulator results will be reported separately. Among the parameters we examined in the laboratory were the influence of symbol overlap on the search task (figure 10.2: see plate) and the influence of accommodation and parallax under overlap conditions (figure 10.4). Overlap was created or avoided by positioning the target and distractors (figure 10.2, left) on, rather than in between, the symbology in the rear layer (figure 10.2, right). A software routine chose from the available placements and then started the next presentation. The figure 10.3 results show that overlap slows the search process down, in particular for the Single-layer condition. The Dual-layer depth difference helps to locate the target, in particular in the overlap condition. It is as if the subjects are able to 'see through' the highly cluttered cockpit display layer shown on the right in figure 10.2 (see plate). These results, which will be published in more detail separately, confirm the generic design goal that symbol overlap should be avoided and demonstrate the potential of true depth to partially mitigate the hindrance that overlap causes.

The data in figure 10.3 confirm several expectations:
1. The depth difference helps to locate the target object (Dual-layer is faster than Single-layer).
2. Overlap greatly increases the reaction time; for the single layer condition it goes through the roof.

[5] The partners in the Flight Deck Strand of the EU Sixth Framework HILAS project are: Smiths Aerospace and BAE SYSTEMS from the UK; NLR, TNO, Noldus and the University of Groningen from the Netherlands; Elbit from Israel; Galileo Avionica and Deep Blue from Italy; STL from Ireland; and Avitronics from Greece.

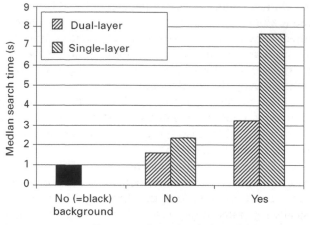

Figure 10.3 Search times for the T target shown in figure 10.2 (see plate) against a black empty rear layer and against the highly cluttered background shown on the right in figure 10.2. This Navigation Display pattern is located either at the same depth plane as the target plus distractors ('Single-layer') or 1.2 cm behind ('Dual-layer'). The target and distractor elements were either all overlapping one of the flight symbols or all not overlapping. The data show a large positive effect from depth difference and a large negative effect from symbol overlap.

3. Therefore, depth difference is particularly useful for highly cluttered displays.
4. Depth difference does not reduce the distraction of the background to zero, but the remaining effect is small in case of no overlap ('No/Dual-layer' compared to 'No background'). If a Dual-layer display can be designed to avoid symbol overlap, symbology may be added to the rear layer almost without cost.

The figure 10.5 data concern the condition of *symbol overlap*, the most confusing condition encountered in symbology displays. The results show that the (secondary) depth cues of Accommodation and Parallax help to disentangle the overlapping symbols. A Dual-layer display therefore has its greatest value in the hardest conditions: when symbols overlap. Phrased differently, figure 10.5 shows that the early vision processes Accommodation and Parallax enhance stereoscopic depth as an attention segregator. Rensink's model in chapter 3 contains a treatment of early vision versus cognitive components of attention. What does this mean for a pilot trying to read his Navigation Display? When a particular symbol needs to be located, focusing on the depth layer containing it will

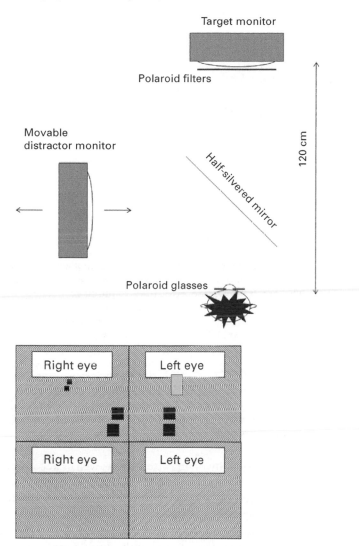

Figure 10.4 Schematic drawing of the experimental set-up on the left and the design of the target monitor on the right. The subject views two monitors superimposed by a half-silvered mirror. One monitor presents the stereoscopic target shown on the *right* viewed through linearly polarized glasses. The other monitor superimposes a 'distractor' which overlaps the two dots that contain the depth information. Its position is indicated by the grey rectangle on the right diagram. The subject's task is to decide which dot is in front, the top or the bottom dot. In this example the correct answer is the bottom dot because it has the larger crossed disparity.

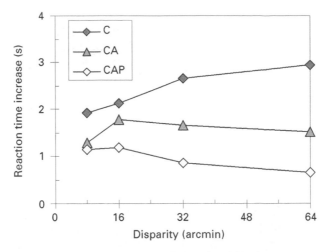

Figure 10.5 The data substantiating the claim that accommodation (A) and motion parallax (P) substantially aid the ease of depth perception. The graph shows the extra time required to perceive the depth relationship of the two adjacent dots superimposed on top of a distracting object at a different depth. Note that the symbol overlap in this experiment is essential. The horizontal axis shows the amount of depth difference between the two planes. The increase in reaction time caused by the distractor is one to two seconds greater for the common type of stereoscopic displays (C: stereoscopic Convergence cue only) than for Dual-layer displays (CAP: Accommodation and Parallax as well as the Convergence depth cue). These results imply that a Dual-layer display is more natural to view and particularly suited for cluttered and/or overlapping symbology.

speed up the search process involving attention as well as accommodation blur. Depth segregation involves a (cognitive) decision component. After the viewer decides which depth plane to look at, the eyes will focus on it by converging appropriately. Along with convergence, focus (accommodation) is automatically adjusted. When looking at the front plane, the rear plane will therefore be seen slightly double and out of focus, enhancing the perceptual separation. The perceptual separation of the two depth planes therefore must involve attentional as well as early-vision physiological mechanisms (eye convergence and accommodation).

10.8   Making use of depth to steer attention

A depth difference can aid the attention allocation process in more ways than one. The main attentional phenomena are that information in front tends to capture the attention first and that the observer is able to limit attention (to a large degree) to either layer at will. In our experiments focusing on cockpit displays like the Navigation Display shown in figure 10.2 (see plate) we exploited both phenomena. We found it particularly useful to place a subset of information in the front layer. Furthermore, the front layer should not contain filled surfaces. A depth split therefore provides an alternative to the 'declutter' algorithms based on the principle of leaving out part of the information. Given that the conspicuity of the important symbols in the front layer is safeguarded, the rear layer may be filled with more information. This alternative way to declutter has a strong appeal in the cockpit, which has limited display space for visualizing the wealth of flight information. The displays decluttered in the classical sense (by leaving out part of the information) force the pilot continuously to anticipate what information will be needed next. Having all flight information nicely ordered, at hand and without clutter eliminates this anticipatory process. The data management task of flying an airplane thus becomes more similar to that of driving a bus.

10.9   Dynamic depth separations

So far we have experimentally addressed *static* divisions between the front and back layers, meaning that the depth location is predictable. In the first of two HILAS flight simulators we placed all information belonging to the outside world on the back layer of the Primary Flight Display and all information belonging to the airplane (which the pilot could influence) on the front layer (figure 10.6: see plate). In the second experiment pertaining to the Navigation Display (figure 10.7: see plate) we placed all information pertaining to objects in the air on the front layer and all information related to the ground on the rear layer. Both divisions are easy to understand, easy to remember and therefore easy to use, but they are static. We have not yet experimentally tested dynamic placement of information in the front layer, and we plan to do so. The examples below show a preview of the potential role of dynamic depth in attention management.

Pilot feedback on the simulator experiments has been that the foremost Navigation Display clutter problem is caused by mutual occlusion of flight information symbols, 'data tags', in congested areas like airports. Of the innumerable two-layer designs a *dynamic depth separation* may work best to alleviate this particular clutter problem. Placing the data tags that in the short term may require action on the front layer and the others that do not form an immediate danger in the rear layer will draw attention to the tags that need action first. Another potential use of a two-layer display is to place warnings in the front layer of a central vehicle display containing the primary (flight) information in the rear. On a standard Single-layer display users would not accept this, due to interference with the primary information.

The research described in this chapter is focused on professional environments like the cockpit. Spin-offs in the consumer domain may well include 'double tasking', such as reading the flight status while watching a movie on a laptop, simultaneously checking SMS and internetting on the mobile phone, or reacting extra fast while playing a video game. The time required to switch fixation between two closely spaced depth planes is negligible compared to the time required to change fixation between two locations on a single-layer display, thereby interrupting the task switching (Toet 2006).

The two central issues in dynamic depth separation are whether the primary information remains easily readable and whether the depth advantage outweighs the uncertainty of where to locate which information. Here we speculate on possible outcomes to facilitate future experiments. Reasonable hypotheses are as follows:

1. In order to keep the location sufficiently predictable, the depth ordering should not be changed too frequently.
2. In order to keep the location sufficiently predictable, the depth ordering should be bounded by easy-to-remember rules.
3. The depth difference should be kept small to facilitate fusional and perhaps attentional changes between layers. With a small (1 cm) depth separation, the user often does not even notice a change in fixation between the two planes.
4. The instruction to the viewer should be to check the front layer regularly for 'important changes'.

The design rules for dynamic depth separations need to be (experimentally) validated and refined. The transition to 'free flight' calls for extra display space in the cockpit to highlight the air-traffic-control tasks that will transition to the pilot, in particular traffic separation and collision avoidance (Verstynen 1980).

10.10   Conclusions

The Dual-layer prototype display makes it possible to evaluate the effectiveness of depth to enhance (symbology) displays without unwanted image degradation. We believe the long-expected breakthrough of stereoscopic 3D displays is held back by a lack of viewing comfort and a lack of depth-quality (Kooi and Toet 2004). Dual-layer displays, consisting of two physically separated depth planes, provide a 'golden standard' with a natural 3D percept that 'pops out' immediately. The experimental results shown in this chapter confirm the value of splitting symbology images in two layers. Information can often be naturally divided into two layers: belonging to self and belonging to the world; frequently viewed and infrequently viewed; friend and foe; above and on or below the surface.[6] While not sufficient to display full 3D pictures, the two depth planes do provide a significant benefit by highlighting important symbology, making it suitable to steer attention allocation.

10.11   Acknowledgements

A number of TNO colleagues have contributed to the experiments mentioned and described, namely Johan Alferdinck, Anne-Marie Brouwer, Sjaak Kriekaard and Janna von Schmid. The HILAS European Union project has given a large impetus to understand life on the flight-deck and to test the Dual-layer display in a flight simulator environment that closely resembles real flight. Three engineers of the GRACE simulator at NLR have been particularly helpful: Martin Joosse, Chris Pols and Jaap Groeneweg.

10.12   References

Baudisch, P. 2008. Designing for small screens, Tutorial held at *MobileHCI 2008*, Amsterdam, 2–5 September

Ellis, S. R., and McGreevy, M. W. 1987. Perspective traffic display format and airline pilot traffic avoidance, *Human Factors* 29: 371–82

Fuchs, G., and Schumann, H. 2004. Visualizing abstract data on maps, in *Proceedings of the 8th International Conference on Information Visualisation IV*, London: 139–45

He, Z. J., and Nakayama, K. 1992. Surfaces vs. features in visual search, *Nature* 359: 231–3

    1995. Visual attention to surfaces in three-dimensional space, in *Proceedings of the National Academy of Sciences of the United States of America* 92: 11155–9

Kooi, F. L. 2003. Multi-plane display for displaying overlapping images. EUR patent application 03078288.2

Kooi, F. L., and Toet, A. 2004. Visual comfort of binocular and 3D displays, *Displays* 25: 99–108

Kooi, F. L., Toet, A., Tripathy, S. P., and Levi, D. M. 1994. The effect of similarity and duration on spatial interaction in peripheral vision, *Spatial Vision* 8: 255–79

---

[6] By comparison, many of the 'full colour' cockpit displays by no means fully exploit their colour gamut and typically display only four to eight colours.

Marr, D. 1982. *Vision: A Computational Investigation into the Human Representation and Processing of Visual Information.* New York: Freeman

Nakayama, K., and Silverman, G. H. 1986. Serial and parallel processing of visual feature conjunctions, *Nature* 320: 264–5

Olmos, O., Wickens, C. D., and Chudy, A. 2000. Tactical displays for combat awareness: An examination of dimensionality and frame of reference concepts and the application of cognitive engineering, *International Journal of Aviation Psychology* 10(3): 247–71

Pastoor, S. 1993. Human factors of 3D displays, *Displays* 14: 150–7

Rosenholtz, R., Li, Y., and Nakano, L. 2007. Measuring visual clutter, *Journal of Vision* 7(2): 1–22

Streefkerk, J. W., van Esch-Bussemakers, M. P., and Neerincx, M. A. 2006. Designing personal attentive user interfaces in the mobile public safety domain, *Computers in Human Behavior* 22: 749–70

Toet, A. 2006. Gaze directed displays as an enabling technology for attention aware systems, *Computers in Human Behavior* 22: 615–47

Treisman, A. M., and Gelade, G. 1980. A feature integration theory of attention, *Cognitive Psychology* 12: 97–136

Verstynen, H. A. 1980. Potential roles for the cockpit traffic display in the evolving ATC system, *Report No. SAE-800736.* Warrendale, PA: Society of Automotive Engineers

Wagner, M., and Hochstein, S. 2000. Visual-search and attention shifts between layers in the 3D environment defined by linear perspective, *Perception* 29 ECVP Abstracts: 14

Wheatley, C., Cook, M. L., and Vidyasagar, T. R. 2004. Surface segregation influences pre-attentive search in depth, *NeuroReport* 15: 303–5

Zon, R., and Roerdink, M. 2007. HCI testing in flight simulator: Set up and crew briefing procedures. Design and test cycles for the future, in D. Harris (ed.), *Engineering Psychology and Cognitive Ergonomics*, Berlin: Springer-Verlag: 867–76

11 Attention management for self-regulated learning: AtGentSchool

Inge Molenaar, Carla van Boxtel,
Peter Sleegers and Claudia Roda

This chapter addresses how an attention-management system can provide personalized support for self-regulated learning and what the effects of this support are on learning. An attention-management system can provide personalized support by capturing and interpretating information from the student's environment. A framework is proposed that will interpret the information and provide dynamic scaffolding for the learner. The essential elements are diagnosing, calibrating and fading scaffolds to the context of the learner. An intervention model supports self-regulated learning processes. In two studies, we have found evidence that an attention-management system can effectively give form to dynamic scaffolding. Dynamic scaffolding has a small- to medium-sized effect on students' performance and a small effect on students' metacognitive knowledge acquisition.

11.1   Introduction

E-learning has incrementally changed education in recent decades. Many new tools and instruments have been introduced to support existing educational practices. Yet only on a small scale have we seen transformative processes in schools. The large changes which have taken place in other sectors have not yet been achieved in education. This can partially be explained by the fact that e-learning solutions are not yet flexible enough to cater for learners' individual needs and demands. We see personalization in many sectors today, but education still seems to hold on to the 'one size fits all' paradigm, even though we know that personalized education is more effective than standardized education (Bloom 1984).

Artificial intelligence has provided personalized solutions, but these programs are mainly applicable to structured domains. Often artificial intelligence programs construct a model of the student's knowledge based on the student's answers to questions. The comparison of the student's knowledge model to a domain knowledge model supports the selection of new assignments and/or support messages for the student. In ill-structured domains, it is difficult to build knowledge models of the student's knowledge because answers are difficult to interpret. Therefore, few personalized solutions are available in ill-structured domains.

Attention management addresses the quest for personalization on a different level. Instead of building models of the domain knowledge and comparing this to the student's knowledge model, it focuses on capturing the user's attentional focus. This attentional focus can be built upon to provide personalized instruction and allow for dynamic support of learning. Attention-management systems integrated with electronic learning environments can provide learners with the help they need to direct and sustain attention to appropriate tools and information. This support can evolve with the student's knowledge and skills and is often referred to in the literature as scaffolding. Although scholars stress the importance of scaffolding self-regulated learning, especially in open electronic learning environments (Azevedo and Hadwin 2005), research into the role and effectiveness of scaffolding in supporting self-regulated learning is scarce.

This chapter addresses two questions. The first is a design-related question: How can an attention-management system enable personalized support, or dynamic scaffolding, of self-regulated learning? In order to answer this question, we describe the theoretical construct of scaffolding and its related dimensions. We will explain how attention management is related to the scaffolding theory and elaborate on the relation between self-regulated learning process and scaffolding. The second question is related to the effectiveness of the system: How does personalized support, or dynamic scaffolding, based on attention management affect students' learning outcomes? In two experimental studies, we assessed the effects of personalized support on different performance indicators of pupils in primary schools.

11.2   Scaffolding

Scaffolding provides assistance to a student on an as-needed basis, fading the assistance as the student's competence increases (e.g., Wood, Bruner and Ross 1976). The scaffolder can be either a human tutor or a tool embedded in the computer environment. Three essential elements for scaffolding descriptions are diagnosis, calibration and fading (Puntambekar and Hübscher 2005). The abilities of the learner must be diagnosed continuously in order to define appropriate scaffolding. This diagnosis supports careful selection, or calibration, of the right scaffolds to support the student and a reduction of support, fading, when the learner masters all aspects of the task.

Within the scaffolding paradigm, there is a distinction between static and dynamic scaffolding (Puntambekar and Hübscher 2005; Molenaar and Roda 2008). Static scaffolding is defined at one moment, constant over time and the same for all students; for instance, one may provide a list of instructions to help users perform a learning activity. Dynamic scaffolding entails pedagogical agents which diagnose, calibrate and fade their support in an individualized manner such that one can monitor the student's progress and provide scaffolds when needed during the learning process. Static scaffolding can support learners to help them increase performance. Dynamic scaffolding has the additional benefit that it can help students learn when to apply certain knowledge or skills during the learning process.

The term scaffolding is often used in cases where static scaffolding is applied: the amount and type of support is fixed and not adjusted on the basis of a diagnosis of the student's learning (Puntambekar and Hübscher 2005). There is no calibration of the scaffolds to the changing needs of the individual student nor any fading of the scaffolding; the scaffolds are permanent and unchanging. We propose using attention management to support dynamic scaffolding, applying diagnosis, calibration and fading based on attentional information from the student's environment.

Next to the distinction between static and dynamic scaffolding, another important issue for the design of scaffolds is the focus of the support. As mentioned above, scaffolding plays a crucial role for learning in largely unguided and open learning environments (Kalyuga, Chandler and Sweller 2001; Kirschner, Sweller and Clark 2006). In these learning environments scaffolding should be directed at self-regulation processes and support students to learn successfully (Azevedo and Hadwin 2005). Self-regulated learning is defined as self-generated thoughts, feelings and behaviours directed at attaining learning goals. It deals with the component processes: cognition, metacognition and regulation of motivation (Ainley and Patrick 2006). Cognitive processes are directed at the acquisition of knowledge while metacognitive processes are directed at monitoring and controlling these processes. Motivation strongly influences learning activities (Boekaerts 1999) and regulation of motivation plays an important role in the attainment of learning goals (Boekaerts 1999; Zimmerman 2002; Ainley and Patrick 2006). In order to scaffold all three component processes, we developed an intervention model from which scaffolds are selected. Before we turn to an explanation of the scaffolding system, we will briefly introduce the reader to some fundamental concepts in human attention that have guided our research.

11.3   Attention

Attention can be defined as the collection of processes regulating the allocation of a human's limited cognitive resources. Attention allows us to select some perceptual input for further processing out of the wide variety of stimuli we continuously receive from the environment, as when, after looking at a landscape, we are capable of describing only some of its characteristics. Attention also controls the allocation of cognitive resources to the processing of multiple tasks, enabling task monitoring and error detection. Finally, attention allows us to create expectations that guide the selection of perceptual stimuli, as when we recognize a person we were waiting for in a crowd.

Attention, or the allocation of cognitive resources, may be controlled either endogenously by volition or exogenously when temporarily directed by external stimuli (Posner 1980; Yantis 1998). For example, when reading this chapter, you are applying endogenous attention because you 'choose' to pay attention to the text; however, a sudden noise may exogenously control your attention and temporarily redirect it to the source of the noise.

In general, attention allocation can be observed at several levels of granularity; that is, we may say that a subject is paying attention to a vertical bar on a screen, to a letter 't', to a word 'table', to a sentence 'the glass is on the table', to a document describing a room layout, to the task of verifying if the description of a room layout corresponds to the room the subject is in, etc. The literature often distinguishes between two granularity levels, the perceptual level and the task level.

We can distinguish several different forms of attention. Focused attention is directed to an individual task or input channel. If the focus is prolonged, then we have sustained attention. Because by focusing on a certain target one excludes others, focused attention implies selective attention (Chun and Wolfe 2001; Driver 2001; Posner 1982). An attention switch is the process by which attention is moved from one target to another. There is always a cost involved in attention switches (Monsell 2003) due both to the uncertainty associated with the task to be performed in response to a stimulus (Spector and Biederman 1976) and to the cost of reconfiguring the current task set (Monsell 2003). Often, rather than switching attention, we are able to allocate attention to multiple tasks or channels at the same time. In this case we talk about divided attention.

The fact that attention plays a fundamental role in learning has been demonstrated in the context of several types of learning processes. Single-task versus dual-task experiments, for example, have demonstrated that implicit learning, the 'nonepisodic learning of complex information in an incidental manner, without awareness of what has been learned' (Seger 1994: 163), requires attention, and it is penalized under dual-task conditions (Shanks, Rowland and Ranger 2005). Similar results (Toro, Sinnett and Soto-Faraco 2005) have been obtained for statistical learning (Saffran, Aslin and Newport 1996). Several experiments (e.g., Ahissar and Hochstein 1993) have also demonstrated the need for focused attention in learning task-relevant information in perceptual learning, that is, the improvement of perceptual abilities after training. Task-related focused attention in perceptual learning generates an alerting process that may also explain the unexpected effect of task-irrelevant learning (Seitz and Watanabe 2005). Finally, the effects of attention on higher-level learning, e.g., the learning of written language or mathematics, are discussed at length in chapter 4 of this book.

Given the role that attention plays in learning processes, attention-management systems – i.e., systems capable of adapting to and supporting human attention processes (Roda and Thomas 2006) – promise to play an essential role in supporting technology-enhanced learning environments. The attentive system research aims at determining the likely utility of given information for a given user in a given context and the costs associated with presenting the information in a certain way (Roda and Nabeth 2007). The utility of attentive systems for learning, such as the one introduced in the next sections, is to detect the attentional focus of the student and interpret this information to support the learning process.

11.4   Scaffolding with attention management

For a detailed technical description of the AtGentSchool system we refer the reader to Molenaar and Roda (2008). In this chapter, we will describe the system's functioning from an educational perspective, which oversimplifies its technical functioning. First, we will explain how the system is related to the scaffolding theory incorporating diagnosis, calibration and fading. Second, we elaborate on the relation between the self-regulated learning process and the interventions the system uses to scaffold the learning process.

11.4.1   AtGentSchool

The AtGentSchool system is an e-learning environment combined with an attention-management system. The e-learning environment incorporated with AtGentSchool is called Ontdeknet, and is focused on supporting students in their collaboration with experts (Molenaar 2003). Ontdeknet is an open learning environment in which assignments are structured in 'projects'. A project consists of a broad overall assignment which is connected to an external expert who will provide the students with specialized information. The assignment is divided into smaller sub-assignments to support collaboration with the experts; students are asked to introduce themselves to the expert, write a goal statement and specify topics of interest on a concept map.

AtGentSchool's attention-management system monitors the students' attentional focus and, based on that information, supplies them with support to enhance their learning. The system's technical design consists of three levels, the input level, the reasoning level and the intervention level. The input level collects the attentional information from the student's environment. Currently, input is based on keystrokes, mouse movements and information about the student's activities in the e-learning environment which is captured by its log. The reasoning level selects a scaffold that is sent to the learner. Different software agents assess the attention information to select the appropriate scaffold. The intervention level determines how the scaffold is communicated to the learner. AtGentSchool uses a three-dimensional animated pedagogical agent powered by Living Actor^{TM} technology (see chapter 6 of this book) for the delivery of scaffolds via text balloons and spoken messages accompanied by the agent's animations and emotions. The student has four icons in the interface by which to communicate with the agent, a question mark to indicate a need for help and three emotional icons indicating a happy, neutral or sad user. This information from the user is used as additional input.

In the section below, we explain how diagnosis, calibration and fading are performed by the AtGentSchool system.

11.4.2 Diagnosis

Diagnosis is defined as the ongoing measurement of the student's current level of understanding to select the appropriate scaffolding (Wood, Bruner and Ross 1976). This entails the evaluation of the user's progress during learning activities. Progress is evaluated based on the student's performance on the learning assignment and/or the student's development of knowledge in the learning domain (Wood, Bruner and Ross 1976). Diagnosis in AtGentSchool is based on the attention information acquired in the student's environment. The system registers the student's progress based on his performance in the learning environment. For example, when the learner browses through a text, the system registers both the viewing of the particular text as well as the browsing behaviour of the student. The information from the electronic learning environment is particularly important because it provides a real-time description of activity on the learning assignment. Based on this information, the learner's progress and experience are registered. For example, if a learner is using the concept map tool in the learning environment and proceeding quickly, filling-in different fields, this information is stored with an indication that the learner is capable of appropriately using the concept map tool. Both the current behaviour of the student as well as the experience and progress are incorporated in the diagnosis.

Additionally, keystrokes and mouse movements provide information beyond the level of involvement in the specific learning task by also measuring the student's activities in the overall environment. For example, no keystrokes or mouse movement registration in a certain timeframe can indicate that the student is idle.

The student's current attentional focus is evaluated on the basis of this input-level information (data related to the performance, progress, experience, keystrokes and mouse movement) and it constitutes the diagnostic component of AtGentSchool.

11.4.3 Calibration

Following diagnosis, calibration is the careful selection of the best scaffold for the student activity (Wood, Bruner and Ross 1976). The system assembles a logical attentional focus based on the learning assignment at hand and creates a list of all possible scaffolds that can support the learner at this instant. The learner's current attentional focus is compared to the logical attentional focus based on the learning assignment. When current and logical attentional focus match, a scaffold is selected to support the learner with his current activities. For example, if a student should introduce himself and is at the screen prompting him to enter the introduction, then, if the system detects that the student is idle, it may support the student by suggesting that he start planning the introduction assignment.

In case of a discrepancy between the current and the logical attentional focus, the system is triggered to select a scaffold that can overcome the discrepancy. For example, if the student has an assignment to introduce himself and the system establishes that he is not on the correct screen, then a focus discrepancy is diagnosed and a scaffold is selected to direct the attention of the learner to the introduction assignment, yet the system will wait to provide the scaffold until it registers that the student is idle.

Calibration has the function of determining the most appropriate scaffold based on the diagnostic information. Scaffolds either support or alter the attentional focus of the student.

11.4.4 Fading

The final element of scaffolding is fading. Fading is the gradual reduction of scaffolds leading to full transfer of tasks and control to the learner (Wood, Bruner and Ross 1976). The nature and amount of fading is highly dependent on the experience of the user: when the student masters all aspects of the tasks, no scaffolds are needed to support the self-regulation of the learner. In AtGentSchool the learner's progress and experience are registered. This information is used to determine whether the scaffold selected in the calibration process should be forwarded to the student. If the system determines that scaffolding is not needed for a student, fading ensures that the scaffold is not sent. For example, when the system registers the student's focus on the introduction assignment, it will send a scaffold only if the student has not worked at the introduction previously. Thus fading, in the AtGentSchool system, is achieved by selecting appropriate scaffolds based on an assessment of the learner's progress and previous experiences. If the diagnostics of the system and the registered user information contradict each other, fading will be reduced. For example, if the learner model indicates that the user is an experienced user and the diagnostics of the system show that the user does not perform the task correctly, the system will reduce the fading and show the supporting scaffold to the user.

To summarize, the attention-management system derives information from the student's environment. Based on this information, an assessment of the attentional focus of the student is made (diagnosis), which is compared to a logical attentional focus based on the learning assignment. This comparison is the basis for the selection of the scaffold (calibration), which is only sent when the student needs support (fading).

Now that we have defined how scaffolds are selected in relation to the attentional focus of the students, we identify what learning processes these scaffolds are supporting.

11.5   The intervention model

An important aspect in ensuring that dynamic scaffolding becomes effective is the focus of the scaffolds. The scaffolds are directed towards three different but related component processes of self-regulated learning: cognition, metacognition and motivation. In order to design scaffolds that are focused on these processes, the AtGentSchool system uses a standardized intervention model (Molenaar and Roda 2008) from which the scaffolds are selected. There is an important difference between interventions and scaffolds. Interventions are the messages that can be shown to the learner to support learning, but they only become scaffolds when they are presented in the right learning context. The intervention model consists of three intervention categories: metacognitive interventions, cognitive interventions and motivational interventions. The intervention categories are further organized by intervention types directed at specific aspects of the main category (see table 11.1 on p. 269 for an overview). The intervention types are general and are transformed in task-related scaffolds depending on the student's context. The different intervention categories are described below; the function of each intervention is discussed, followed by an explanation of how the intervention is used in the learning process and relates to the attentional focus of the student.

11.5.1 *Metacognitive interventions*

Metacognition is defined as knowledge about, and regulation of, one's cognitive activities (Flavell 1979). Metacognitive activities are categorized as preparatory activities such as orientation and planning, executive activities such as monitoring and evaluation, and closing activities such as reflection (Zimmerman 2002; Veenman, van Hout-Wolters and Afflerbach 2006). Orientation on a learning assignment supports a detailed view of the task at hand and the activation of prior knowledge about the task. Planning a learning assignment entails dividing it into subtasks and deciding on the strategies to be followed to complete the subtasks. Through monitoring activities, students check the correctness of their learning. Evaluation activities enable students to react to failures and misunderstandings. Reflection about the learning procedures and strategies provides grounds for future enhancement.

Metacognitive interventions are directed at supporting and triggering metacognitive learning activities. These interventions can scaffold the learning process when they are shown to the learner at times when metacognitive activities are normally executed in the learning process. AtGentSchool supports three forms of scaffolds per learning assignment: orientation scaffolds, planning scaffolds and monitoring scaffolds.

Orientation is best performed just before task selection; thus when the attentional focus of the students is about to change towards a new assignment, students are shown a scaffold with which to focus on the assignment. An example of an orientation intervention for the 'goal statement' assignment is: 'Your expert would like to know what your learning goal is; could you tell him? Please click here to write your learning goal.'

Planning is done just before starting a learning assignment; therefore, planning interventions are implemented just after the attentional focus of the student shifts from one assignment to another. The following sentence is an example of a planning intervention (figure 11.1: see plate) for the 'goal statement' assignment: 'Here you will write your learning goal; for example, "I like to learn everything about David." Just kidding, good luck.'

Finally, monitoring should be performed during and after execution of the assignment, just before the attentional focus of the student moves away from the assignment. The following sentence is an example of a monitoring intervention for the 'goal statement' assignment: 'I'll go directly to your expert and explain what you would like to learn.'

11.5.2   *Cognitive interventions*

Cognitive activities are directed towards the acquisition of knowledge (Nelson 1996), cognitive support can provide the knowledge and skills necessary to perform an assignment (Garner 1987) and cognitive interventions are shown to learners when there is an indication that they are experiencing problems with the current assignment. Indications of problems could be an idle user, when there are no keystrokes or mouse movements, or when the user indicates he needs help via a question mark icon in the interface. The selection of the cognitive support is determined by the attentional focus of the learner. Two different types of cognitive interventions are distinguished: cognitive support interventions and cognitive resource interventions. Cognitive support is directed towards helping the learner with the current learning activity whereas cognitive resource interventions provide students with links to resources in the learning environment that can help them perform the task. For example, a message to the user saying 'What do you already know about the subject you are going to study?' is a cognitive support intervention for the assignment 'write a concept map'; an example of a cognitive resource intervention for the same learning task would be: 'Need some ideas? You can read the introduction diary of the expert.'

11.5.3   *Motivational interventions*

Motivation strongly influences learning activities (Boekaerts 1999), and motivational support can increase learners' motivation. Motivational interventions are directed at increasing learners' motivation to work on

Table 11.1 *A summary of the intervention categories and types*

Intervention category	Intervention type	Description
Metacognitive	MC orientation	Introduces the learning assignment to the learner
Metacognitive	MC planning	Asks the learner to plan the learning assignment
Metacognitive	MC monitoring	Provides feedback to the learner about the learning activity performed
Cognitive	Cognitive support	Provides additional explanation to the learner
Cognitive	Cognitive resources	Provides additional explanation by redirecting the learner to another learning resource containing additional information
Motivation	Motivation support	Provides a motivational incentive to the learner
Motivation	ES happy	Reacts to a happy learner
Motivation	ES sad	Reacts to a sad learner
Motivation	ES neutral	Reacts to a neutral learner

the learning assignment. They are shown when there is an indication that the user is having a motivational experience. Indication of motivational experiences can occur when users indicate their motivation to the agent. Also motivational interventions are triggered when the user is idle and there are no new cognitive interventions for this user available. The selection of a motivational support intervention is determined on the basis of the attentional focus of the learner. General motivational interventions are implemented in the system as motivational support. An example is: 'You can do it! Just start writing.' Additionally, when the user indicates his current emotional state with happy, neutral or sad smileys, the agent mirrors the state of the user by showing an animation and expression that resembles the user's state. These three forms of emotional feedback lead to three emotional support interventions where the embodied agent responds to a user's notification of a happy, neutral or sad emotional state. The three intervention categories and nine intervention types are summarized in table 11.1.

Relationships are established between the attentional focus of the learner, the learning assignment and the scaffolds selected. Both the cognitive and motivational scaffolds are selected on the basis of the assignment that is currently in the attentional focus of the learner. They can also be triggered by the 'user reaction' icons, the question mark and emotional icons. Metacognitive (MC) scaffolds, on the other hand, do not have a direct relation with the assignment currently in the attentional focus of the students. MC interventions provide pre-task, on-task or post-task support; they are presented to the learner when he/she changes focus. Thus, when the learner is about to select a sub-assignment, the MC orientation intervention could be shown. At the start of the assignment an MC planning intervention could be shown, whilst MC monitoring interventions may appear during execution. Thus the positioning of metacognitive scaffolds in the learning process is connected to the registered changes in the learner's attentional focus. This allows for dynamic support of the students' metacognitive activities through AtGentSchool.

It is more difficult to position cognitive interventions effectively in relation to the information about attentional focus the system currently retrieves. Input to the AtGentSchool system currently only provides information allowing limited inferences about the cognitive activities of the student. The system knows which activity the student is working on but has no information about the student's knowledge-building process. This means that AtGentSchool can position the adequate cognitive support in relation to the current task and the progress of the student, but it is unable to align the cognitive interventions with the knowledge-acquisition process. The question mark icon in the interface is currently the most important indicator that the students need additional support. Thus AtGentSchool can provide cognitive interventions to support the cognitive activities but cannot adjust support to the knowledge-building process. Also the trigger of cognitive support is partially dependent on the students' ability to monitor their own cognitive activities. This means that the positioning of cognitive interventions based on the current registration of attentional focus in AtGentSchool is limited.

Motivational interventions are similarly difficult to position in relation to current information about the student's attentional focus. The input in AtGentSchool provides no information about the students' motivational state other than the information students provide voluntarily via the icons in the interface. Based on this input we can support students on the motivational level, but the trigger of this support is largely dependent on the students' ability to monitor their own motivational states. For the motivational interventions as well, we can conclude that the current registration of the attentional focus in AtGentSchool only supports motivational scaffolding to a limited degree.

So far, we have addressed the question: How can an attention management system enable personalized support, or dynamic scaffolding, of self-regulated learning? We have discussed how the AtGentSchool system uses the information from the student's environment to interpret the student's attentional focus. Based on this attentional focus, scaffolds that can support the students' self-regulated learning process are selected using the processes of diagnosis, calibration and fading. Thus in AtGentSchool, the attention-management system allows for dynamic scaffolding to support the learners. We predict that the AtGentSchool system in its current form is particularly capable of scaffolding the metacognitive activities of the students, whereas it will only be effective at scaffolding cognitive and motivational activities to a lesser degree. In the next section we will address the second question: What is the effect of personalized support, or dynamic scaffolding, based on attention management on students' learning outcomes? In order to answer this question, we report the findings of two experimental studies directed at assessing the effects of dynamic scaffolding on students' learning outcomes.

11.6   The effects of dynamic scaffolding

Earlier studies showed that scaffolding supports and elicits self-regulated learning and that self-regulated learning enhances learning performance (Azevedo and Hadwin 2005). However, these studies did not assess the effects of dynamic scaffolding performed by an attention-management system on learning outcomes. Therefore, systematic research into the effectiveness of dynamic scaffolding performed by an attention-management system on different learning outcomes is lacking. We draw on the earlier work of two experimental studies to examine the effects of dynamic scaffolding with an attention-management system on student learning in an open e-learning environment. We predict that students receiving dynamic scaffolds will outperform students who are not supported with respect to learning outcomes. Furthermore, as discussed earlier, we expect that the attention-management system will be especially effective in supporting the metacognitive activities of the students and to a lesser extent their cognitive and motivational activities. By examining this problem we contribute to a deeper understanding of the way personalized support based on attention management works and the conditions under which this support can be effective.

The two experimental studies described below were conducted at two different moments in time. The findings of the first study were used for designing the second study. Both studies use an experimental design to assess the effects of dynamic scaffolding. In both studies group performance and students' domain knowledge are measured as learning outcomes. Yet, the two studies differ in some aspects. The first study was conducted in the Czech Republic. Students worked in pairs, and each pair was assigned its own teacher. The second study was conducted in the Netherlands. Students worked in triads instead of pairs and all classes were taught by the same teacher. Additionally, more and different outcome measurements were incorporated.

In the second study, students' metacognitive knowledge was measured. Measuring metacognitive knowledge tests the expectation that the system is especially effective in supporting metacognitive activities.

11.7   Study 1: pairs in the Czech Republic

11.7.1   Method

In the first study a total of 134 students from 4 schools divided over 5 classes in the Czech Republic participated. The students were in the 5th grade, with ages ranging from 10.5 to 11.4. The teachers grouped students into 55 dyads within their classes based on the principle of heterogeneity, balancing gender, school performance, reading and computer abilities. The pairs in all classes were randomly assigned to one of two conditions. The first condition formed the control group of 27 dyads and received no scaffolds. The second condition formed the experimental group of 28 dyads and was supported by scaffolding interventions. The conditions were equally divided over the classes. The dyads in the experimental group received scaffolds supporting their metacognition, cognition and motivation as described above. The scaffolds were provided by a virtual agent. The dyads in the control group did see the virtual agent but did not receive any form of support from the agent.

The total duration of the experiment was 6 lessons of 45 minutes each. During the lessons, pairs worked on an assignment called 'Would you like to live abroad?' The goal of the assignment was for the students to explore New Zealand, write a paper on the findings and decide if they would like to live in that country. The pairs worked on one computer with an electronic learning environment (Ontdeknet) in which they had access to an inhabitant of the country, their expert. They could consult the expert by posing questions and reading the information section which contained information about the country written by the expert. The assignment to write a paper about the country was preceded by three preparation assignments: introducing the pair, writing a goal statement and specifying topics of interest in a concept map. All assignments were integrated in the working space of the pairs where they also wrote their papers.

In the first lesson the students were given instructions about the task. All students received the same instructions and all pairs spent the same time working on the assignment (4 hours). The work of the dyads was stored in the learning environment. In the final lesson, students finished the assignment and the domain knowledge of individual students was measured.

11.7.2 Measurements

The effects on the learning outcomes were assessed via two performance measurements: group performance and students' domain knowledge. Group performance was measured by scoring the couples' work on the paper and the number of questions posed to the expert. The paper was evaluated by two researchers who mutually gave a grade for the quality of the paper. The grade was based on the number of issues covered and the researchers' interpretation of the percentage of self-formulated text. The number of issues was scored by counting the topics covered in the paper. The maximum score was 3 points. The score for the questions posed to the expert was simply based on the number of questions asked. Students' domain knowledge was measured individually by a curriculum-based knowledge test with 15 true/false items related to New Zealand. Students received 1 point for each correct answer and 0 points for incorrect answers. Cronbach's alpha, which is an indicator of the validity of the test, was 0.83 for the knowledge test. The effect sizes were calculated using the effect size estimate r, following Rosenthal (1991), defining 0.1 as a small effect, 0.3 as a medium effect and 0.5 as a large effect.

11.7.3 Results

The effect of dynamic scaffolding on the learning performance of the pairs was assessed by comparing the control group with the experimental group. This showed that scaffolding did have a significant effect on students' performance on the paper. An effect size of $r = 0.26$ indicates a medium positive effect of scaffolding on group performance on the paper. Also, with respect to the number of questions asked there was a significant effect of scaffolding. An effect size of $r = 0.21$ shows a small to medium positive effect of scaffolding on the number of questions asked. These findings with respect to group performance confirm our prediction that attention-based scaffolding does significantly affect group performance and has a small to medium positive effect on group performance.

The effect of dynamic scaffolding on domain knowledge in comparing the control group with the experimental group reveals that scaffolding did not have a significant effect on individual students' domain knowledge. The effect size $r = 0.08$ for the knowledge test does indicate a small positive effect of dynamic scaffolding. With regard to domain knowledge, the findings do not confirm our expectations.

11.8   Study 2: triads in Dutch schools

11.8.1   Method

In the second study, a total of 156 students from 3 schools divided over 6 classes participated. Of the students, 27 were in the 4th grade (aged 9–10), 82 were in the 5th grade (aged 10–11) and 47 were in the 6th grade (aged 11–12) of primary education. The teachers grouped the students into 52 triads within their classes based on the principle of heterogeneity, balancing gender, school performance, reading and computer abilities. Each triad was randomly assigned to one of two conditions: the first control group of 16 triads had no scaffolds, while the second experimental group of 36 triads was supported with scaffolds. The conditions were equally divided over the classes. The triads in the experimental group received scaffolds supporting their metacognition, cognition and motivation as described above. The scaffolds were provided by a virtual agent. The triads in the control group did see the virtual agent but did not receive any form of metacognitive support from the agent.

The total duration of the experiment was 8 lessons of 1 hour each. During the lessons, triads worked on an assignment called 'Would you like to live abroad?' The goal of the assignment was to explore a country of choice (New Zealand or Iceland), write a paper on the findings and decide if the students would like to live in that country. The triads worked on one computer with an electronic learning environment (Ontdeknet) under the same conditions as in Study 1.

In the first lesson, the students were only given instructions about the task. All students received the same instructions and all triads spent the same amount of time working on the assignment (6 hours). The triads' performance was stored in the learning environment. In the final lesson the domain and metacognitive knowledge of the individual students was measured. All lessons were taught by the same researcher to prevent teaching discrepancies.

11.8.2   Measurements

Group performance was measured by scoring the triad's work on the paper and the number of questions posed to the expert. The paper was evaluated by one researcher who gave a grade for the quality of the paper. The grade was based on the number of issues covered and the percentage of self-formulated text; the students could copy and paste information given by the inhabitant, or expert. The number of issues was scored by counting the topics covered in the paper. Of the papers, 28 per cent were scored by two independent researchers (Cohen's kappa = 0.75). The percentage of copying was measured using Wincopyfind 2.6. This percentage was reversed into a copy score; less copying resulted in a higher copy score. The paper grade was calculated by adding the topics score to the copy score. The maximum paper score was 6 points. The score for the questions posed to the inhabitant was simply based on the number of questions asked.

Students' domain knowledge was measured individually on four different levels: recall, knowledge, application and transfer. Recall was measured by asking students to make a concept map with as many topics as they could think of related to the country they investigated in 5 minutes. For each correct proposition, 1 point was assigned. Knowledge was measured by a curriculum-based test with 40 true/false/question mark items related to the country the students studied. Students received 1 point for each correct answer and 0 points for a question mark or an incorrect answer. The question mark option was integrated to prevent gambling; we told the students they would receive −1 point for each incorrect answer. Cronbach's alpha was 0.93 for the New Zealand test and 0.88 for the Iceland test. The application of the acquired knowledge was measured by asking the students to formulate the advantages and disadvantages of the country they studied. Again 1 point was assigned for each correct advantage and disadvantage. Of the application tasks, 10 per cent were scored by two independent researchers, leading to a kappa of 0.84 for the advantages and a kappa of 0.89 for the disadvantages. The transfer assignment was to write down as many topics as possible that one would need to consider when moving to another country. For each reasonable topic, 1 point was assigned.

Finally, metacognitive knowledge was measured by asking the students to imagine that they were going to do the same assignment again. They were asked to write down steps to be taken and how they would proceed on this assignment. The answers were scored against a full procedural overview made by the researchers. The full procedural overview consisted of 18 steps; examples of steps were 'activate prior knowledge' and 'division of tasks in the group'. The maximum score was 18 points. Of the questionnaires, 10 per cent were scored by two independent researchers to reliably establish a kappa of 0.83.

11.8.3 Results

The findings showed that scaffolding did not have a significant effect on group performance. However, the effect size r = 0.19 indicates a small to medium positive effect of scaffolding on group performance on the paper. Also, with respect to the number of questions asked there was no significant effect of scaffolding, but again the effect size r = 0.21 does show a small to medium positive effect of scaffolding on the number of questions asked. These findings with respect to group performance do not confirm our expectations: scaffolding does not significantly affect group performance, but it does have a small to medium positive effect on group performance.

The findings also showed that dynamic scaffolding did not have a significant effect on individual students' domain knowledge. Specifically, we did not find a significant effect of scaffolding on free recall (r = 0.03), the knowledge test of New Zealand (r = 0.01), the knowledge test of Iceland (r = 0.08), the application of knowledge (r = 0.06) or the transfer of knowledge (r = 0.03). The effect size for the knowledge test of Iceland does indicate a small positive effect of dynamic scaffolding. With regard to domain knowledge, the findings do not confirm our expectations.

Finally, a significant effect was found with regard to students' metacognitive knowledge. The results reveal a small positive effect (r = 0.16) of scaffolding on the amount of metacognitive knowledge acquired. This finding confirms our expectations: scaffolding does have positive effects on the amount of metacognitive knowledge individual students acquired.

11.9   Discussion

We began this chapter by proposing that attention management could be used to personalize education. We have discussed how AtGentSchool enables personalized support, or dynamic scaffolding, during learning generated by an attention-management system and what the effect of such support is on learning outcomes.

We described how the AtGentSchool system uses attention management dynamically to scaffold self-regulated learning. The attention-management system derives information from the student's environment. Based on this information, an assessment or diagnosis of the student's attentional focus is made and then compared to a logical attentional focus based on the learning assignment. This comparison is the basis for the selection of the scaffold, or calibration, which is only sent when the student is fading and needs the support. AtGentSchool uses an intervention model directed at supporting self-regulated metacognitive, cognitive and motivational learning processes. The different scaffolds are shown to the user based on diagnosis, calibration and fading decisions made by the attention-management system.

Secondly, we addressed the effect the AtGentSchool system has on students' learning outcomes. We found evidence that AtGentSchool can be used effectively to give form to dynamic scaffolding. The results of the two studies concur with respect to the effect sizes found on group performance. Dynamic scaffolding has a small to medium effect on the performance of students; both the quality of the papers they write and the number of questions they ask the inhabitant increase. In the first study the effects were significant, while in the second study they were not significant.

We did not find effects of dynamic scaffolding on the domain knowledge of the students in either of our studies. This is consistent with other findings in scaffolding studies which also did not find an effect on domain knowledge measured with a recall task or knowledge test (Lin and Lehman 1999; Bannert 2006). This also confirms our expectation that there are limits to the system's efficacy in relation to cognitive scaffolding.

The second study also incorporated the measurement of individual students' metacognitive knowledge acquisition. We found a significant positive small effect of dynamic scaffolding on the metacognitive knowledge students acquired. This finding suggests that the current AtGentSchool system is particularly effective at supporting metacognitive activities.

Naturally, more research is needed in different domains and different learning environments to assess the overall generalizability of these results with regard to the effectiveness of attention management for dynamic scaffolding. We suspect that the current input into our system is rather too limited to support the diagnosis of both the cognitive and motivational processes of students. Registering more and different information from the student's environment allows us to accumulate a better representation of the learner's attentional focus. This could enhance our ability to position interventions in relation to the cognitive and motivational processes. For example, the effectiveness of cognitive scaffolds could be enhanced by using eye tracking, which would give a better diagnosis of learners' current cognitive processes. Further, a webcam could be used to assess the students' emotional states, providing useful information for the diagnosis of their motivation. Research focused on new input variables can address these issues. The calibration process relates the students' attentional focus and the selected intervention; for example, it could send a planning intervention at the start of a task. Again the system could be enhanced with respect to cognitive scaffolding; for instance, when we know more about the knowledge model of the learner, we can adjust the cognitive scaffolds to the knowledge model by providing more elaborate interventions for low-level students.

Finally, adjustments could be made in the presentation of scaffolds to the user. The form and modality of the scaffolds can be adjusted to make them more effective: for example, statements versus questions or virtual agents versus text messages. In our studies we have used the virtual agent as a scaffolder, but one can think of many other possible modalities such as text interventions, agent interventions or interventions by robots. The effects of the modalities are largely unknown. Additionally, with respect to the virtual agent, we know very little about the usage of its emotions, appearance, animations and their effects on learning outcomes.

Our findings show that AtGentSchool is a solution that supports learning on a personalized level, especially with respect to support for metacognitive processes. As we mention in the discussion, we have grounds to assert that with improvement in registration of the attentional focus of the learner, improvements could be expected with respect to cognitive and motivational scaffolding. Thus attention management could be a solution that would support learning on a personalized level. Artificial intelligence has traditionally struggled with ill-structured domains, resulting in few personalized solutions for these fields. Attention-management systems are domain-independent and thus can also be used for ill-structured domains. This means that learning systems augmented with an attention-management system could be an interesting path of exploration that would enhance the availability of personalized learning solutions.

11.10   Acknowledgements

This research was supported by a grant from the National Scientific Organization of the Netherlands (NWO) 411-04-102 and from the European Commission under the FP6 Framework project AtGentive IST 4-027529-STP. We acknowledge the contribution of all project partners to the development of the AtGentSchool scaffolding system.

11.11   References

Ahissar, M., and Hochstein, S. 1993. Attentional control of early perceptual learning, in *Proceedings of the National Academy of Sciences of the United States of America* 90(12): 5718–22

Ainley, M., and Patrick, L. 2006. Measuring self-regulated learning processes through tracking patterns of student interaction with achievement activities, *Review of Educational Psychology* 18: 267–86

Azevedo, R., and Hadwin, A. F. 2005. Scaffolding self-regulated learning and metacognition: Implications for design of computer-based scaffolding, *Instructional Science* 33: 367–79

Bannert, M. 2006. Effects of reflection prompts when learning with hypermedia, *Journal of Educational Computing Research* 4: 359–75

Bloom, B. 1984. The 2 sigma problem: The search for methods of group instruction as effective as one-to-one tutoring, *Educational Researcher* 13: 3–16

Boekaerts, M. 1999. Motivated learning: Studying student * situation transactional units, *European Journal of Psychology of Education* 14(4): 41–55

Chun, M. M., and Wolfe, J. 2001. Visual attention, in E. B. Goldstein (ed.), *Blackwell's Handbook of Perception*. Oxford: Blackwell: 272–310

Driver, J. 2001. A selective review of selective attention research from the past century, *British Journal of Psychology* 92: 53–78

Flavell, J. 1979. Metacognition and cognitive monitoring: A new area of cognitive-developmental inquiry, *American Psychologist* 34: 906–11

Garner, R. 1987. *Metacognition and Reading Comprehension*. Norwood, NJ: Ablex

Kalyuga, S., Chandler, P., and Sweller, J. 2001. Learner experience and efficiency of instructional guidance, *Educational Psychology* 21: 5–23

Kirschner, P. A., Sweller, J., and Clark, R. E. 2006. Why minimal guidance during instruction docs not work: An analysis of the failure of constructivist, discovery, problem-based, experiential, and inquiry-based teaching, *Educational Psychologist* 4: 75–86

Lin, X., and Lehman, J. D. 1999. Supporting learning of variable control in a computer-based biology environment: Effects of prompting college students to reflect on their own thinking, *Journal of Research in Science Teaching* 36: 837–48

Molenaar, I. 2003. Knowledge exchange from citizens to learners through online collaboration. In D. Lassner and C. McNaught (eds.), *Proceedings of World Conference on Educational Multimedia, Hypermedia and Telecommunications 2003*, Chesapeake, VA. AACE: 894–9

Molenaar, I., and Roda, C. 2008. Attention management for dynamic and adaptive scaffolding, *Pragmatics and Cognition* 16(2): 225–71

Monsell, S. 2003. Task switching, *Trends in Cognitive Sciences* 7(3): 134–40

Nelson, T. 1996. Consciousness and metacognition, *American Psychologist* 51: 102–29

Posner, M. 1980. Orienting of attention, *Quarterly Journal of Experimental Psychology* 32: 3–25

1982. Cumulative development of attention theory, *American Psychologist* 37: 168–79

Puntambekar, S., and Hübscher, R. 2005. Tools for scaffolding students in a complex environment: What have we gained and what have we missed? *Educational Psychologist* 40(1): 1–12

Roda, C., and Nabeth, T. 2007. Supporting attention in learning environments: Attention support services, and information management, in *Proceedings of the Second European Conference on Technology Enhanced Learning, EC-TEL 2007*, Crete: 277–91

Roda, C., and Thomas, J. 2006. Attention aware systems: Theories, applications, and research agenda, *Computers in Human Behavior* 22(4): 557–87

Rosenthal, R. 1991. *Meta-Analytic Procedures for Social Research* (rev. edn). Newbury Park, CA: Sage

Saffran, E. R., Aslin, R. N., and Newport, E. L. 1996. Statistical learning by 8-month-old infants, *Science* 274(5294): 1926–8

Seger, C. A. 1994. Implicit learning, *Psychological Bulletin* 115(2): 163–96

Seitz, A., and Watanabe, T. 2005. A unified model for perceptual learning, *Trends in Cognitive Sciences* 9(7): 329–34

Shanks, D. R., Rowland, L. A., and Ranger, M. S. 2005. Attentional load and implicit sequence learning, *Psychological Research* 69(5): 369–82

Spector, A., and Biederman, I. 1976. Mental set and mental shift revisited, *American Journal of Psychology* 89(4): 669–79

Toro, J. M., Sinnett, S., and Soto-Faraco, S. 2005. Speech segmentation by statistical learning depends on attention, *Cognition* 97(2): B25–B34

Veenman, M. V. J., van Hout-Wolters, B. H. A. M., and Afflerbach, P. 2006. Metacognition and learning: Conceptual and methodological considerations, *Metacognition and Learning* 1: 3–14

Wood, D., Bruner, J., and Ross, G. 1976. The role of tutoring in problem solving, *Journal of Child Psychology and Psychiatry and Allied Disciplines* 17: 89–100

Yantis, S. 1998. Control of visual attention, in H. Pashler (ed.), *Attention*. London: University College London Press: 223–56

Zimmerman, B. J. 2002. Becoming a self-regulated learner: An overview, *Theory into Practice* 42(2): 64–70

12 Managing attention in the social web: the AtGentNet approach

Thierry Nabeth and Nicolas Maisonneuve

By transforming the Web into a massive social space, Web 2.0 has opened a vast set of opportunities for people to interact with one another using online social networking, blogs, wikis or social bookmarking. But at the same time such a phenomenon has created the conditions for a massive social interaction overload: people are being overwhelmed by solicitations and opportunities to engage in social exchange but they have few means by which to deal effectively with this new level of interaction. The objective of this chapter is to investigate the use of ICT (information and communication technologies) to support online social interactions in a more attention-effective way. This is achieved by adapting to a social context a general model (Roda and Nabeth 2008) which defines four levels of attention support: perception, deliberation, operation and metacognition. We then describe how the support of social attention has been operationalized with the implementation of the attention-aware social platform AtGentNet, and tested in the context of communities of learners and professionals. After discussing the results of the experimentation, this chapter concludes by reflecting on how this approach can be generalized to support the interaction of people in the social web in general.

12.1 Introduction: addressing the social interaction overload

The social web, an essential component of the Web 2.0 vision, which refers to the use of the Internet for facilitating online social activities (Chi 2008), has totally reinvented the Web as a massive participatory social space. In Web 2.0 (O'Reilly 2005), people are engaged in a variety of interactions with others: they use blogs, wikis (Cunningham and Leuf 2001) and other social media to participate in the creation of content; they employ social bookmarking (Golder and Huberman 2006; Halpin, Robu and Shepherd 2006; Marlow *et al.* 2006), reputation systems (Resnick *et al.* 2000), RSS feeds (Gill 2005) and other massively distributed collaborative mechanisms to filter, share, aggregate and annotate resources; they maintain constant contact with others using instant messaging or micro-blogging systems; and finally, people use social networking (Boyd and Ellison 2007) or dating services to manage relationships.

The advantages of a more social web are undeniable: people's roles have been transformed from passive consumers of resources into active participants (much content is generated by users), and this new setting has considerably augmented the availability, processing and circulation of knowledge (since everyone is potentially an active participant in these knowledge processes). Besides, these processes exist without supervision, relying on concepts such as emergence or collective intelligence (Tapscott and Williams 2007; O'Reilly 2005; Weiss 2005; McAfee 2006) to make the coordination happen without apparent effort.

Yet at the same time, this new setting has come at a cost: whereas with Web 1.0 people were overwhelmed with information, Web 2.0 has come with a tremendous level of interaction, subjecting people to massive social interaction overload. Participating in social media such as blogs and wikis, as a consumer, and even more as a contributor, is a time-consuming activity (Perez 2008). People are also subject to frequent social solicitations originating from multiple sources and available in multiple forms (invitations to connect to online social networking services, invitations to chat, invitations to become part of a group, invitations to comment, etc.). The social web provides a fragmented (quasi-schizophrenic) perception of the environment, and its users are kept in a state of 'continuous partial attention' (Stone 2006) reinforced by the fear of being disconnected from the social sphere and becoming marginalized. Finally, people are under constant pressure to develop their social relationships (Granovetter 1973), since the associated social capital (Burt 1997) is acknowledged as a determining factor of success in the knowledge economy (Nardi, Whittaker and Schwarz 2000; Thomas, Kellogg and Erickson 2001).

Managing all these social interactions and solicitations represents a daunting and seemingly impossible task: how to deal with the different solicitations and limit the level of interaction, knowing that some of them will be critical. How much time and attention can one dedicate to these social interactions without risking overlooking something important or having one's attention totally consumed in unproductive activities? In particular, we know that with Web 2.0 people's cognitive capabilities have not changed: the short-term or working memory of the human brain is still limited to a maximum capacity to manipulate 7 ± 2 concepts (Miller 1956) and, more importantly related to social interaction, the maximum number of stable interpersonal relationships that a person can effectively manage is 150 (Dunbar 1992).

The objective of this chapter is to provide some answers to these questions in the context of a social platform, AtGentNet, that was elaborated to support the interactions of groups of learners engaged in a blended learning programme.

The first part of this chapter briefly describes principles for supporting attention based on a model of *attention support* at four levels: *perception, deliberation, operation* and *metacognition*. We then describe how these principles can be adapted to support attention in a social context. In the next section we describe how these principles have been operationalized in the social platform AtGentNet, via the design of an architecture and a series of mechanisms supporting social attention at different levels. We then report on how this platform was tested for supporting the online interaction of a group of learners engaged in a blended learning programme. Finally, we conclude by reflecting on how this approach can be generalized to support the interaction of people in the social web in general, and we identify further lines of evolution.

12.2   Managing attention

12.2.1   Attention in the information and knowledge economy

The questions of social interaction overload are neither new nor only related to the social web. Similar questions had already surfaced as a major concern with the advent of the information and knowledge economy (Drucker 1999).

The old industrial economy was characterized by the scarcity of information and by the important cost of accessing it. At this time, people and organizations had no difficulties managing information and the critical factor for the success of companies was the capacity to access capital. The advent of the knowledge economy at the end of the twentieth century totally transformed this situation: in the information and knowledge economy, information is abundant and even overflowing (Goldhaber 1997). Knowledge is also subject to continuous regeneration and transformation (Senge 1990), and is socially constructed via social interaction (Argyris and Schon 1978; Kogut 2008). In this context, the new requirement for success has become the capability to process effectively large amounts of information with limited resources constituted mainly by people's time, i.e., the attention they can dedicate to accomplishing their tasks. In the information economy, *attention* has therefore become one of the most important aspects of human and organizational productivity (Ocasio 1997; Simon 1971), the most successful organizations being the ones that are the most capable in allocating their attention effectively and therefore more capable in dealing with information overflow (Davenport and Beck 2001) and adapting to a changing environment

(Ocasio 1993). The importance of attention for knowledge-intensive activities has thus been acknowledged in a variety of sectors, such as venture capitalism (Gifford 1997), libraries (Bridges 2008) and advertising (Huberman and Wu 2007).

In the social web, opportunities to interact with others have flourished everywhere: people use blogs to express opinions and engage in discussions with others, they use wikis to contribute to the creation of collective knowledge, they use micro-messages (via microblogging systems such as Twitter) to express and to follow people's current thinking, and make use of online social networking services to develop and maintain relationships. In the social web, the abundance of information has been complemented by the abundance of social interaction, *attention* remaining however the scarcest resource. In this context, the more successful organizations will be the ones in which people are able to deal the most effectively with a high and rich level of social interactions and to optimize the use of attention for supporting social interaction.

12.2.2   Supporting attention: a four-level model

Different models and mechanisms have been proposed to support attention. At an organizational level approaches and methods have been proposed for helping companies and people to manage their attention in a more effective way. At the technical level ICT has been used to provide operational support to attention management.

At the organizational level, Davenport and Beck (2001) have proposed an approach and an assessment tool (AttentionScape) to help individuals and organizations determine and optimize how they allocate their attention along three axes (Beck and Davenport 2001): (1) aversive/attractive – aversive attention is paid when people are afraid of the consequences of not paying attention; attractive attention is given to elements people like and expect to be pleasant; (2) captive/voluntary – people pay voluntary attention to things they find innately interesting, but attention is held captive when people have something thrust upon them; (3) front of mind/back of mind – front of mind is related to an active and conscious allocation of cognitive resources (like reading a textbook), whereas back of mind is related to a partial, unconscious allocation of these resources (like listening to music in the background while reading a book). This notion of *peripheral attention* is also present in the term 'continuous partial attention' coined by Linda Stone (2006) to describe the dominant mode of attention nowadays when people are under a continuous state of vigilance given the use of the new communication tools (SMS, Chat, messengers). Stone also distinguishes between two modes of management of people's time: the *tactical mode* where 'all is about tasks prioritization' and 'optimization *efficiency*'; and the *strategic mode* where 'all is about *intention*, making choices as to what *does* and *does not* get done'. She stresses that the *tactical mode* is mostly in use today, and calls for a development of the *strategic mode*. Finally, Ashkenas (2007) proposes to address the attention overload by working on the reduction of complexity in organization by: (1) making simplification a goal; (2) simplifying the organizational structure; (3) pruning and simplifying products and services; (4) disciplining business and governance processes; and (5) simplifying personal patterns.

At the technical level, different approaches have been proposed to use ICT to support attention. Bier and colleagues (1993: 73) have proposed the Magic Lens concept as 'filters that modify the presentation of application objects to reveal hidden information, to enhance data of interest, or to suppress distracting information'. More generally, 'attentive user interfaces' have been proposed in order to increase the effectiveness of human–computer interaction (Vertegaal 2003). Specifically, four main types of attentive user interfaces have been identified (Vertegaal *et al.* 2006): visual attention, turn management, interruption decision interfaces and visual detail management interfaces. Huberman and Wu (2008) introduced the automatic configuration mechanism resulting in the most relevant information being presented to limited attention users. Finally, Anicic, Stojanovic and Apostolou (2008) propose the use of Enterprise Attention Management Systems that consist in attention-aware platforms such as Workflow, Content Management System (CMS) and the GroupWare System (GWS). Their attention model relies on the idea of proactively supporting the user in reacting to changes respecting the user's context and preferences. Practically, their system is an event-based system which tracks and mines events (such as the addition of a new document or someone opening a document), and manages alerts in an attention-effective way.

A brief analysis of these different approaches and tools indicates that attention can be supported in a variety of ways, such as by filtering the noise, by making the information more relevant (via personalization), by minimizing distraction through notification management, by reducing the required level of vigilance (e.g., through the use of personal organizers), or by helping people to assess the level and nature of the attention that they dedicate to their activities (e.g., what is done with Attention-Scape).

Roda and Nabeth (2008) have proposed a holistic framework for integrating in a single model the different means of supporting attention. This model proposes that attention can be supported at four different levels: (1) the perception level; (2) the deliberative level; (3) the operational level; (4) the metacognitive level. The support of attention at the *perceptual level* consists in enhancing people's perceptive capabilities. It relies on the idea of filtering the irrelevant or less important information, of emphasizing the most important information, and of presenting interruptions at the appropriate level of prominence. The support of attention at the *deliberative level* consists in helping people in their decision making. The support of attention at the *operational level* consists in reducing the effort needed to accomplish tasks. For instance, some mechanisms may automate a task or reduce the number of steps required to accomplish a task. Finally the *metacognitive* support consists in helping people to improve their attention allocation practices. Thus mechanisms can be used to allow people to assess their current practices, such as visualizing how they allocate their attention, and to situate their practices. Other mechanisms can allow people to experiment with new practices. Finally, yet other mechanisms can be used to stimulate motivation, for instance by increasing the perception of self-efficacy (Bandura 1994), or by providing the means to compare their practices with others.

12.3   Managing social attention

In this section, we discuss how the four-level model of supporting attention of Roda and Nabeth (2008) can be adapted to support the management of attention in a social context. More specifically, for each level (perception, deliberation, operation and metacognition), we will introduce a set of mechanisms that can be used to support people in better allocating their attention when interacting with others. However, we first provide a rapid overview of theories and works relevant to the support of attention in a social context and that have informed the work presented here.

12.3.1   Relevant theories and research

Psychology and Sociology have proposed a number of theories relevant to the management of attention in a social context, and, in particular, that associate limitations or a cognitive effort with the establishment and maintenance of social relationships.

First, the anthropologist and evolutionary biologist Robin Dunbar (1992), based on an extrapolation of a study of groups of primates, has found a maximum number of 150 as the cognitive limit of the number of stable interpersonal relationships that humans can effectively maintain. This limitation, which does not apply only to the offline world, suggests that it is illusory to think that people are able to manage a very large number of relationships, unless some of these relationships are very loose, and not really used. Thus the value of the many hundreds of relationships that some persons record in online networking services, or micro-blogging systems, is most probably unrealistic.

Second, there exist a number of theories that have tried to explain how people manage their relationships and that induce some limits in their number, such as the *social exchange theory* (Thibaut and Kelley 1959) and the *social behaviour as exchange theory* (Homans 1958). Both these theories derive from the application of economic theories of rational choice that attribute a cost to establishing and maintaining a social relationship. More specifically, the *social exchange theory* proposes that voluntary relationships depend on their participants receiving satisfactory outcomes, and that a person's commitment to an existing relationship is proportional to his/her satisfaction in this relationship and to the investment he/she has already put into this relationship, and it is inversely proportional to potential alternative relationships. A relationship therefore generates value but it also has a cost, and there exists a limit at which the cost of a relationship overtakes the benefit. The *social behaviour as exchange theory* is even more radical, since it explains how people interact socially in terms of negotiated exchanges between parties. We can presume, since negotiating has a cost, that people will find some limit to the number of people with whom they can establish fruitful relationships.

Another direction of research is related to the augmentation of social cognition. This consists in 'enhancing the ability of a group to remember, think, and reason' (Chi *et al.* 2008: 11), increasing usability and facilitating the navigation of the information via social imitation and mimesis (Erickson 2009). Social cognition augmentation also relates to the concepts of social navigation (Dieberger *et al.* 2000) and social foraging (Chi, Pirolli and Lam 2007; Giraldeau and Caraco 2000). Mechanisms providing social cognition augmentation also influence the levels of motivation of individuals and groups. Motivation may be increased via social stimulation through techniques such as social comparison (Harper *et al.* 2007) and increased perception of self-efficacy in a social context (Bandura 2001). Such reinforcement may be obtained by displaying the value of contribution to the community (Rashid *et al.* 2006), or by allowing the exposure of personal information (Tufekci 2008) and flattering people's egos (Joinson 2008; Nishikant, Konstan and Terveen 2005). More generally, these mechanisms intervene to support collective intelligence (Yuan *et al.* 2007).

Finally, from a more operational perspective, we can observe the integration in many social platforms of a number of mechanisms supporting the management of a large number of interactions. For instance, the social networking system LinkedIn or the micro-blogging system Twitter aggregate in a single linefeed all the activities originating from a user's acquaintances, reducing the cognitive effort required to keep track of them. Wikipedia offers the possibility, via the 'watch list', to track in a single place the changes happening in a set of pages that the user puts under observation, considerably reducing the effort required to follow the pages that are the more relevant to this user. Finally, we can mention personal information management (PIM) systems such as electronic address books, or more simply the SMS in mobile phones, that definitively allow a user to be more attention effective in the management of social relationships. In all these cases, however, the driving force behind the design of these tools has not been the support of social attention but only the desire to increase personal efficiency.

12.3.2   An application of the four-level model

12.3.2.1 Enhancing social perception   Erickson and Kellogg (2000) proposed *social translucence* as an approach to enhance the perception of social activity in online environments. Social translucence consists in making participants and their activities visible to one another. The role of social translucence is to inform, to create awareness and to enforce accountability (Erickson and Kellogg 2003). By enhancing social perception, it also contributes to the coordination of groups as well as stimulating participation (Vassileva and Sun 2007). A variety of mechanisms can be used, and have been invented as part of Web 2.0, to make the social activity more visible. Erickson (2009) refers to these mechanisms as social proxies, i.e., 'minimalist graphical representation that portrays socially salient aspects of an online interaction'. Examples of such mechanisms include: presence features in instant messaging systems; notification in email systems; lists of contributors' and items' popularity in online communities; social connectedness and life-activity feeds in online social networking services; and tagging in collaborative bookmarking services (Marlow *et al.* 2006).

12.3.2.2 Supporting deliberation   Deliberation support consists in assisting users to choose the most effective approach to adopt for interacting with others. Guidance can be offered by mechanisms based on high-level visualization to help the decision process. It can also suggest approaches to maximize the impact of the actions, such as the application of principles derived from the diffusion of innovation theory (Rogers 2003) or the use of viral marketing techniques (Subramani and Rajagopalan

2003). Mechanisms may include: (1) methods and tools to analyse social networks (Cross, Borgatti and Parker 2002) so as to identify the most important nodes; (2) reputation indicators (Resnick *et al.* 2000) allowing users to assess the risks attached to a potential interaction and decide the value of engaging in a social exchange (Thibaut and Kelley 1959); or (3) indicators allowing users to select information and actions having maximum impact but requiring a minimum of effort. In the latter cases, users may be guided by elements such as the novelty or popularity of the items (Wu and Huberman 2008).

12.3.2.3 Providing operational support   Operational support is aimed at reducing the cognitive effort required to accomplish a social interaction task by reducing the number of steps required or by automating the task. For example, this may consist in suggesting to a user that he affiliate to a group matching his observed interests. By making people's interests more visible, or by using the introductions and recommendation mechanisms, the cognitive effort related to the weaving of social ties is reduced. Other approaches may consist in selecting a tool to reduce the amount of effort to communicate, such as the use of social media like blogs, wikis or RSS feeds. The usage of these tools will result in a reduction of effort from the 'communicator', and less distraction for target users. Other examples include organizer services that assist people in managing their agenda, reducing their 'back of mind' cognitive load from the necessity to remember appointments or friends' birthdays. Finally, in a similar line, watch mechanisms, such as those offered by Wikipedia, allow a user to keep track of changes in resources with minimal effort.

12.3.2.4 Metacognition   Support for metacognition consists of awareness mechanisms as well as other mechanisms that influence users' motivation. Awareness mechanisms provide people with the possibility to examine how they have behaved in the past when interacting with others, and represent useful tools for improving their practices. Motivational mechanisms play a role in motivating people to interact or to participate. The first category of mechanisms includes tools to allow people to assess how they have dedicated their time during social activities, such as the AttentionScape system previously mentioned, as well as statistical tools to visualize their activities. The second category of mechanisms may indicate the popularity of one's contributions, and more generally the impact level. This effectiveness assessment intervenes at the level of motivation of the users since it contributes to increase the perception of self-efficacy (Bandura 2001). This effect has, for instance, been demonstrated by Huberman, Romero and Wu in the case of user-generated content on

Table 12.1 *Supporting attention at different levels*

Level	Support of social attention	Examples of mechanisms
Perception	Make the social activity more visible (social translucence); filter the information and personalize the interaction	Presence mechanisms; notification mechanisms; popularity indicators (such as most-accessed document)
Deliberation	Inform and guide users in deciding about actions that are the most attention-effective (require less effort and have the most impact)	Reputation indicators; involvement indicators (e.g., most-active contributors); social network visualization and analysis; impact indicators (e.g., 'who reads me'); tactical advice
Operation	Reduce the cognitive effort required to accomplish a task or conduct an activity, for instance the need to remember	Automated group affiliation; watch lists; adoption of more attention-effective communication tools (such as blogs, RSS); organizer services
Metacognition	Help users to assess the attention effort needed in conducting some activities so as to help them to learn to become more attention-effective	Display of statistics of attention allocation; comparison with other people's practices; indicators of the level of impact; strategic advice

YouTube: 'the productivity exhibited in crowdsourcing exhibits a strong positive dependence on attention, measured by the number of downloads. Conversely, a lack of attention leads to a decrease in the number of videos uploaded and the consequent drop in productivity' (Huberman, Romero and Wu 2009a: 1).

12.3.2.5 Discussion and summary   A mechanism may provide attentional support at different levels at the same time. Thus a mechanism that makes the social activity more visible will intervene both in enhancing user perception, helping the users' decision making, and in providing him with feedback allowing him to improve his practice. This makes the applicability to a social context of our four-level model of attention support less straightforward than if we had been able to assign each mechanism to a single level. However, the application of this model remains useful since it ensures that attention support is done at all levels, and not only at the level of perception as is usually the case in systems focusing essentially on the user interface.

Table 12.1 provides a summary of the support of attention at different levels.

12.4 AtGentNet: a social attention effective platform

12.4.1 Overview

AtGentNet is a Web 2.0 social platform elaborated in the context of the EU research project AtGentive which is aimed at supporting users' social attention in community platforms (Roda and Nabeth 2006). This platform is used to support both collaboration and social networking in different contexts, such as blended learning (Nabeth et al. 2008), knowledge exchange in communities and collaboration in groups. AtGentNet incorporates a mix of features supporting online interaction by reducing the level of attention needed for people's interaction.

AtGentNet appears as a community portal (see figure 12.1 (in plate section)), and provides the communication and social network infrastructure supporting the interaction of members as well as their networking. It includes forums, bulletin boards, chat space, search, tagging, profiles, groups and membership management. AtGentNet also includes a series of mechanisms providing basic attention support, and in particular translucence mechanisms, such as the display of the statistics of activities of the participants, the list of the most popular resources, the list of the most active contributors, the list of the more regular visitors, etc. AtGentNet is enhanced by an intelligent agent generating different interventions that are proposed in one of the portlets (a dedicated area in the user interface) or delivered via an artificial character embodying the artificial agent. More details about these mechanisms will be provided later in this chapter.

12.4.2 The design

AtGentNet is composed of two main elements: (1) a collaborative/social platform providing a variety of means (including an artificial character) to support people's interaction and networking; (2) an external agent module able to provide proactive and intelligent support to attention. This agent module consists of a perception layer and a reasoning layer. The function of the perception layer is to observe and to mine the activity of the community originating from the platform. The reasoning layer uses this information to generate a series of advanced proactive interventions.

This architecture allows a very good decoupling between a community platform and the advanced mechanisms. The platform is only aware of the agent module via the Application Programming Interface (API). This agent-based approach, also adopted in Nabeth et al. (2005) to stimulate participation in virtual communities, moves the intelligence to an external module, increasing modularity and reusability. The platform and the agent module can be used independently in a totally different context. Yet, the two systems appear seamlessly integrated into an agent-enhanced social platform as presented in figure 12.2 (see plate).

12.4.2.1 The platform   The platform was implemented in the Lotus Domino technology, which provides an environment well adapted for the design of collaborative applications. The application logic was implemented mainly using the Java programming language.

This platform provides a ReST (Representational State Transfer) based API (Fielding and Taylor 2002) which opens its data and activities to any external third-party services willing to monitor the community's activity, and allows the receipt of any attention-related interventions from them. More precisely, this API provides:

• *Access to the resources of the community*: This API gives access (through an XML representation) to a variety of items in the platform, such as: (1) the documents, including both content and meta-information such as tags, dates and statistical data; (2) the users' profiles, with identification, basic description, dates, statistical information, competence and interest; (3) and general information about the community, e.g., the list of members or of the most popular documents.

• *Access to the activity of the community*: The platform exports several Atom RSS feeds representing the events happening in the platform, such as: (1) document-centric events (all the activity related to a specific document, e.g., creation, view, comment); (2) user (or group)-centric events, i.e., all the activity of a given member (view of a user's profile, creation, tagging or comment on a document); (3) tag-centric events, i.e., all the activity associated with a tag (document tagged).

• *The possibility to execute external interventions*: External components can create interventions to notify users about information or make suggestions (guidance). Interventions may later be delivered in the form of a message displayed in a portlet (dedicated area of the user interface), notifying the user about the availability of new information in the platform (information that has been inferred or obtained from other sources), or the execution of an animation by an artificial character (an embodied agent).

Subscription to the community's activity (a list of events) allows an external entity to monitor the community's activity in real time. The decoding of this information is facilitated by the tagging of each event according to different aspects: the type of actions, and the resources and users involved in the interaction. Such tagging can contribute to a better visualization (advanced RSS readers are taking advantage of the tags when visualizing information), but can also be exploited for automatic processing by external programs (such as agents).

12.4.2.2 The external agent

The agent is an external component that has been implemented using the Java programming language, and that runs on a Tomcat web server (which was installed on a different computer in the different tests that were conducted). As indicated previously, this agent was developed separately so as to reduce the complexity of the whole system and provide the maximum of flexibility.

This external agent observes the activity of the community and generates attention-related interventions. An intervention is constituted by a predicate (corresponding to the identification of a particular state) and an action or suggestion. For instance, if a new user has not completed his profile, the agent sends a reminder to complete it. The external agent can generate different types of interventions from basic to advanced. Examples of interventions include task reminders (e.g., completing a user profile), notification of collective or individual bursts of attention related to a resource (e.g., many community members have recently commented on a document), and advice about the user's practices related to his/her attention management (e.g., suggesting that he/she should be more focused on a topic, or, on the contrary, that he/she should broaden his/her attention span to other topics).

The cycle of functioning of this agent can be summarized by the following steps (see figure 12.2):

1. The users interact with the platform, generating digital traces (Latour 2007).
2. The agent observes the community's activity using AtGentNet's API.
3. This agent (via the perception layer) mines this information (Anjewierden and Efimova 2006; Wolpers et al. 2007; May, George and Prévôt 2008) and conducts operations such as data fusion and pattern matching, making use of heuristics and user profiling (Nabeth 2008).
4. The agent generates a personalized intervention (Pierrakos et al. 2003; Mobasher 2007) and sends it to the platform using the API (the interface used for inter-program communication). The platform then executes this intervention, displaying the result using either an embodied character or a portlet (a small dedicated area in the computer–human interface).

12.4.3 Mechanisms supporting social attention in AtGentNet

AtGentNet integrates a variety of mechanisms supporting attention implemented directly at platform level, or via the agent module. These mechanisms are designed to provide a user-centric perspective of the system.

12.4.3.1 Social perception support   Social translucence: AtGentNet is designed so as to make the social dimension and social activity visible (social translucence) and to reinforce the idea that the environment is primarily about social interaction and networking and not about managing documents. Pictures of participants, traces of their activities and resource popularity indicators are displayed to convey the feeling of people's participation. For instance, the home page displays the list of members who have recently connected as well as the list of the most popular documents (see figure 12.1). The display of a document includes pictures of the author and of recent readers. The display of the page associated with a tag includes the document annotated with this tag but also the pictures of authors who have most frequently used this tag. Finally, many statistics are available, such as a list of the most active contributors or a list of people who connect most often.

Abstract view of the social dimension of a list of items: The platform is also able to abstract information at the community level on three dimensions: people, resources and concepts (i.e., tags). For instance, when a list of postings is displayed, a member can immediately see an aggregated view of the most popular authors of items in the list, of the concepts associated with these items, and of the most popular item included in the list.

Reporting of bursts of attention: The agent module informs members of abnormal levels of attention received by documents they have authored. This category of mechanisms may be extended in the future to notify members of abnormal levels of attention given to concepts they have shown an interest in.

12.4.3.2 Deliberation   support   Assessing the social impact of actions: AtGentNet provides the possibility for members to assess the social impact of their actions. For instance, when posting a document, an author can see not only the number of visits but also who the readers are. Members can also know which people they are getting the most attention from (see 'people who read me' or 'my profile visitor' in figure 12.3 (in plate section)).

Such information allows a user to decide more confidently whether to engage in interactions with another user. At the community level, this information may be useful in determining the most effective interaction tactics. For instance, an author may decide to target people who have already paid attention to documents he/she has produced (e.g., people who have read several documents authored by this user).

Assessing the attention given to others: The platform makes each member aware of people he/she is dedicating most of his/her attention to. For instance, the platform displays the members receiving most of the user's attention ('people I read': see figure 12.3). The platform also allows users to determine documents or concepts (tags) to which they are dedicating most of their attention as a consumer ('tags of my last readings') or as a contributor ('tags of my postings') (figure 12.4: see plate).

Network visualization: Displaying the relationships between members and resources (such as authorship of a document, readership of a document, contribution to concepts, social relationships, etc.) provides an alternative way to navigate the maze of information and to facilitate the decision-making process.

12.4.3.3 Operational support AtGentNet makes available a number of mechanisms for operational support, such as assisting users in accomplishing a task or reducing the number of steps needed to execute an operation. For instance, in the latter case, the platform is designed so as to allow users to access rapidly the most relevant information (e.g., the home page provides the list of the last unread messages, and the 'clickable' tags facilitate navigation through the information).

Reminder to complete a task: The agent module intervenes to provide assistance to users in accomplishing some tasks, such as in managing assignments in reading documents, or in reminding them of the importance of completing their user profile.

Presentation of the community by an embodied character: The agent detects the creation of new accounts and presents the platform to the new user using an embodied character (see figure 12.1). The agent may also notify the community as a whole of a new member, facilitating the establishment of social relationships.

Aggregation of information: The exporting of RSS feeds also contributes to reducing the cognitive load of users. RSS readers, by aggregating different sources of information in a single place, reduce the number of pages that a user needs to consult.

Watch list: AtGentNet implements the watch list feature, allowing a user to track, in a single place, the activities related to documents, tags or people. A user may use this feature to know who is reading/replying to some documents, or to know of the activity of the members of a group (e.g., the date of their last connection, or the number of documents they have created).

Tracking inattentive members: Furthermore, the agent can notify an author about (inattentive) members who have not yet read a document assigned to them. This feature can be especially useful to teachers for supervising students.

12.4.3.4 Metacognition

Finally, many of the mechanisms provided by AtGentNet allow users to reflect about their behaviour from a perspective of self-improvement, but also contribute to their motivation (and therefore influence the level of attention they dedicate in interacting with others).

More specifically, these mechanisms include the social translucence visualization tools, the assessment of the impact of actions, and the availability of many statistics indicating usage of the platform (how often the person connects, how much she contributes and when, or what are her different types of actions).

Users' intention versus users' attention: It is important to distinguish between the information that people declare (such as acquaintances or competence) and the information that reflects their real actions, the latter being what really matters (Huberman, Romero and Wu 2009b). For instance, a user may state a particular interest in a topic but never read a document on this topic, or a user may indicate an expertise on a subject but never provide any input on this subject. The AtGentNet platform displays on one page the aggregated list of tags of the documents that a user has read or has authored (figure 12.4). The display of this information in parallel with information that the user has explicitly declared (such as stated competence, stated interest or list of acquaintances) helps to identify dissonances in her attention allocation.

Tracking the diversity of social attention: The agent also notifies users when they read only contributions generated by the same group of members, since this is associated with low social diversity. The objective of this intervention is to augment the cohesion and the social cognition of the whole community.

12.4.3.5 Summary

Table 12.2 summarizes (incompletely) and categorizes the different mechanisms by level (P: perception; D: deliberation; O: operation; MC: metacognition), and indicates how strongly the mechanism supports this level (X: strong support; x: limited support).

Table 12.3 below summarizes the different (proactive) agent interventions.

Table 12.2 *Mechanisms of support at different levels*

Mechanism	P	D	O	MC	Comments (and examples)
Pictures of participants	X			x	*P*: Using pictures of participants in many different places as traces of their activities *MC*: Contributing to motivation
Abstract view of the social dimension of a list of items (tags or documents)	X				*P*: Making visible the social dimension of the resources. Facilitating social serendipity (via social navigation)
An agent is reporting a burst of activity at the community or an individual level	x	X		x	*P*: Notifying an abnormally high level of activity from the community or from a user *D*: Engaging more confidently in an interaction with people who seem interested *MC*: Such a burst of attention is an indicator in the assessment of his influence in the community or among certain members (individual level)
Showing the members who are getting a user's attention (list of 'people I read') + Showing the social impact of a user (list of 'people who read me')	x	X		X	*P*: Social translucence: showing the related social impact at the community and member levels of contributions of a user *D*: Engaging in interactions more confidently and augmenting the social cognition of the community globally thanks to social reciprocity factors (if A knows that B pays attention to him, by reciprocity he will be influenced in his decision making by paying more attention to B) *MC*: Providing a way for a user to evaluate and improve his strategy of communication
Visualizing the social network	x	X			*P*: Allowing users to discover a hidden social relationship *D*: such a tool supports users in identifying the more useful contacts
Reminder about completing the user profile			X		*O*: Reducing the cognitive effort to remember

(cont.)

Table 12.2 *(cont.)*

Mechanism	P	D	O	MC	Comments (and examples)
Presentation of the community			X		*O*: Educating users about how to use the platform
Watch mechanism			X		*O*: Facilitating and reducing the cognitive effort to follow a discussion
Tracking inattentive members	x			X	*P*: For the author: providing a view of the inattentive members of his posting (i.e., showing the non-activity) *MC*: for the inattentive members: Such a mechanism provides a way to be aware of their behaviour and change their attention management
Assessing user intention vs. user observed attention				X	*MC*: Such a tool provides a way to detect good or bad practices in attention management by showing similarity or dissonance between what is declared by the user (e.g., the interest the user has indicated in his profile) and his real foci of attention (e.g., the subjects of the documents that this user has read)
Tracking social diversity				X	*MC*: Assessing his management of his social attention and providing suggestions to reduce or open his social attention to other members
Basic statistics about attention allocation				X	*MC*: Some general statistics (number of posts read, written, tags used, people watched etc.) help the user to assess his attention allocation

12.5   AtGentNet: application in a blended learning scenario

12.5.1   *The context*

The AtGentNet platform, and the mechanisms supporting attention in a social context, were tested in a pilot test that took place during a period of six months in 2007, in the context of the ITM (International Trade Management) vocational training programme (Nabeth *et al.* 2008). In this programme, the participants attend series of local seminars, joint international seminars and monthly meetings with an expert coach.

Table 12.3 *Agent interventions*

Role	Condition	Action	Attention support
Presentation: Presentation of the platform: guidance about how to use the platform (using an artificial anthropomorphic character)	Detection of an event: the creation of a user's account	Propose a tutorial about the platform (using an artificial character)	An overall presentation of the platform will help the user to be more effective in using the platform
Profile completion: Reminder about the completion of the user's profile	At the second connection of a new user to the platform	Remind user to complete his/her profile (notification)	A good user profile is important to get the attention of others
Deadline approaching: Alert inattentive members to read a posting close to its deadline	A few days before the deadline date of a posting, detection of the inattentive members who haven't read a document yet	Remind each inattentive member to read the document (notification)	Reminder reduces the cognitive load related to back of head attention
Tracking inattention: Report to the author of a posting the set of inattentive members to it after a given deadline	At the posting's deadline date, detection of the members who still haven't viewed the posting	Report to the author of the posting about the set of inattentive members	Assist the user in managing the completion of the assignment to a given audience
Tracking readership: Report to the author that someone responded to his/her posting	Detection of a response (event 'creating' + relationship with a parent posting)	Notification to the author	Contribute to the awareness of the impact of a contribution. Notification of relevant information
Collective burst of attention: Abnormal collective interest in a posting or in a user's profile	Detection of an abnormally large audience for a posting (or a user profile)	Suggestion to have a look at this resource	Contribute to collective awareness

(cont.)

Table 12.3 *(cont.)*

Role	Condition	Action	Attention support
Personal burst of attention: Abnormal interest from a specific user in a posting or in a user's profile	Detection of an abnormally high number of views of a user for a posting (or a user profile)	Notification to the author of the resource of this special interest from a user	Contribute to introduce or reinforce link between members. Contribute to the awareness of the impact of an individual contribution
Low social diversity: A lack of openness to others was observed	Detection of the diversity of the user's attention in the last two weeks	Suggestion to open up to other people	Contribute to create awareness of others

The objective of these meetings is the elaboration of an export business plan.

The role of AtGentNet was to provide a learning platform to be used between the different sessions, so as to make the physical sessions more effective. The platform therefore enabled the transformation of this programme into a blended programme, i.e., taking place both offline and online. The platform was used before the sessions to inform the participants and to deliver some materials to them, but also to contribute to the familiarization of the participants with one another and with the faculty members. The assumption was that this familiarization process would create trust that would contribute to the motivation of the participants, and would help in the building of a common understanding and facilitate communication (Clark and Brennan 1991). The platform was also used after the sessions to consolidate the work conducted during the sessions, and to support knowledge exchange and confrontation of ideas afterwards. The AtGentNet platform appeared to be particularly adapted to support the context of the ITM programme: the participants of this programme are 'isolated' because of their geographical location, because they travel a significant part of their time and because of the size of their organization (SMEs), which makes them unlikely to exchange knowledge with colleagues of similar expertise.

This pilot involved the participation of sixty people from nine countries (Greece, Hungary, Iceland, Lithuania, Namibia, Norway, Slovenia, South Africa and Sweden) and seven faculty members (one each from

Denmark, China, France, South Africa, the Netherlands and two from the UK), and was launched at the first international seminar that took place at Lidköping, Sweden in May 2007. This seminar provided the opportunity to present the participants with the ITM concept and to introduce them to the platform. Participants were told that they would be able to use the platform as an interaction space to use between the seminars to strengthen their social relationships and to exchange knowledge (such as experiences) once they returned to their respective countries. After this seminar, participants were organized into groups and received an account to connect to the platform. The first group was provided with access to a legacy collaborative platform that only provided basic communication capability, and was not analysed. The second group (the control group) was provided with access to a restricted version of the new social network platform that only offered a subset of the functionalities. The last group (the experimental group) was given access to the full functionalities of the new platform, and in particular to the more advanced mechanisms supporting attention (proactive agent interventions; watch list; advanced indicators).

Different actions were then initiated to stimulate the participants into engaging in interactions so as to generate a maximum of data for our analysis. These actions included: a first phase of familiarization; a series of small, light assignments related to the course; and finally an online role-playing collaborative business game to boost participation. This game had been designed in the context of another European research project, L2C (Angehrn and Nabeth 2006). The data collected for analysis during this AtGentNet pilot consisted of the log files of the activities of the users; the responses to a series of questionnaires filled in by participants; and some post-trial telephone interviews. The data were analysed using statistical analysis (for the log files), but more qualitative methods were also used, not only because the small size of the sample did not always lead to conclusions that would be statistically significant, but also so as to allow a higher level of analysis (Rudman and Zajicek 2007).

12.5.2   The results

Before analysing the results, it is important to mention that one of the main issues for the utilization of social platforms is the question of participation. The fact that the profile of the population participating in our test consisted of busy managers made the problem even more difficult: such participants connect to the platform in the first place only if they consider that they will receive tangible value from the interaction. It is for this reason that the project decided to organize a simulation game, so as to overcome the cold-start effect and allow participants to assess the value of the platform in the context of a very engaging activity.

A very noticeable difference was observed in the patterns of system use before and after the simulation game was organized: before the game, the participants in the experimental group (who had access to the more sophisticated mechanisms) were consistently showing more activity than the participants in the control group (who only had access to the basic mechanisms). The observation of the difference in usage between the two groups after the simulation indicated a less pronounced difference.

The advanced mechanisms (provided by the agent module) mainly appear to play a role in increasing the perceived value of the platform, and therefore the likeliness that a participant will reconnect later. This can be considered as relatively disappointing, since we can imagine that this element will fade once the novelty effect is over, and the project was investigating the possibility of providing advanced support to attention (and not only basic and passive support to attention). More work needs to be accomplished to design such mechanisms, but we can also expect that more maturity from the users will improve the situation.

The data extracted from the log files provided a number of other findings. 'Lurking' at other people's profiles (as an indicator of social interest) represents a behavioural pattern that is very important, and extensively used: people connect to the platform not so much to interact with others but to get information about others. This behaviour was later confirmed on the Alumni platform that was set up: people connect to the platform in the first place to get information about other users. This is something that is consistent with the large adoption of online social networking services such as LinkedIn and Facebook that we can observe today.

The data extracted from the questionnaires and the telephone interviews helped to refine, elaborate on and add to the previous findings. The participants described themselves as busy people strongly involved with their regular work, and unable to justify dedicating time to an activity which did not generate tangible value. The comparison of the answers originating from the two groups indicates that the more advanced platform helps the understanding of the use of the platform, but also eases access to documents, confirming users' interest in mechanisms that help them to be more efficient. The participants in the two groups liked the ability of the platform to help them maintain business and social connection with the other participants. They also expressed their interest in being able to get in touch with the lecturers, as well as having the possibility to collaborate with colleagues they had met at the seminar. However, on the last point, the observation shows that they engaged in these activities mostly when they had been organized and had clearly benefited (such as in the case of the game), and they were reluctant to engage in informal interactions.

Finally, all the participants indicated that they found the interface too complex. The reason for this complexity lies in an underestimation of the level of distraction of displaying too much information on a page resulting from the desire to provide a maximum of social translucence to the system. The interface of the second version of the prototype was simplified so as to address this problem.

12.6   Discussion and conclusion

This project generated a number of findings that could be derived from the design of the social platform AtGentNet supporting attention at the social level and from the empirical study that was conducted to evaluate this platform in the context of supporting a blended learning programme.

12.6.1   Attention: a high-level concept that is difficult to operationalize directly in a technical platform

We first have to point out the difficulty we experienced in this project in trying to map the concept of attention into a technical implementation that would make sense to users. Attention refers to a relatively abstract concept that is grounded in the cognitive sciences, and that cannot easily be transformed into something tangible that is directly manipulated by end users. Thus, if people understand the meaning of social interaction overload, and even are confronted with its reality in their work, they may not be ready to integrate this concept directly into their day-to-day operational thinking. People need to 'manipulate' concepts that are more concrete, that do not require from them too great a mental effort or too high a level of abstraction. During this project, we therefore evolved in our objectives from designing a platform aimed at supporting people's social attention to a more operational vision of designing a social platform that would be more effective at supporting people's interactions with others. Thus, in its final version, the AtGentNet platform offers users a variety of mechanisms (described in this chapter) that allow them to communicate with each other more effectively, to use the social information to identify relevant data, and to assess the impact of their actions. Intelligent mechanisms are also used in the form of agents that are able to observe people's activities and reason on them, and intervene proactively. It should be noted, however, that the idea of supporting attention remained present during the whole project, and proved very valuable for guiding the design: attention represents indeed a very valuable approach for reasoning about the many aspects of knowledge-intensive activities, and it concerns more than just the time that people spend on a task. Our focus on attention also allowed us to address in a holistic way the different aspects a knowledge worker is confronted with, such as perception and bias, cognitive overload and interruption.

The evaluation of attention also represented an important challenge. Attention, even when referring to long-term attention, cannot easily be measured directly, since much of the associated data is not currently accessible, and would probably require monitoring the brain itself or capturing people's actions over a long period of time. Yet, we found that the capture and exploitation of people's activities (i.e., collecting and processing the digital traces that people leave when they interact) that we were able to conduct in AtGentNet proved that meaningful data were already available, and that it could be used for profiling people's attention, reasoning about this attention, and providing support for people's interactions that is attention effective. Of course, more progress will need to be made on this subject, and in particular in knowing how to extract from these digital traces the data representing people's attention. We have reason to believe that we are only at the beginning, and that attention-aware systems will increasingly be available: the development of Web 2.0, and more generally of the information society, is making available an increasingly large amount of traces that can be exploited to monitor people's activities, even if some restrictions linked to the protection of people's privacy may apply. Web 2.0 has also created conditions in which people have to be very effective in managing their interactions with others, and we do not expect this to change in the future.

12.6.2   Implementing the four-level model

This project offered us the possibility to assess the value of the four-level model of attention proposed by Roda and Nabeth (2008) by providing an interesting context: the support of attention in a social platform.

We were able to verify that support of social attention according to the four levels (perception, deliberation, operation and metacognition) made sense since we could find for each level a set of meaningful mechanisms supporting attention. We were also able to implement meaningful mechanisms at the four different levels. The technical architecture appears to have been functioning very well, and in line with our expectations. In particular, the separation of the advanced mechanisms, using an external agent, from the platform that was providing only the communication capability proved to be valuable.

However, we were confronted by a number of findings that we had not anticipated.

First, we found that mechanisms may provide support to attention at several levels at the same time. Actually, this does not come as too much of a surprise, but it makes the application of the four levels of attention support a little more complex than we had originally thought.

Second, and more interestingly, we found that the support of attention at different levels may sometimes conflict, and that more work needs to be conducted to understand better the relationship between the support of attention at different levels. In the first version of the prototype, we made important use of translucence mechanisms. Our intention was to inform the user as much as possible using a minimum number of steps. In other words, we wanted to maximize support at the operational level and reduce the number of steps required for accessing this information. Unfortunately this approach proved to be counter-productive since it generated information overload, and resulted in reducing the 'quality of the perception' of the users. At the same time we are observing that Web 2.0 sites are proposing a richer and more complex interface. Online networking services such as LinkedIn and Facebook display a large quantity and variety of information on the same page, such as the activity stream, suggestions to make connections to other people, or applications (such as slides). It will be interesting to follow this evolution towards richer and more complex user interfaces, and to see if people will learn to use them effectively or, on the contrary, if the provider of these services will have to go back to the design of simpler interfaces.

Third, we found that the less sophisticated mechanisms, such as the ones contributing to social translucence, have proved to be the most effective. This is somewhat disappointing if we consider that the first objective of this research was to investigate how to provide advanced support to attention, and in particular to explore how proactive and intelligent mechanisms implemented by an agent could be used for this purpose. Yet at the same time we were able to observe that the most advanced mechanisms were having a positive impact. Besides, we have to admit that we only implemented a limited set of advance mechanisms supporting attention, and that the mining and exploitation of digital traces (a core element of our research) is a subject under important investigation by the research community (Anjewierden and Efimova 2006; Wolpers et al. 2007; May, George and Prévôt 2008) and represents a very promising direction for further work.

Our general conclusion is that the application of this model is functioning, but appears to have been less straightforward to achieve than anticipated, since we found that different mechanisms supporting attention could intervene at different levels at the same time. We also could only scratch the surface of supporting the highest level (meta-cognition support) of attention, and of supporting people's attention more intelligently. However, this work did not come to a dead end, but on the contrary revealed or confirmed lines for further research, such as supporting people's attention in a social context, and the exploitation of all the digital traces that are becoming available and for which an 'attention' approach appears to be particularly fruitful.

12.7   References

Angehrn, A. A., and Nabeth, T. 2006. The L2C project: Learning to collaborate through advanced SmallWorld simulations, in *Proceedings of the 1st European Technology Enhanced Learning Conference*, 1–4 October 2006, Crete: 452–7

Anicic, D., Stojanovic, N., and Apostolou, D. 2008. Enterprise attention management system, in M. Hepp, N. Stojanovic, K. Hinkelmann, D. Karagiannis, and R. Klein (eds.), *Proceedings of the 3rd International Workshop on Semantic Business Process Management (SBPM 2008) in conjunction with the 4th European Semantic Web Conference (ESWC 2008)*, Tenerife, 2 June 2008

Anjewierden, A., and Efimova, L. 2006. Understanding weblog communities through digital traces: A framework, a tool and an example, in R. Meersman *et al.* (eds.), *On the Move to Meaningful Internet Systems 2006: OTM 2006 Workshops*, Montpellier: 279–89

Argyris, C., and Schon, D. 1978. *Organizational Learning: A Theory of Action Perspective*. Reading, MA: Addison-Wesley

Ashkenas, R. 2007. Simplicity-minded management: A practical guide to stripping complexity out of your organization, *Harvard Business Review* 85(12): 101–9

Bandura, A. 1994. Self-efficacy, in V. S. Ramachaudran (ed.), *Encyclopedia of Human Behavior*. New York: Academic Press: vol. IV: 71–81
    2001. Social cognitive theory: An agentic perspective, *Annual Review of Psychology* 52: 1–26

Beck, J. C., and Davenport, T. H. 2001. How corporate leaders can help their companies manage the scarcest resource of all: Attention; Accenture point of view, August 2001. Retrieved 20 November 2008 from: www.accenture.com/Global/Research_and_Insights/Outlook/By_Alphabet/HowAttention.htm

Bier, E. A., Stone, M. C., Pier, K., Buxton, W., and DeRose, T. D. 1993. Toolglass and magic lenses: The see-through interface, in *Proceedings 20th Annual Conference on Computer Graphics and Interactive Techniques*, Anaheim: 73–80

Boyd, D., and Ellison, N. 2007. Social network sites: Definition, history, and scholarship, *Journal of Computer-Mediated Communication* 13(1): article 11

Bridges, K. 2008. Librarians and the attention economy; Library Philosophy and Practice, March 2008. Retrieved 19 November 2008 from: http://libr.unl.edu:2000/LPP/bridges3.htm

Burt, R. 1997. The contingent value of social capital, *Administrative Science Quarterly* 42(2): 339–65

Chi, E. H. 2008. The social web: Research and opportunities, *IEEE Computer* 41(9): 88–91

Chi, E. H., Pirolli, P., and Lam, S. K. 2007. Aspects of augmented social cognition: Social information foraging and social search, in *Proceedings Human–Computer Interaction International Conference*, Beijing: 60–9

Chi, E. H., Pirolli, P., Suh, B., Kittur, A., Pendleton, B., and Mytkowicz, T. 2008. Augmented social cognition, in *Proceedings of the AAAI Spring Symposium on Social Information Processing*, Stanford University, 26 March 2008. AAAI Press

Clark, H., and Brennan, S. 1991. Grounding in communication, in B. Resnick, S. Levine and S. Teasley (eds.), *Perspectives on Socially Shared Cognition*. Washington, DC: APA: 127–49

Cross, R., Borgatti, S. P., and Parker, A. 2002. Making invisible work visible: Using social network analysis to support strategic collaboration, *California Management Review* 44(2): 25–46

Cunningham, W., and Leuf, B. 2001. *The Wiki Way. Quick Collaboration on the Web*. Reading, MA: Addison-Wesley

Davenport, T. H., and Beck, J. 2001. *The Attention Economy*. Harvard Business School Press

Dieberger, A., Dourish, P., Höök, K., Resnick, P., and Wexelblat, A. 2000. Social navigation: Techniques for building more usable systems, *Interactions* 7(6): 36–45

Drucker, P. F. 1999. Knowledge worker productivity: The biggest challenge, *California Management Review* 1(2): 79–94

Dunbar, R. 1992. Neocortex size as a constraint on group size in primates, *Journal of Human Evolution* 20: 469–93

Erickson, T. 2009. 'Social' systems: Designing digital systems that support social intelligence, *AI & Society* 23(2): 147–66

Erickson, T., and Kellogg, W. A. 2000. Social translucence: An approach to designing systems that support social processes, *ACM Transactions on Computer–Human Interaction* 7(1): 59–83

2003. Social translucence: Using minimalist visualizations of social activity to support collective interaction, in K. Höök, D. Benyon and A. Munro (eds.), *Designing Information Spaces: The Social Navigation Approach*. Berlin: Springer: 17–42

Fielding, R. T., and Taylor, R. N. 2002. Principled design of the modern web architecture, *ACM Transactions on Internet Technology* 2(2): 115–50

Gifford, S. 1997. Limited attention and the role of the venture capitalist, *Journal of Business Venturing* 12(6): 459–82

Gill, K. E. 2005. Blogging, RSS and the information landscape: A look at online news, in *Proceedings WWW 2005*, Chiba, Japan

Giraldeau, L.-A., and Caraco, T. 2000. *Social Foraging Theory*. Princeton, NJ: Princeton University Press

Golder, S., and Huberman, B. A. 2006. Usage patterns of collaborative tagging systems, *Journal of Information Science* 32(2): 198–208

Goldhaber, M. H. 1997. The attention economy and the net, *First Monday* 2(4)

Granovetter, M. 1973. The strength of weak ties, *American Journal of Sociology* 78(6): 1360–80

Halpin, H., Robu, V., and Shepherd, H. 2006. The dynamics and semantics of collaborative tagging, in K. Möller, A. de Waard, S. Cayzer, M.-R. Koivunen, M. Sintek and S. Handschuh, *SAAW'06, CEUR Workshop Proceedings*, Atlanta

Harper, M., Li, X., Chen, Y., and Konstan, J. 2007. Social comparisons to motivate contributions to an online community, *Persuasive Technology Conference*, Palo Alto, CA

Homans, G. C. 1958. Social behavior as exchange, *American Journal of Sociology* 63: 597–606

Huberman, B. A., Romero, D. M., and Wu, F. 2009a. Crowdsourcing, attention and productivity, *Journal of Information Science* 35(6): 758–65

2009b. Social networks that matter: Twitter under the microscope, *First Monday* 14(1)

Huberman, B. A., and Wu, F. 2007. Comparative advantage and efficient advertising in the attention economy, *Proceedings of the 22nd European Conference on Operational Research (EURO XXII)*

2008. The economics of attention: Maximizing user value in information-rich environments, *Advances in Complex Systems* 11(4): 487–96

Joinson, A. N. 2008. Looking at, looking up or keeping up with people? Motives and use of Facebook, in *Proceedings of the SIGCHI Conference on Human Factors in Computing Systems*, Florence: 1027–36

Kogut, B. 2008. *Knowledge, Options and Institutions*. Oxford: Oxford University Press

Latour, B. 2007. Beware, your imagination leaves digital traces, *Times Higher Literary Supplement*, 6 April 2007

Marlow, C., Naaman, M., Boyd, D., and Davis, M. 2006. Position paper, tagging, taxonomy, Flickr, Article, ToRead, Collaborative Web Tagging Workshop, in *Proceedings WWW 2006*, Edinburgh, 22 May 2006

May, M., George, S., and Prévôt, P. 2008. A closer look at tracking human and computer interactions in web-based communications, *International Journal of Interactive Technology and Smart Education (ITSE)* 5(3): 170–88

McAfee, A. P. 2006. Enterprise 2.0: The dawn of emergent collaboration, *Sloan Management Review* 47(3): 21–8

Miller, G. 1956. The magical number seven, plus or minus two, *Psychological Review* 63: 81–97

Mobasher, B. 2007. Data mining for web personalization, in P. Brusilovsky, A. Kobsa and W. Nejdl (eds.), *The Adaptive Web: Methods and Strategies of Web Personalization*. Berlin: Springer: 90–135

Nabeth, T. 2008. User profiling for attention support for school and work, in M. Hildebrandt and S. Gutwirth (eds.), *Profiling the European Citizen*. Dordrecht: Springer: 185–200

Nabeth, T., Karlsson, H., Angehrn, A., and Maisonneuve, N. 2008. A social network platform for vocational learning in the ITM worldwide network, *IST Africa 2008*, Windhoek, Namibia, 14–16 May 2008

Nabeth, T., and Roda, C. 2006. Les espaces sociaux virtuels: Approches, pratiques émergentes et perspectives, in A. Bounfour (ed.), *Capital Immatériel, Connaissance et Performance.* Paris: L'Harmattan: 225–65

Nabeth, T., Roda, C., Angehrn, A., and Mittal, P. K. 2005. Using artificial agents to stimulate participation in virtual communities, in *Proceedings of the IADIS International Conference CELDA (Cognition and Exploratory Learning in Digital Age)*, Porto: 391–4

Nardi, S. W., Whittaker, S., and Schwarz, H. 2000. It's not what you know, it's who you know: Work in the information age, *First Monday* 5(5)

Nishikant, K., Konstan, J., and Terveen, L. 2005. How peer photos influence member participation in online communities, in *Proceedings ACM CHI 2005*, Portland, OR, 2–7 April 2005: 1525–8

Ocasio, W. 1993. The structuring of organizational attention and the enactment of economic adversity: A reconciliation of theories of failure-induced change and threat-rigidity, Working Paper (Sloan School of Management), Retrieved 20 November 2008 from: http://hdl.handle.net/1721.1/2473: 3577–93

    1997. Towards an attention-based view of the firm, *Strategic Management Journal* 18: 187–206

O'Reilly, T. 2005. What is Web 2.0? Design patterns and business models for the next generation of software, Retrieved 30 September 2005 from: www.oreillynet.com/pub/a/oreilly/tim/news/2005/09/30/what-is-web-20.html

Perez, S. 2008. Real people don't have time for social media, ReadWriteWeb, Retrieved 16 April 2008 from: www.readwriteweb.com/archives/real_people_dont_have_time_for_social_media.php

Pierrakos, D., Paliouras, G., Papatheodorou, C., and Spyropoulos, C. D. 2003. Web usage mining as a tool for personalization: A survey, *User Modeling and User-Adapted Interaction* 13: 311–72

Rashid, A. M., Ling, K., Tassone, R. D., Resnick, P., Kraut, R., and Riedl, J. 2006. Motivating participation by displaying the value of contribution, in *CHI '06: Proceedings of the SIGCHI Conference on Human Factors in Computing Systems.* New York: ACM Press: 955–8

Resnick, P., Zeckhauser, R., Friedman, E., and Kuwabara, K. 2000. Reputation systems, *Communications of the ACM* 43(12): 45–8

Roda, C., and Nabeth, T. 2006. Poster: The AtGentive project: Attentive agents for collaborative learners, in *Proceedings ECTEL 2006, First European Technology Enhanced Learning Conference*, Crete, 1–4 October 2006

    2008. Attention management in organizations: Four levels of support in information systems, in A. Bounfour (ed.), *Innovation and Information Systems.* Routledge: 214–33

Rogers, E. 2003. *Diffusion of Innovations* (5th edn). New York: Free Press

Rudman, P., and Zajicek, M. 2007. Final evaluation report, AtGentive Project, Deliverable D4.4. Retrieved 9 July 2010 from: www.calt.insead.edu/LivingLab/AtGentive/Wiki/?D4.4

Senge, P. 1990. *The Fifth Discipline: The Art and Practice of the Learning Organization.* New York: Doubleday

Simon, H. A. 1971. Designing organizations for an information rich world, in M. Greenberger (ed.), *Computers, Communications and the Public Interest*. Baltimore: Johns Hopkins Press: 38–52

Stone, L. 2006. Linda Stone's thoughts on attention and specifically, continuous partial attention. Retrieved 20 November 2008 from: http://continuouspartialattention.jot.com/WikiHome

Subramani, M. R., and Rajagopalan, B. 2003. Knowledge-sharing and influence in online social networks via viral marketing, *Communications of the ACM* 46(12): 300–7

Tapscott, D., and Williams, A. D. 2007. *Wikinomics: How Mass Collaboration Changes Everything*. New York: Penguin

Thibaut, J. W., and Kelley, H. H. 1959. *The Social Psychology of Groups*. New York: Wiley

Thomas, J. C., Kellogg, W. A., and Erickson, T. 2001. The knowledge management puzzle: Human and social factors in knowledge management, *IBM System Journal* 40(4): 863–84

Tufekci, Z. 2008. Can you see me now? Audience and disclosure management in online social network sites, *Bulletin of Science, Technology and Society* 11(4): 544–64

Vassileva, J., and Sun, L. 2007. Using community visualization to stimulate participation in online communities, *e-Service Journal* 6(1): 3–40

Vertegaal, R. 2003. Attentive user interfaces, *Communications of the ACM* 46(3): 30–3

Vertegaal, R., Shell, J. S., Chen, D., and Mamuji, A. 2006. Designing for augmented attention: Towards a framework for attentive user interfaces, *Computers in Human Behavior* 22(4): 771–89

Weiss, A. 2005. The power of collective intelligence, *netWorker* 9(3): 16–23

Wolpers, M., Najjar, J., Verbert, K., and Duval, E. 2007. Tracking actual usage: The attention metadata approach, *Educational Technology and Society* 10(3): 106–21

Wu, F., and Huberman, B. A. 2008. Popularity, novelty and attention, in *Proceedings of the 9th ACM Conference on Electronic Commerce* (Chicago, 8–12 July 2008). New York: ACM Press: 240–5

Yuan, W., Chen, Y., Wang, R., and Du, Z. 2007. Collective intelligence in knowledge management, in L. Xu, A. Tjoa and S. Chaudhry (eds.), *Research and Practical Issues of Enterprise Information Systems II*. Boston: Springer: vol. I: 651–5

Index of authors cited

Cited authors are listed at the corresponding page whether their name explicitly appears or not (their name may be part of the *et al.* list).

Index